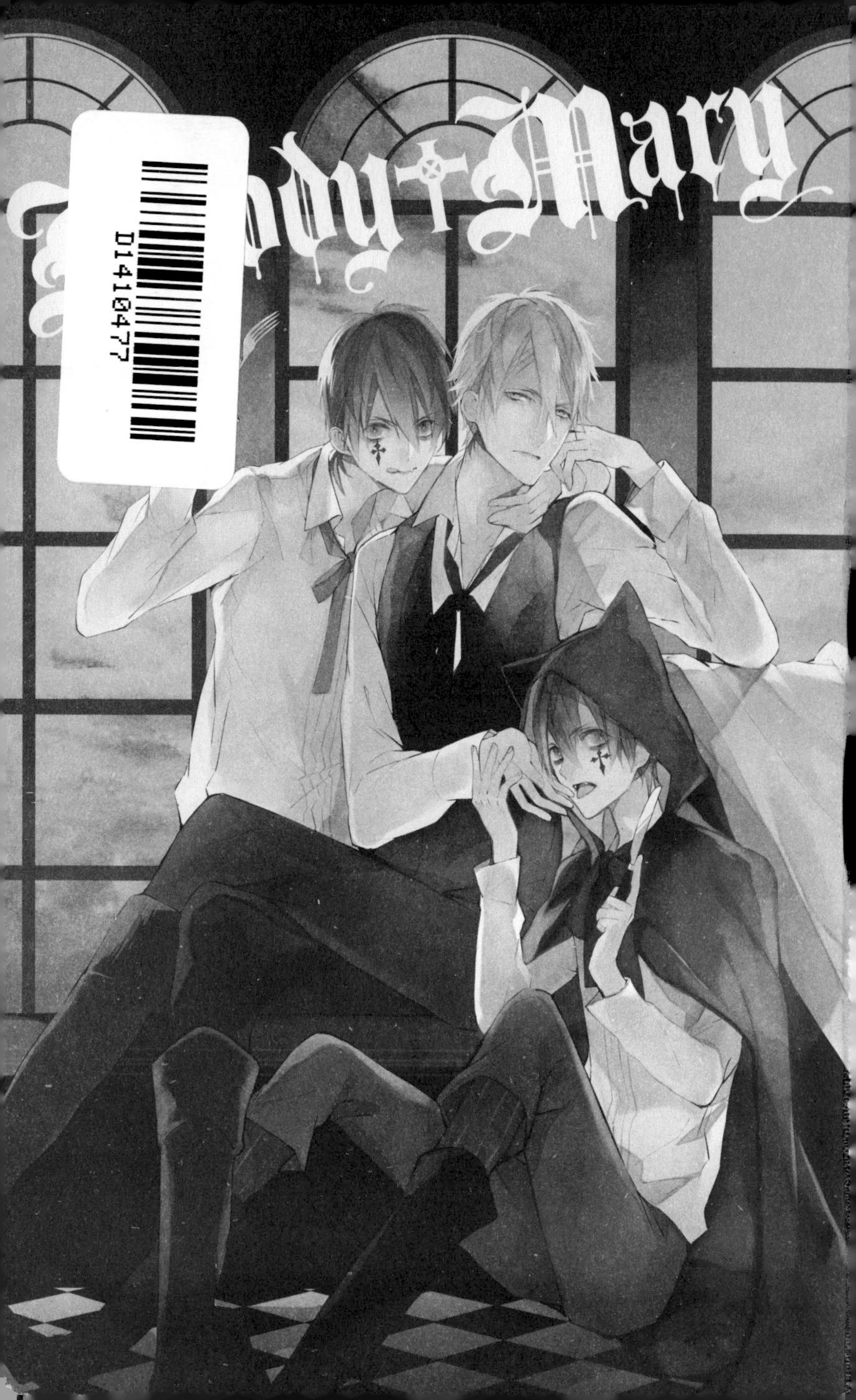
Mary

# Bloody † Mary

## ⑦ contents

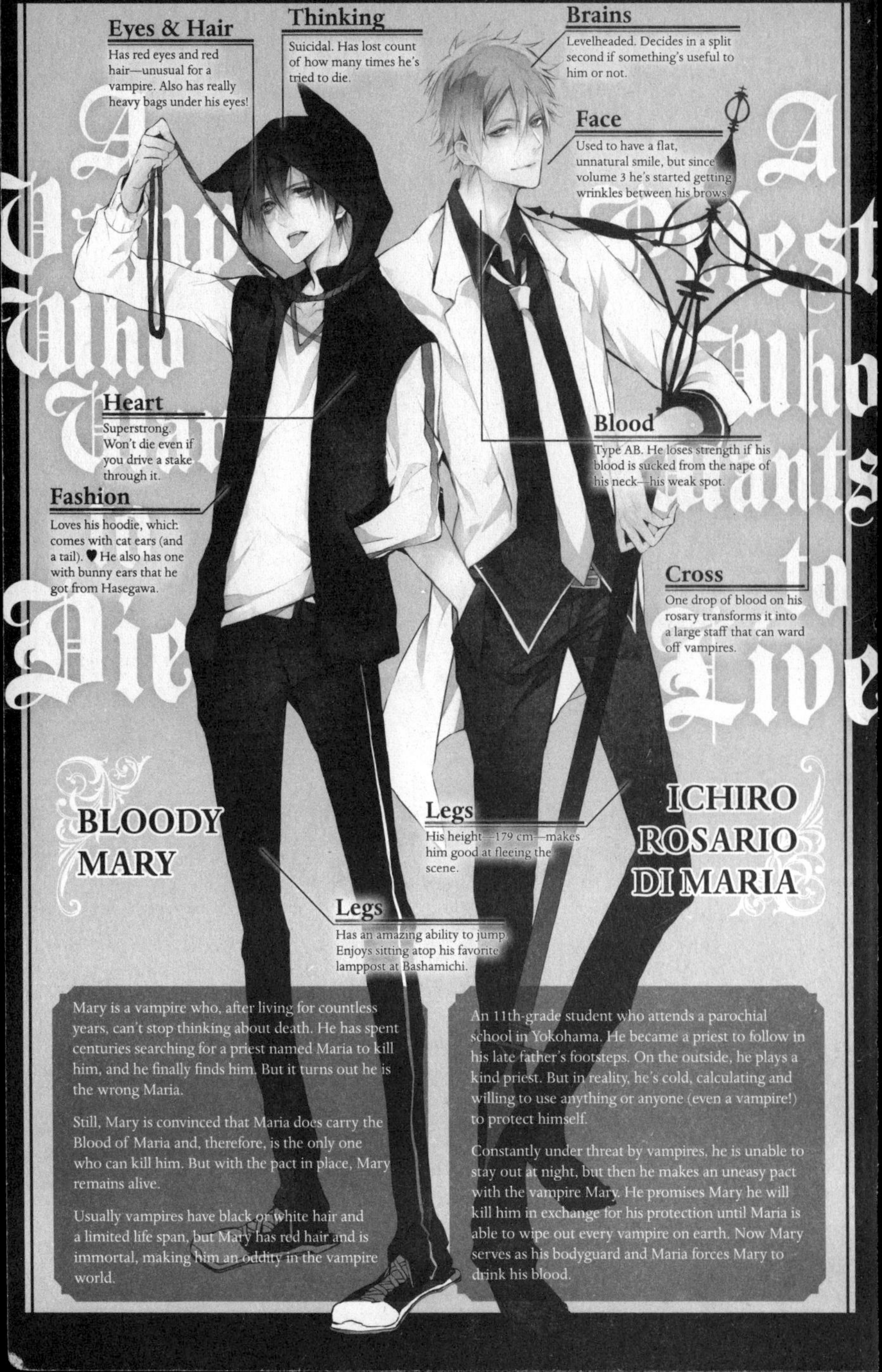
Eyes & Hair
Has red eyes and red hair—unusual for a vampire. Also has really heavy bags under his eyes!
Thinking
Suicidal. Has lost count of how many times he's tried to die.
Brains
Levelheaded. Decides in a split second if something's useful to him or not.
Face
Used to have a flat, unnatural smile, but since volume 3 he's started getting wrinkles between his brows.
Heart
Superstrong. Won't die even if you drive a stake through it.
Blood
Type AB. He loses strength if his blood is sucked from the nape of his neck—his weak spot.
Fashion
Loves his hoodie, which comes with cat ears (and a tail). ♥ He also has one with bunny ears that he got from Hasegawa.
Cross
One drop of blood on his rosary transforms it into a large staff that can ward off vampires.
BLOODY MARY
ICHIRO ROSARIO DI MARIA
Legs
His height—179 cm—makes him good at fleeing the scene.
Legs
Has an amazing ability to jump. Enjoys sitting atop his favorite lamppost at Bashamichi.

Mary is a vampire who, after living for countless years, can't stop thinking about death. He has spent centuries searching for a priest named Maria to kill him, and he finally finds him. But it turns out he is the wrong Maria.

Still, Mary is convinced that Maria does carry the Blood of Maria and, therefore, is the only one who can kill him. But with the pact in place, Mary remains alive.

Usually vampires have black or white hair and a limited life span, but Mary has red hair and is immortal, making him an oddity in the vampire world.

An 11th-grade student who attends a parochial school in Yokohama. He became a priest to follow in his late father's footsteps. On the outside, he plays a kind priest. But in reality, he's cold, calculating and willing to use anything or anyone (even a vampire!) to protect himself.

Constantly under threat by vampires, he is unable to stay out at night, but then he makes an uneasy pact with the vampire Mary. He promises Mary he will kill him in exchange for his protection until Maria is able to wipe out every vampire on earth. Now Mary serves as his bodyguard and Maria forces Mary to drink his blood.

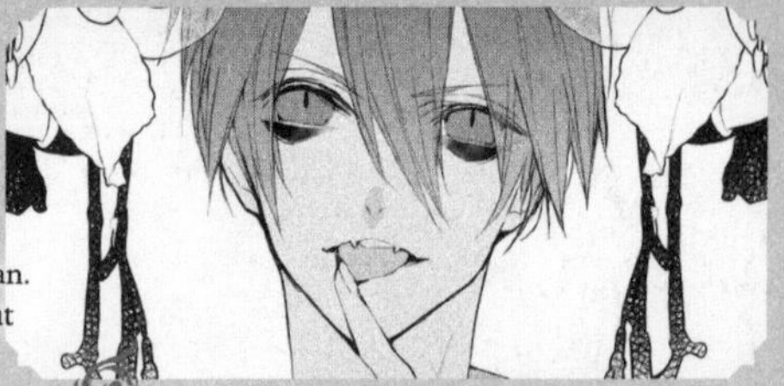

## "MARY"

He was the twin brother of Mary (the masochist) when they were both still human. It's not clear how he became a vampire, but the skeleton of "Mary" was locked away in Hydra's castle for a long time. But then she set it aflame, reducing it to ashes.

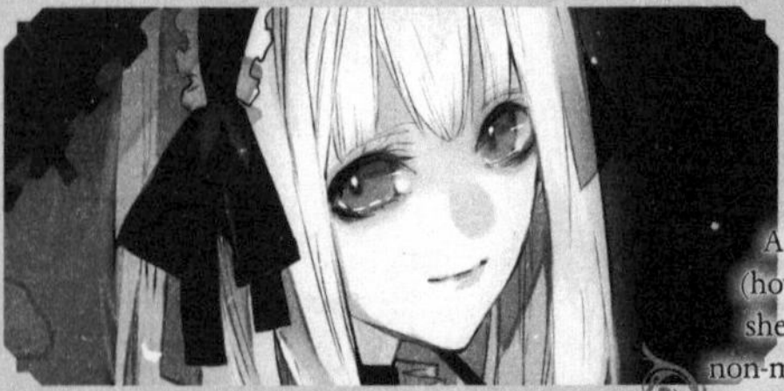

## HYDRA

A vampire who takes the form of a little girl (however, her real age is unknown). It appears she has some deep connection to "Mary" (the non-masochistic one) and persistently affixes the "Bloody" part to masochist Mary's name. She's considering killing Mary for the sake of "Mary."

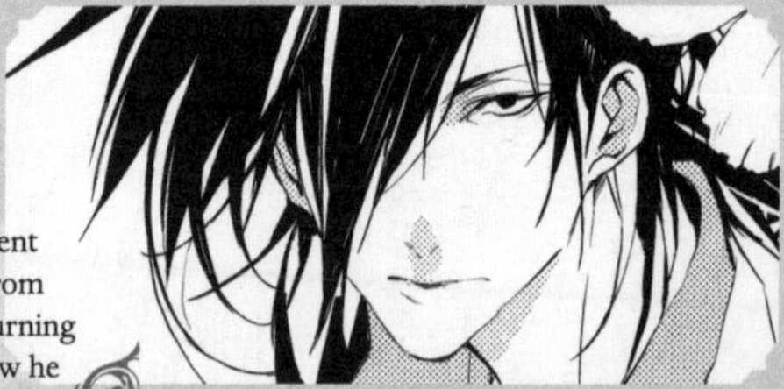

## SHINOBU

Maria's uncle. After his sister's death, he went to England to learn how to protect Yusei from vampires and the Sakurabas. But upon returning to Japan, Yusei had already been killed. Now he does all he can to protect Maria instead. But recently his job has been comforting Mary, who's being treated coldly by Maria.

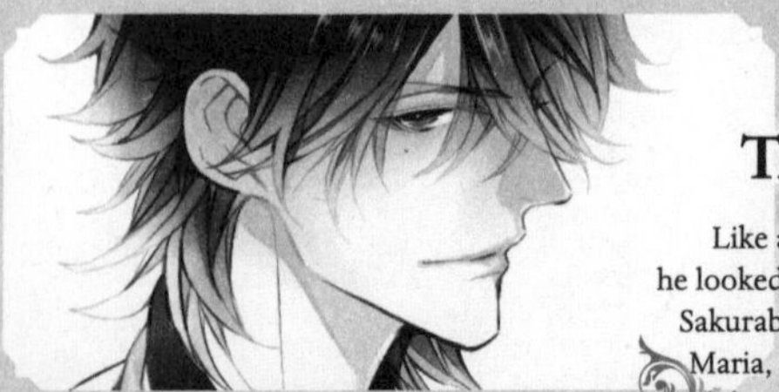

## TAKUMI SAKURABA

Like an older brother to Maria. After Yusei died, he looked after Maria, who had been taken in by the Sakurabas. Under the control of Yzak, he betrayed Maria, but now he's committed to uncovering the dubious actions of Yzak and the Sakuraba family. He's guided by a strong sense of right and wrong.

## Even a masochist could understand it

# What M has remembered about "Mary"

## Cast of Characters

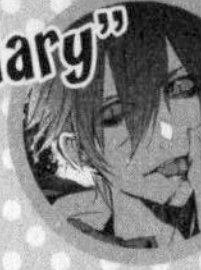
"Mary"

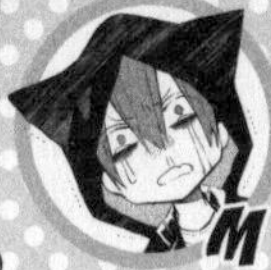
M

Note: Since "Mary" and Mary are so intermingled, Mary (the masochistic one) will be referred to as M from now on.

"Mary" and M were two brothers born as twins (their original human names are unknown).
The two lost their parents and grew up in the church.
One day, foster parents were found for them, and they were to two separate households.
However, "Mary" was worried about the sickly M and gave M his own name of "Mary," even though M wasn't thrilled about it.
After that, M was taken to the wealthy Howard family.
Even after the two were separated, "Mary" would sneak into the Howard estate to go visit M.

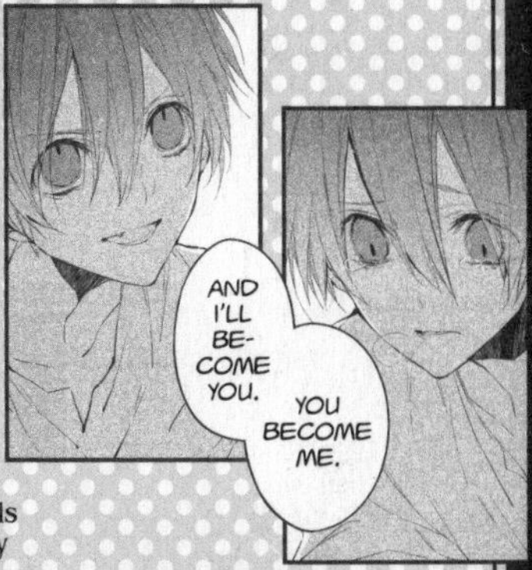
AND I'LL BECOME YOU.
YOU BECOME ME.

### One Day

The two of them tested their courage by going into the woods where vampires were rumored to be. But along the way, they got separated, and M, who collapsed, found himself back in town while "Mary" went missing.

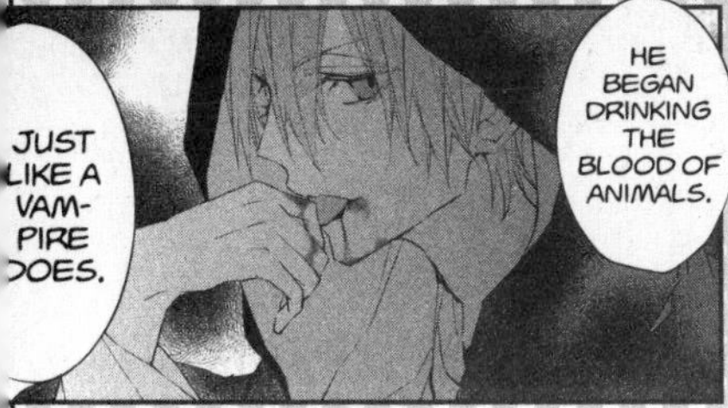
HE BEGAN DRINKING THE BLOOD OF ANIMALS.
JUST LIKE A VAMPIRE DOES.

### A Few Days Later

"Mary" suddenly reappeared, but he was acting just like a vampire—going out only at night and drinking the blood of small creatures.
This continued for some years until one day "Mary" declared that he was "ready to become a vampire," thwarted M's attempts to stop him, and disappeared.
But he promised M that he'd "never leave him alone."

### Then Time Went On

"Mary," completely soaked in blood, appeared on the balcony of the Howard home.
He tells M he's come for him.
Feeling that "Mary" had broken his promise to him, M refuses tells him off by telling "Mary" that he hates him.

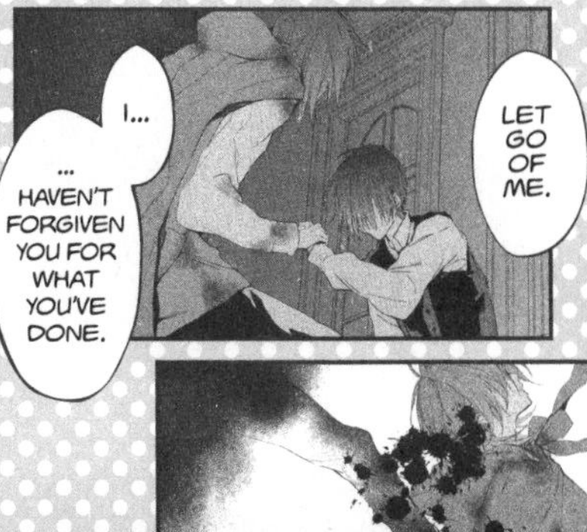
LET GO OF ME.
I...
...HAVEN'T FORGIVEN YOU FOR WHAT YOU'VE DONE.

### Immediately Following

"Mary" is attacked by a gang of vampires and dragged down.
That's where M's memories of "Mary" abruptly end...

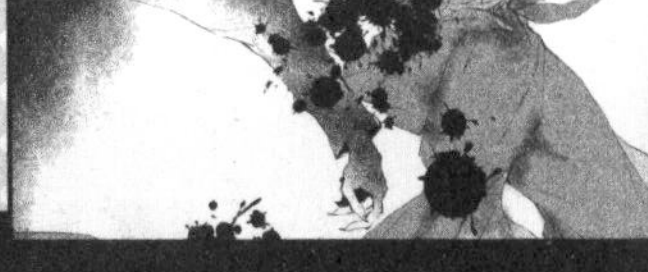

# Bloody✝Mary

FOR THOSE WHO DON'T WANT TO WASTE ANY TIME LEARN-ING THESE THREE'S NAMES, PLEASE REFER TO PAGE 163!

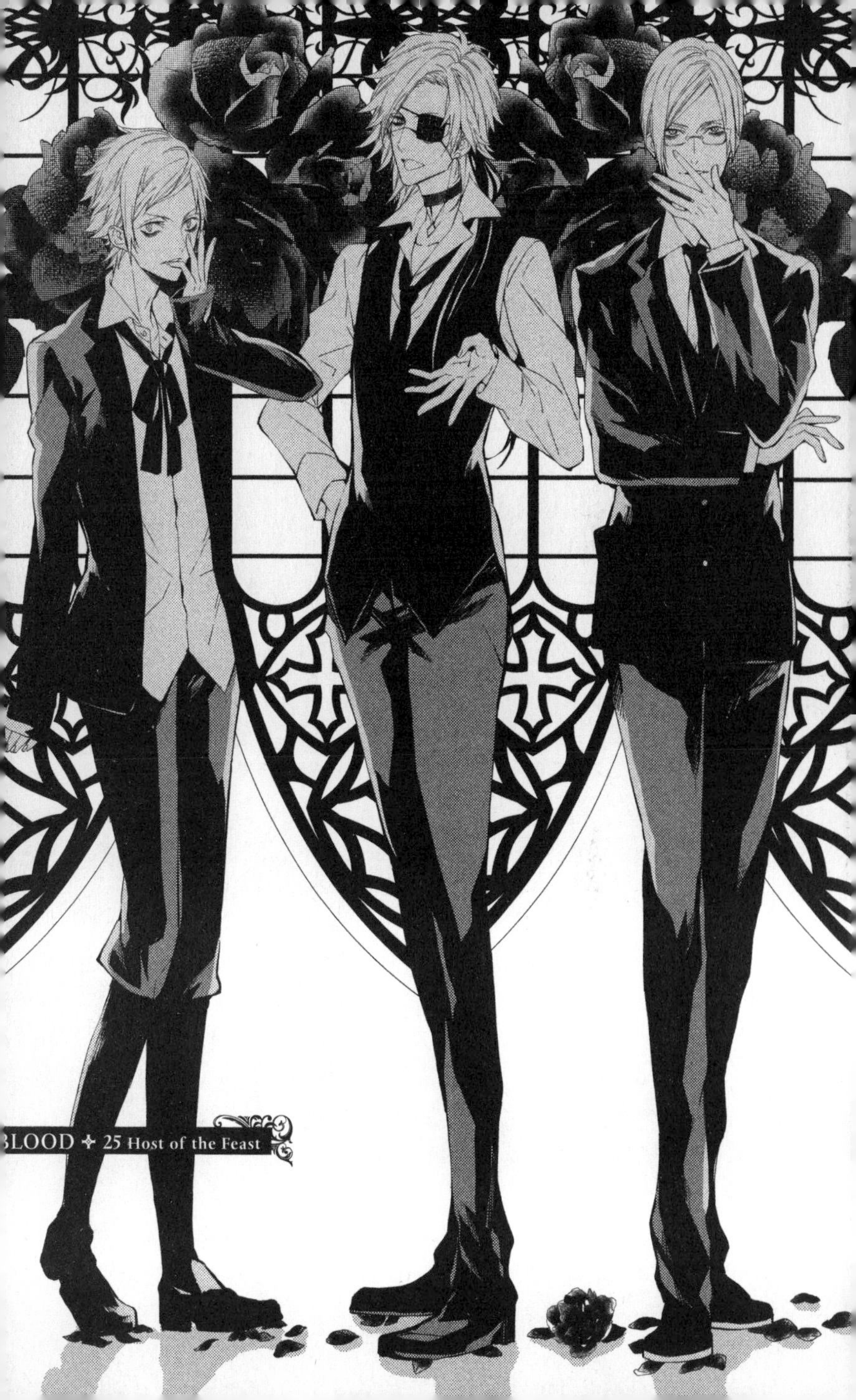
BLOOD ✦ 25 Host of the Feast

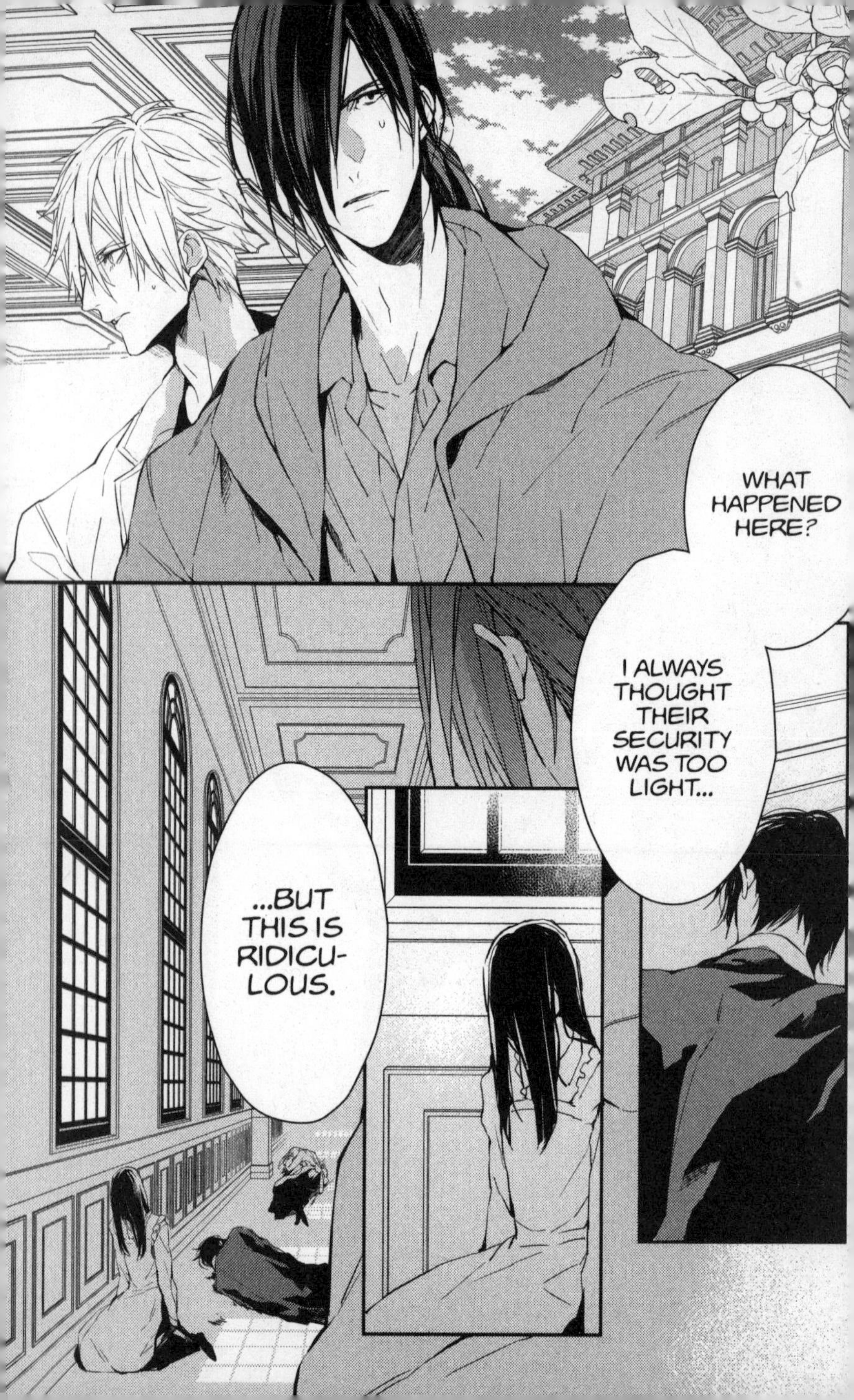
WHAT HAPPENED HERE?
I ALWAYS THOUGHT THEIR SECURITY WAS TOO LIGHT...
...BUT THIS IS RIDICU-LOUS.

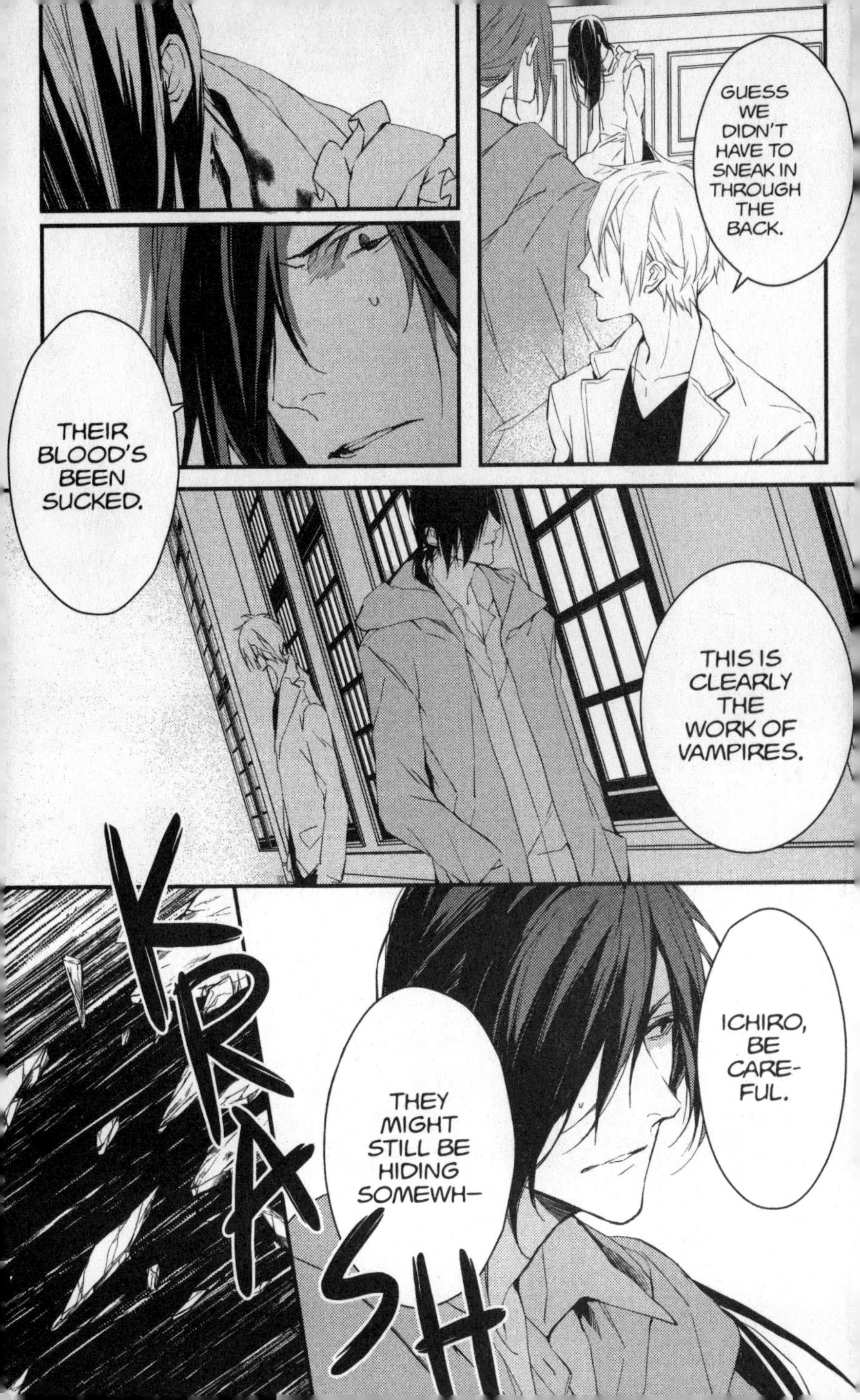
GUESS WE DIDN'T HAVE TO SNEAK IN THROUGH THE BACK.
THEIR BLOOD'S BEEN SUCKED.
THIS IS CLEARLY THE WORK OF VAMPIRES.
ICHIRO, BE CARE-FUL.
THEY MIGHT STILL BE HIDING SOMEWH-
KRASH

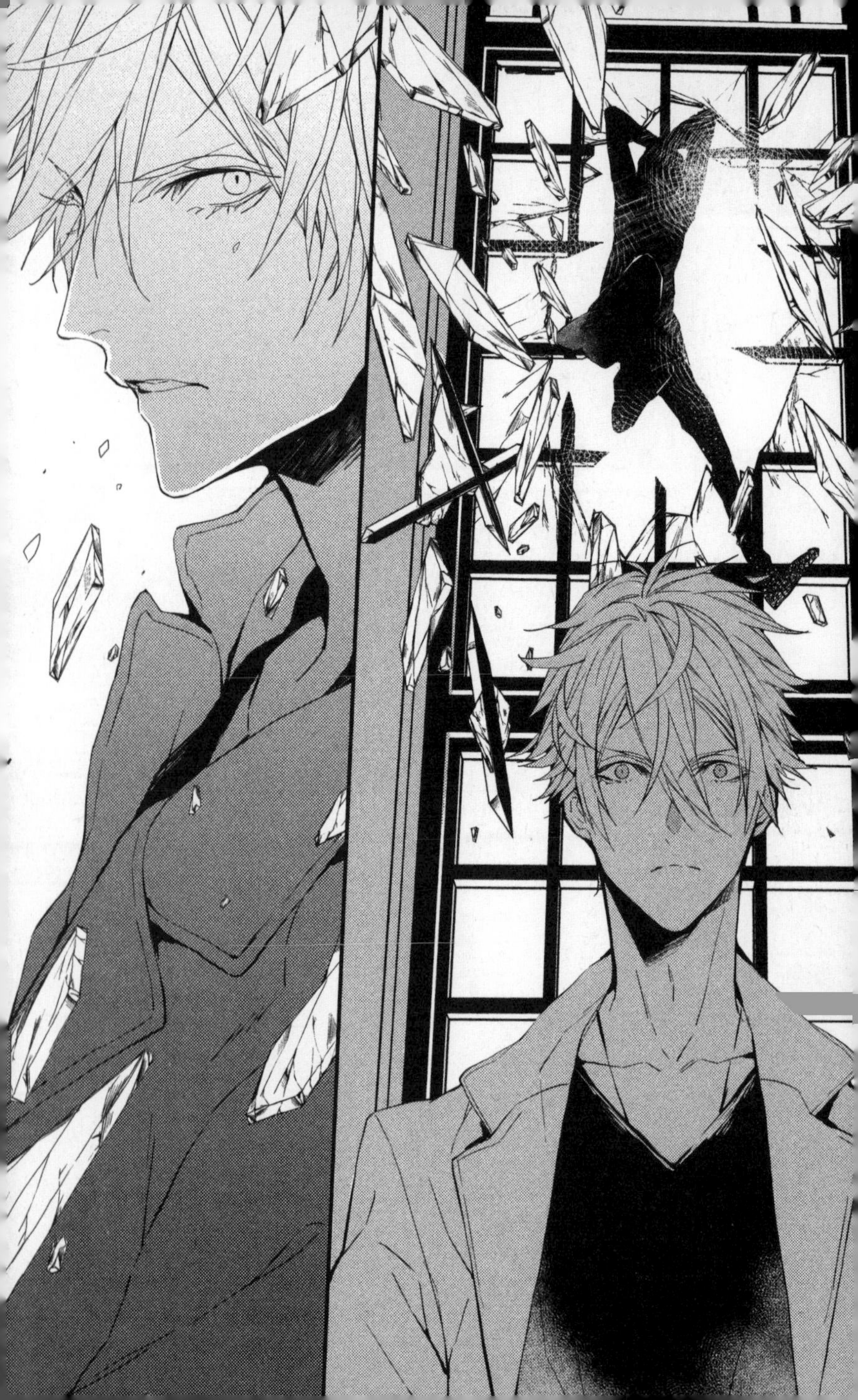

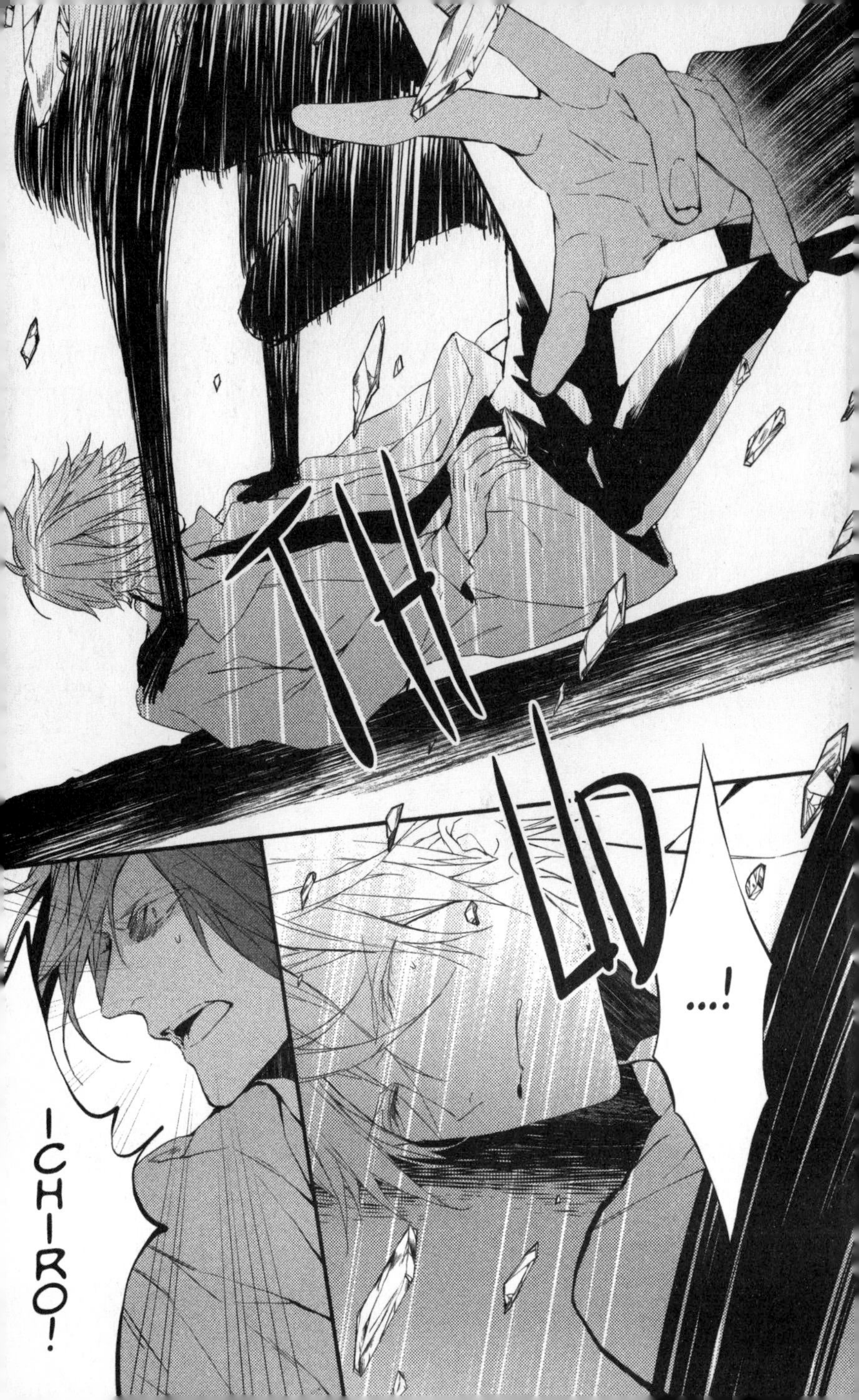
THUD
...!
ICHIRO!

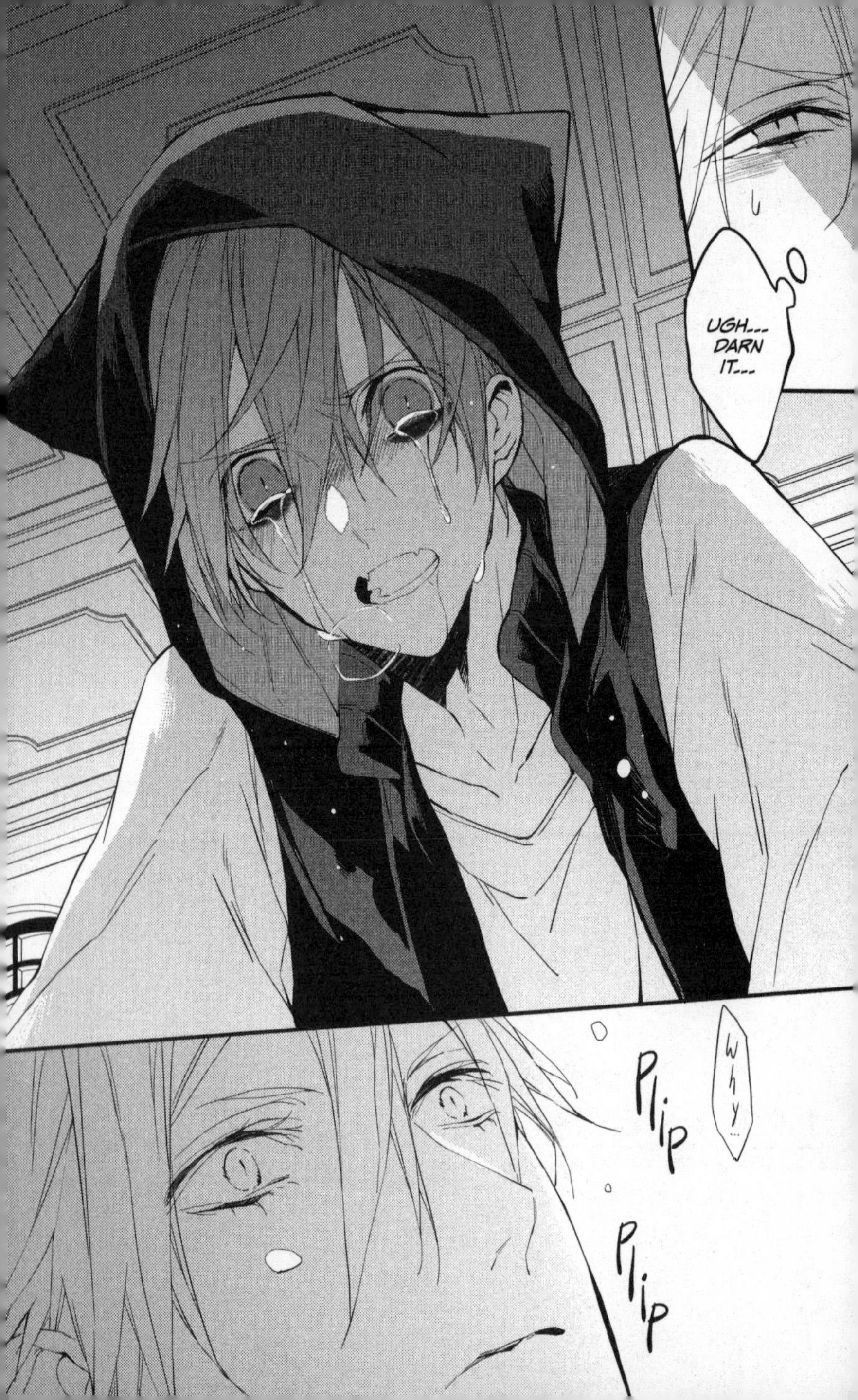
UGH... DARN IT...
Why...
Plip
Plip

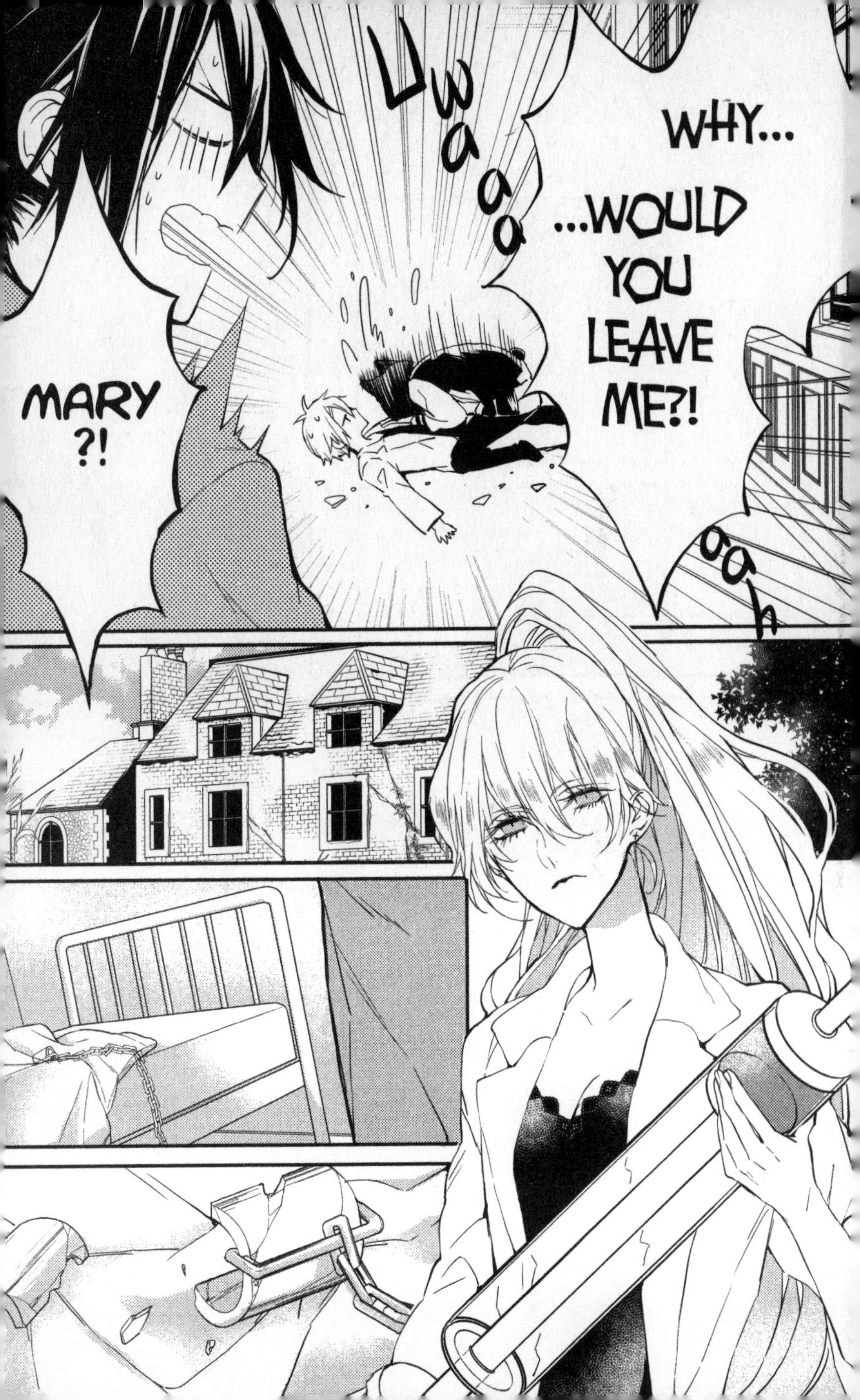
WHY...
...WOULD YOU LEAVE ME?!
Uwaaa
oon
MARY ?!

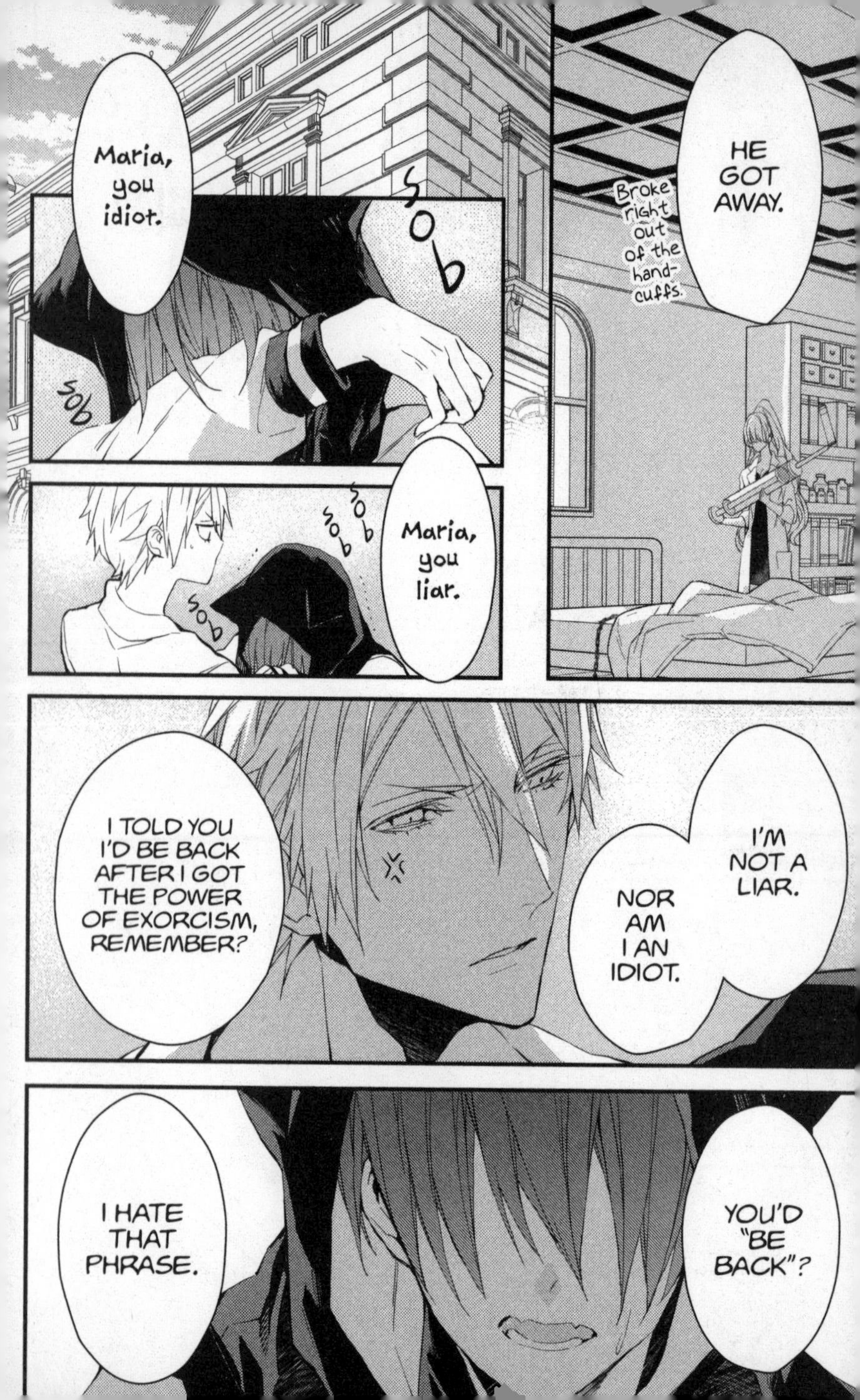
HE GOT AWAY.
Broke right out of the hand-cuffs.
Maria, you idiot.
sob
sob
Maria, you liar.
sob
sob
sob
I'M NOT A LIAR.
NOR AM I AN IDIOT.
I TOLD YOU I'D BE BACK AFTER I GOT THE POWER OF EXORCISM, REMEMBER?
YOU'D "BE BACK"?
I HATE THAT PHRASE.

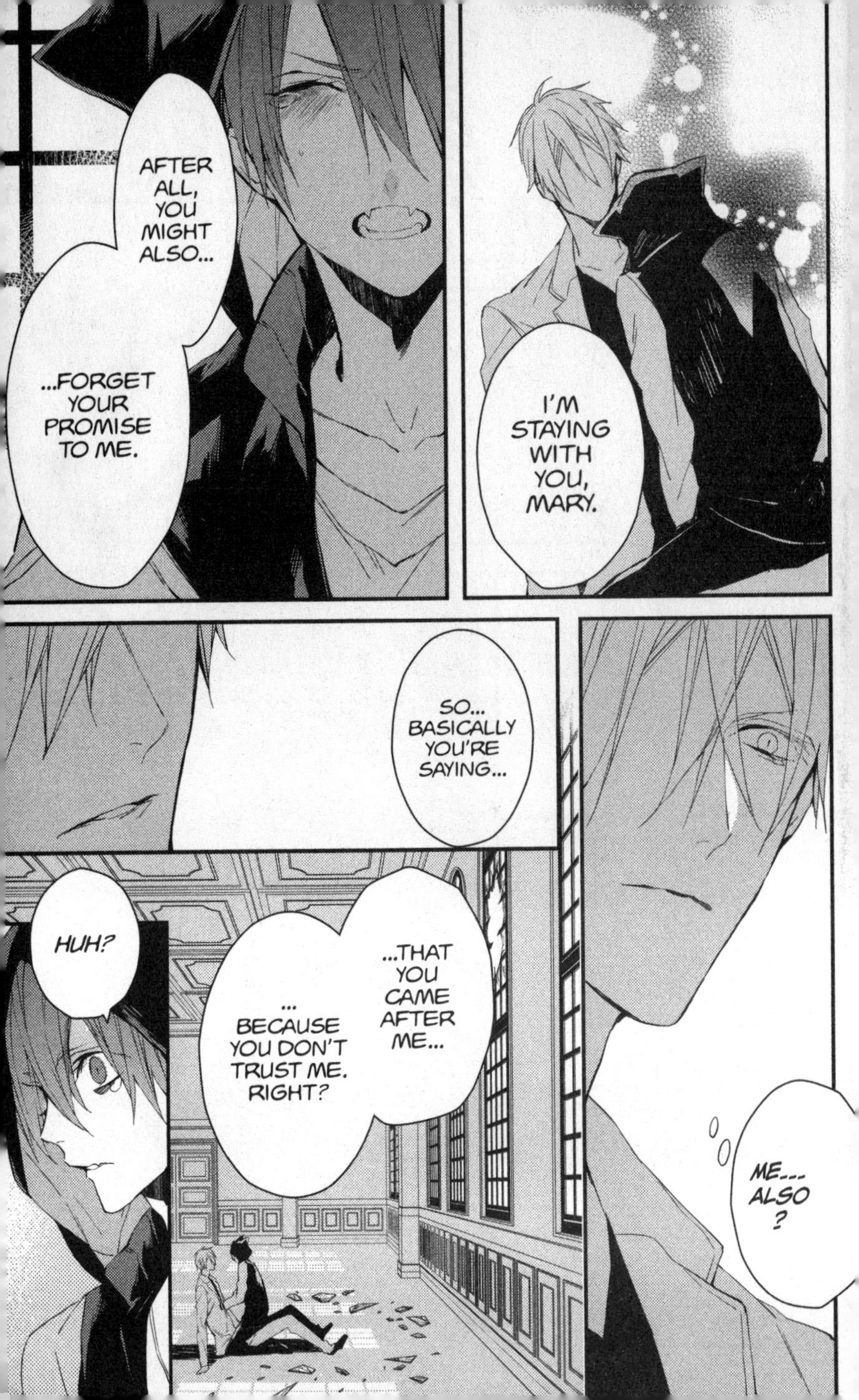
I'M STAYING WITH YOU, MARY.
AFTER ALL, YOU MIGHT ALSO...
...FORGET YOUR PROMISE TO ME.
ME... ALSO?
SO... BASICALLY YOU'RE SAYING...
...THAT YOU CAME AFTER ME...
...BECAUSE YOU DON'T TRUST ME. RIGHT?
HUH?

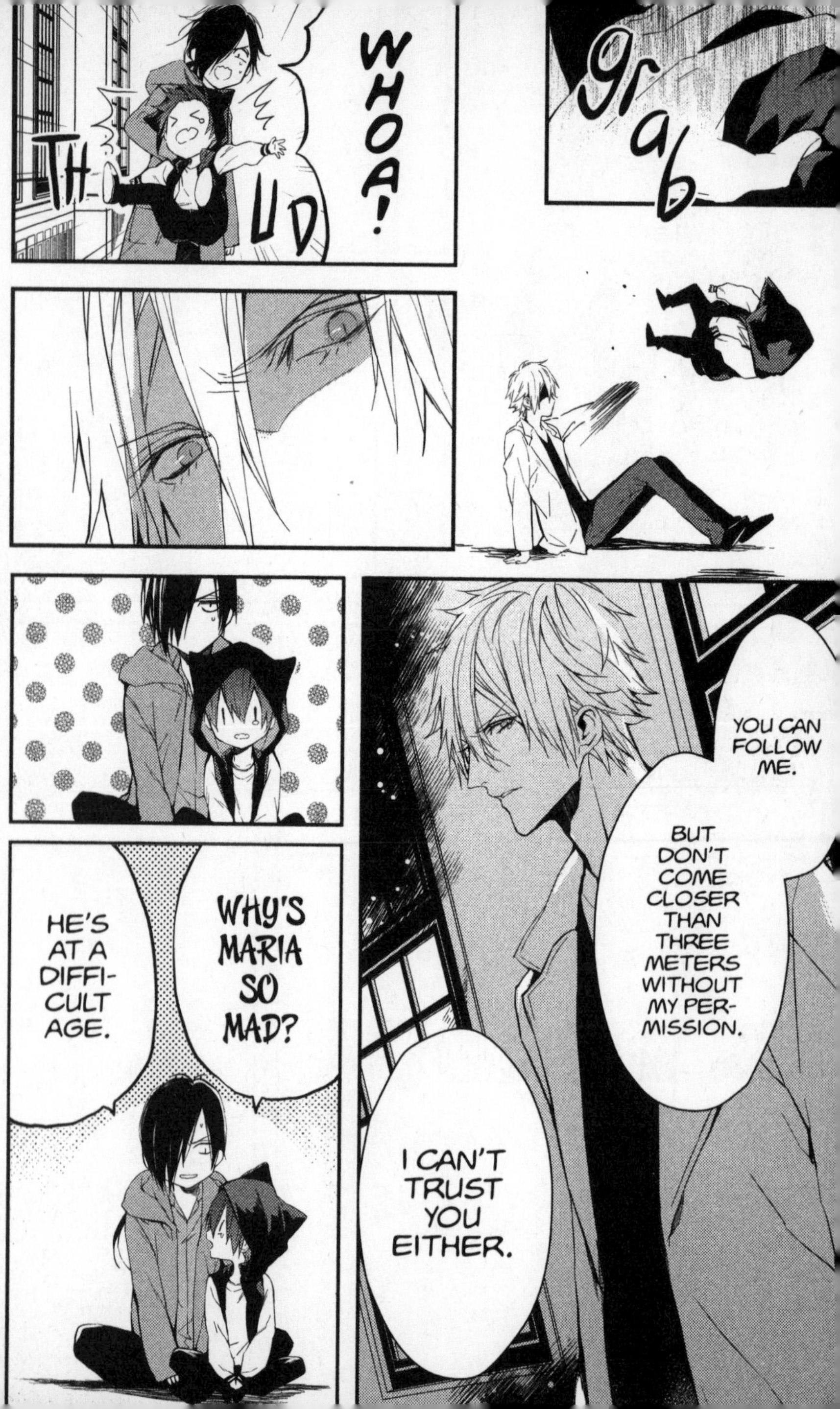
grab
WHOA!
THUD
YOU CAN FOLLOW ME.
BUT DON'T COME CLOSER THAN THREE METERS WITHOUT MY PERMISSION.
I CAN'T TRUST YOU EITHER.
WHY'S MARIA SO MAD?
HE'S AT A DIFFICULT AGE.

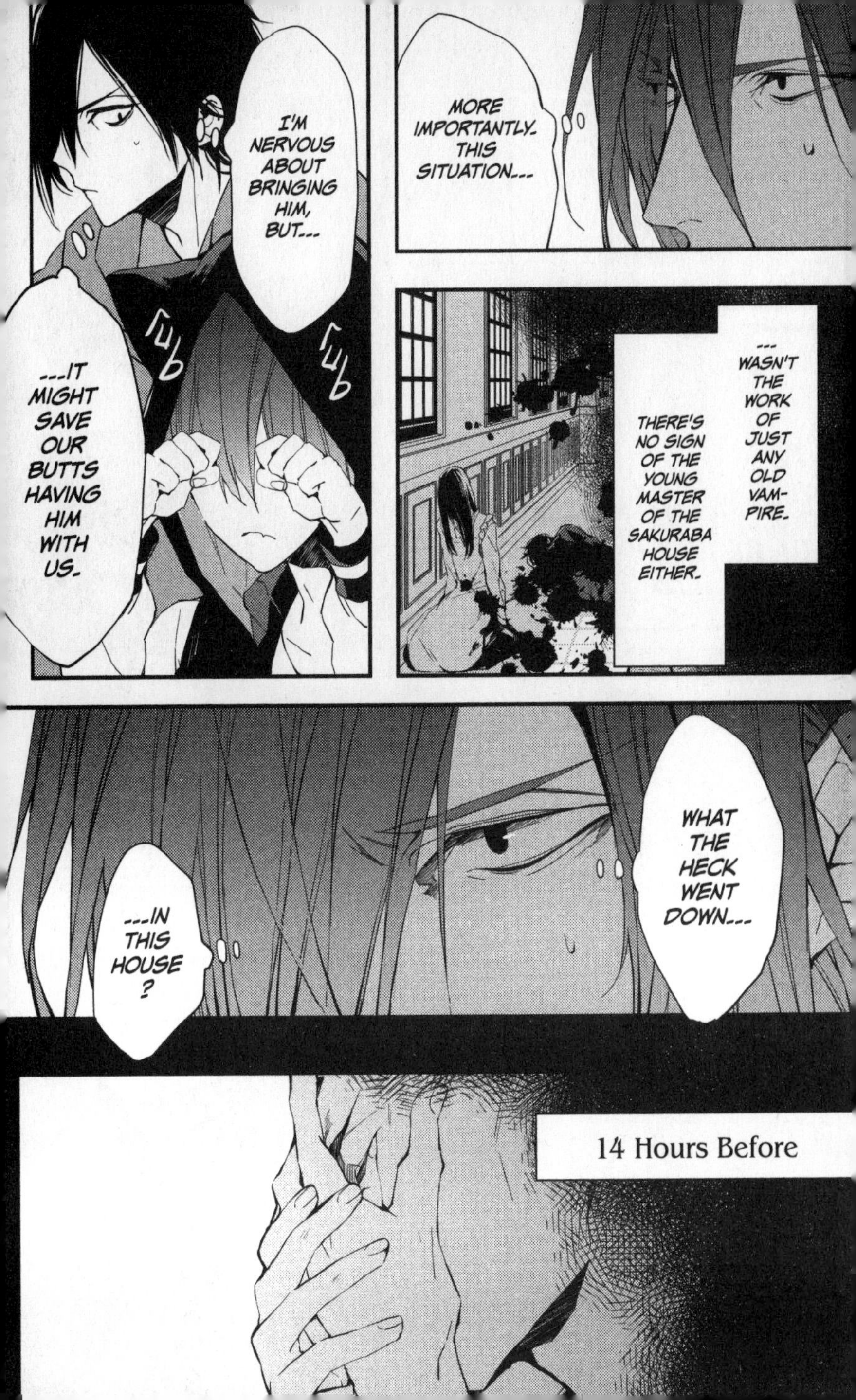
MORE IMPORTANTLY... THIS SITUATION...
...WASN'T THE WORK OF JUST ANY OLD VAMPIRE.
THERE'S NO SIGN OF THE YOUNG MASTER OF THE SAKURABA HOUSE EITHER.
I'M NERVOUS ABOUT BRINGING HIM, BUT...
rub
rub
...IT MIGHT SAVE OUR BUTTS HAVING HIM WITH US.
WHAT THE HECK WENT DOWN...
...IN THIS HOUSE?
14 Hours Before

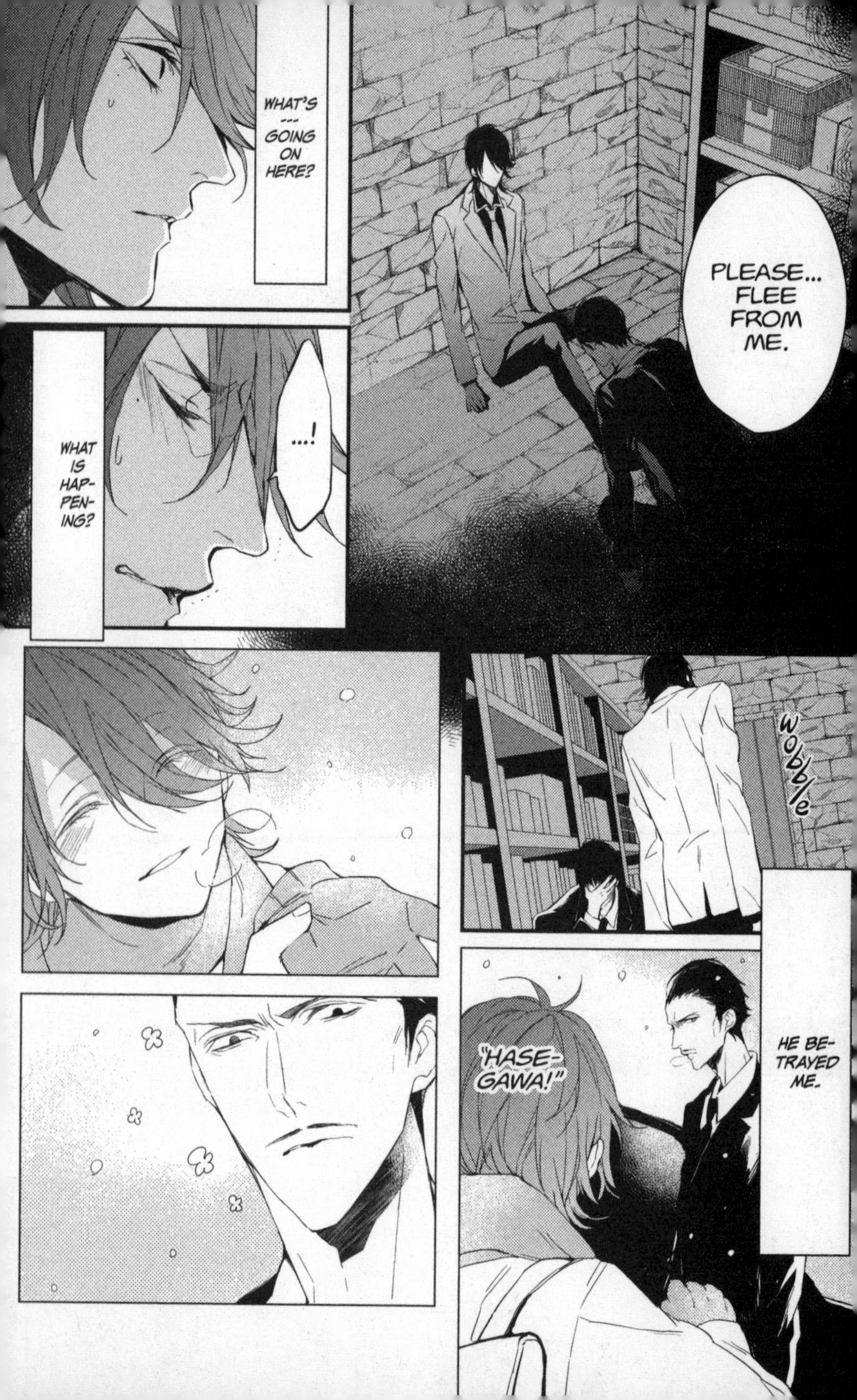
PLEASE... FLEE FROM ME.
WHAT'S --- GOING ON HERE?
...!
WHAT IS HAP-PEN-ING?
wobble
HE BE-TRAYED ME.
"HASE-GAWA!"

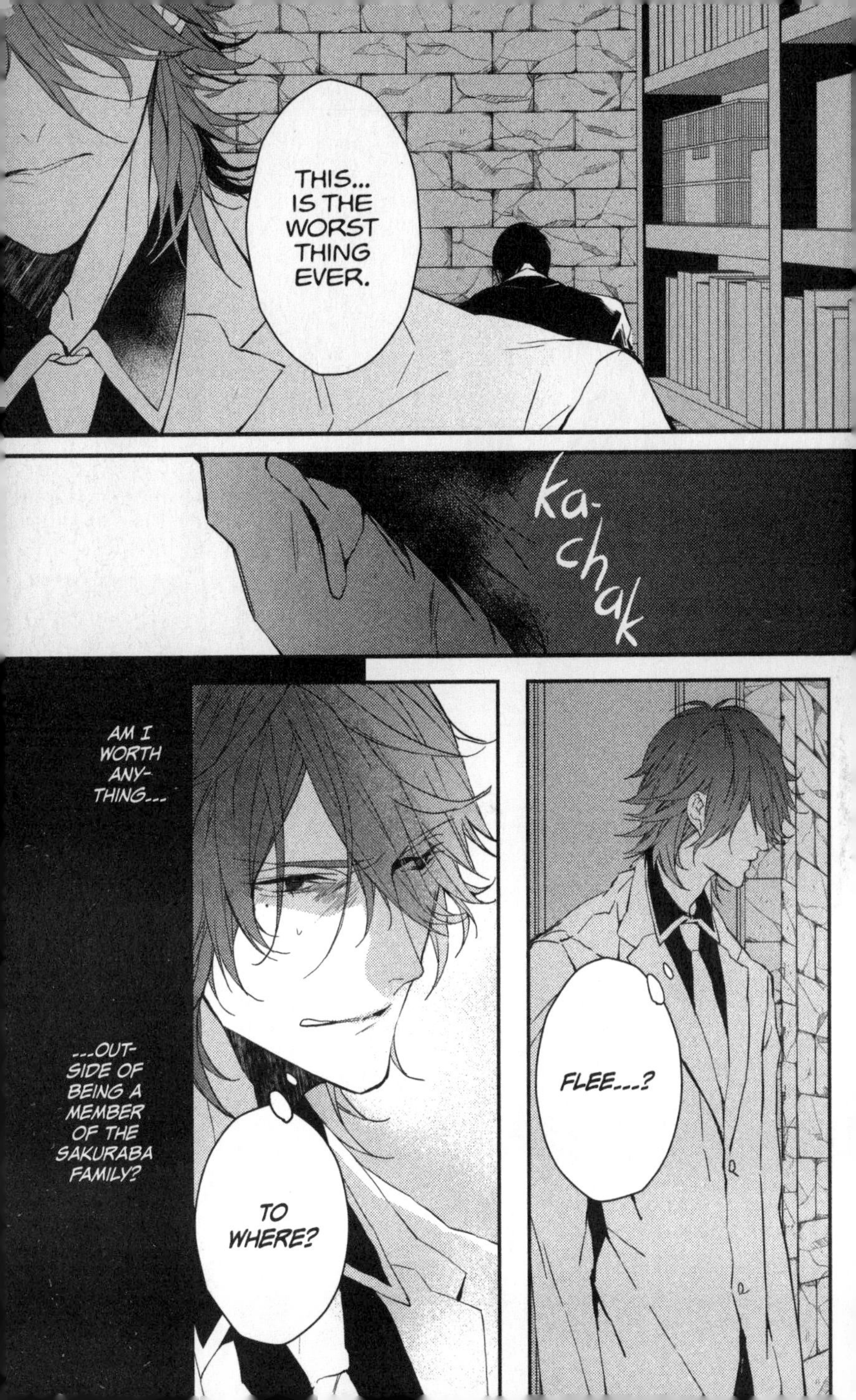
THIS... IS THE WORST THING EVER.
ka-chak
FLEE...?
AM I WORTH ANYTHING...
...OUTSIDE OF BEING A MEMBER OF THE SAKURABA FAMILY?
TO WHERE?

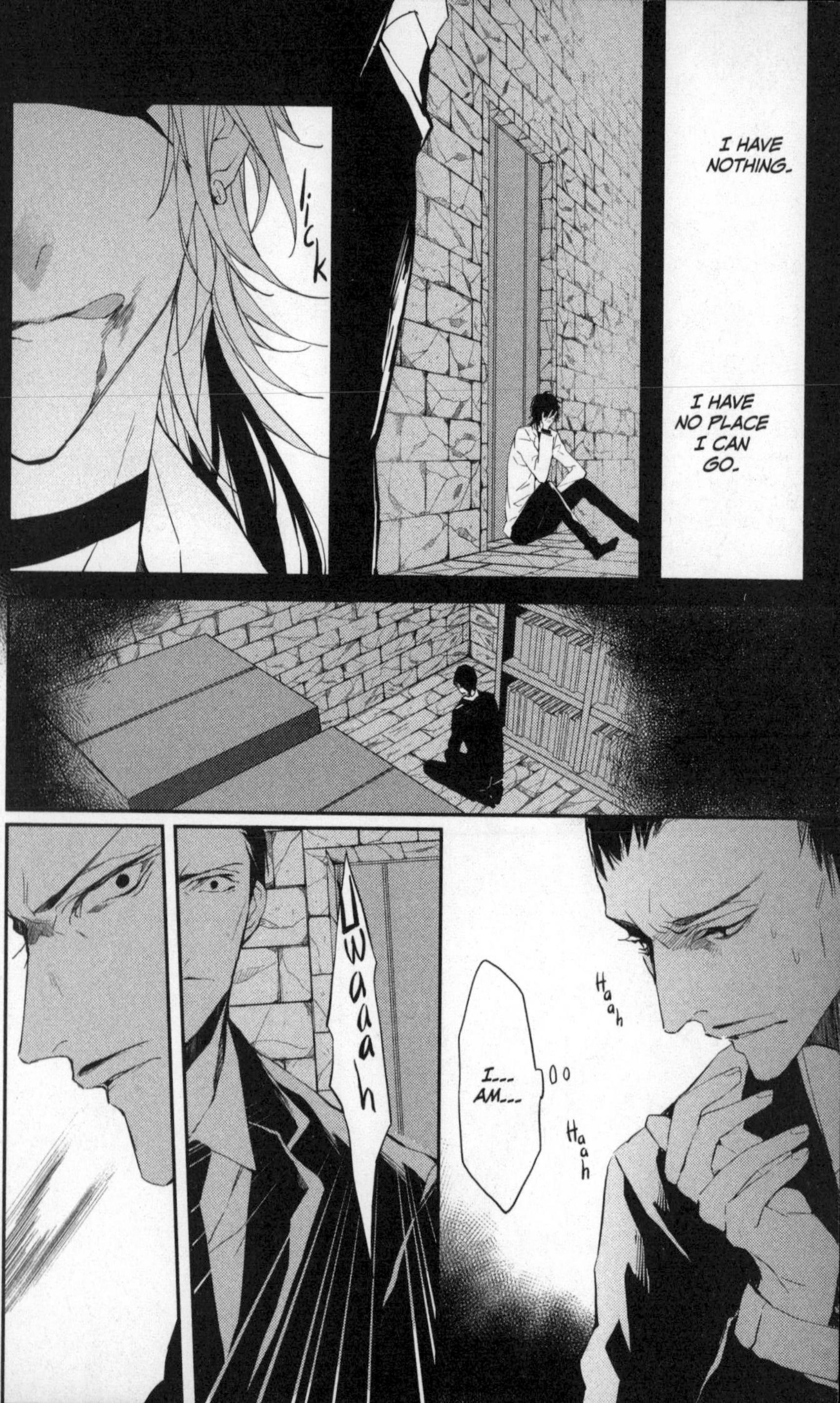
I HAVE NOTHING.
I HAVE NO PLACE I CAN GO.
lick
Haaah
I... AM...
Haaah
Uwaaaah

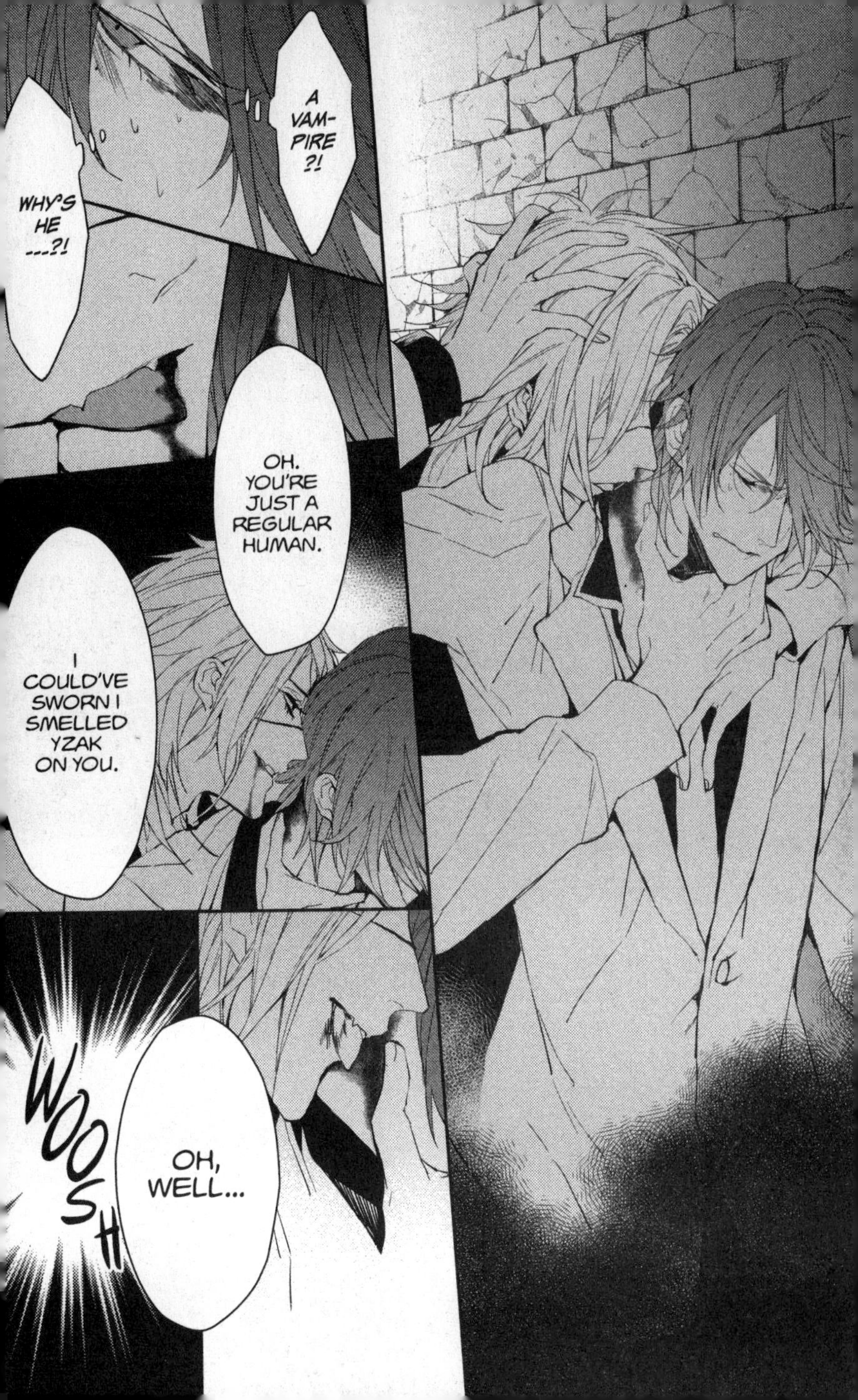
A VAMPIRE?!
WHY'S HE ---?!
OH. YOU'RE JUST A REGULAR HUMAN.
I COULD'VE SWORN I SMELLED YZAK ON YOU.
OH, WELL...
WOOSH

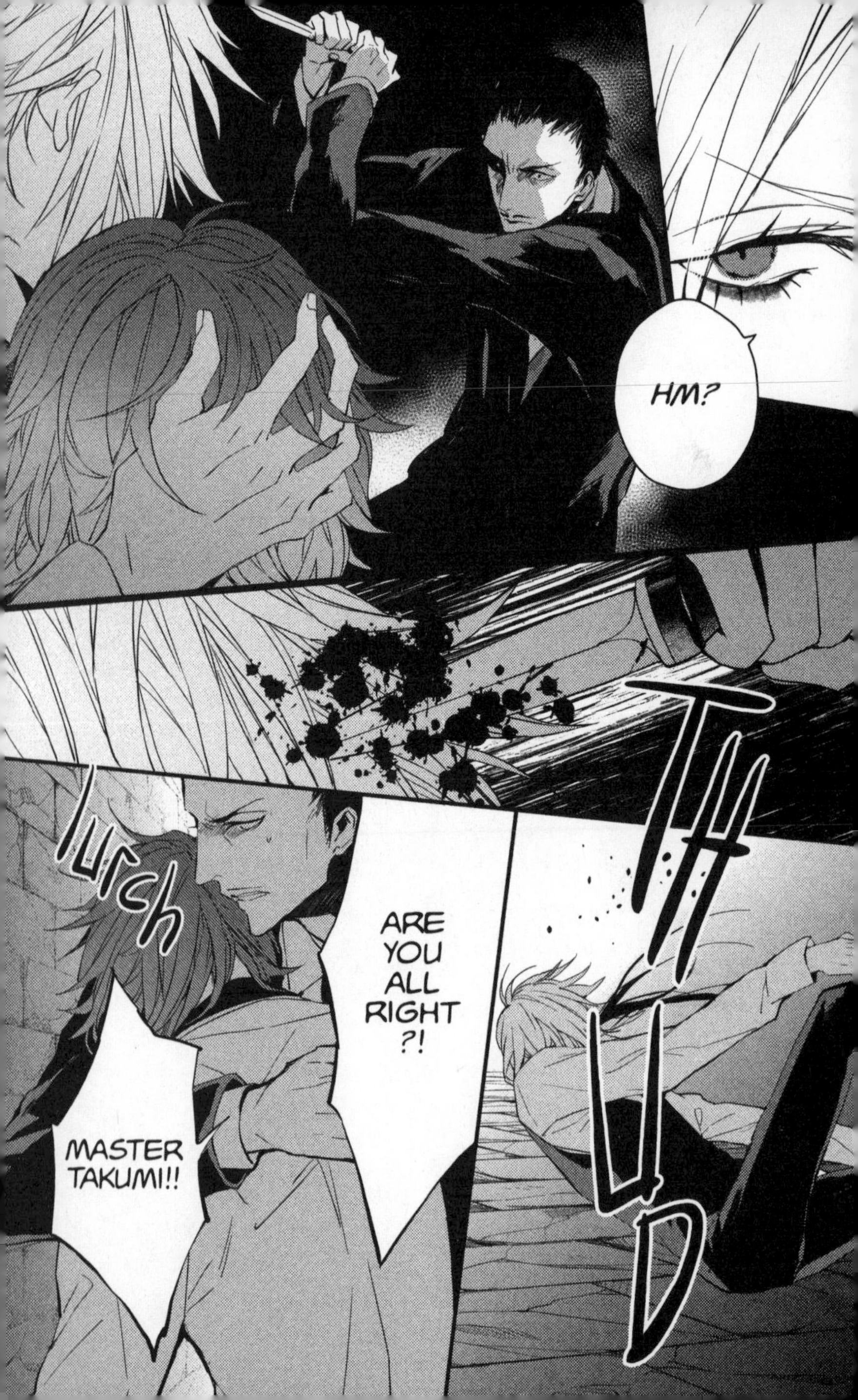
HM?
THUD
ARE YOU ALL RIGHT?!
MASTER TAKUMI!!
lurch

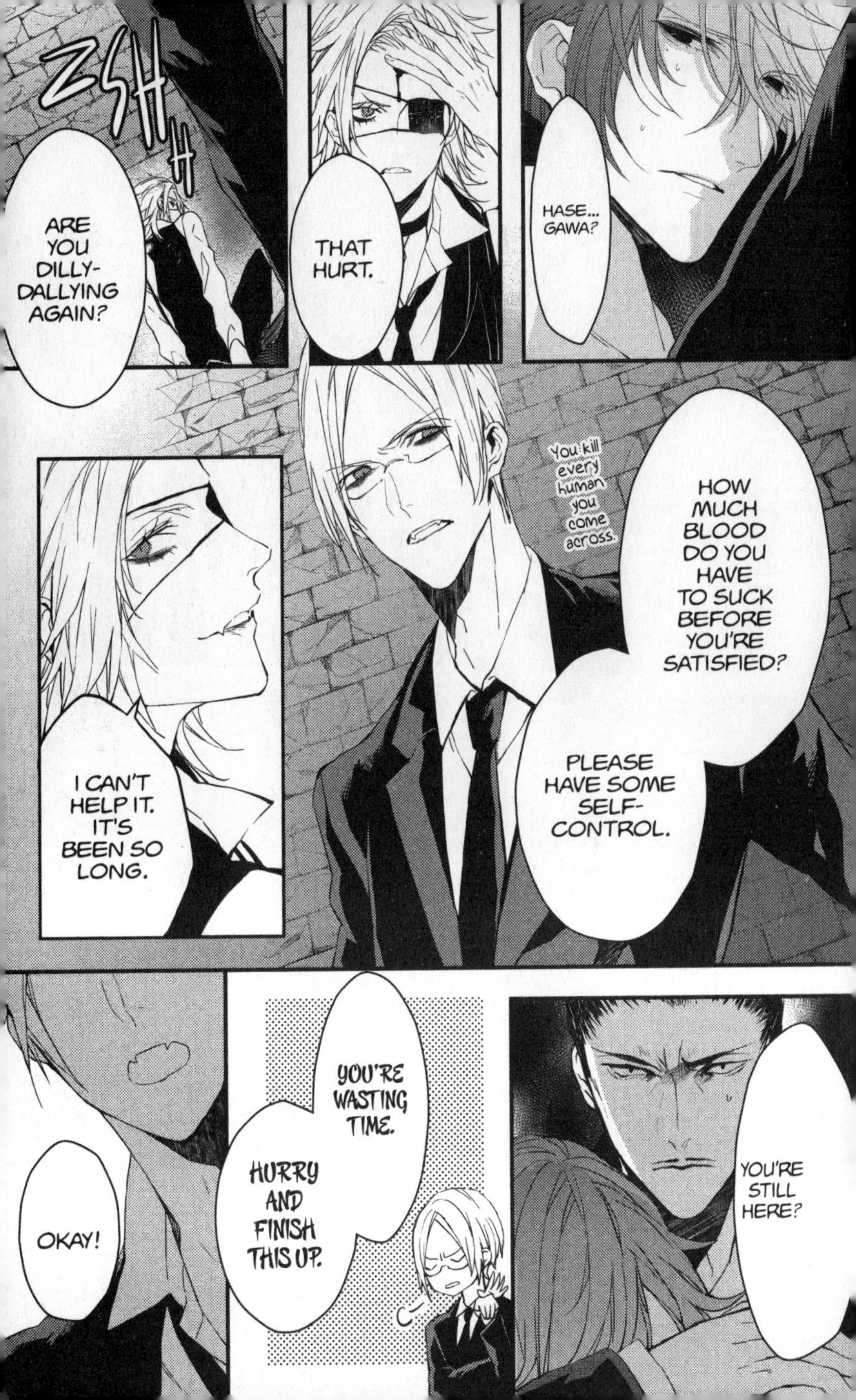
HASE... GAWA?
THAT HURT.
ZSHH
ARE YOU DILLY-DALLYING AGAIN?
HOW MUCH BLOOD DO YOU HAVE TO SUCK BEFORE YOU'RE SATISFIED?
You kill every human you come across.
PLEASE HAVE SOME SELF-CONTROL.
I CAN'T HELP IT. IT'S BEEN SO LONG.
YOU'RE STILL HERE?
YOU'RE WASTING TIME.
HURRY AND FINISH THIS UP.
OKAY!

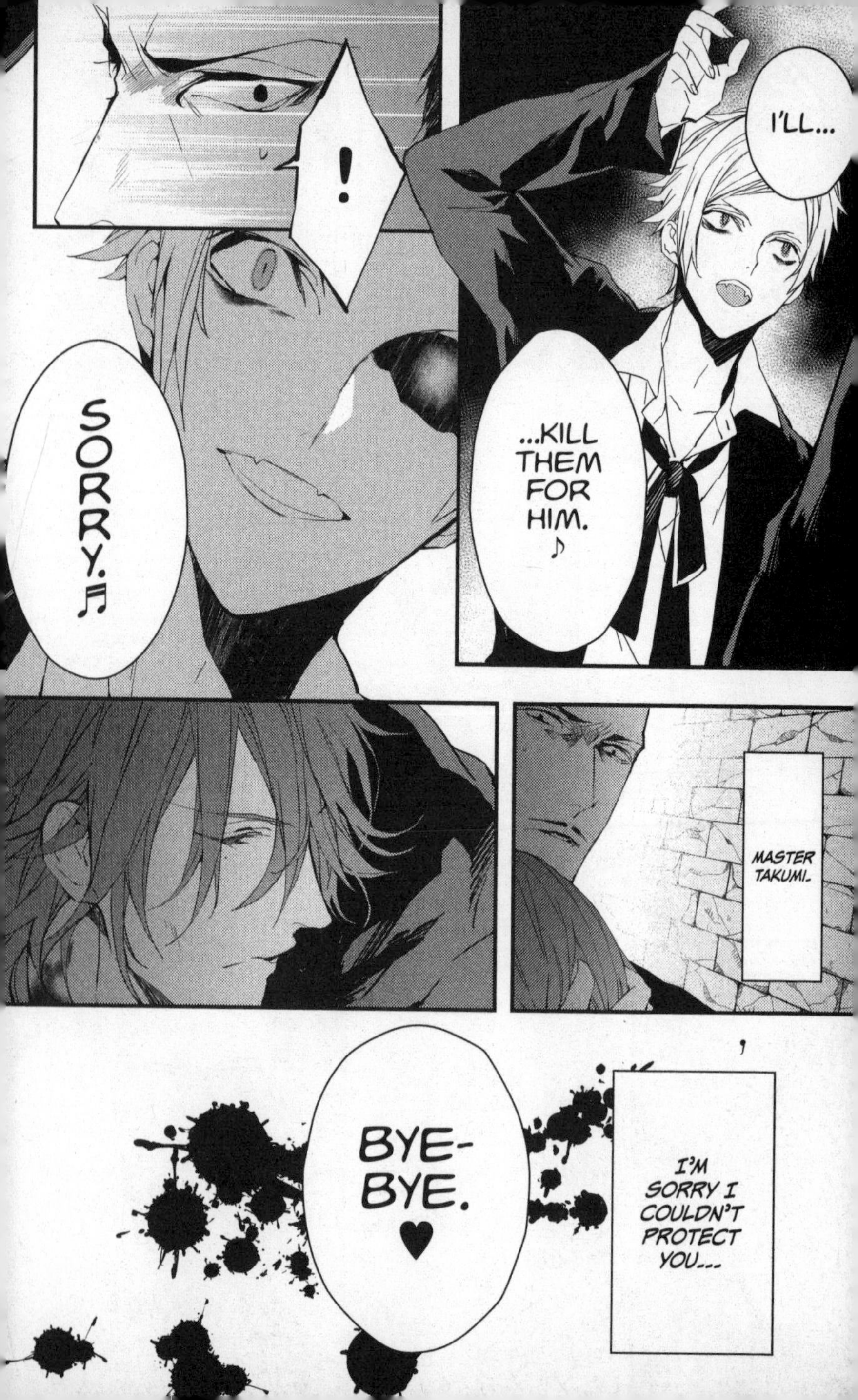
I'LL...
...KILL THEM FOR HIM. ♪
!
SORRY. ♬
MASTER TAKUMI...
I'M SORRY I COULDN'T PROTECT YOU...
BYE-BYE. ♥

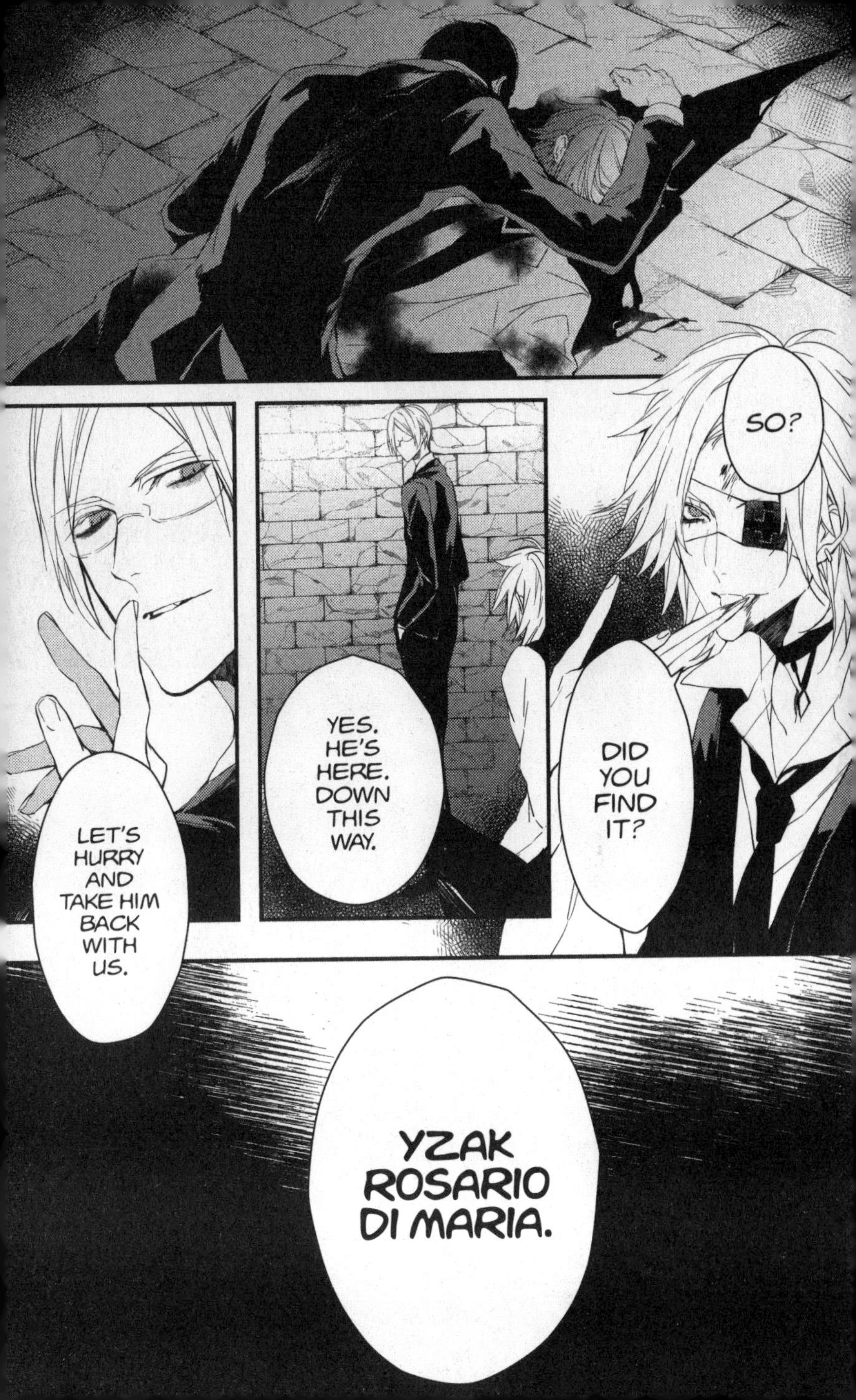
SO?
DID YOU FIND IT?
YES. HE'S HERE. DOWN THIS WAY.
LET'S HURRY AND TAKE HIM BACK WITH US.
YZAK ROSARIO DI MARIA.

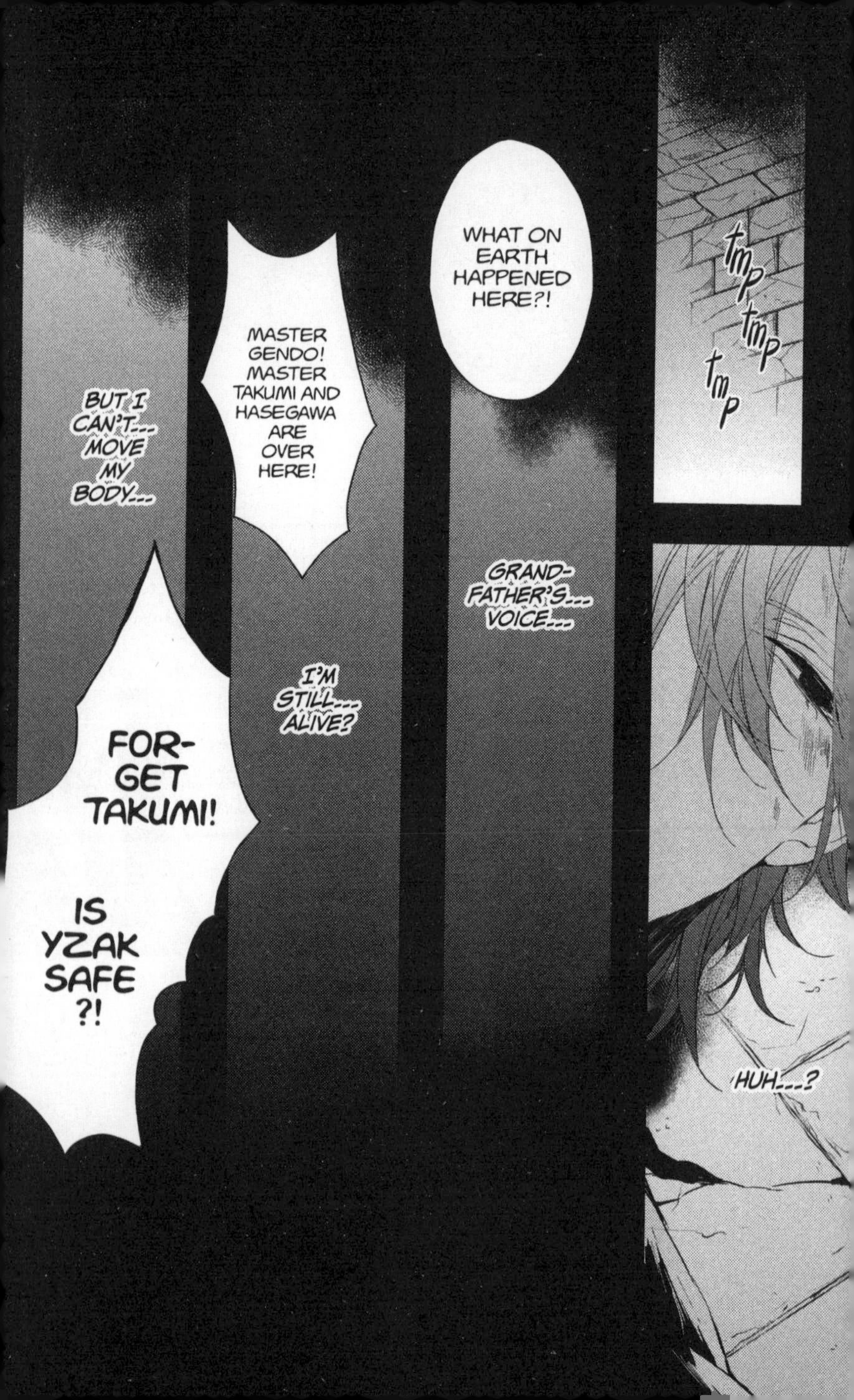
tmp tmp tmp
HUH...?
WHAT ON EARTH HAPPENED HERE?!
GRAND-FATHER'S... VOICE...
MASTER GENDO! MASTER TAKUMI AND HASEGAWA ARE OVER HERE!
I'M STILL... ALIVE?
BUT I CAN'T... MOVE MY BODY...
FOR-GET TAKUMI!
IS YZAK SAFE ?!

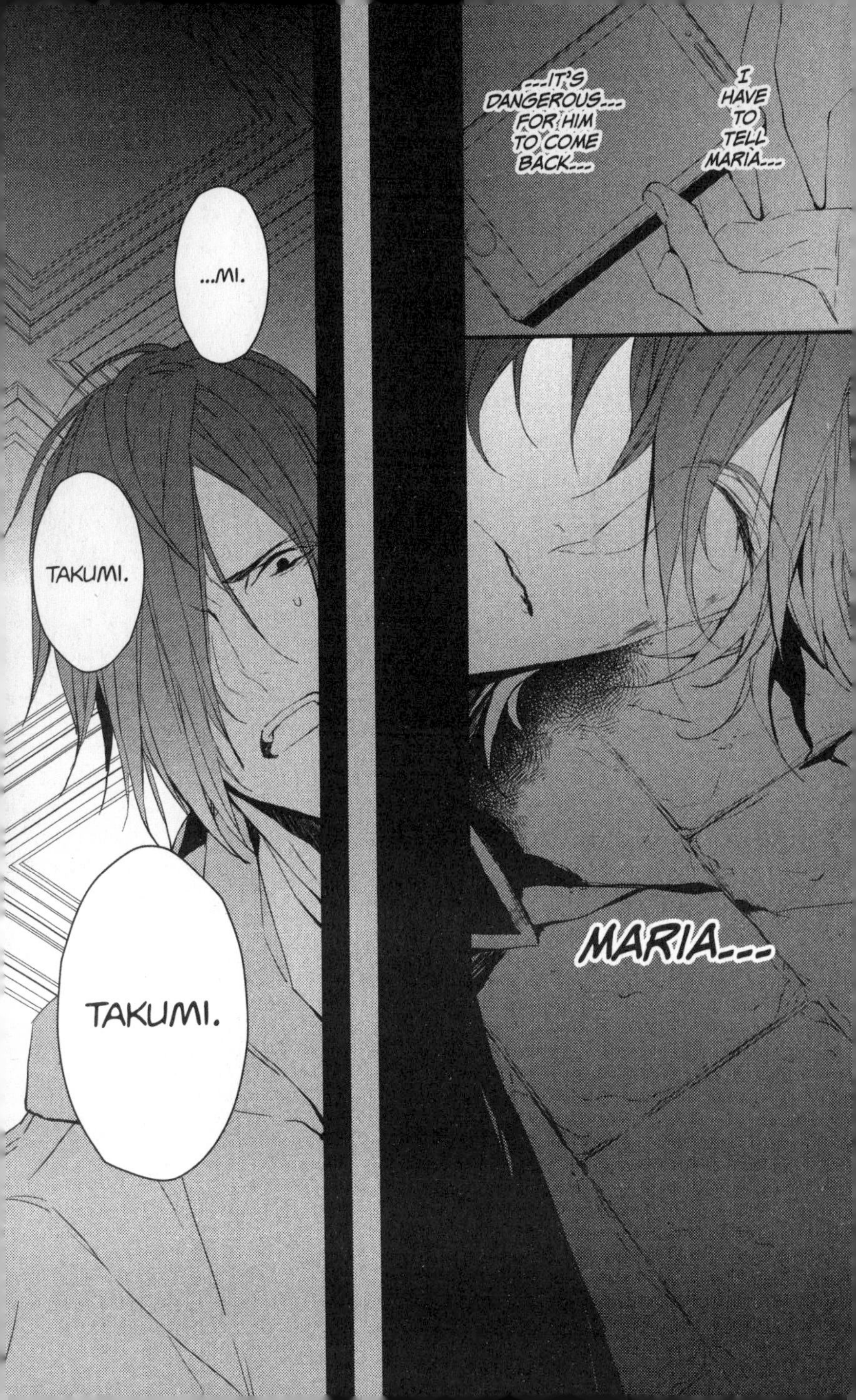
I HAVE TO TELL MARIA...
...IT'S DANGEROUS... FOR HIM TO COME BACK...
MARIA...
...MI.
TAKUMI.
TAKUMI.

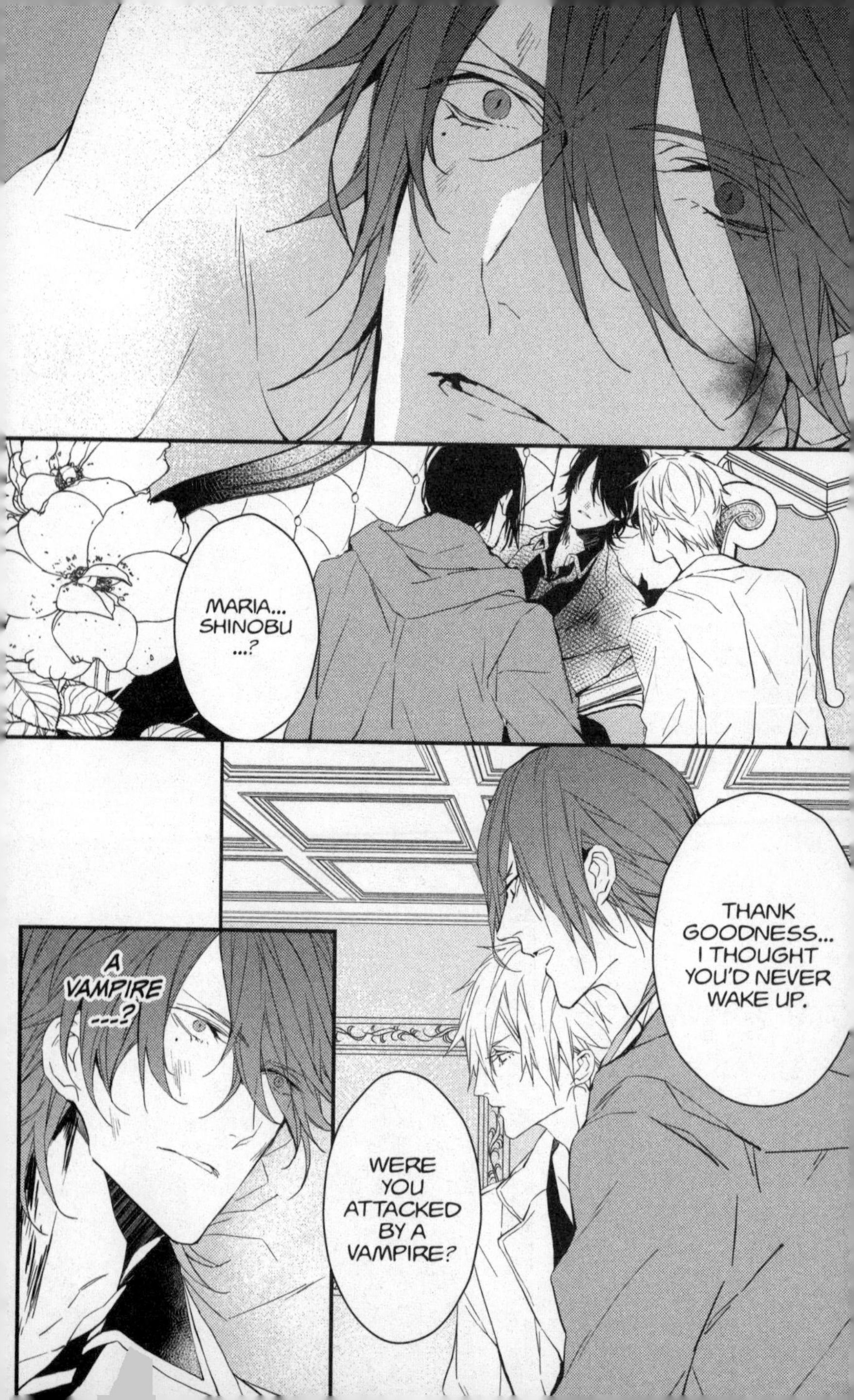
MARIA... SHINOBU ...?
THANK GOODNESS... I THOUGHT YOU'D NEVER WAKE UP.
WERE YOU ATTACKED BY A VAMPIRE?
A VAMPIRE ---?

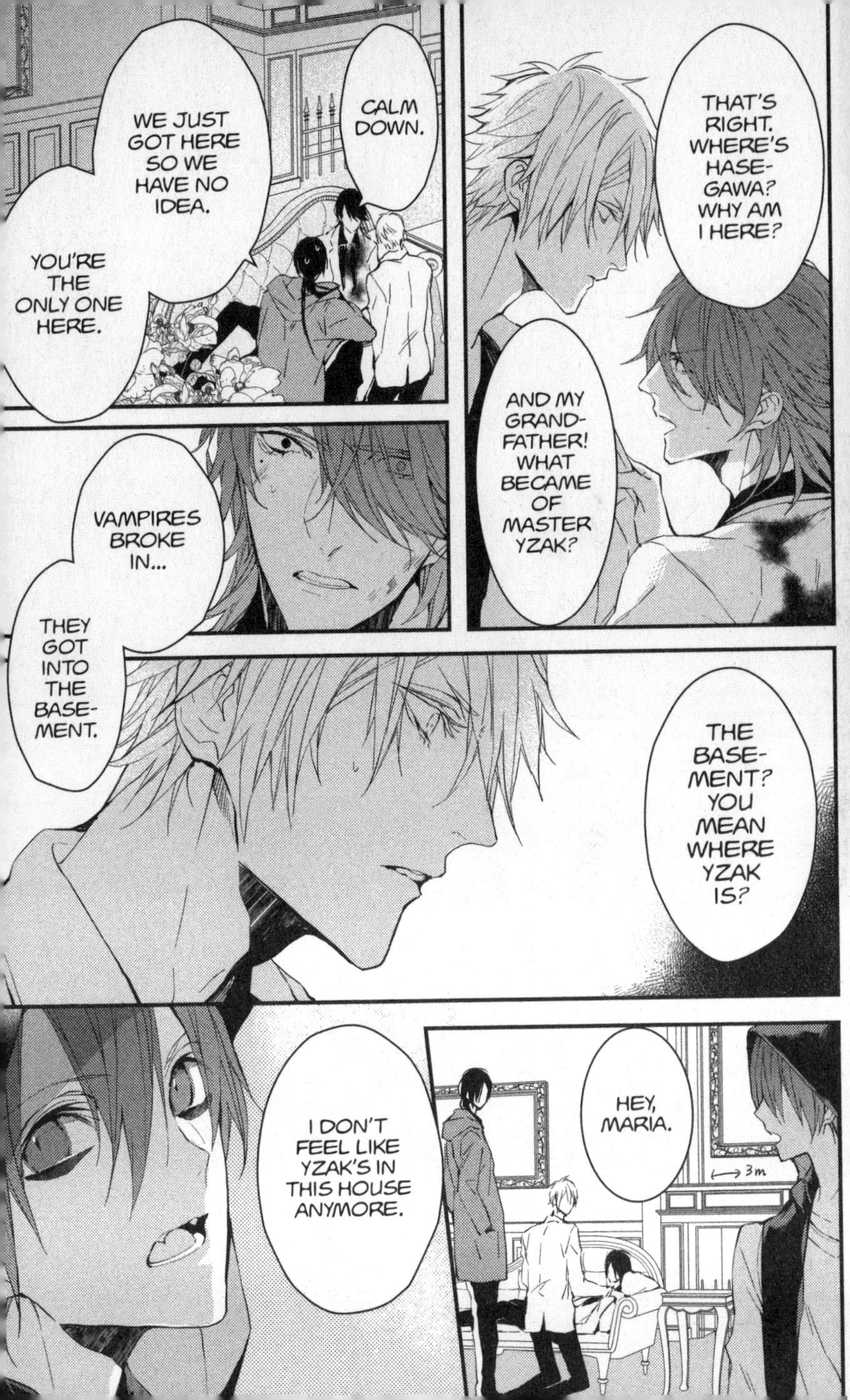
THAT'S RIGHT. WHERE'S HASEGAWA? WHY AM I HERE?
AND MY GRANDFATHER! WHAT BECAME OF MASTER YZAK?
CALM DOWN.
WE JUST GOT HERE SO WE HAVE NO IDEA.
YOU'RE THE ONLY ONE HERE.
VAMPIRES BROKE IN...
THEY GOT INTO THE BASEMENT.
THE BASEMENT? YOU MEAN WHERE YZAK IS?
HEY, MARIA.
3m
I DON'T FEEL LIKE YZAK'S IN THIS HOUSE ANYMORE.

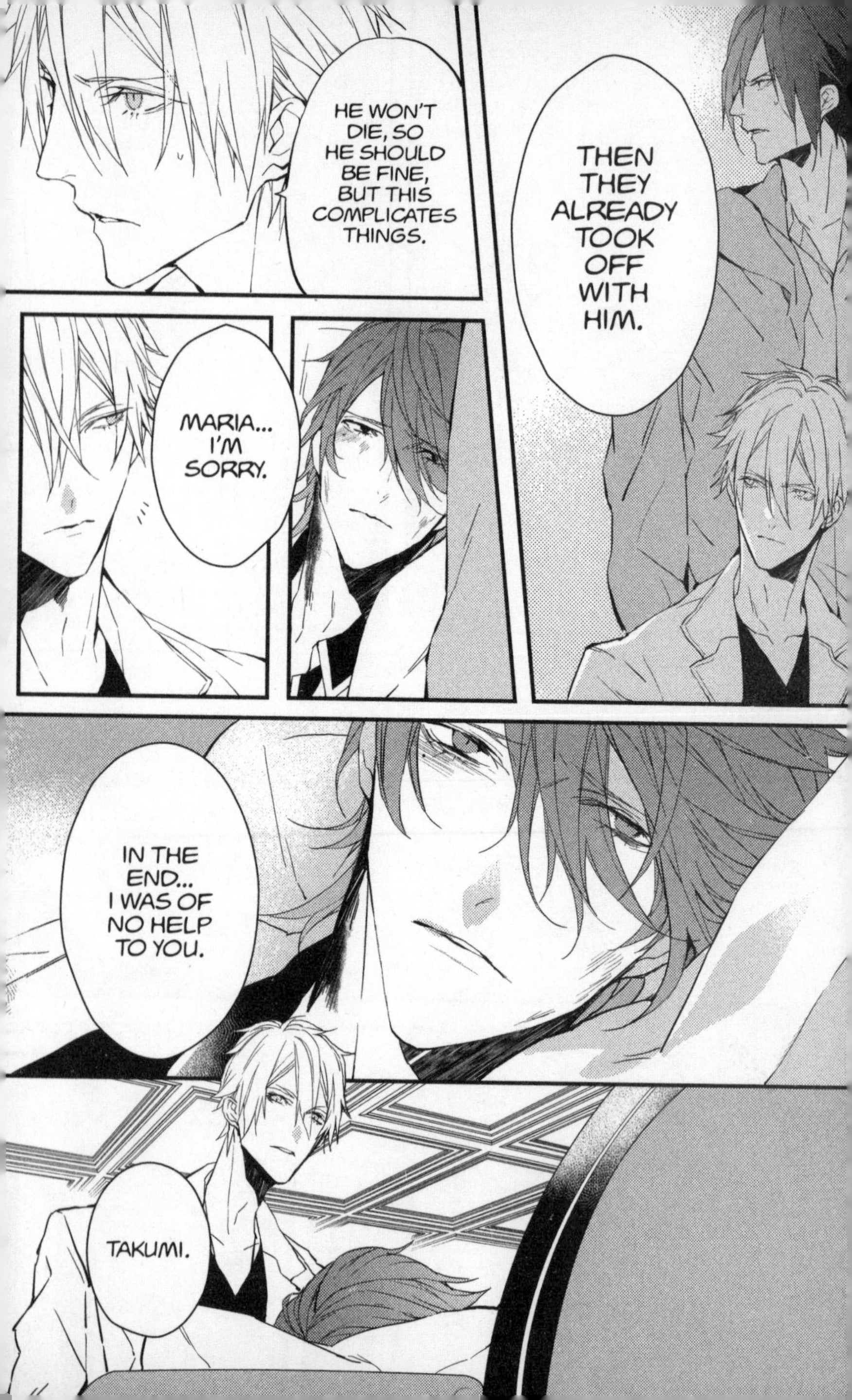
THEN THEY ALREADY TOOK OFF WITH HIM.
HE WON'T DIE, SO HE SHOULD BE FINE, BUT THIS COMPLICATES THINGS.
MARIA... I'M SORRY.
IN THE END... I WAS OF NO HELP TO YOU.
TAKUMI.

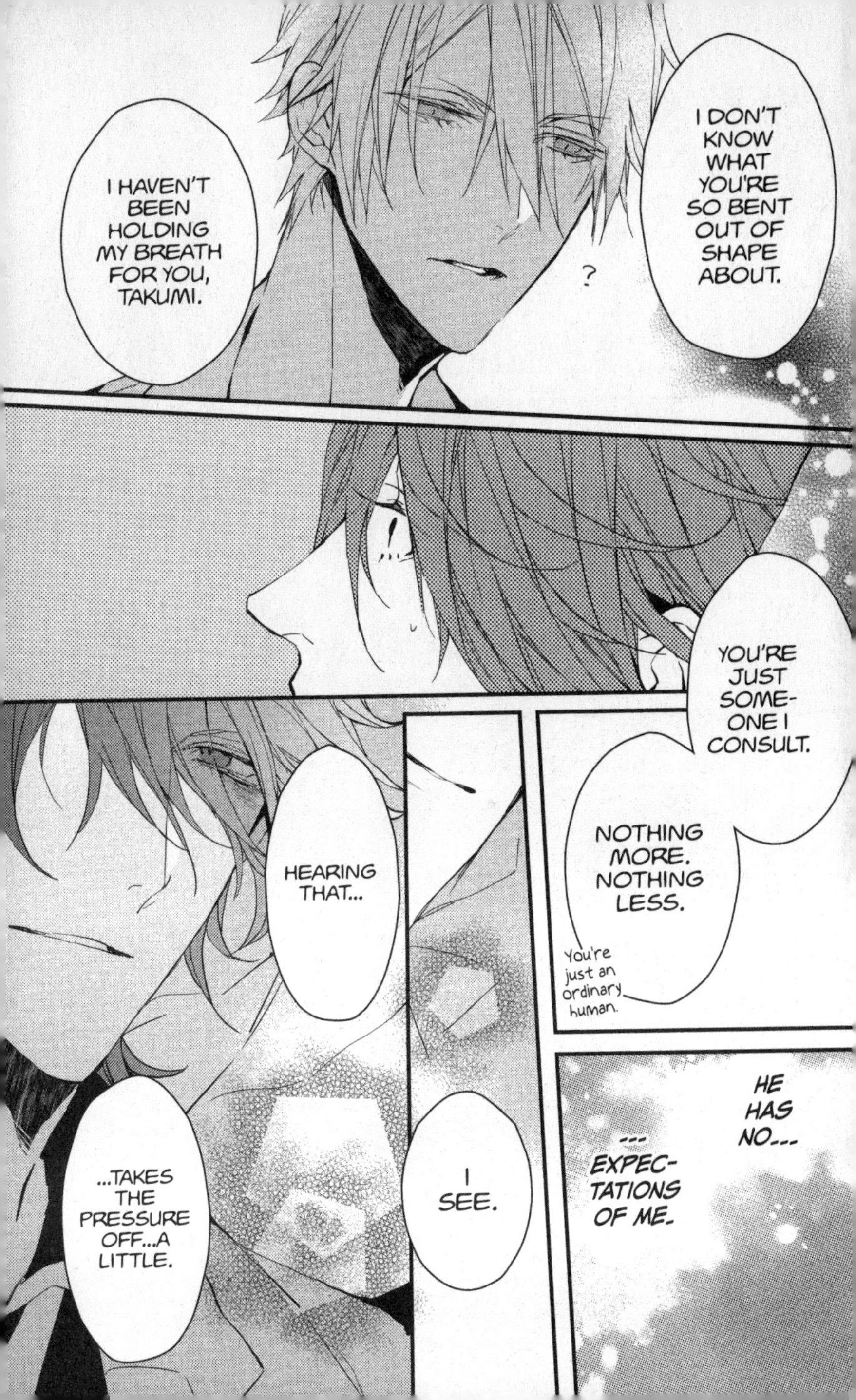
I DON'T KNOW WHAT YOU'RE SO BENT OUT OF SHAPE ABOUT.
?
I HAVEN'T BEEN HOLDING MY BREATH FOR YOU, TAKUMI.
YOU'RE JUST SOME-ONE I CONSULT.
NOTHING MORE. NOTHING LESS.
You're just an ordinary human.
HEARING THAT...
HE HAS NO...
...EXPECTATIONS OF ME.
I SEE.
...TAKES THE PRESSURE OFF...A LITTLE.

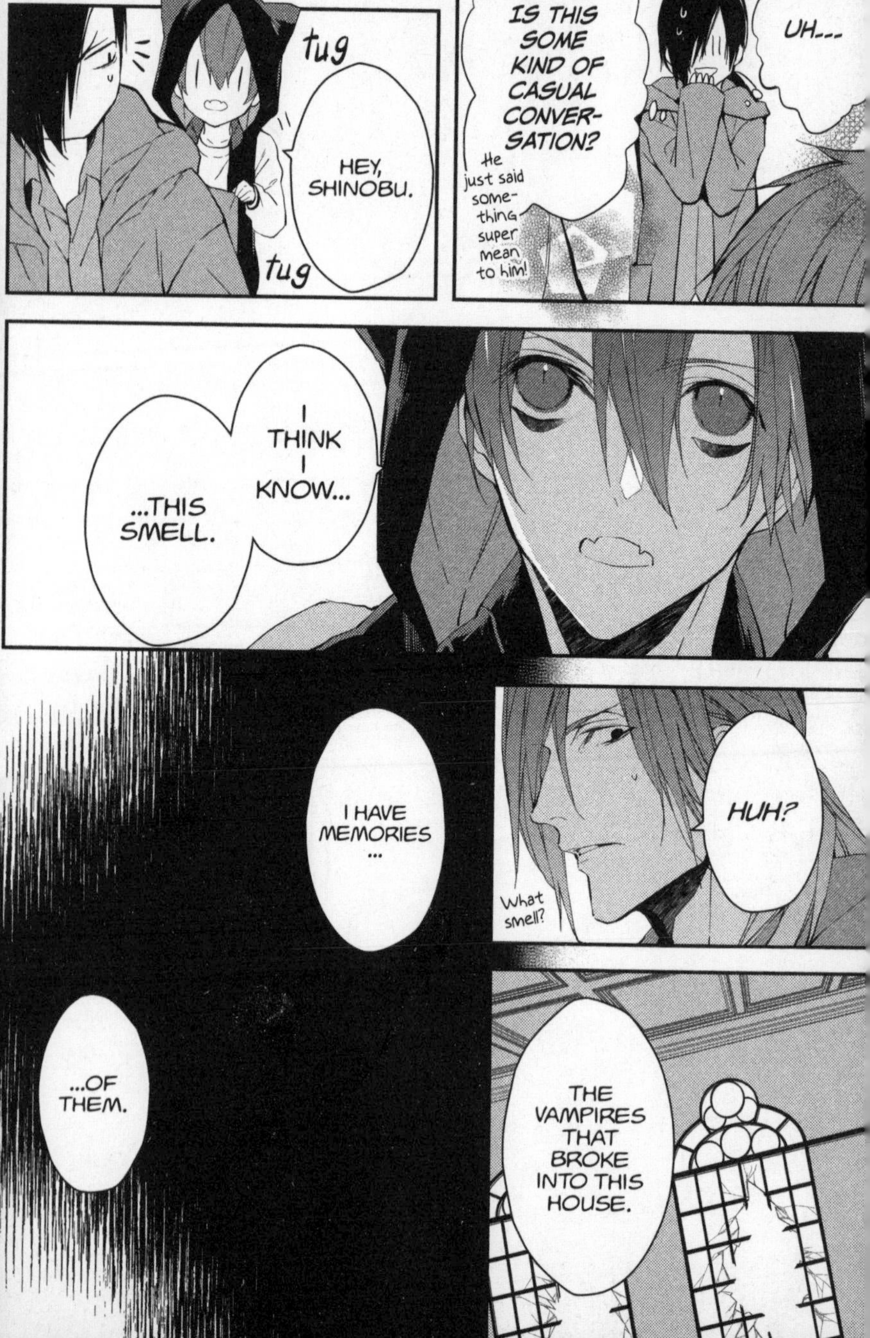
UH...
IS THIS SOME KIND OF CASUAL CONVER-SATION?
He just said some-thing super mean to him!
tug
HEY, SHINOBU.
tug
I THINK I KNOW...
...THIS SMELL.
HUH?
What smell?
I HAVE MEMORIES...
...OF THEM.
THE VAMPIRES THAT BROKE INTO THIS HOUSE.

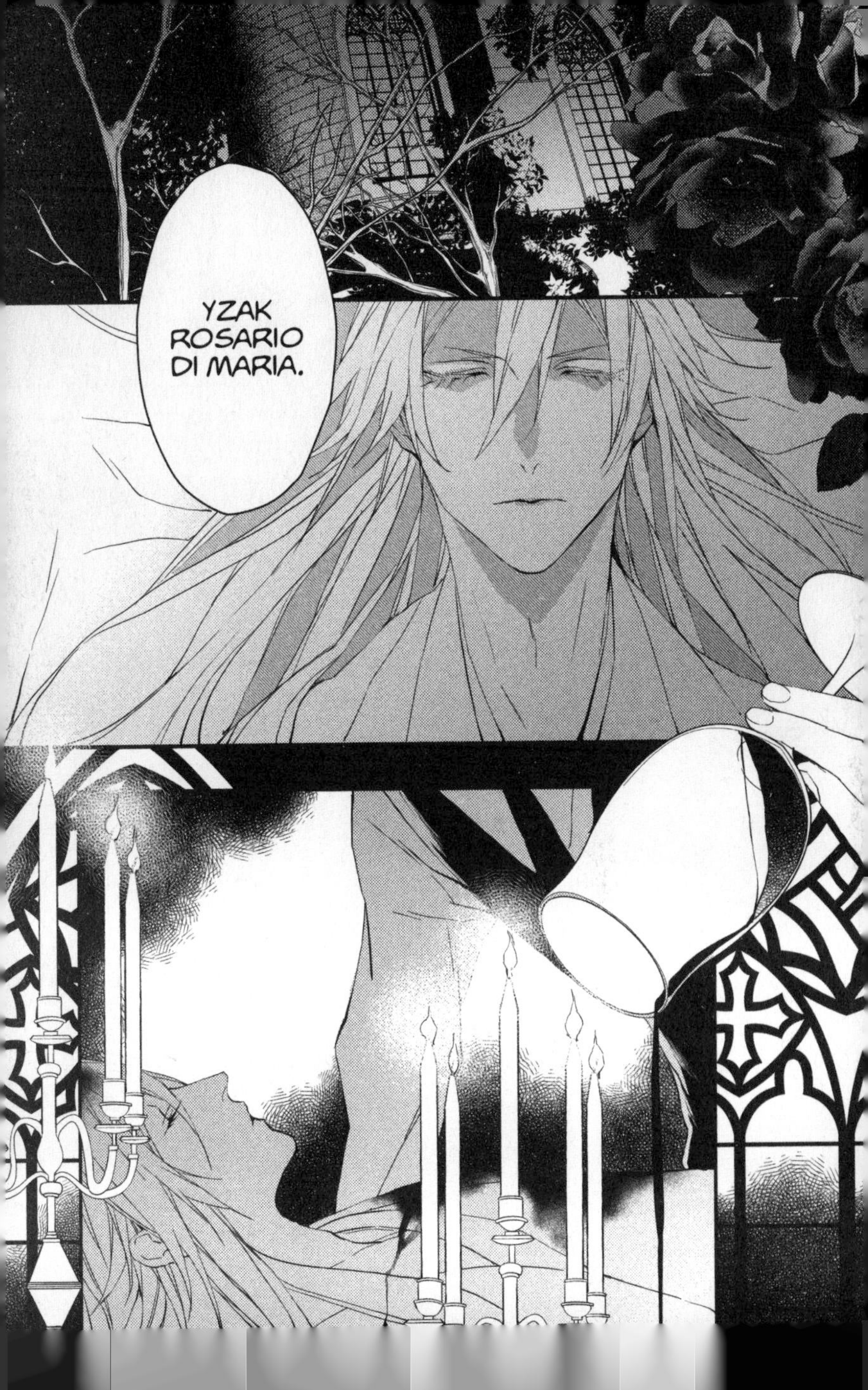
YZAK ROSARIO DI MARIA.

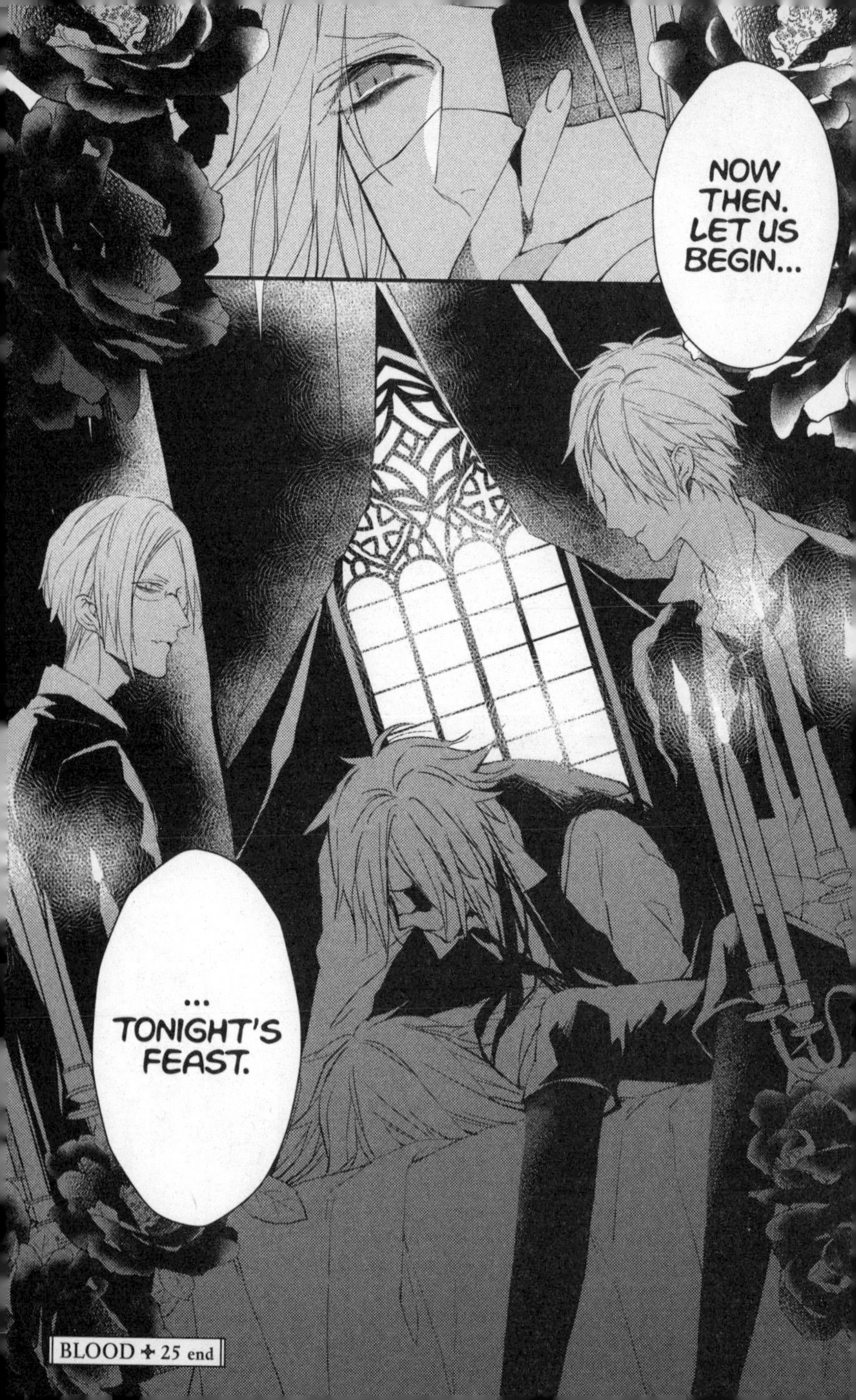
NOW THEN. LET US BEGIN...
... TONIGHT'S FEAST.
BLOOD ✣ 25 end

Bloody+Mary

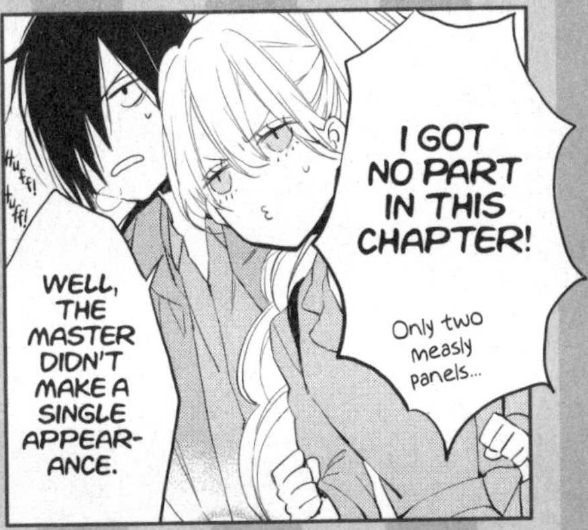
I GOT NO PART IN THIS CHAPTER!
Only two measly panels...
Huff! Huff!
WELL, THE MASTER DIDN'T MAKE A SINGLE APPEAR-ANCE.

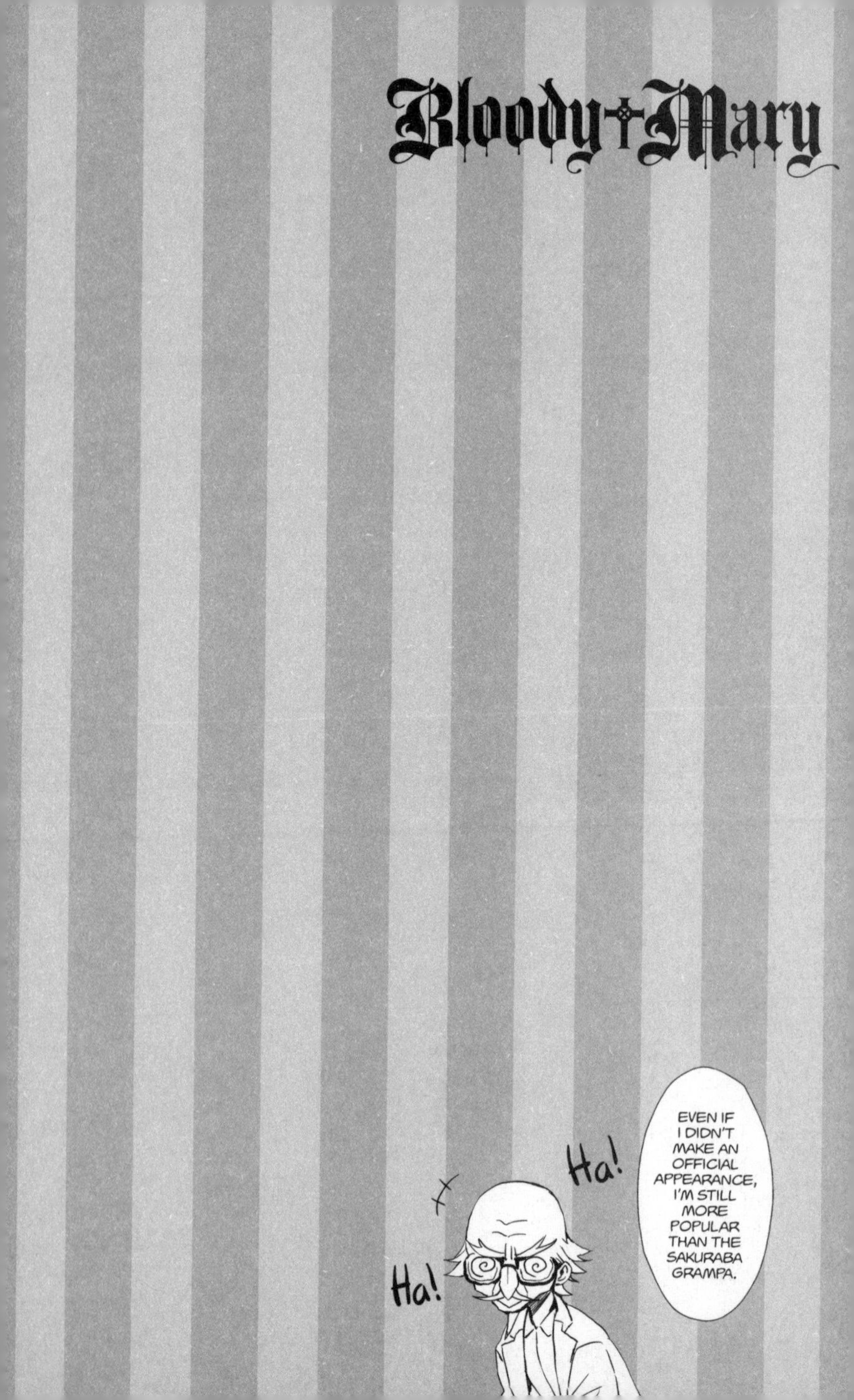
Bloody+Mary
EVEN IF I DIDN'T MAKE AN OFFICIAL APPEARANCE, I'M STILL MORE POPULAR THAN THE SAKURABA GRAMPA.
Ha!
Ha!

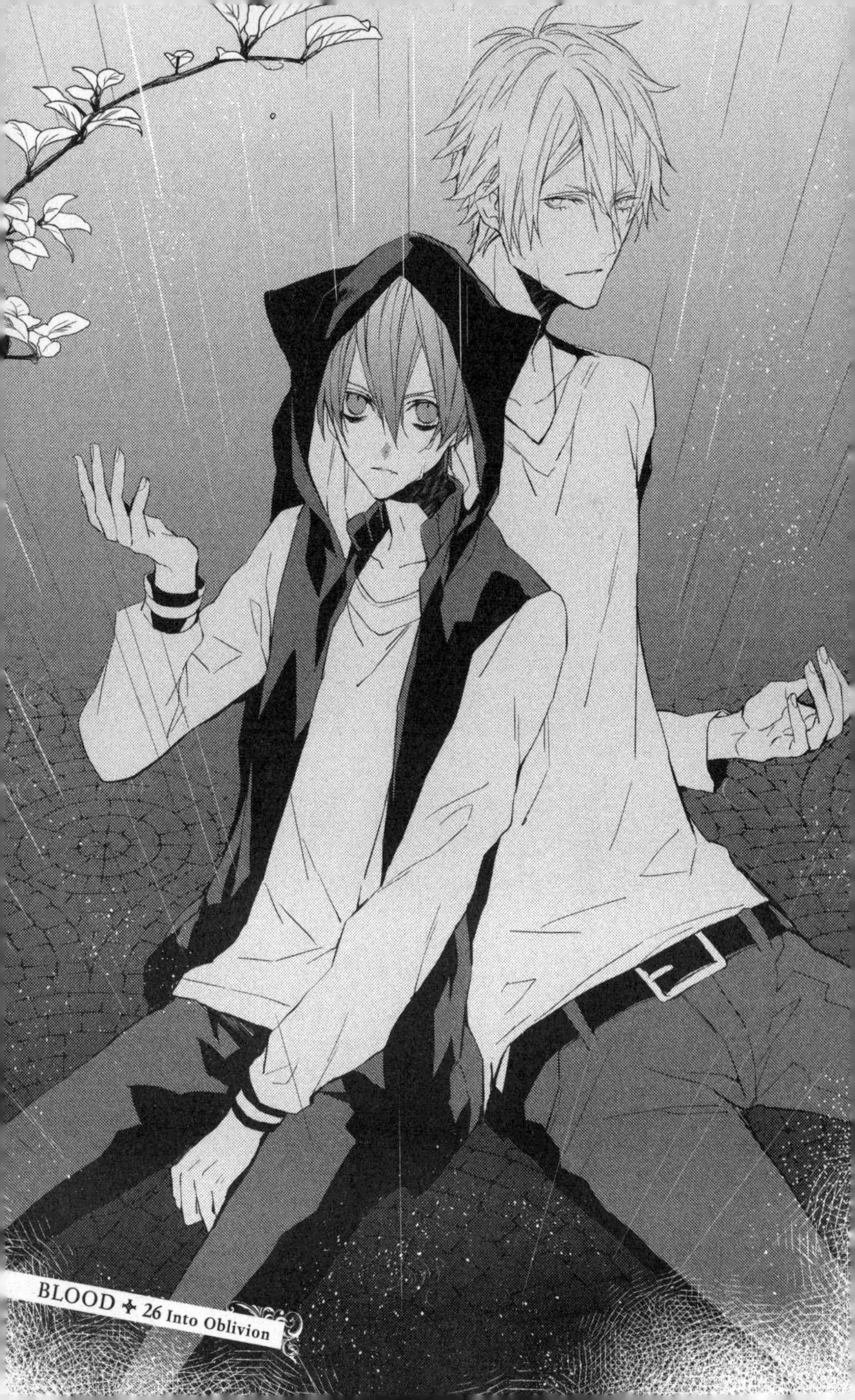
BLOOD ✦ 26 Into Oblivion

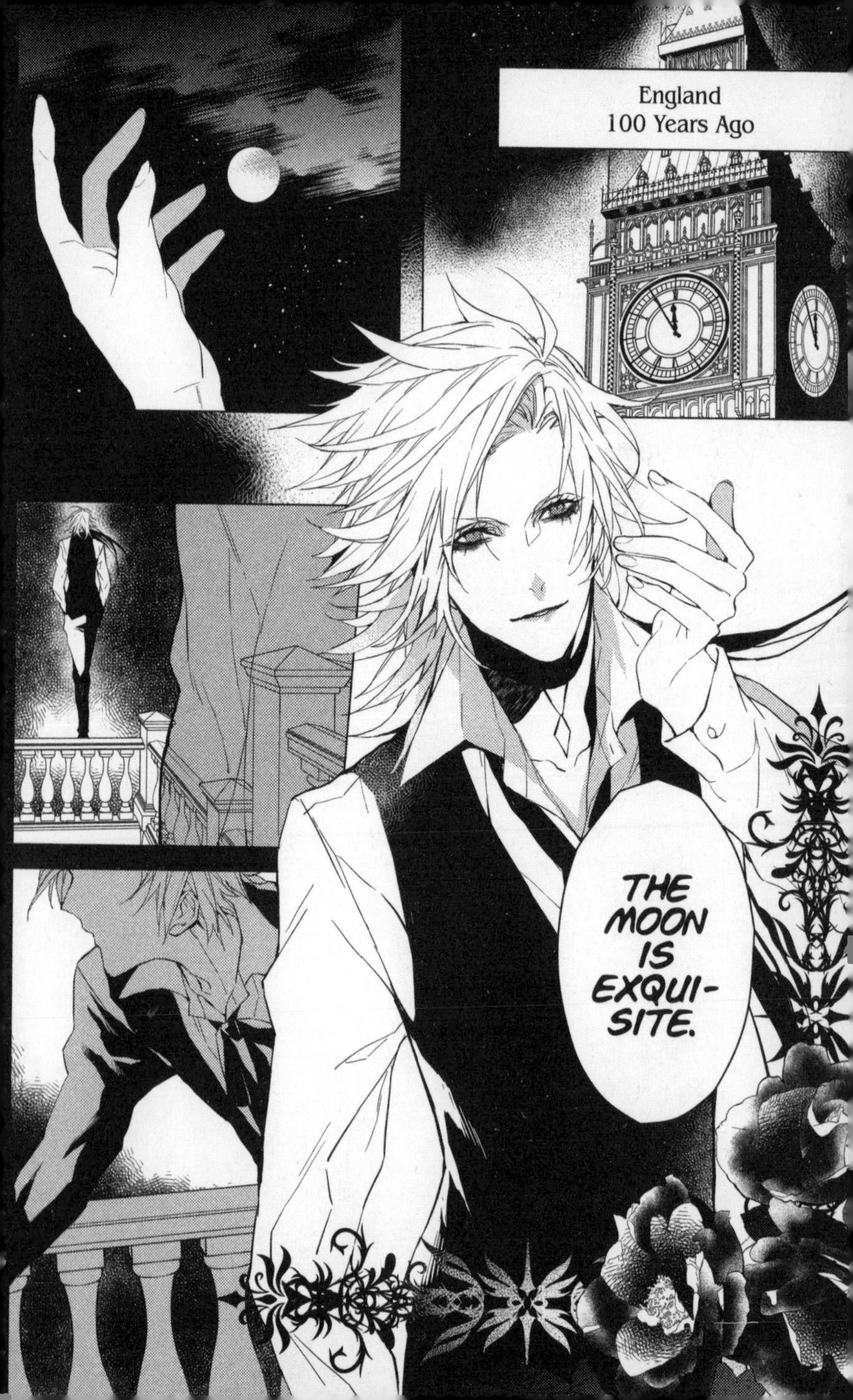
England
100 Years Ago
THE MOON IS EXQUI-SITE.

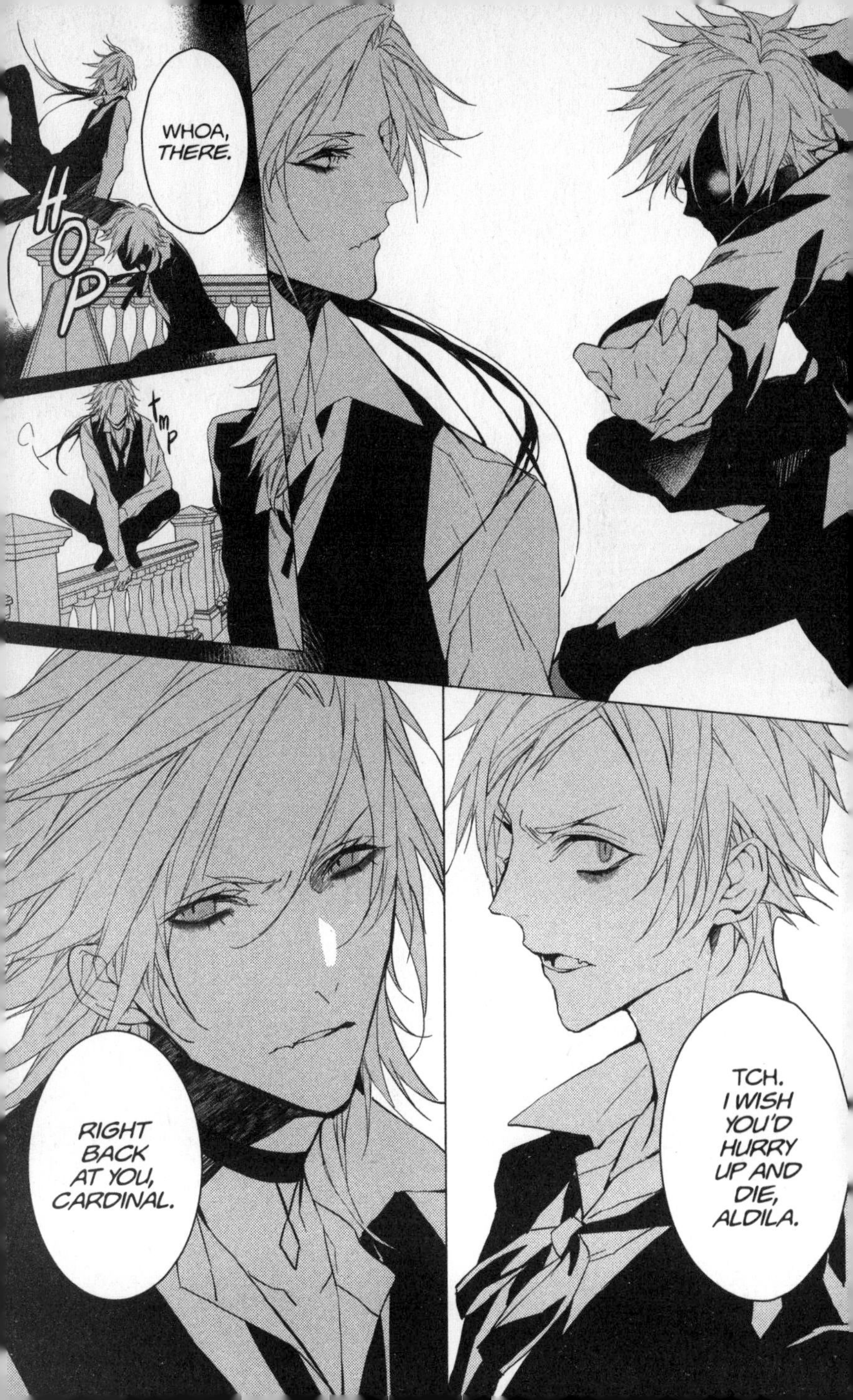
WHOA, THERE.
HOP
tmp
TCH. I WISH YOU'D HURRY UP AND DIE, ALDILA.
RIGHT BACK AT YOU, CARDINAL.

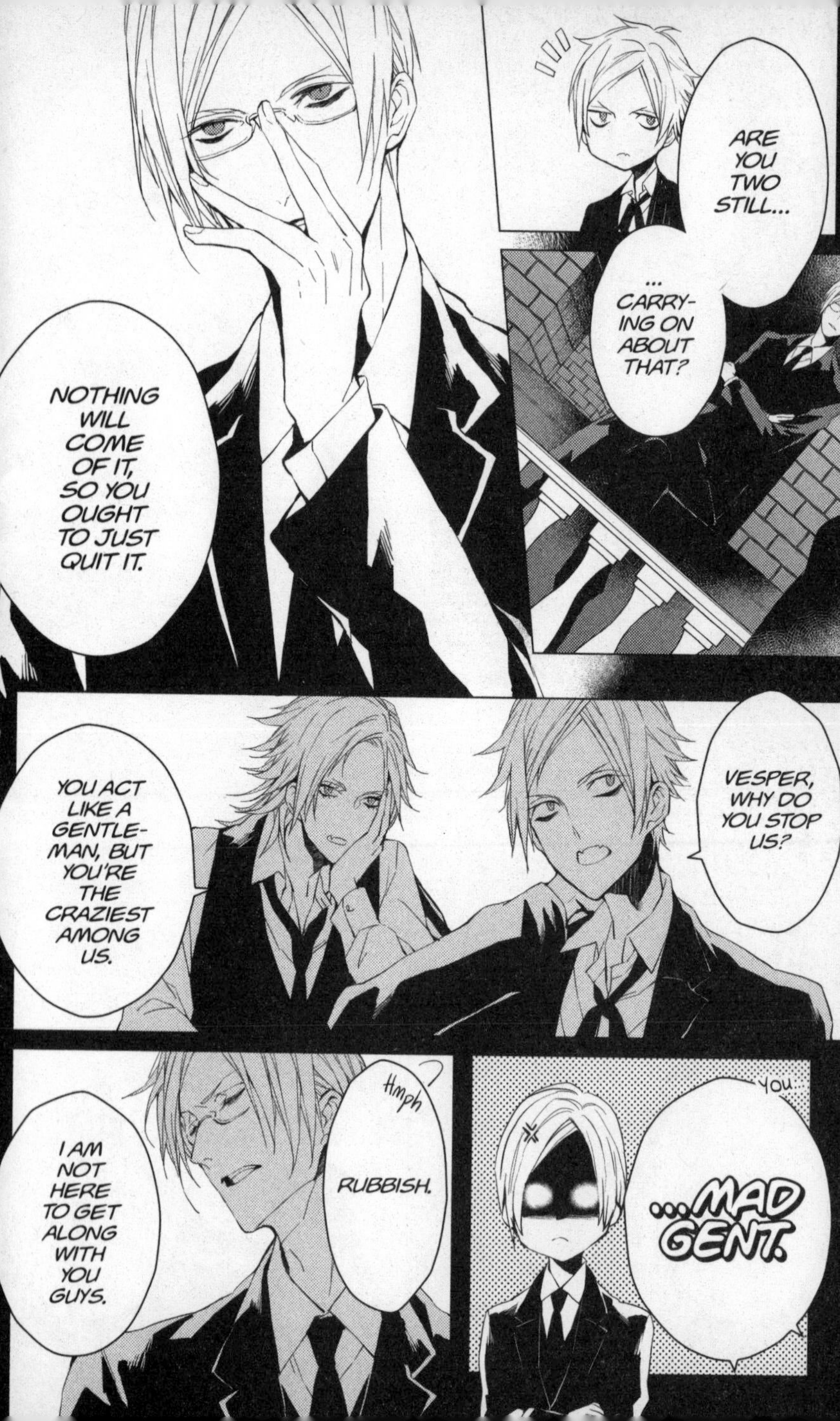
ARE YOU TWO STILL...
...CARRYING ON ABOUT THAT?
NOTHING WILL COME OF IT, SO YOU OUGHT TO JUST QUIT IT.
VESPER, WHY DO YOU STOP US?
YOU ACT LIKE A GENTLEMAN, BUT YOU'RE THE CRAZIEST AMONG US.
YOU...
...MAD GENT.
Hmph
RUBBISH.
I AM NOT HERE TO GET ALONG WITH YOU GUYS.

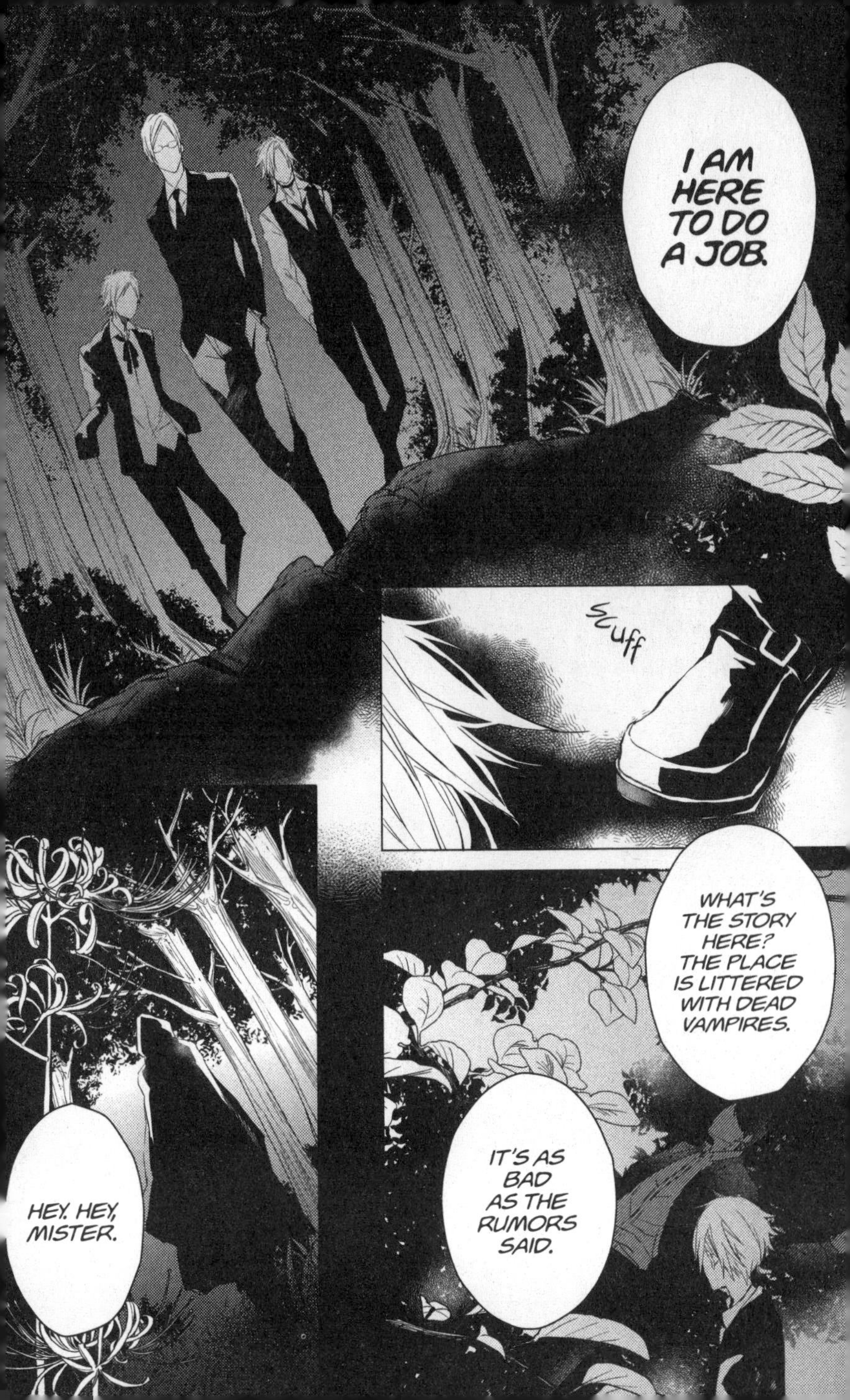
I AM HERE TO DO A JOB.
SCUFF
WHAT'S THE STORY HERE? THE PLACE IS LITTERED WITH DEAD VAMPIRES.
IT'S AS BAD AS THE RUMORS SAID.
HEY. HEY, MISTER.

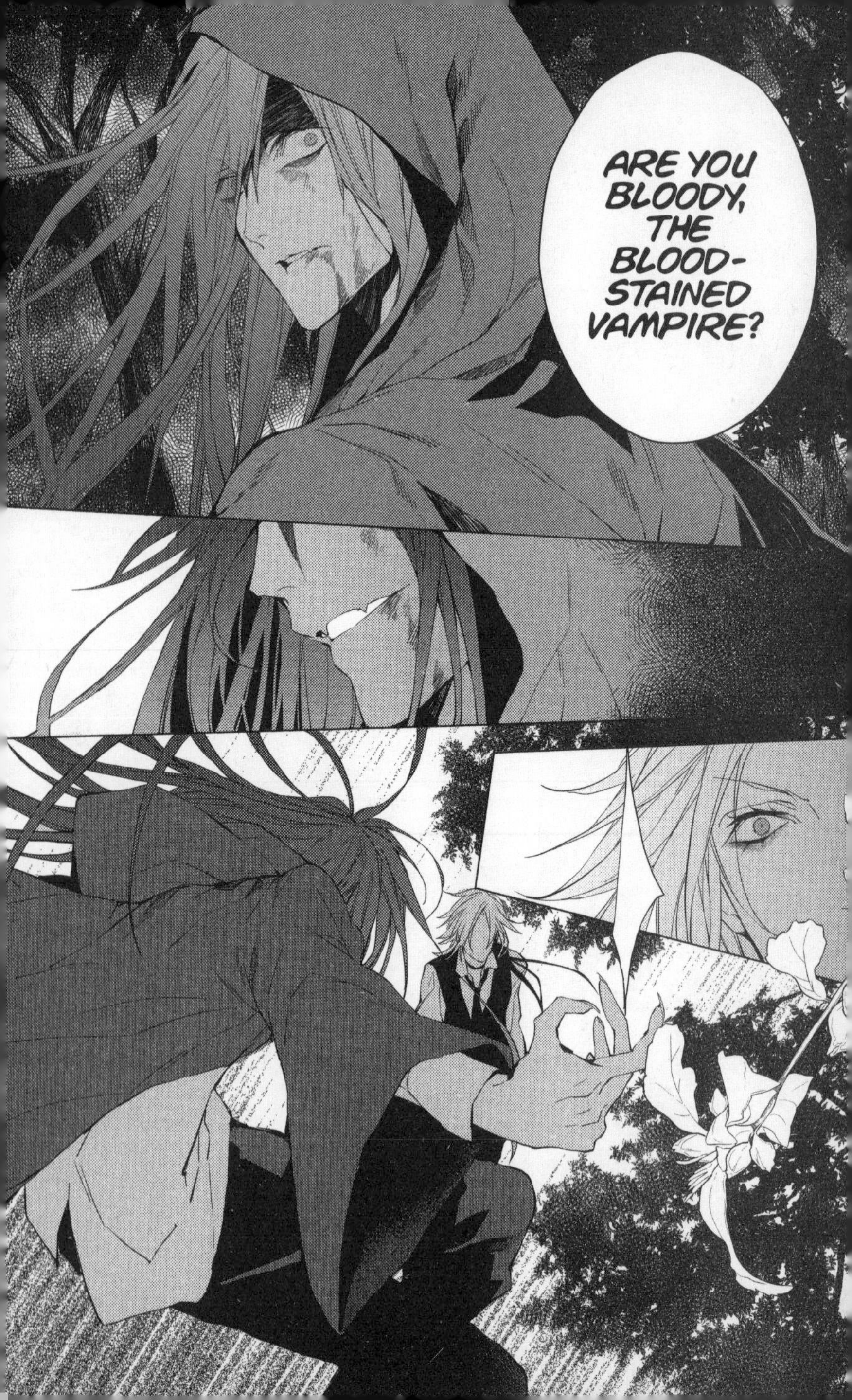
ARE YOU BLOODY, THE BLOOD-STAINED VAMPIRE?

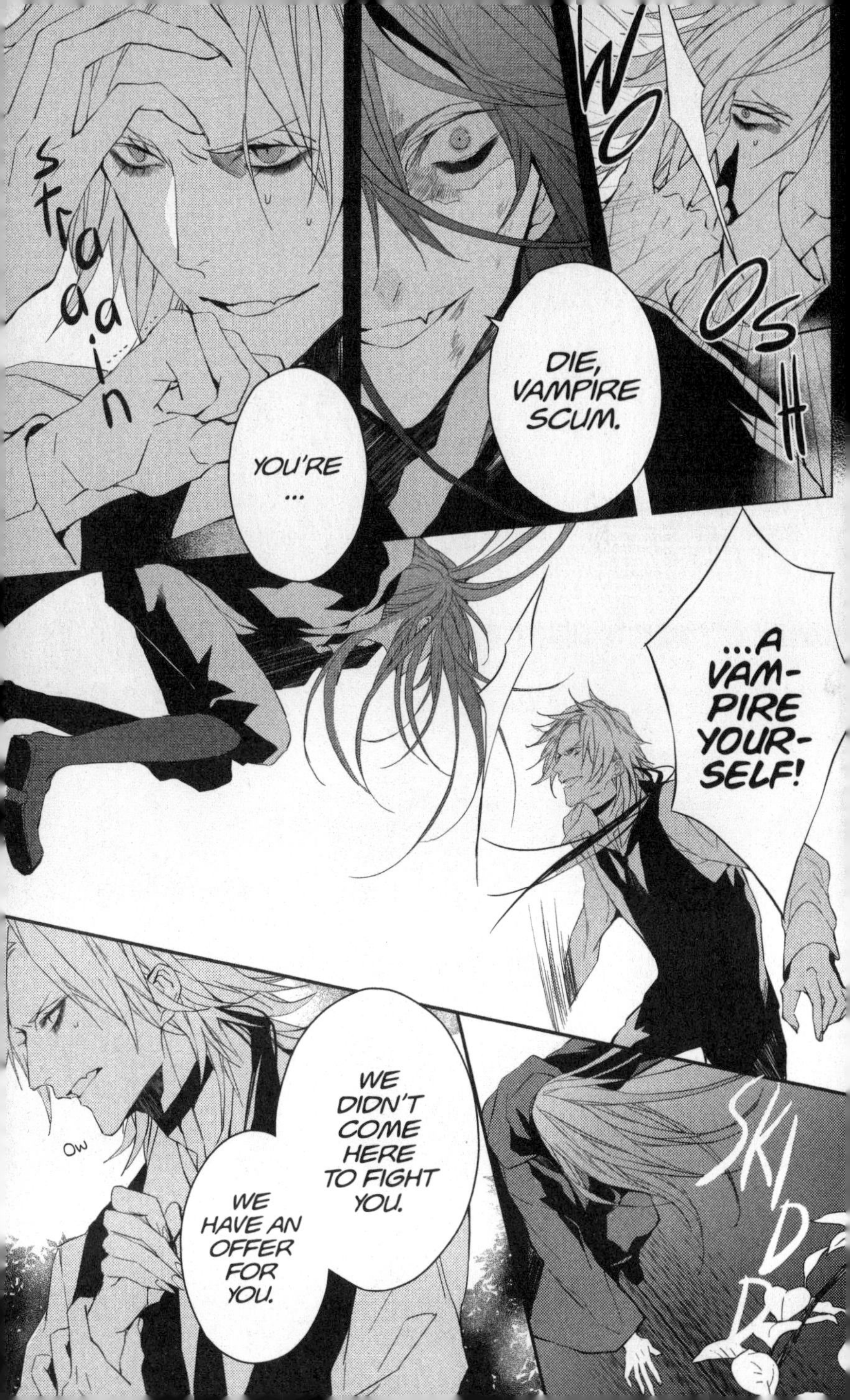
WOOSH
DIE, VAMPIRE SCUM.
straaain
YOU'RE ...
...A VAMPIRE YOURSELF!
SKIDD
WE DIDN'T COME HERE TO FIGHT YOU.
WE HAVE AN OFFER FOR YOU.
Ow

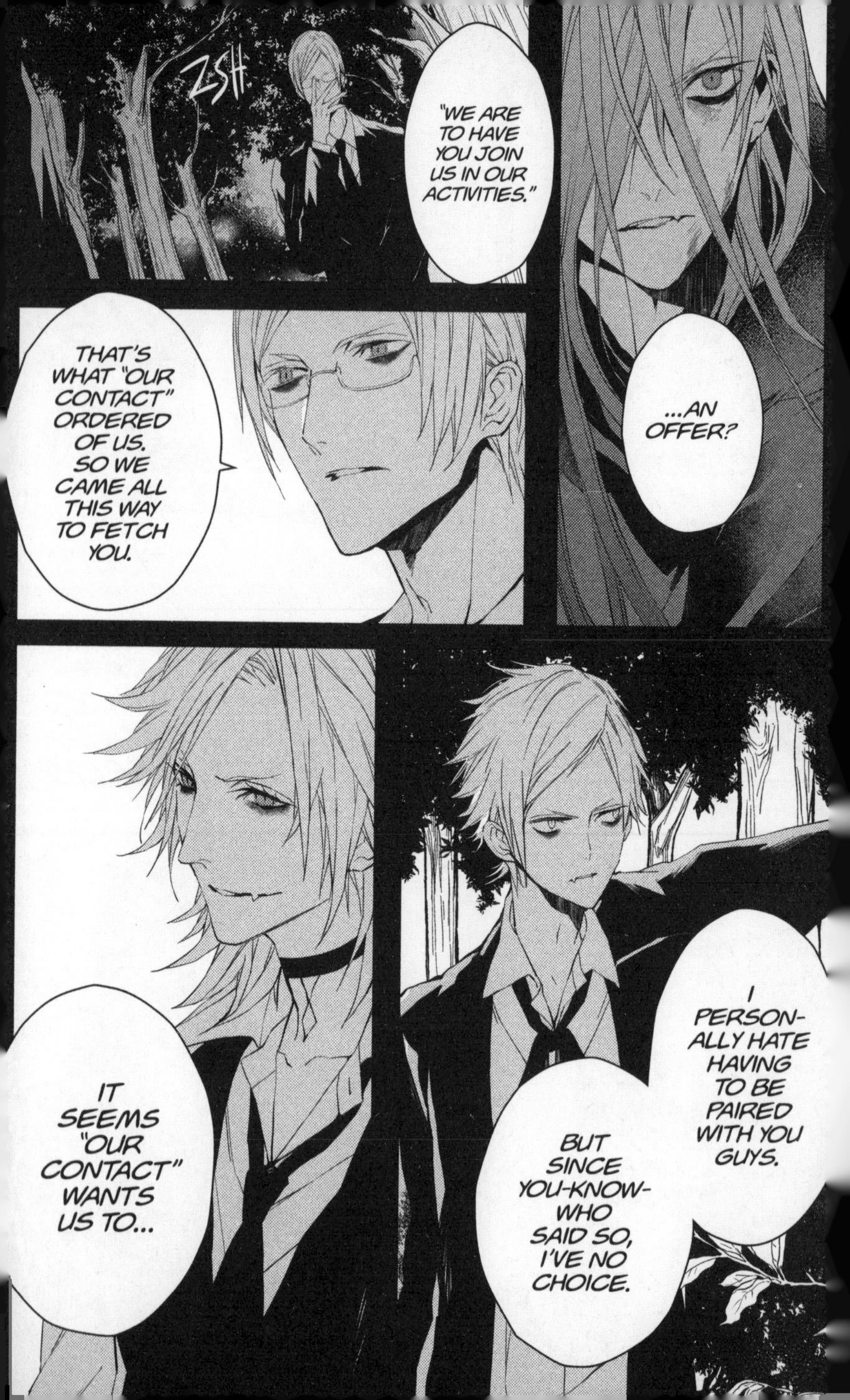
...AN OFFER?
"WE ARE TO HAVE YOU JOIN US IN OUR ACTIVITIES."
ZSH
THAT'S WHAT "OUR CONTACT" ORDERED OF US. SO WE CAME ALL THIS WAY TO FETCH YOU.
I PERSONALLY HATE HAVING TO BE PAIRED WITH YOU GUYS.
BUT SINCE YOU-KNOW-WHO SAID SO, I'VE NO CHOICE.
IT SEEMS "OUR CONTACT" WANTS US TO...

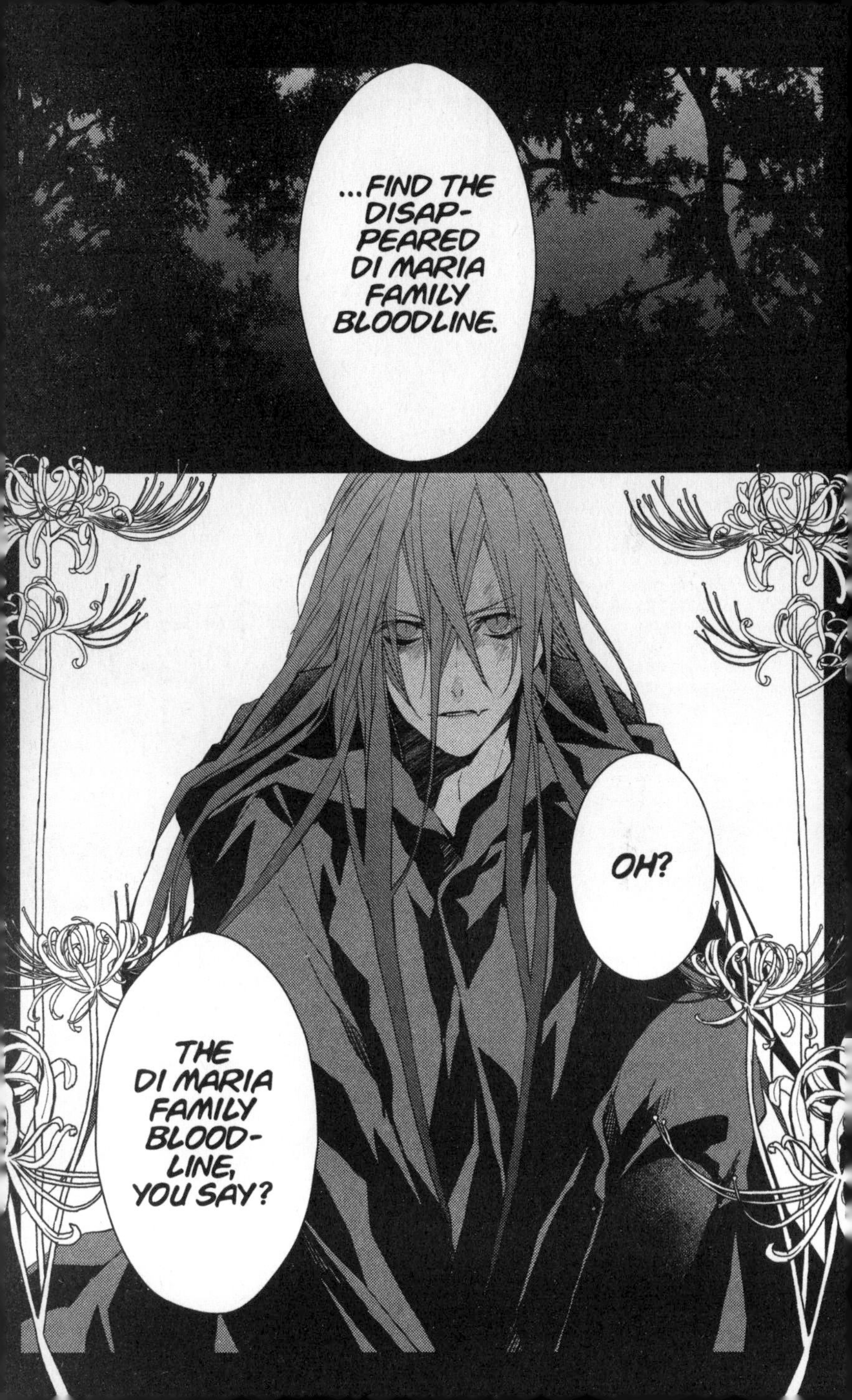
...FIND THE DISAP-PEARED DI MARIA FAMILY BLOODLINE.
OH?
THE DI MARIA FAMILY BLOOD-LINE, YOU SAY?

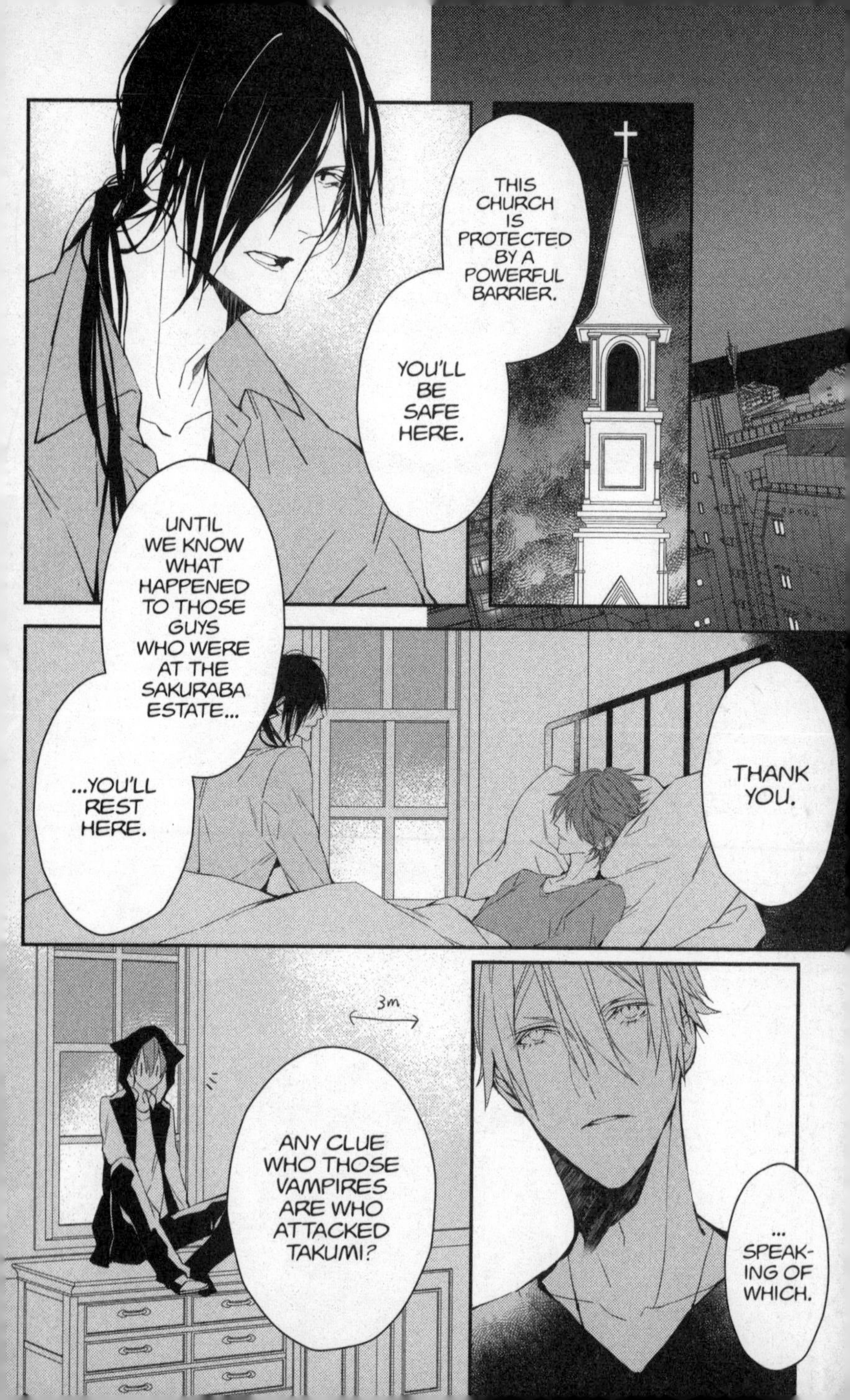
THIS CHURCH IS PROTECTED BY A POWERFUL BARRIER.
YOU'LL BE SAFE HERE.
UNTIL WE KNOW WHAT HAPPENED TO THOSE GUYS WHO WERE AT THE SAKURABA ESTATE...
...YOU'LL REST HERE.
THANK YOU.
... SPEAK-ING OF WHICH.
3m
ANY CLUE WHO THOSE VAMPIRES ARE WHO ATTACKED TAKUMI?

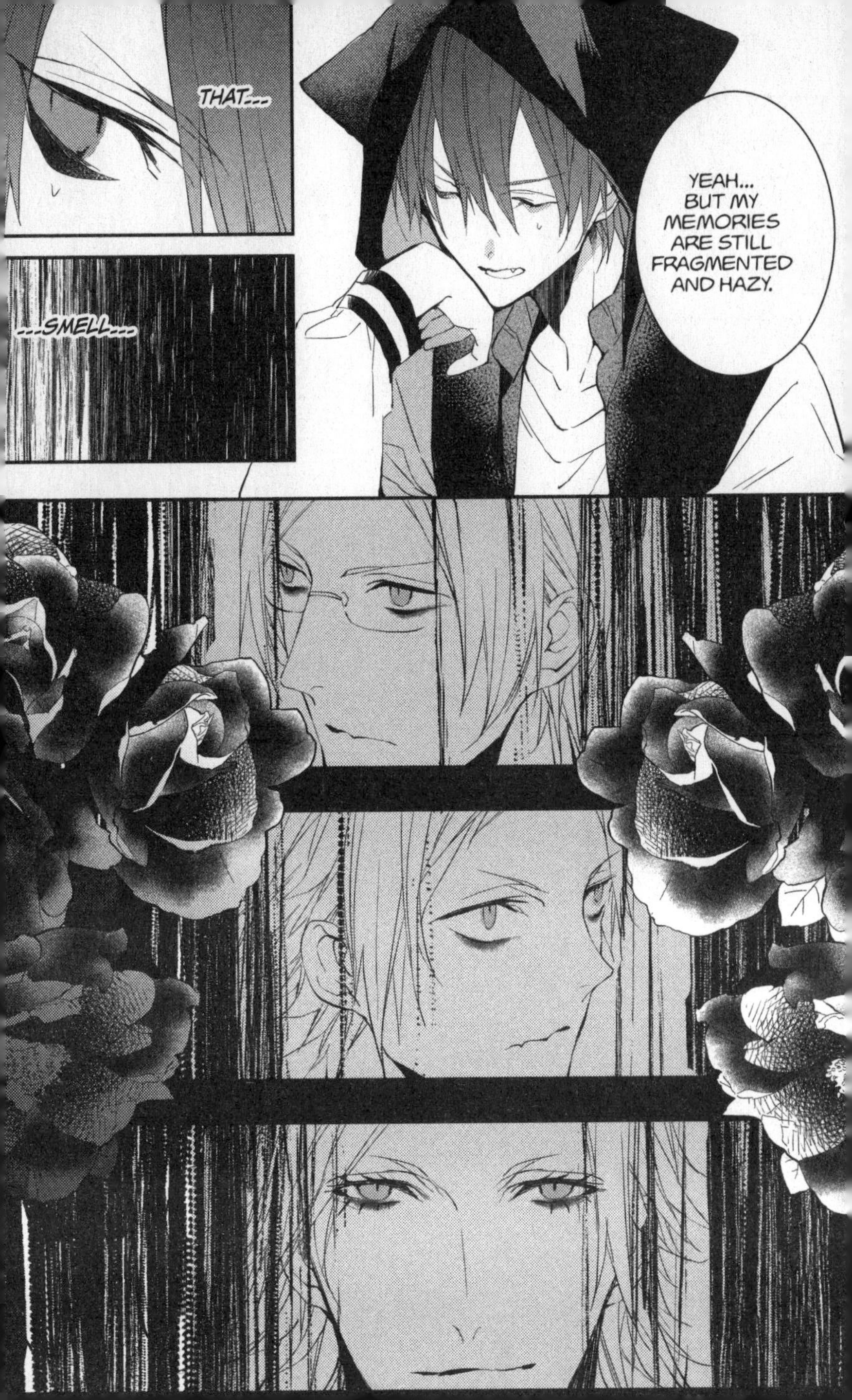
YEAH... BUT MY MEMORIES ARE STILL FRAGMENTED AND HAZY.
THAT...
...SMELL...

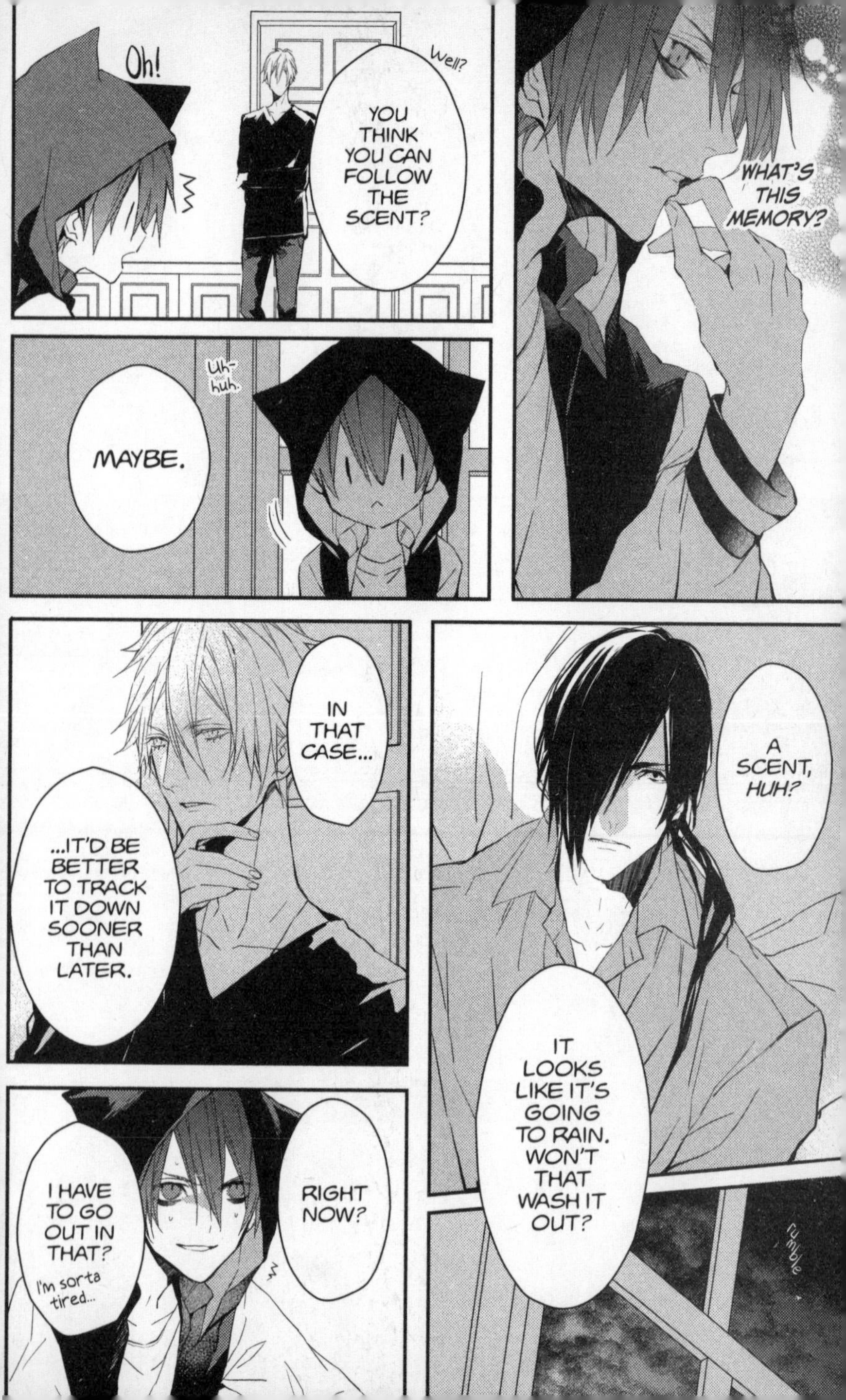
WHAT'S THIS MEMORY?
Well?
YOU THINK YOU CAN FOLLOW THE SCENT?
Oh!
Uh-huh.
MAYBE.
A SCENT, HUH?
IT LOOKS LIKE IT'S GOING TO RAIN. WON'T THAT WASH IT OUT?
rumble
IN THAT CASE...
...IT'D BE BETTER TO TRACK IT DOWN SOONER THAN LATER.
RIGHT NOW?
I HAVE TO GO OUT IN THAT?
I'm sorta tired...

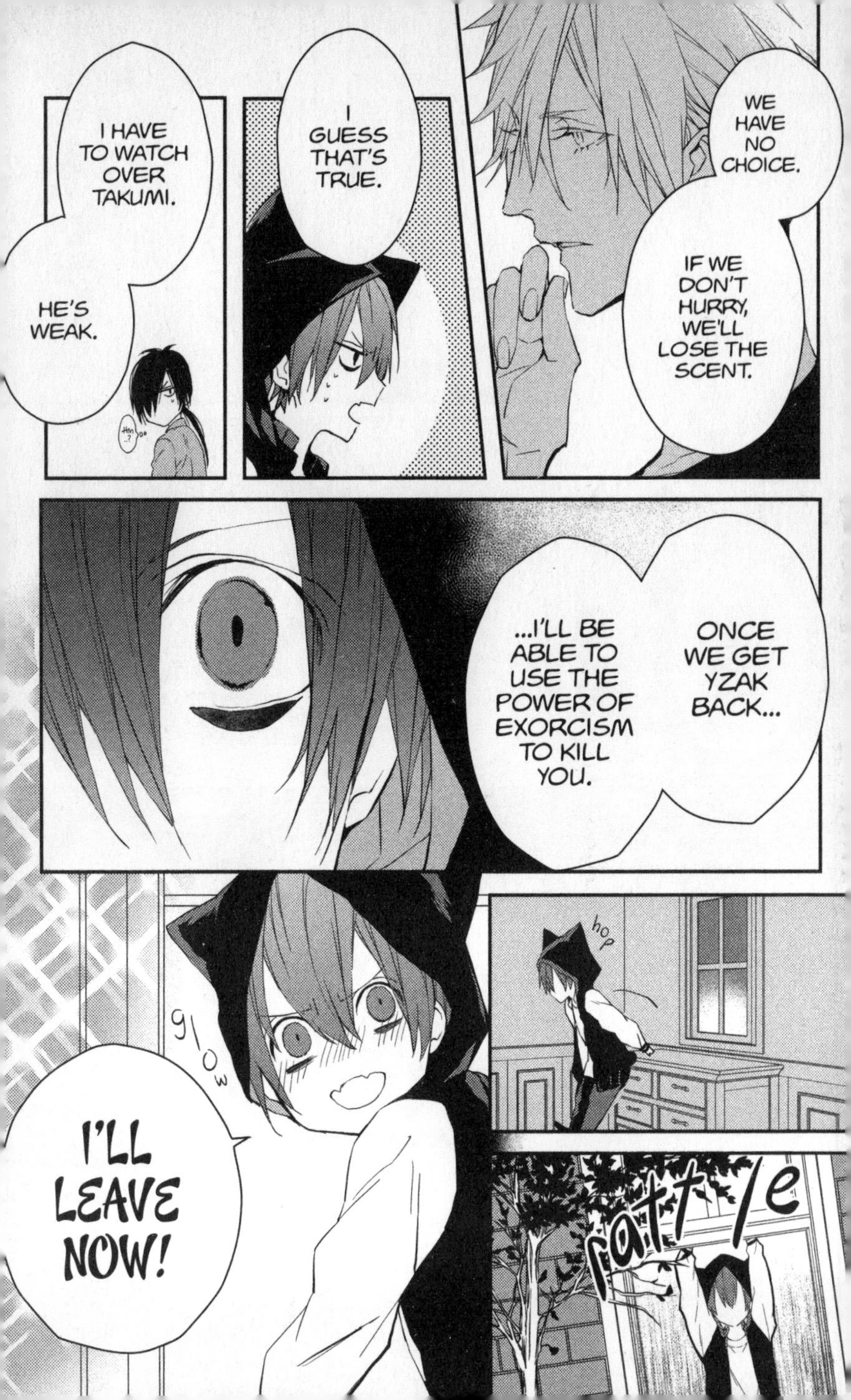
WE HAVE NO CHOICE.
IF WE DON'T HURRY, WE'LL LOSE THE SCENT.
I GUESS THAT'S TRUE.
I HAVE TO WATCH OVER TAKUMI.
HE'S WEAK.
ONCE WE GET YZAK BACK...
...I'LL BE ABLE TO USE THE POWER OF EXORCISM TO KILL YOU.
hop
rattle
glow
I'LL LEAVE NOW!

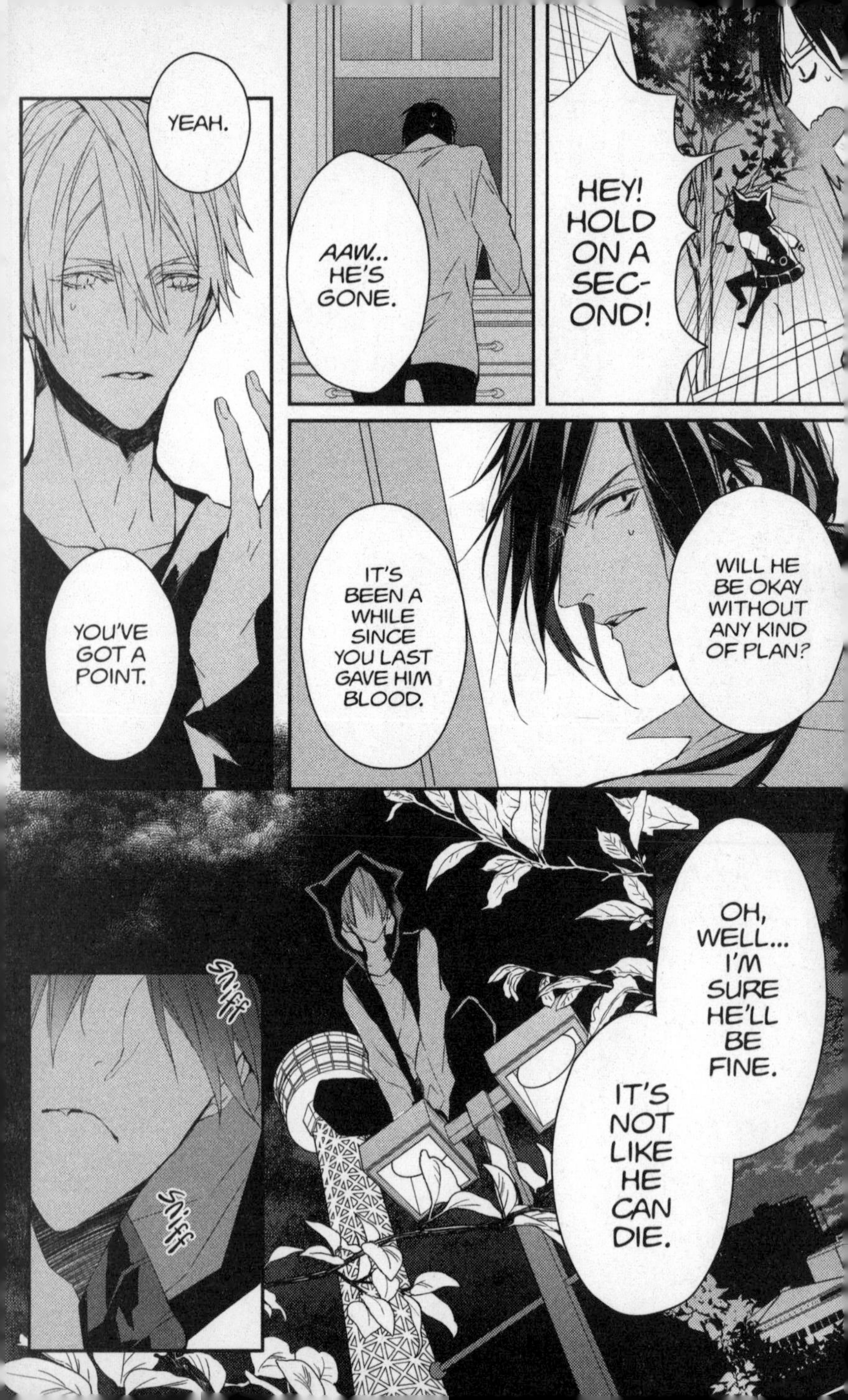
HEY! HOLD ON A SEC-OND!
AAW... HE'S GONE.
WILL HE BE OKAY WITHOUT ANY KIND OF PLAN?
IT'S BEEN A WHILE SINCE YOU LAST GAVE HIM BLOOD.
YEAH.
YOU'VE GOT A POINT.
OH, WELL... I'M SURE HE'LL BE FINE.
IT'S NOT LIKE HE CAN DIE.
Sniff
Sniff

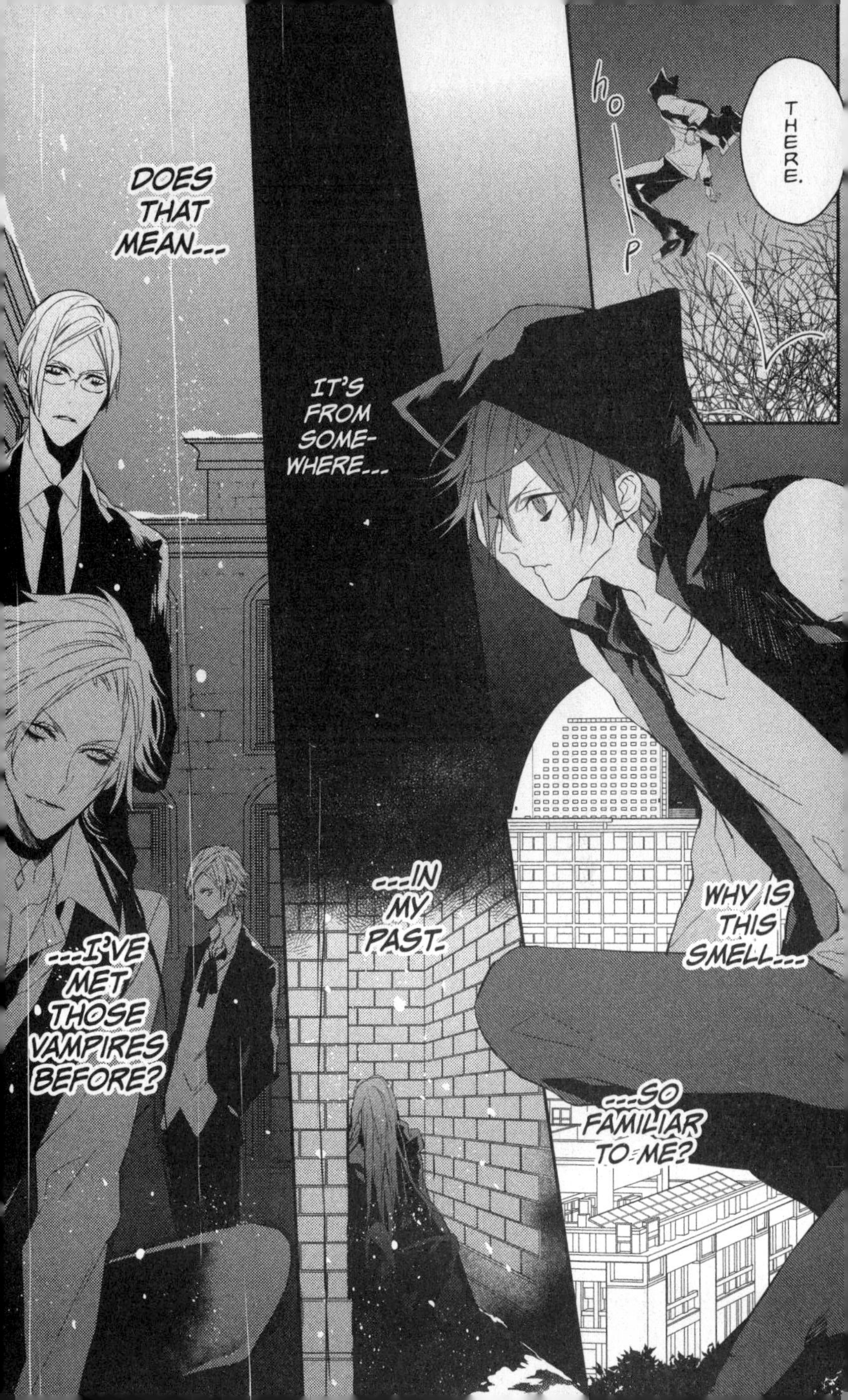
THERE.
hop
WHY IS THIS SMELL...
...SO FAMILIAR TO ME?
IT'S FROM SOME-WHERE...
...IN MY PAST.
DOES THAT MEAN...
...I'VE MET THOSE VAMPIRES BEFORE?

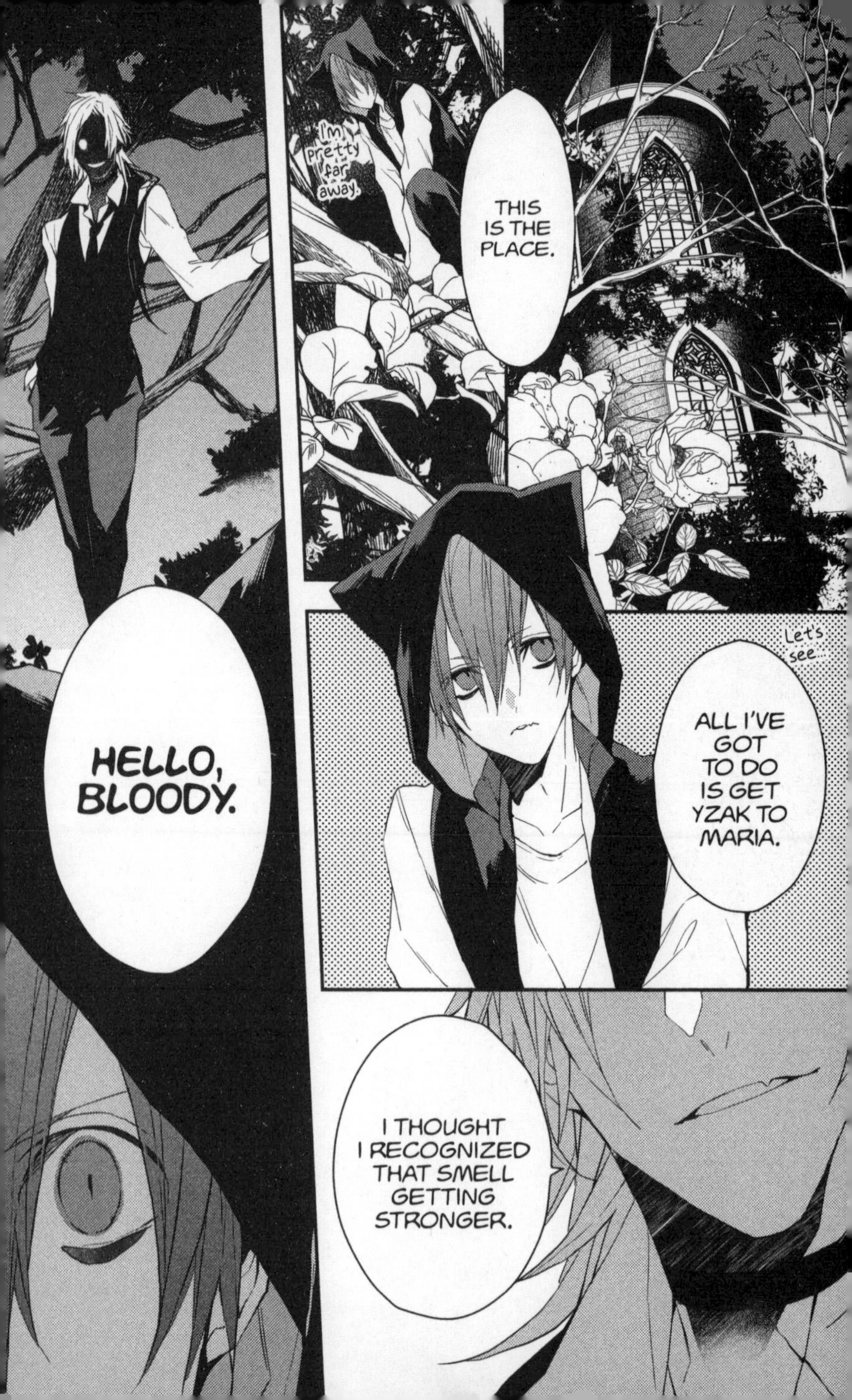

THIS IS THE PLACE.
I'm pretty far away.
Let's see...
ALL I'VE GOT TO DO IS GET YZAK TO MARIA.
I THOUGHT I RECOGNIZED THAT SMELL GETTING STRONGER.
HELLO, BLOODY.

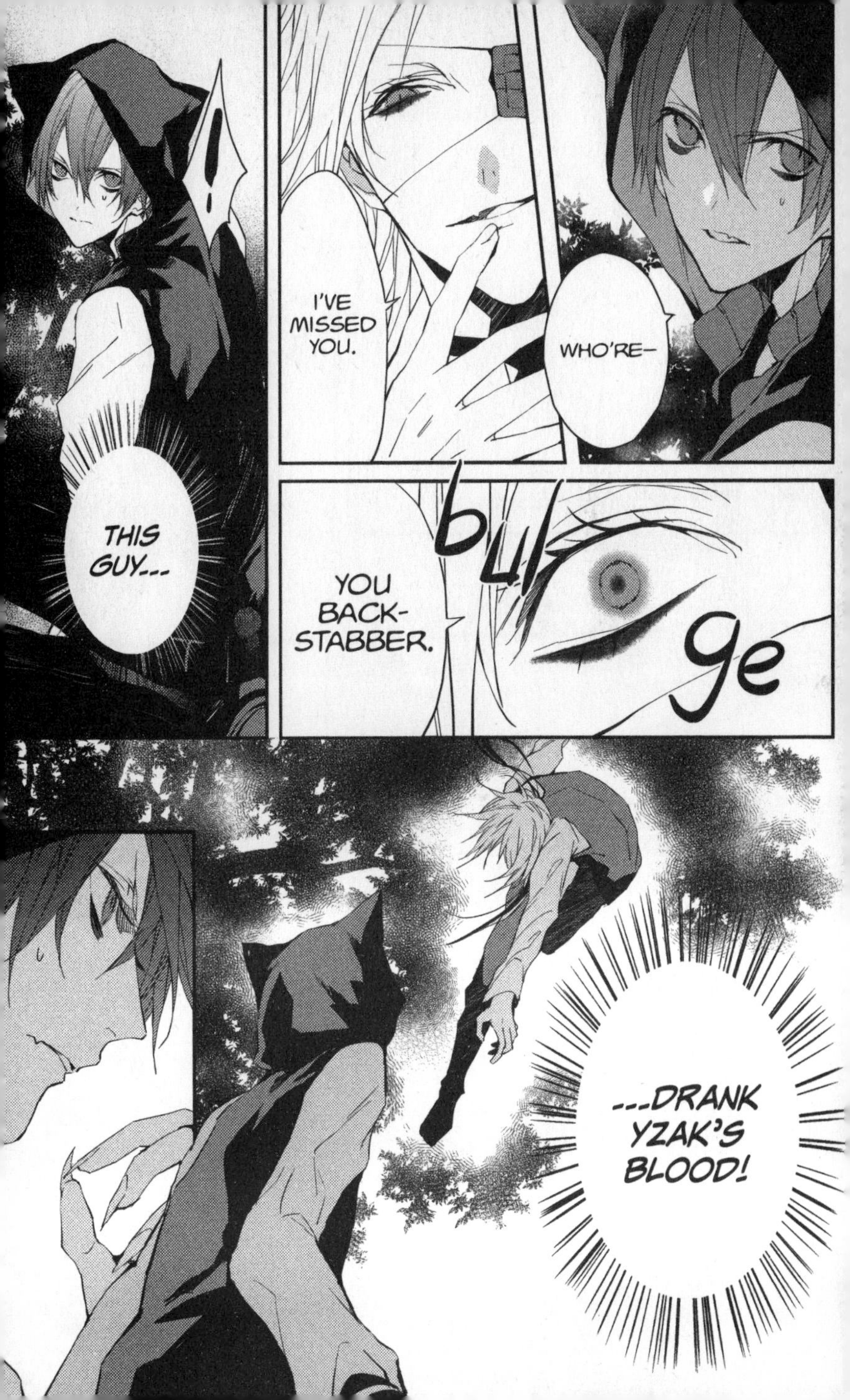
WHO'RE–
I'VE MISSED YOU.
bulge
YOU BACK-STABBER.
THIS GUY...
...DRANK YZAK'S BLOOD!

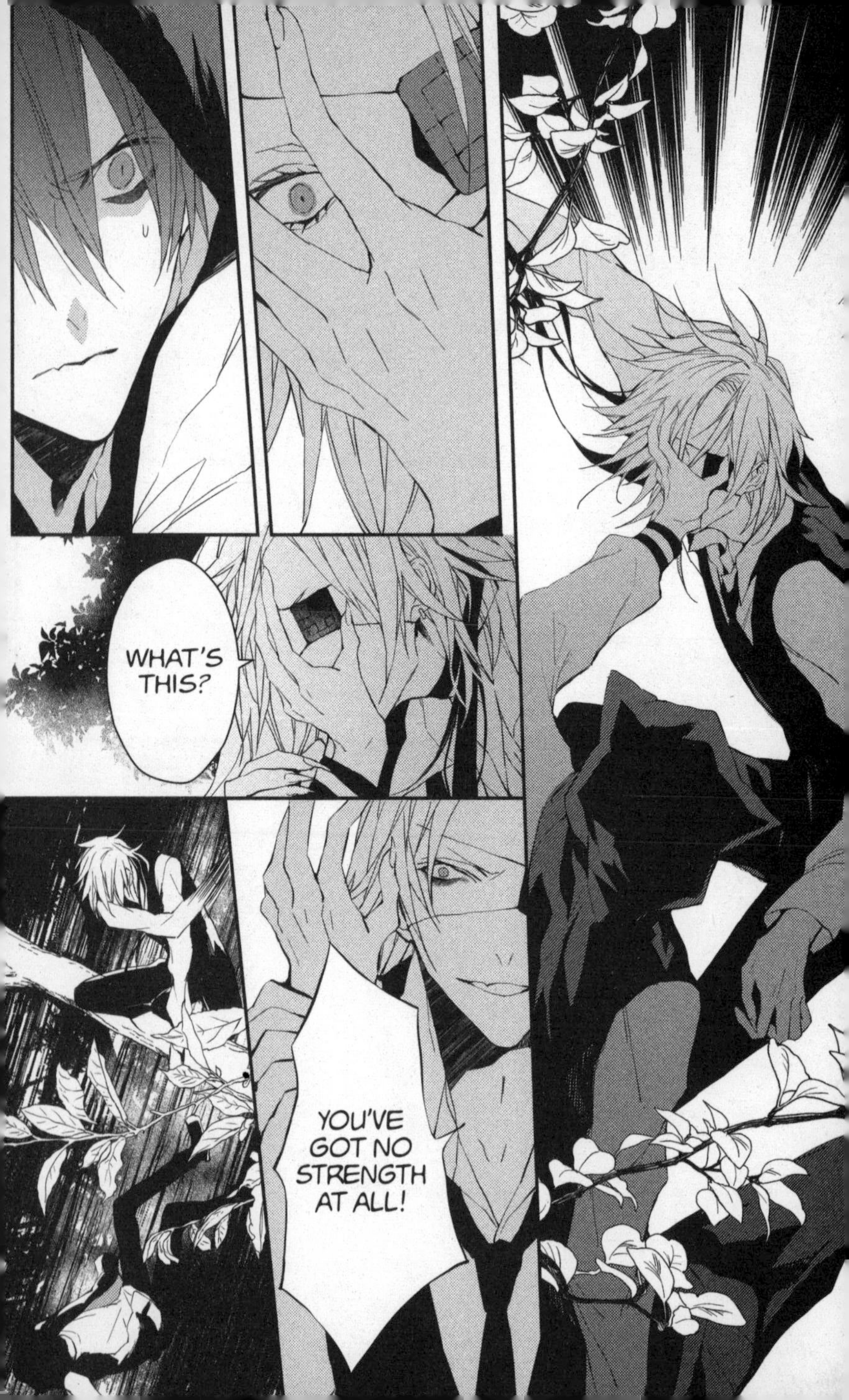
WHAT'S THIS?
YOU'VE GOT NO STRENGTH AT ALL!

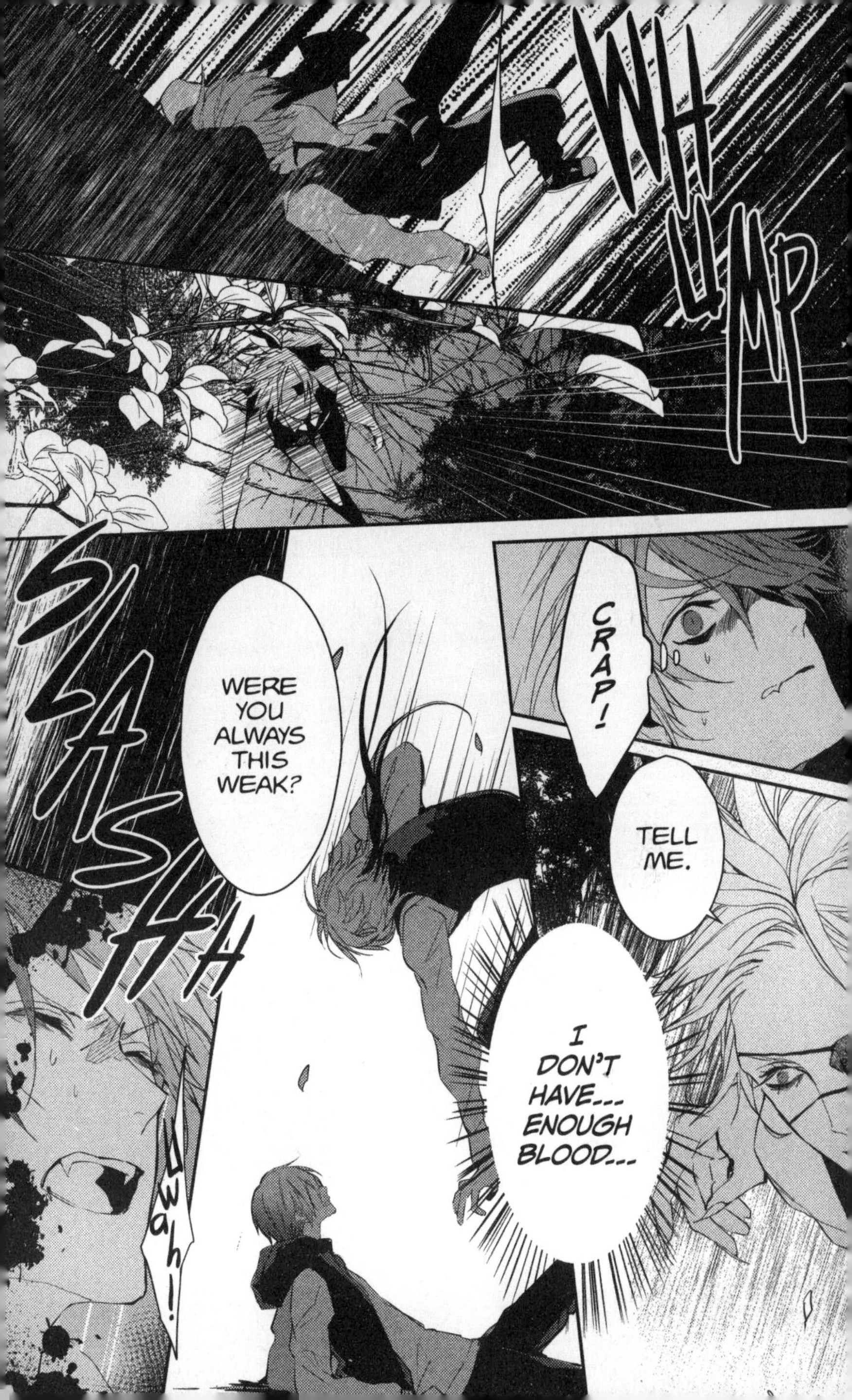
WHUMP
CRAP!
TELL ME.
I DON'T HAVE... ENOUGH BLOOD...
SLASHH
WERE YOU ALWAYS THIS WEAK?
Uwah!

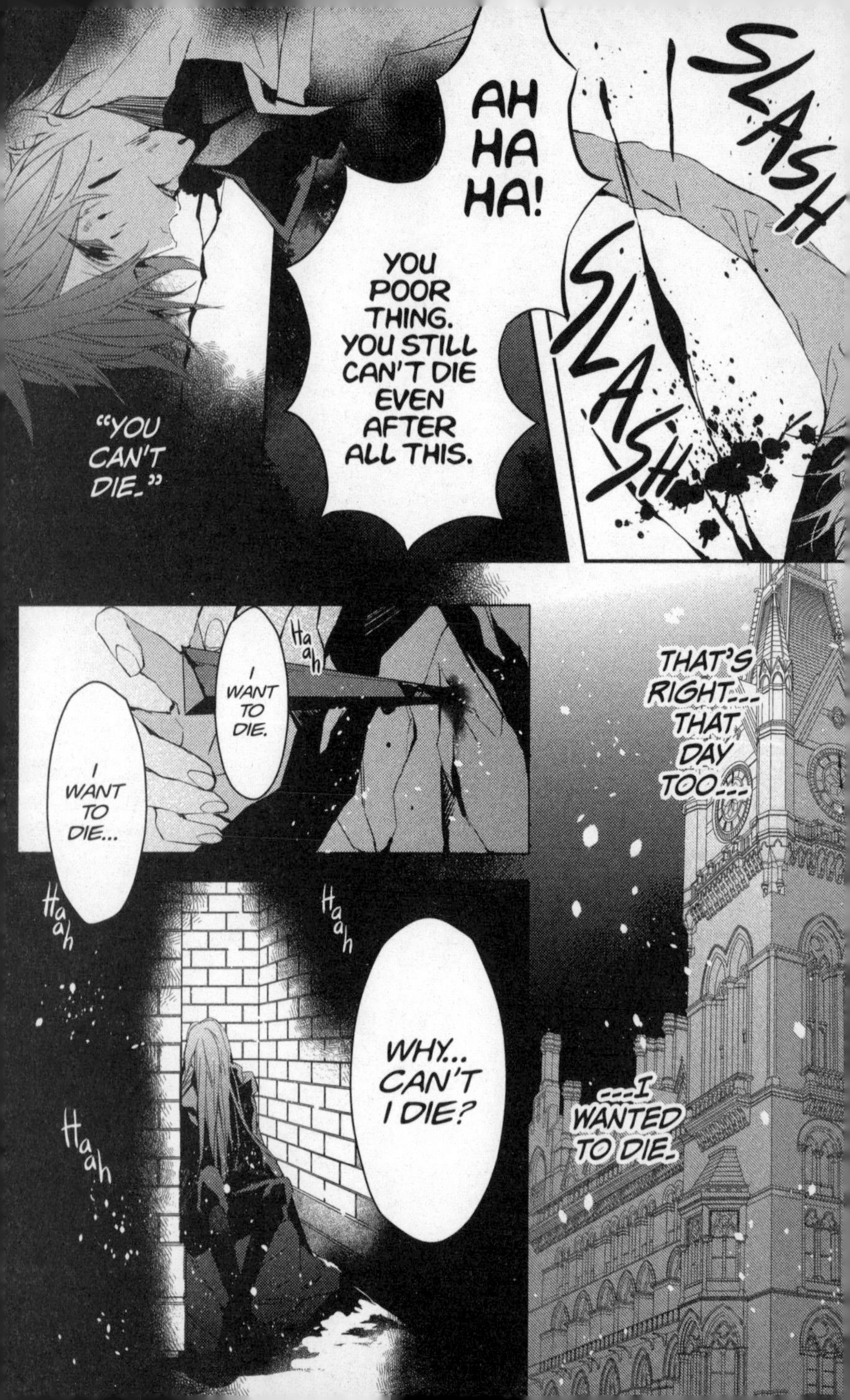
SLASH
SLASH
AH HA HA!
YOU POOR THING. YOU STILL CAN'T DIE EVEN AFTER ALL THIS.
"YOU CAN'T DIE."
THAT'S RIGHT... THAT DAY TOO...
...I WANTED TO DIE.
Haah
I WANT TO DIE.
I WANT TO DIE...
Haah
WHY... CAN'T I DIE?
Haah
Haah

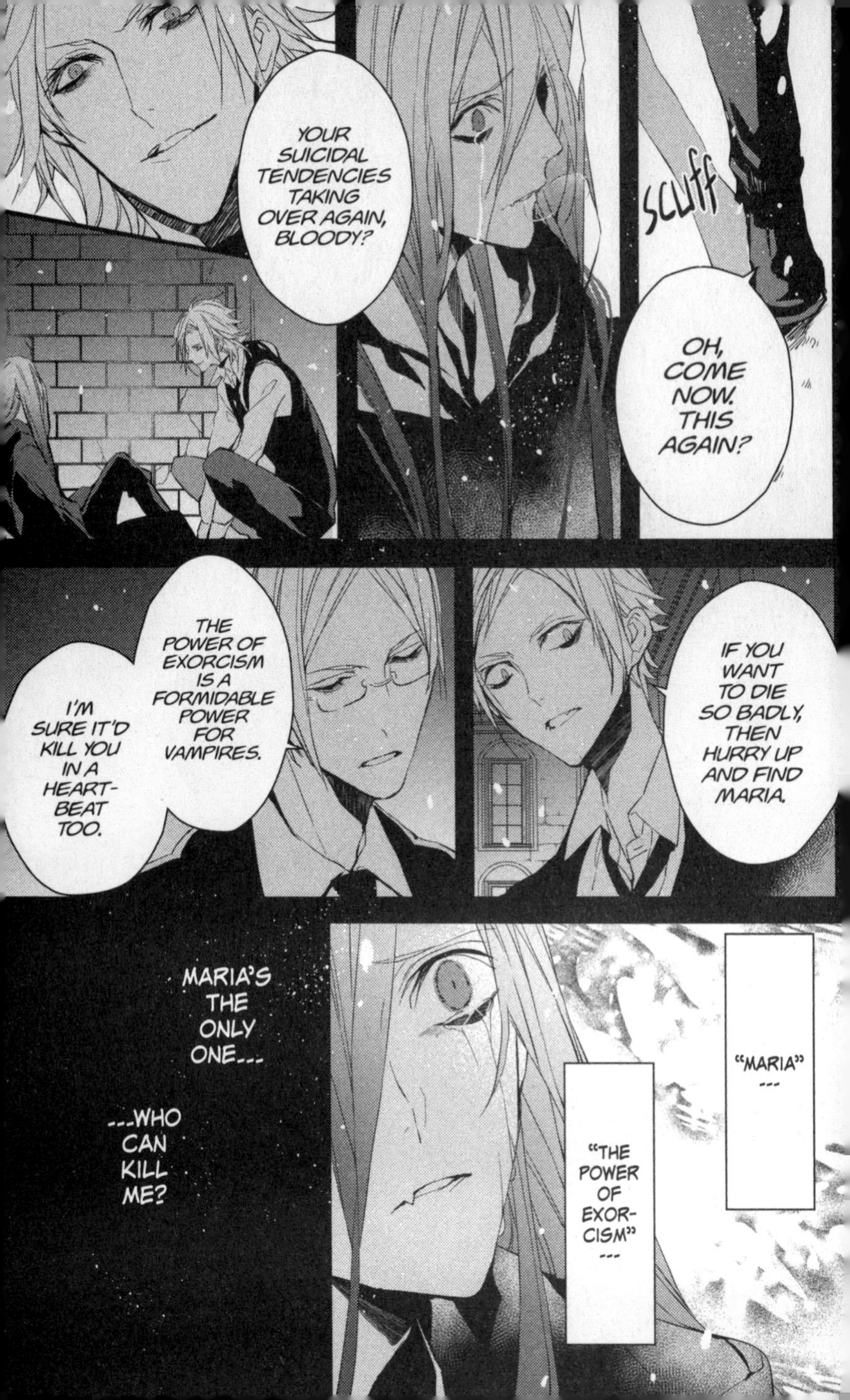
SCUFF
OH, COME NOW. THIS AGAIN?
YOUR SUICIDAL TENDENCIES TAKING OVER AGAIN, BLOODY?
IF YOU WANT TO DIE SO BADLY, THEN HURRY UP AND FIND MARIA.
THE POWER OF EXORCISM IS A FORMIDABLE POWER FOR VAMPIRES.
I'M SURE IT'D KILL YOU IN A HEART-BEAT TOO.
"MARIA"---
"THE POWER OF EXOR-CISM"---
MARIA'S THE ONLY ONE...
...WHO CAN KILL ME?

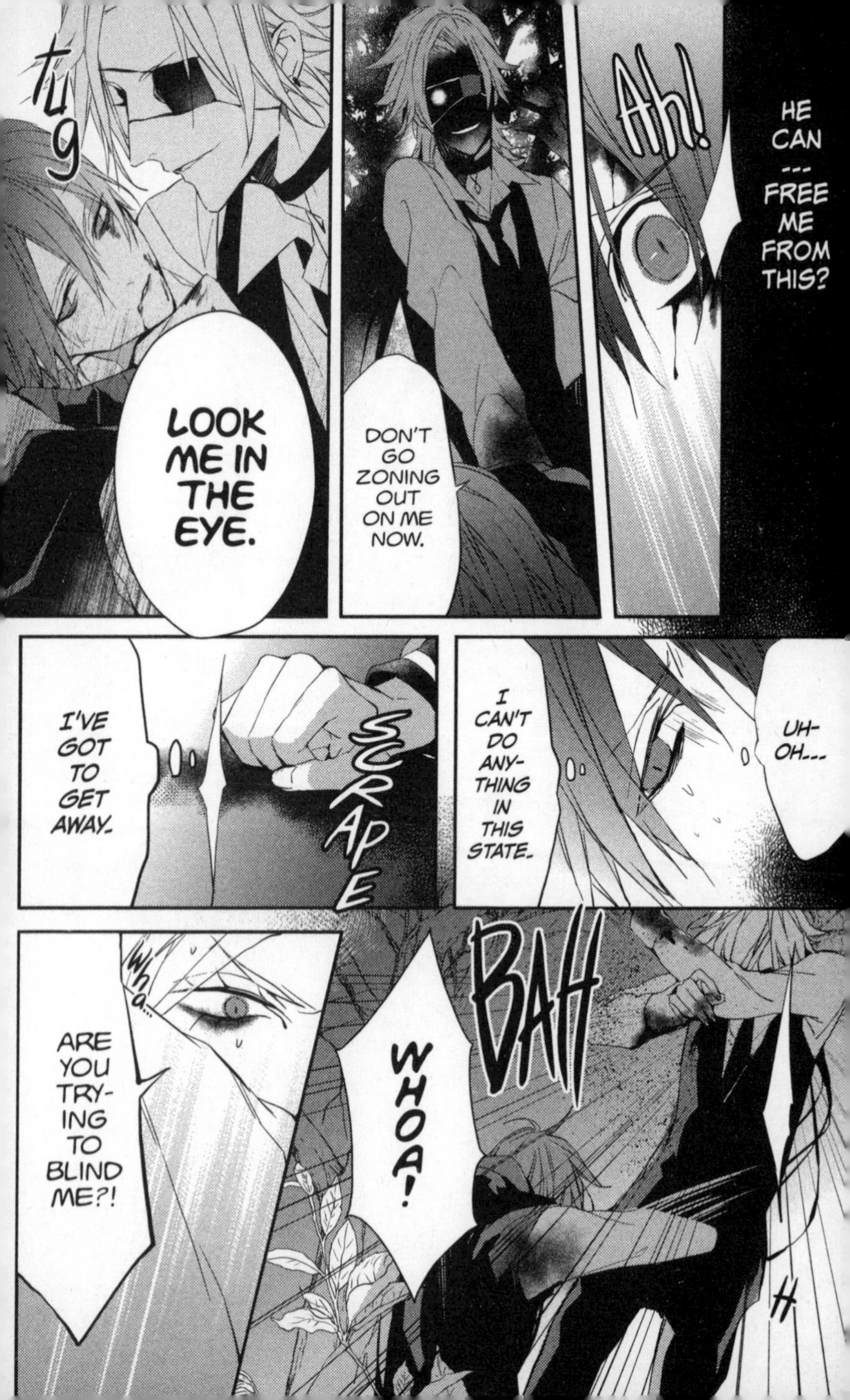
HE CAN --- FREE ME FROM THIS?
Ah!
DON'T GO ZONING OUT ON ME NOW.
tug
LOOK ME IN THE EYE.
UH-OH...
I CAN'T DO ANYTHING IN THIS STATE...
SCRAPE
I'VE GOT TO GET AWAY...
BAH
WHOA!
Wha...
ARE YOU TRYING TO BLIND ME?!

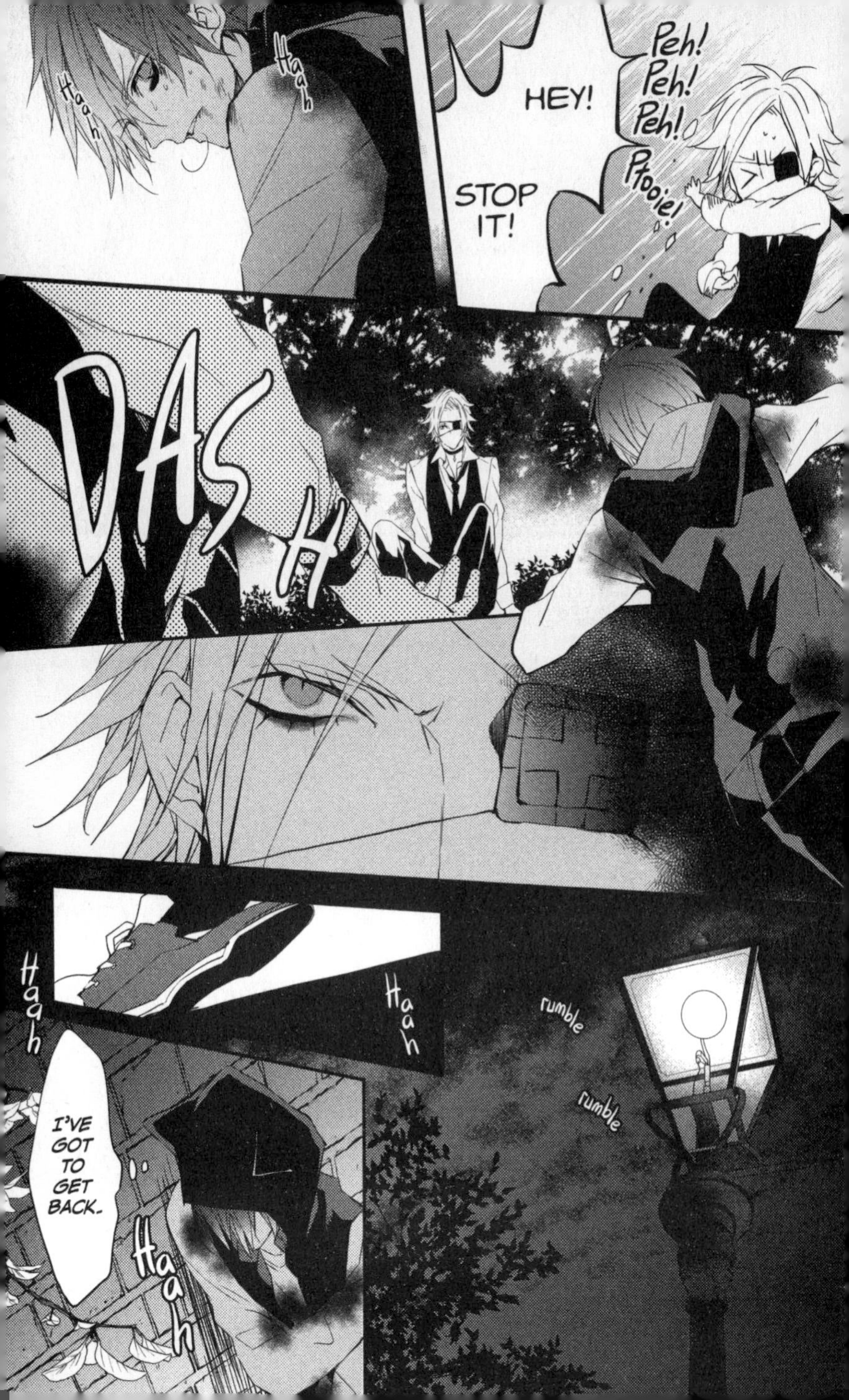
Peh! Peh! Peh! Ptooie!
HEY!
STOP IT!
Haaah
Haaah
DASH
rumble
rumble
Haaah
Haaah
I'VE GOT TO GET BACK.
Haaah

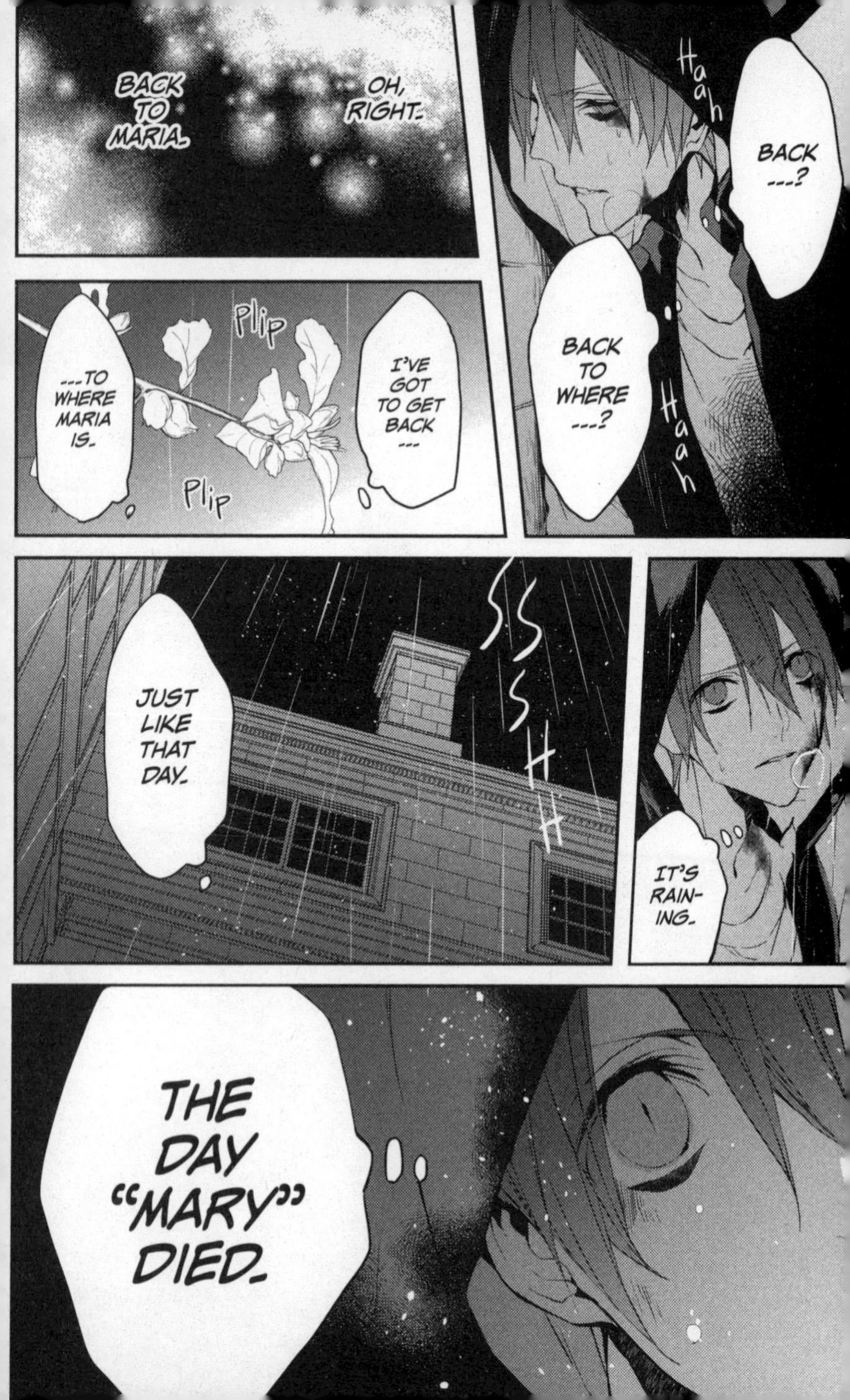
Haah
BACK---?
BACK TO WHERE---?
Haah
OH, RIGHT.
BACK TO MARIA.
I'VE GOT TO GET BACK---
Plip
---TO WHERE MARIA IS.
Plip
IT'S RAIN-ING.
SSHH
JUST LIKE THAT DAY.
THE DAY "MARY" DIED.

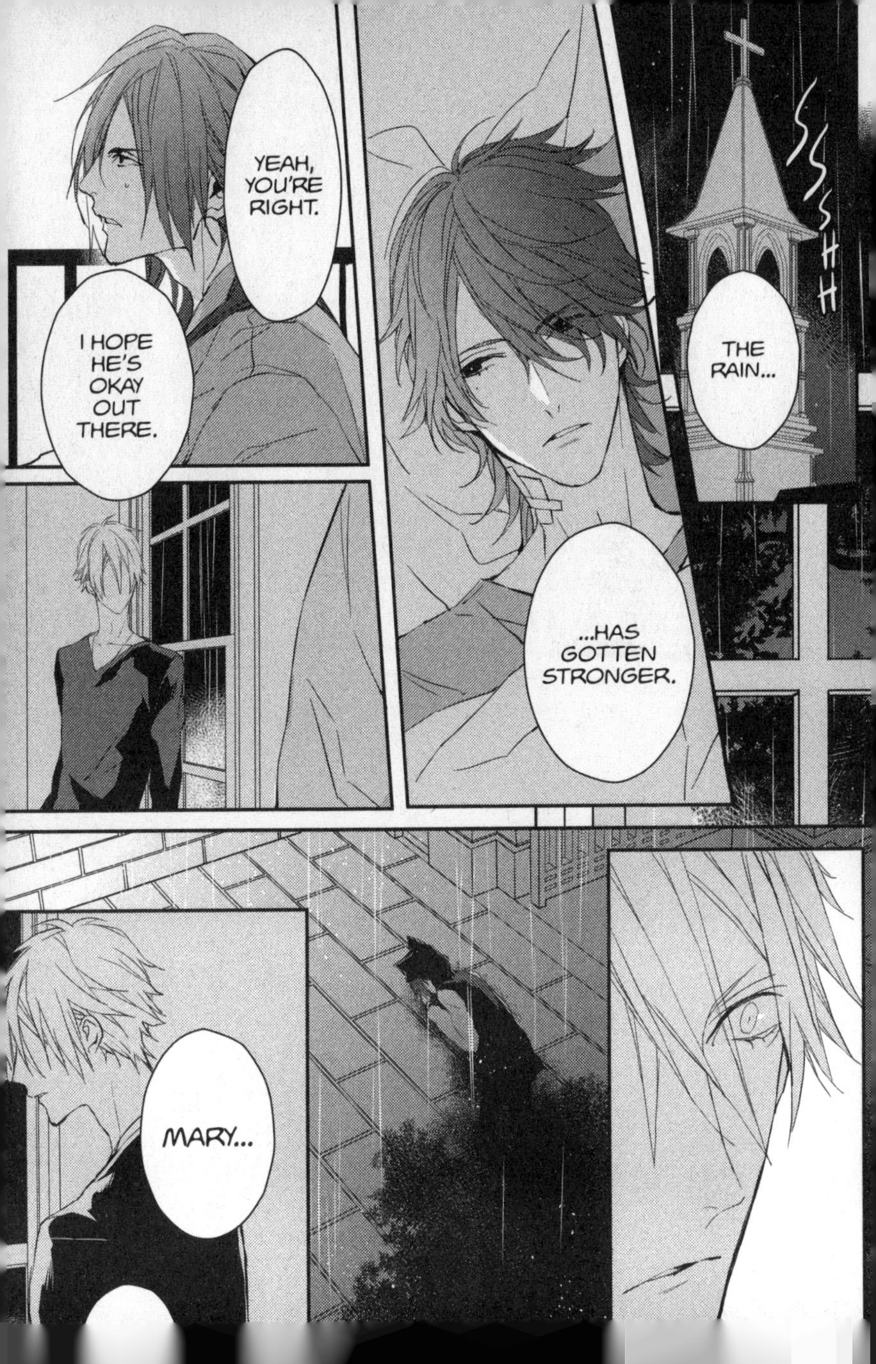
SSSHH
THE RAIN...
...HAS GOTTEN STRONGER.
YEAH, YOU'RE RIGHT.
I HOPE HE'S OKAY OUT THERE.
MARY...

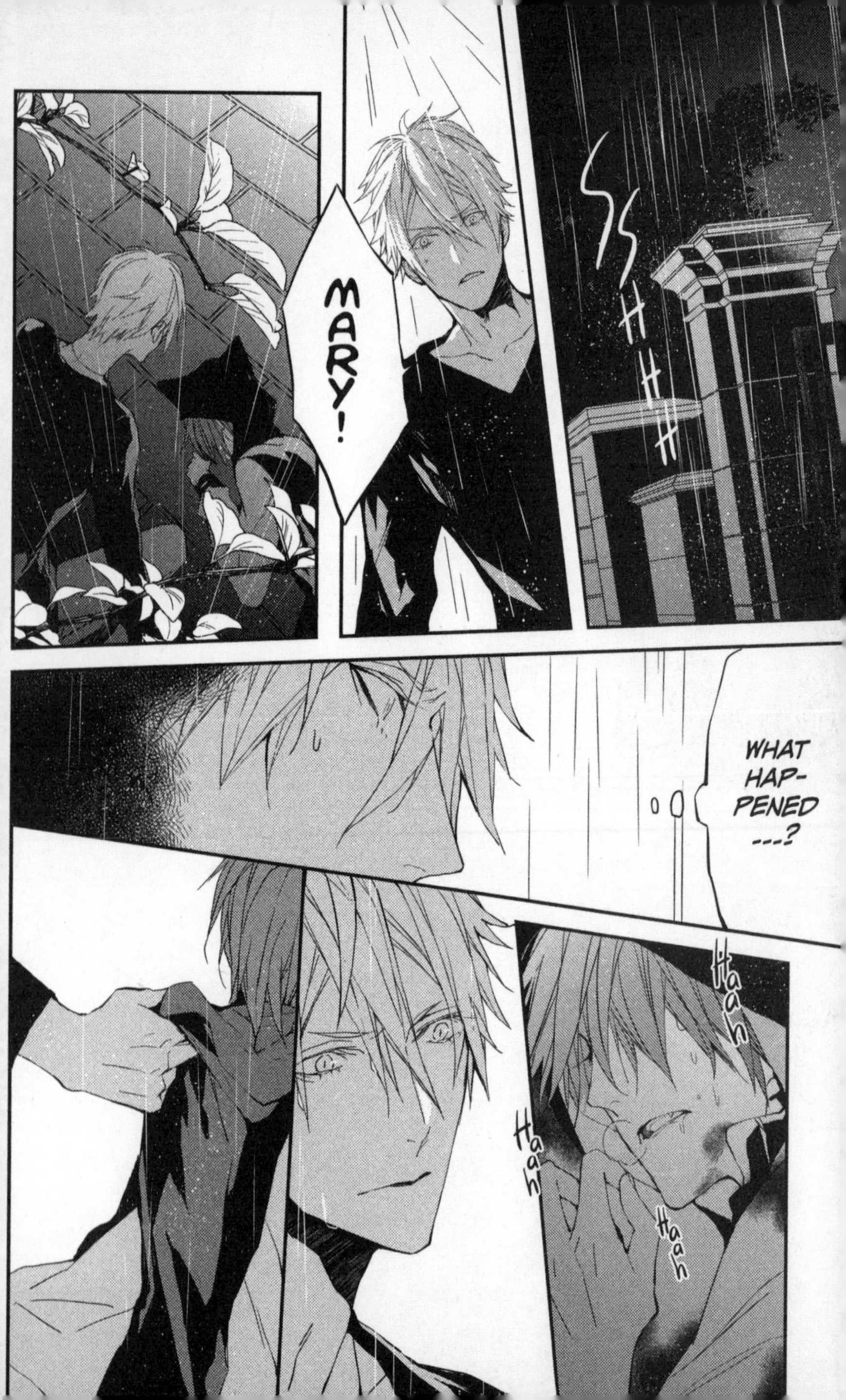
SSHHHH
MARY!
WHAT HAP-PENED---?
Haah
Haah
Haah

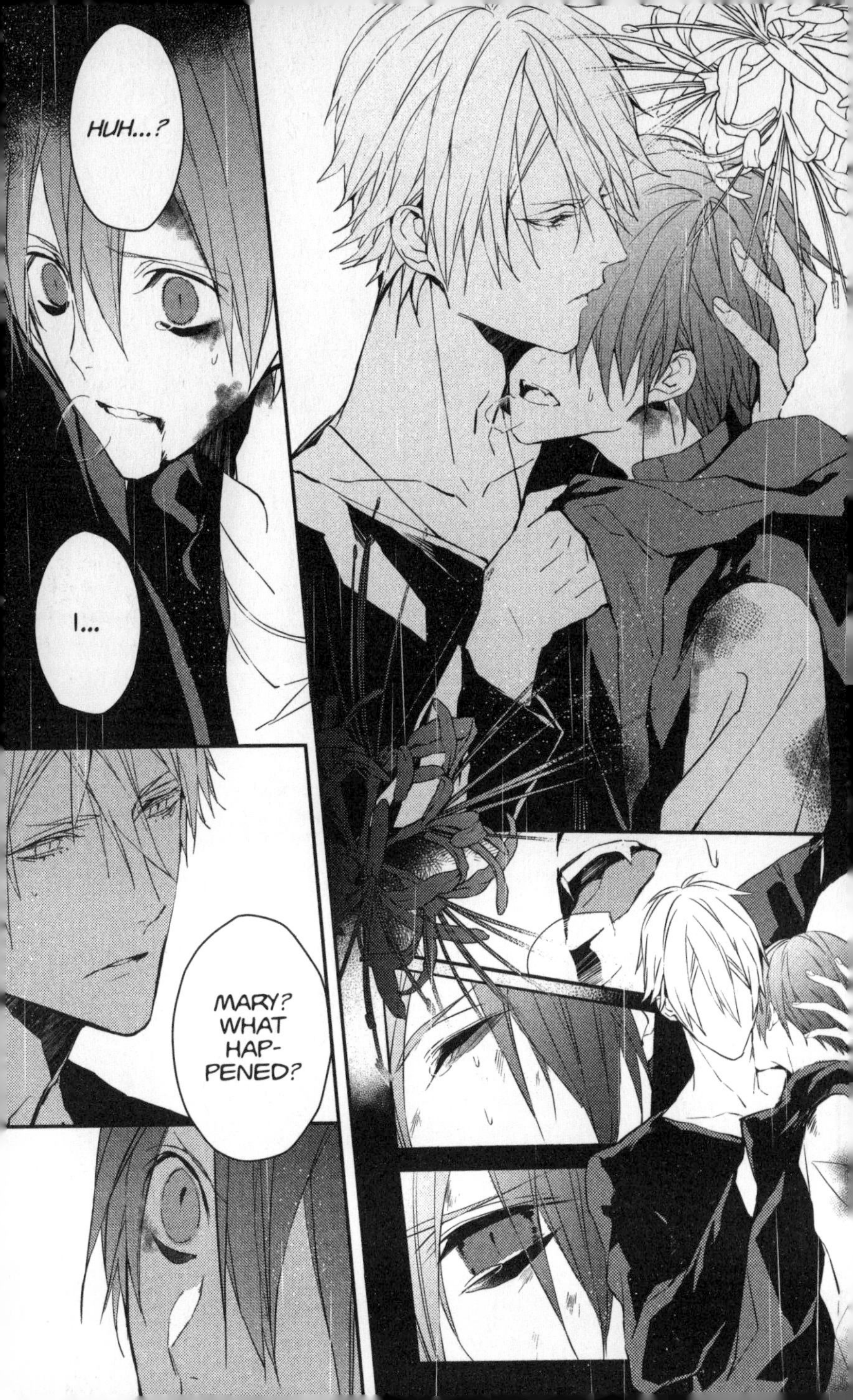
HUH...?
I...
MARY? WHAT HAP-PENED?

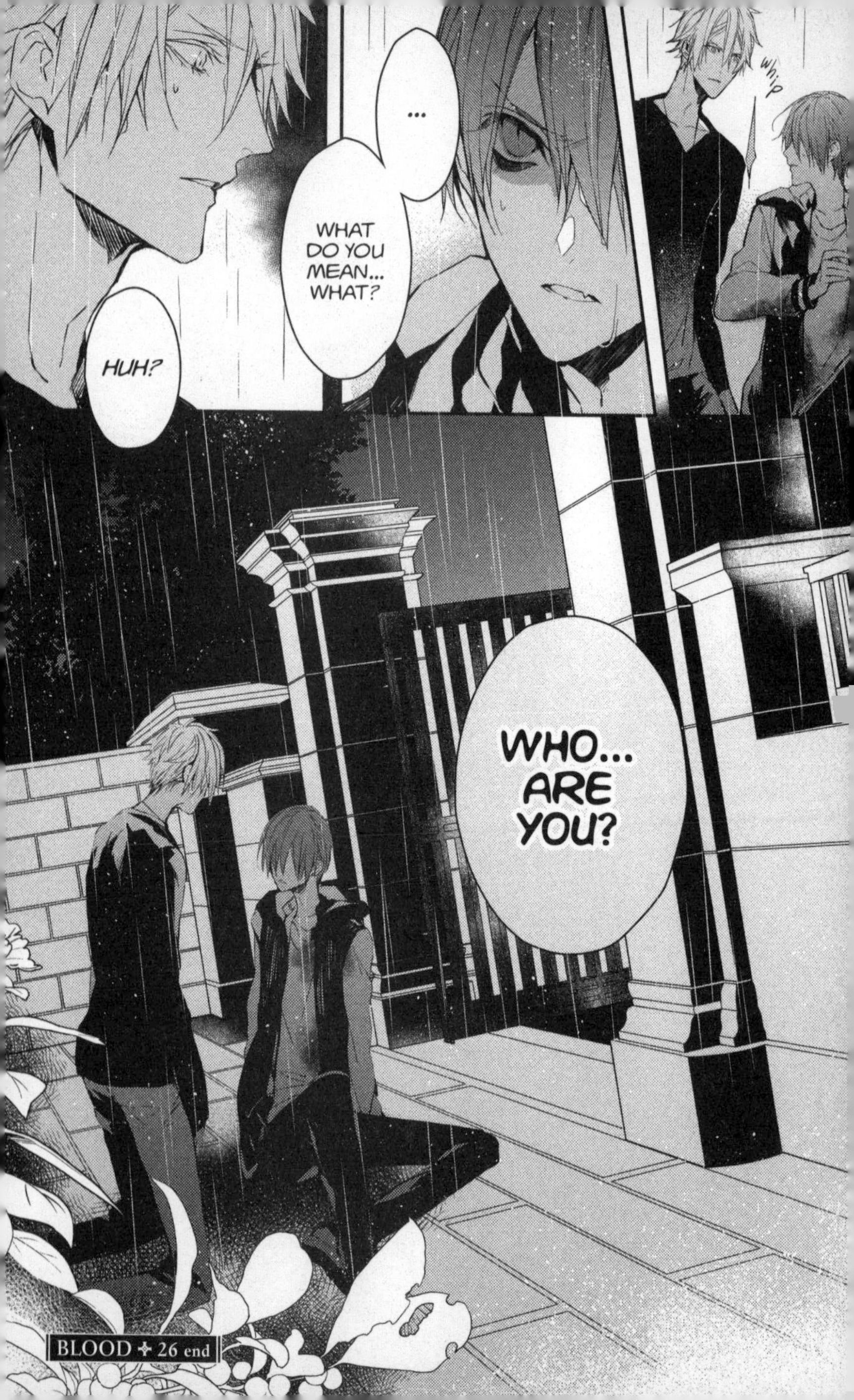
whip
...
WHAT DO YOU MEAN... WHAT?
HUH?
WHO... ARE YOU?
BLOOD ✦ 26 end

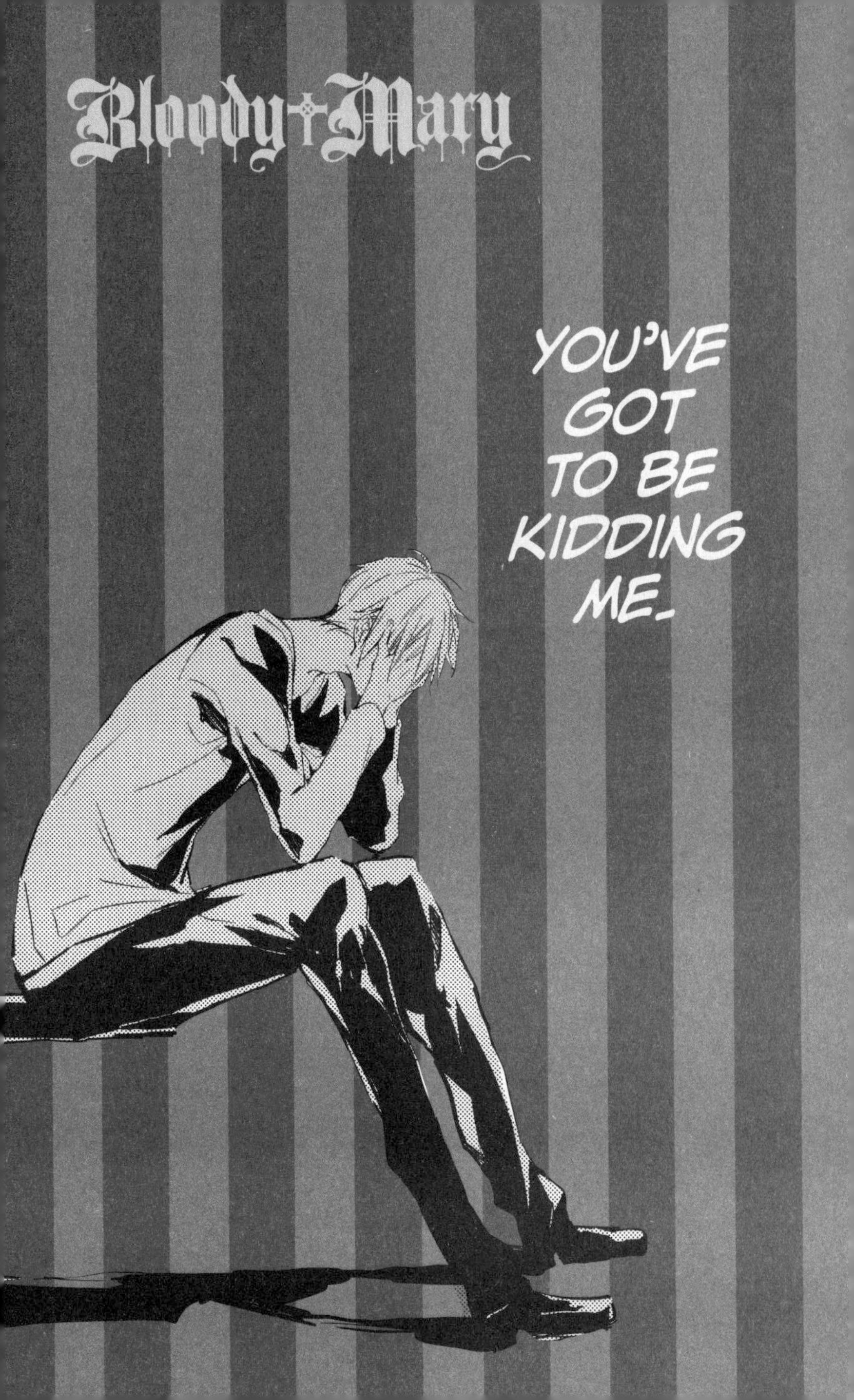
Bloody+Mary
YOU'VE GOT TO BE KIDDING ME_

# Bloody✝Mary

ARE YOU GUYS DOING THAT THING? WEARING TRENDY GLASSES?

PLEASE SHUT UP WITH YOUR NON-SENSE.

Ouchie...

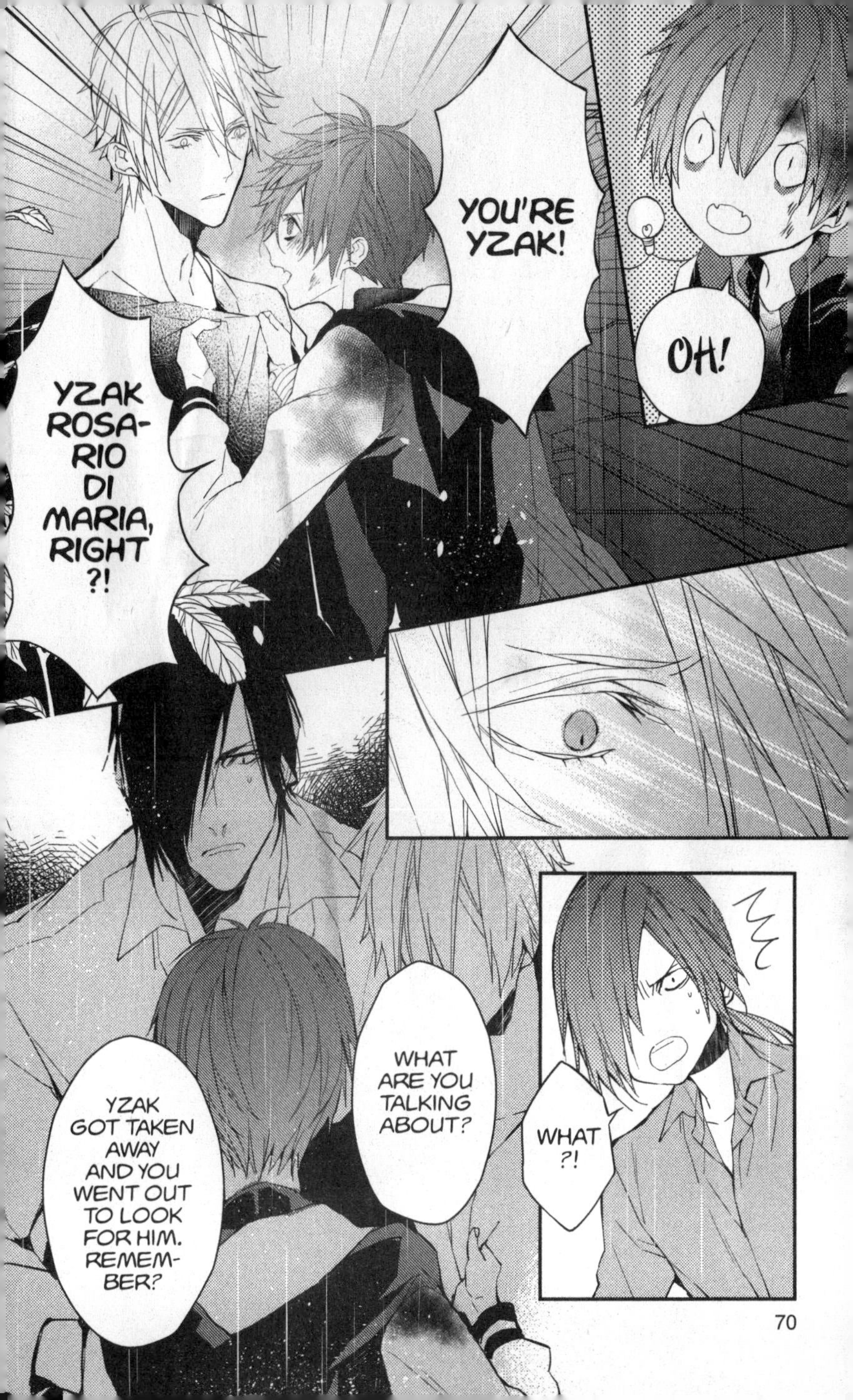
OH!
YOU'RE YZAK!
YZAK ROSARIO DI MARIA, RIGHT?!
WHAT?!
WHAT ARE YOU TALKING ABOUT?
YZAK GOT TAKEN AWAY AND YOU WENT OUT TO LOOK FOR HIM. REMEMBER?

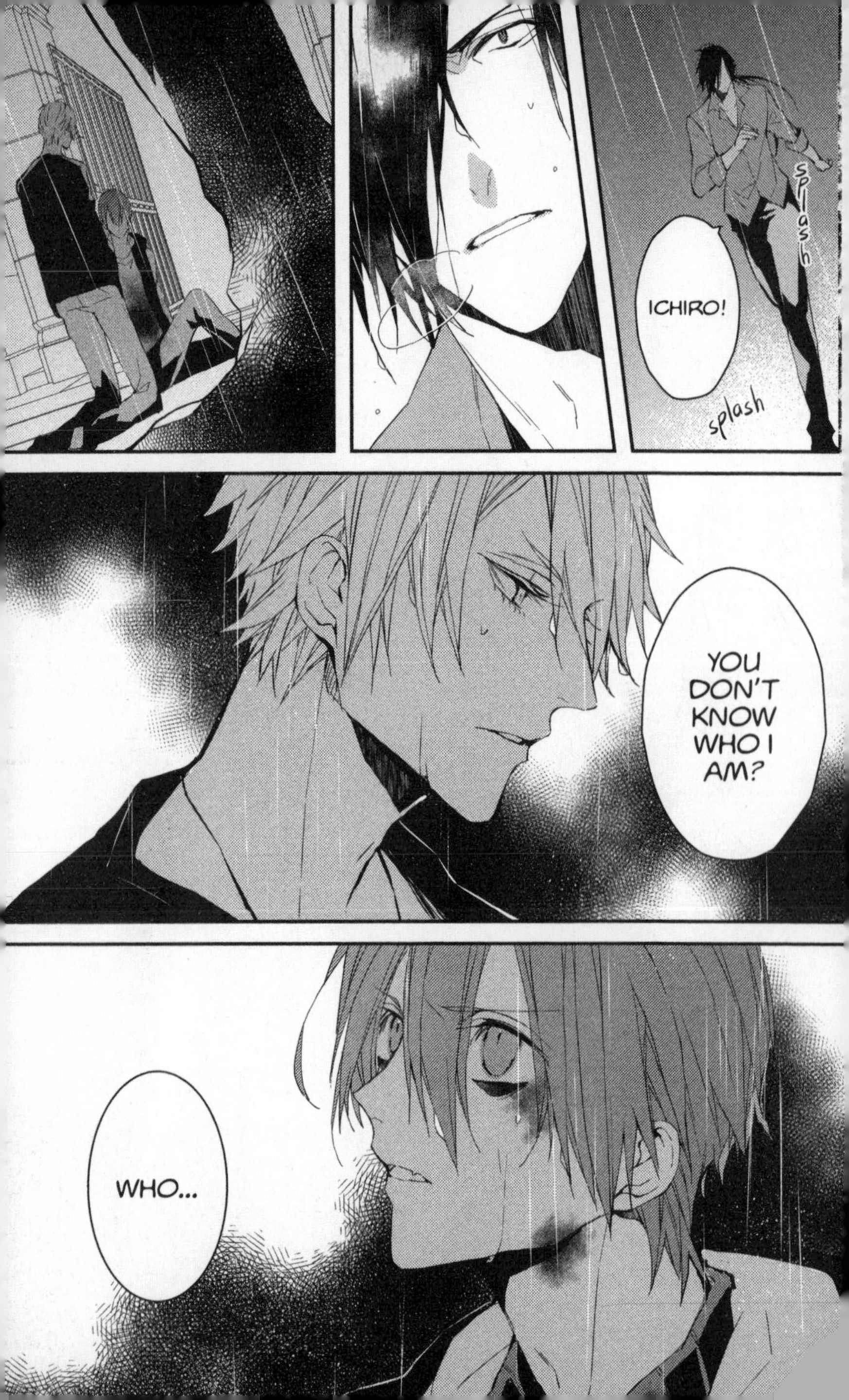
splash
ICHIRO!
splash
YOU DON'T KNOW WHO I AM?
WHO...

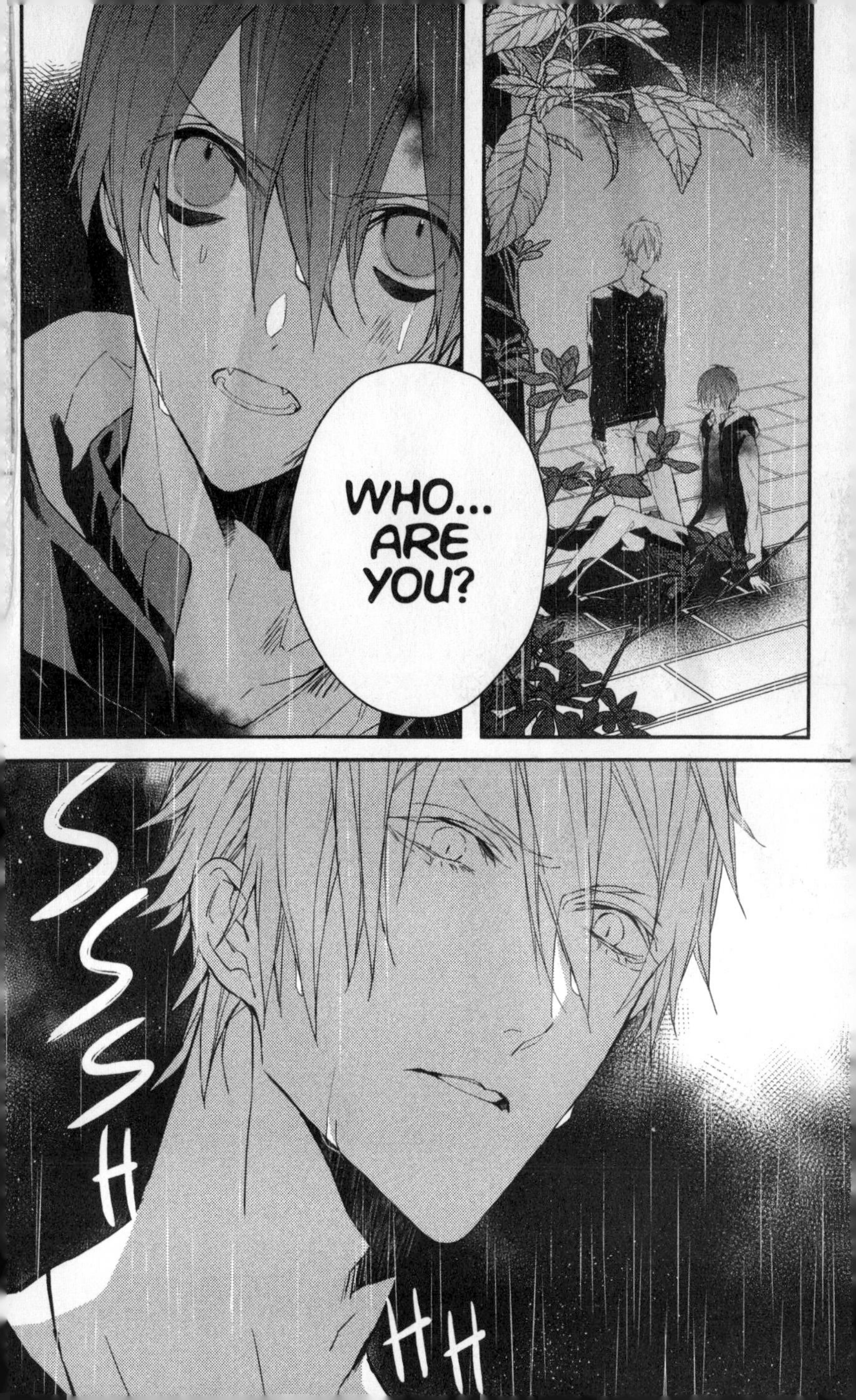
WHO... ARE YOU?
SSSHHHH

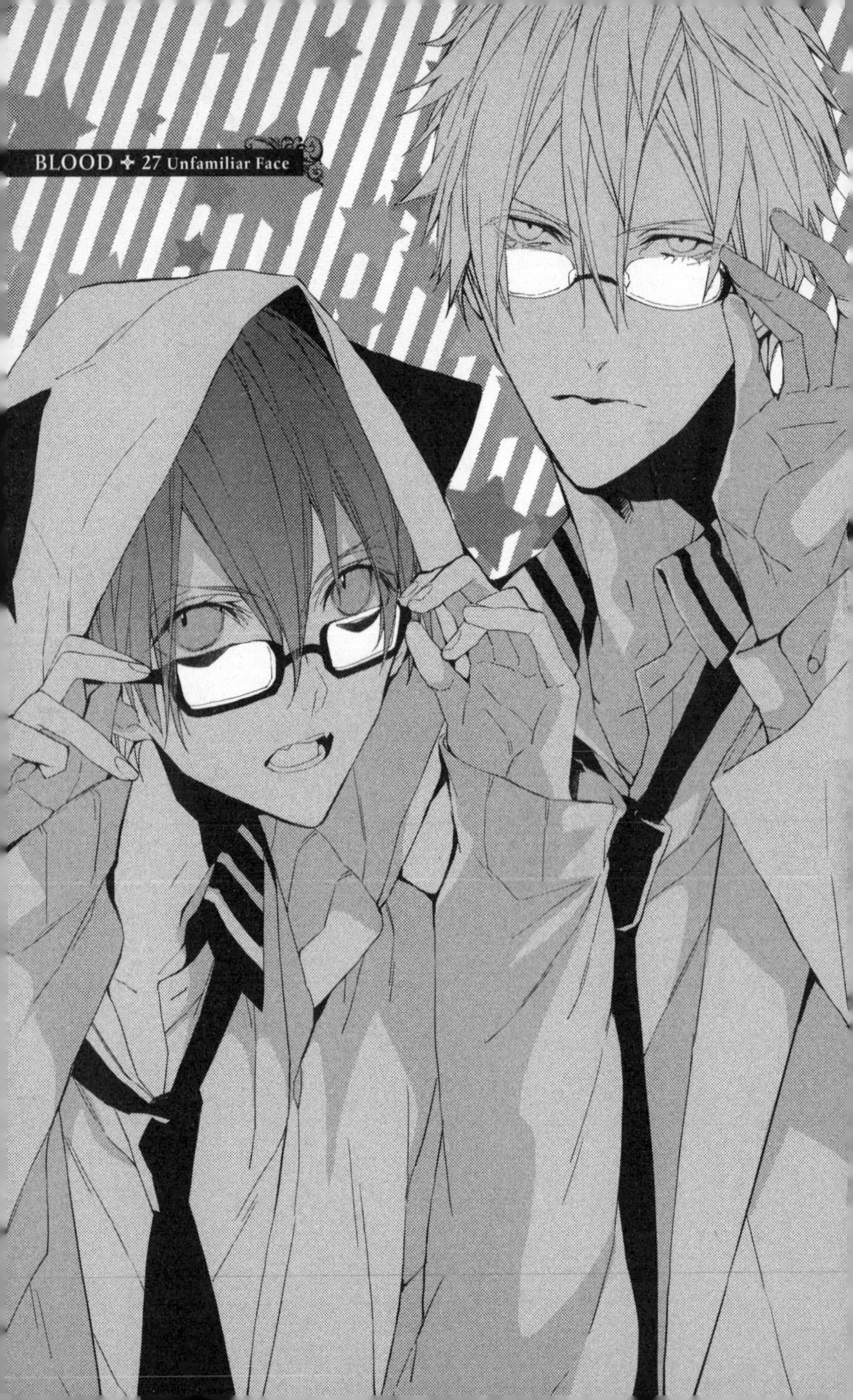
BLOOD ✣ 27 Unfamiliar Face

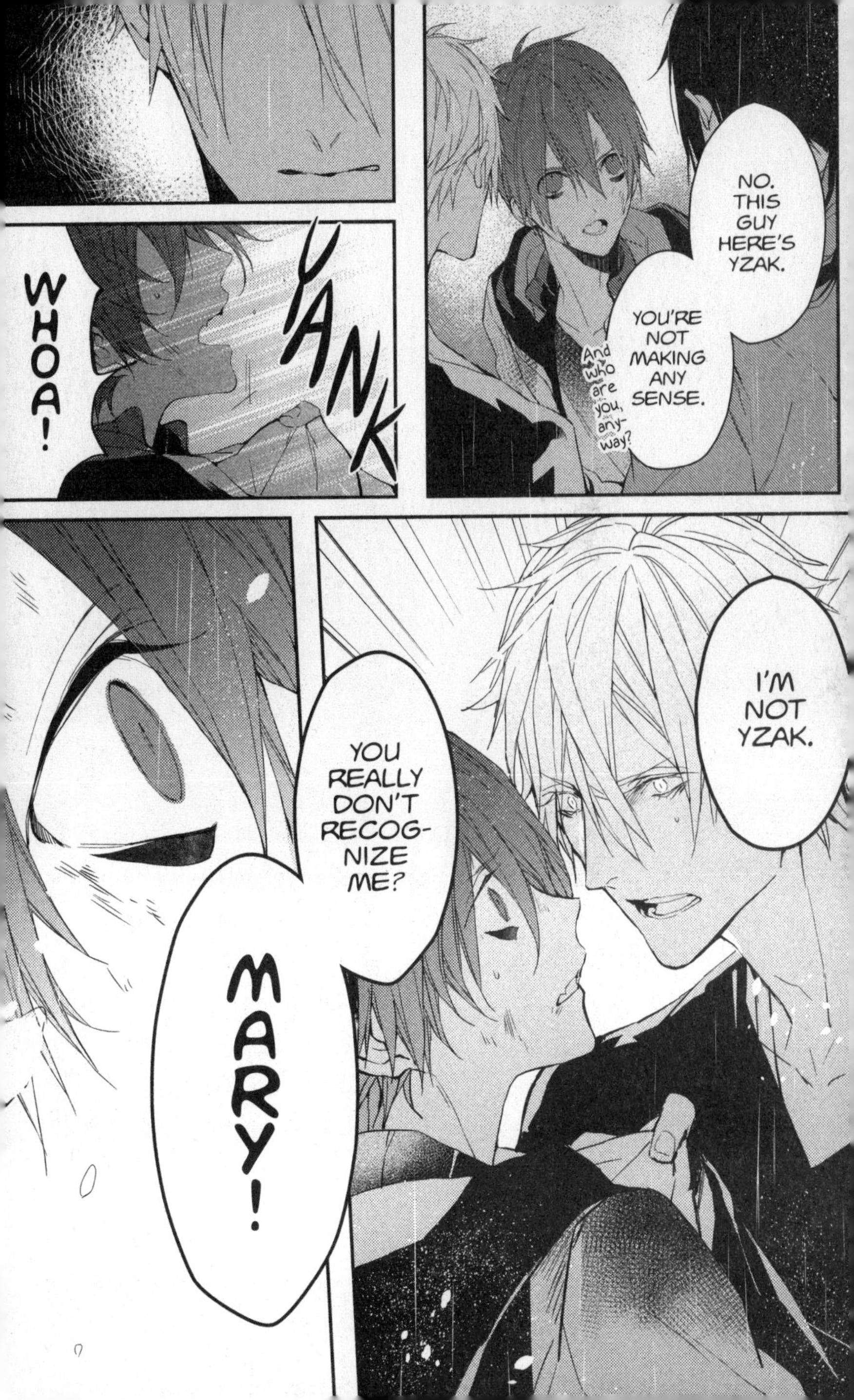
NO. THIS GUY HERE'S YZAK.
YOU'RE NOT MAKING ANY SENSE.
And who are you, anyway?
YANK
WHOA!
I'M NOT YZAK.
YOU REALLY DON'T RECOG-NIZE ME?
MARY!

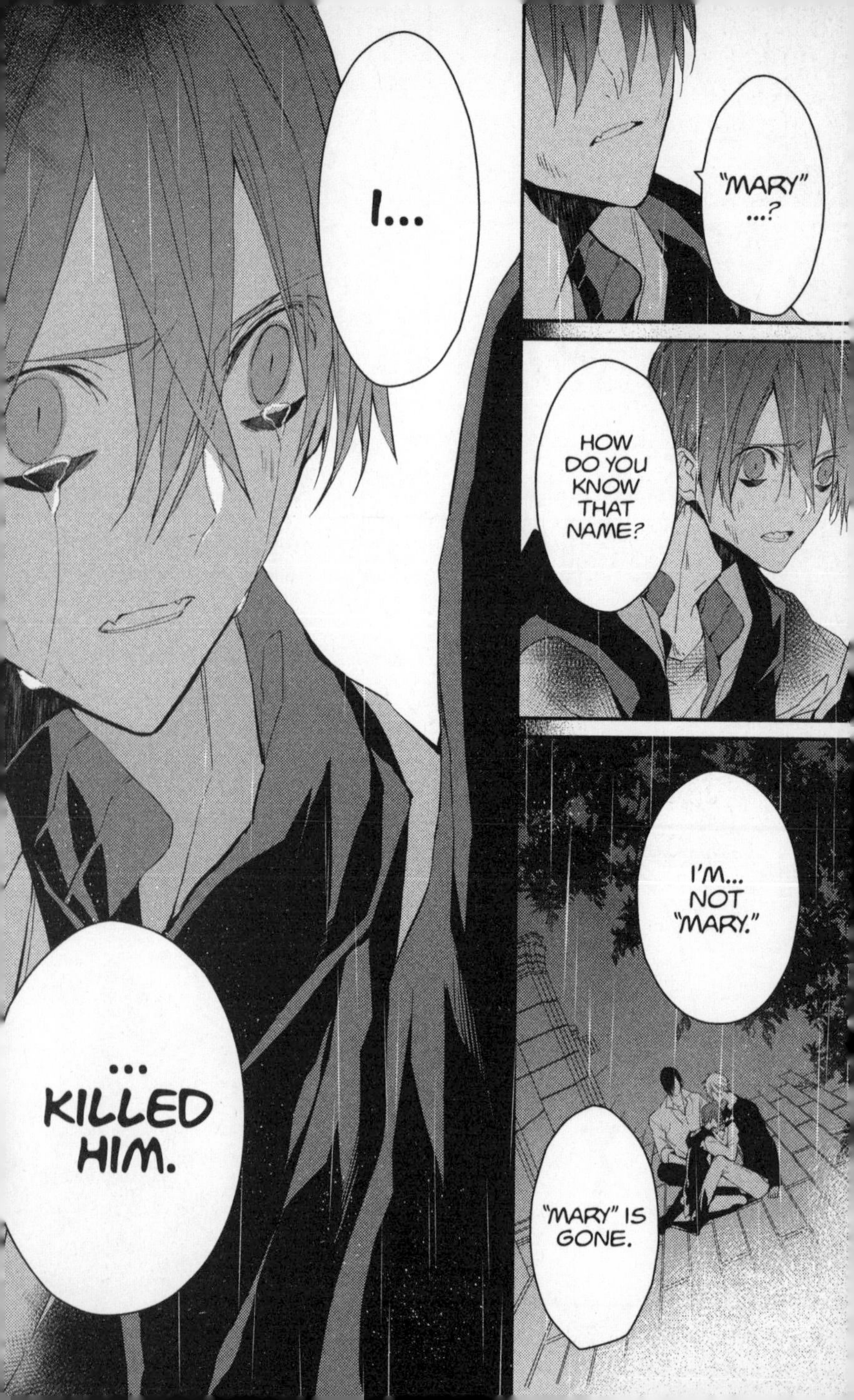
"MARY" ...?
HOW DO YOU KNOW THAT NAME?
I'M... NOT "MARY."
"MARY" IS GONE.
I...
...KILLED HIM.

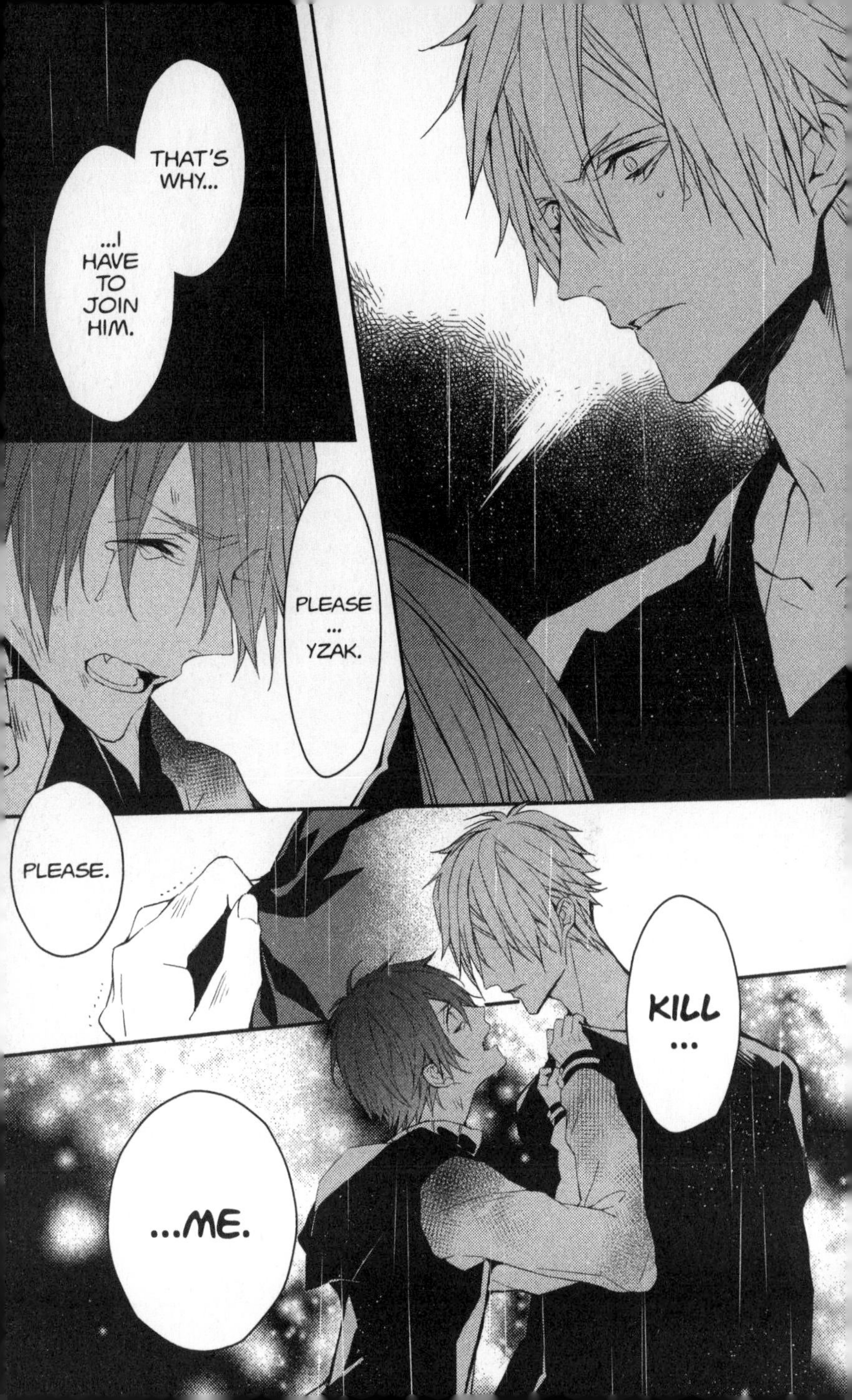
THAT'S WHY...
...I HAVE TO JOIN HIM.
PLEASE ... YZAK.
PLEASE.
KILL ...
...ME.

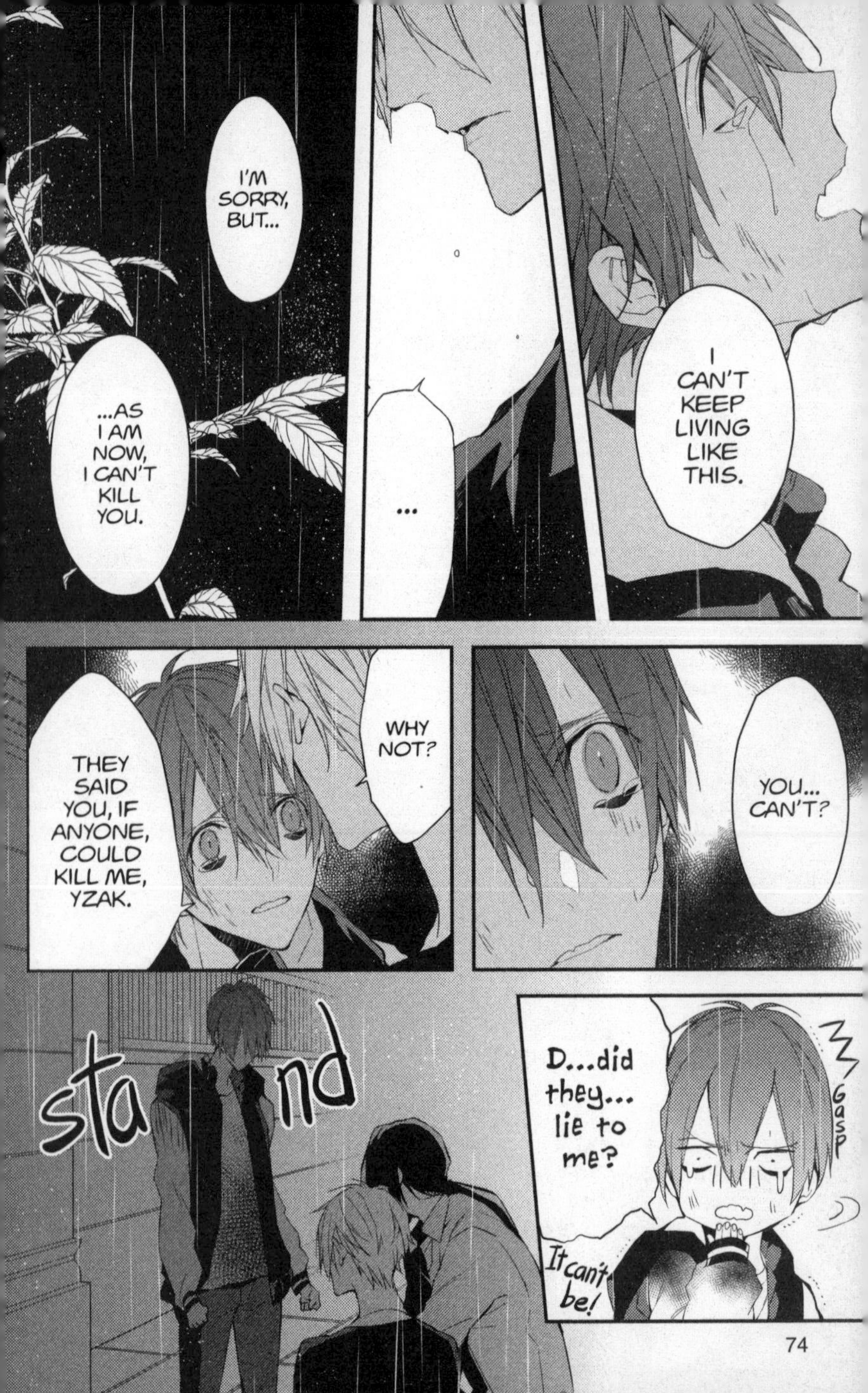
I CAN'T KEEP LIVING LIKE THIS.
...
I'M SORRY, BUT...
...AS I AM NOW, I CAN'T KILL YOU.
YOU... CAN'T?
WHY NOT?
THEY SAID YOU, IF ANYONE, COULD KILL ME, YZAK.
D...did they... lie to me?
Gasp
It can't be!
stand

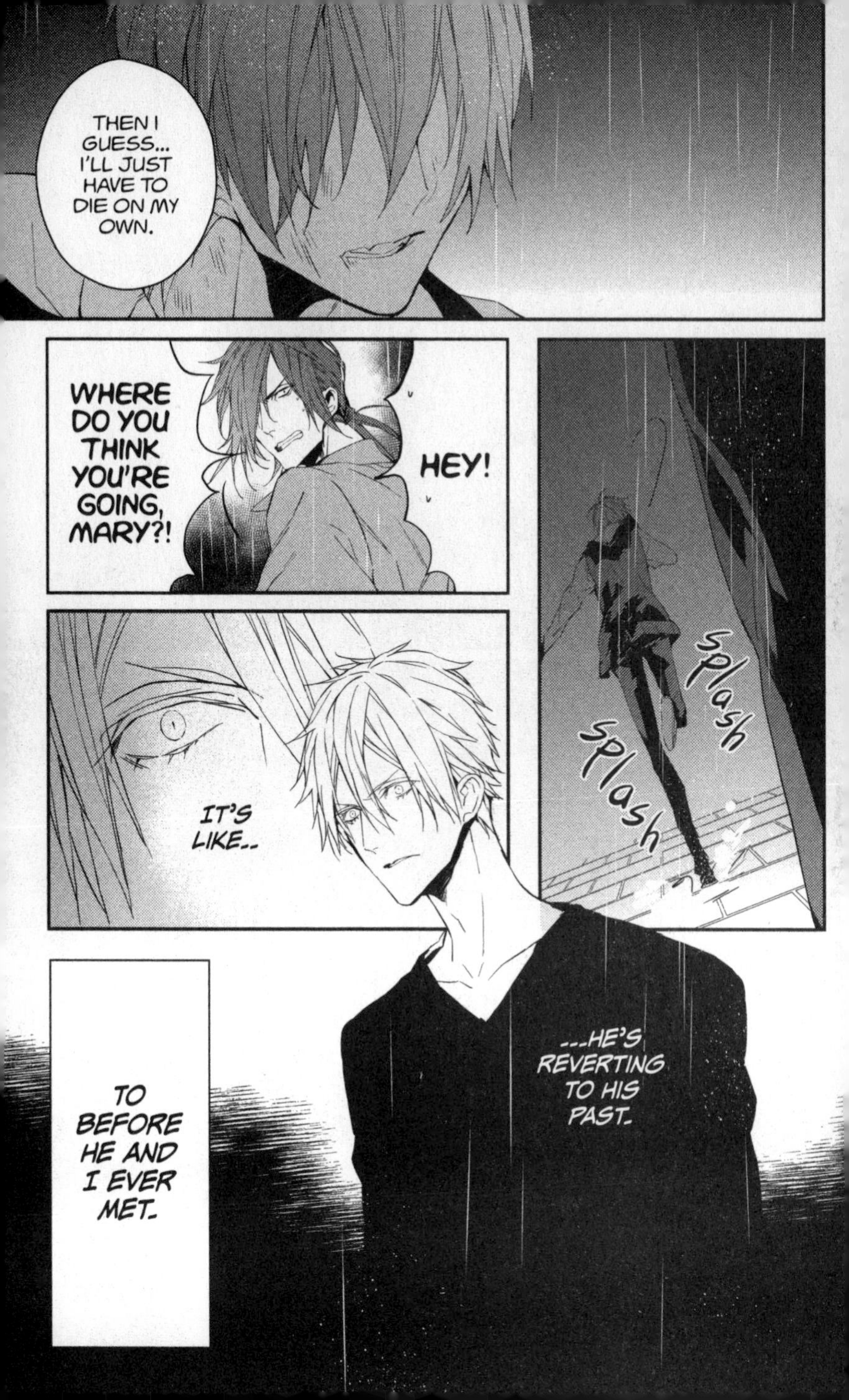
THEN I GUESS... I'LL JUST HAVE TO DIE ON MY OWN.
splash
splash
HEY!
WHERE DO YOU THINK YOU'RE GOING, MARY?!
IT'S LIKE...
...HE'S REVERTING TO HIS PAST.
TO BEFORE HE AND I EVER MET.

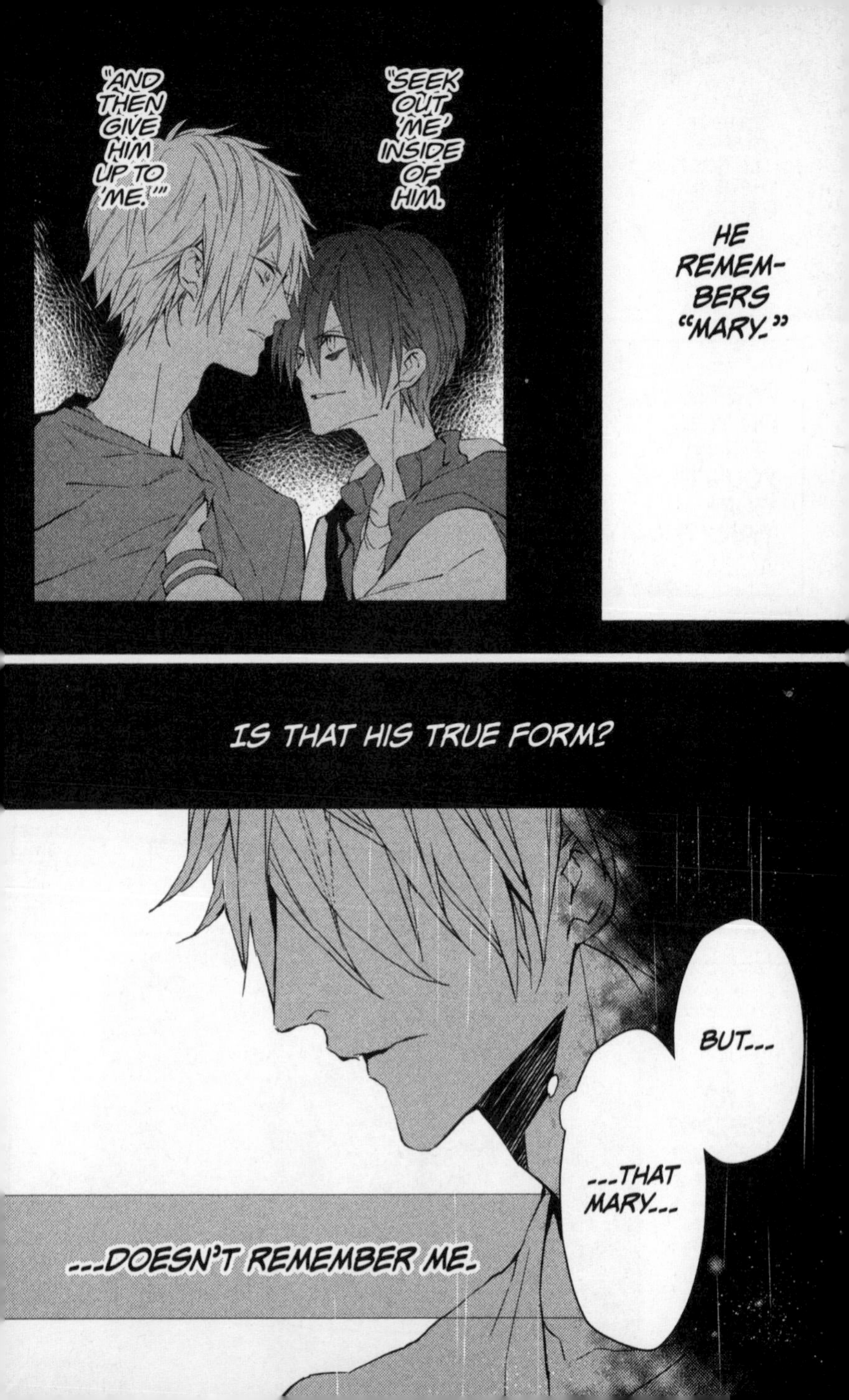
HE REMEMBERS "MARY."
"SEEK OUT 'ME' INSIDE OF HIM.
AND THEN GIVE HIM UP TO 'ME.'"
IS THAT HIS TRUE FORM?
BUT...
...THAT MARY...
...DOESN'T REMEMBER ME.

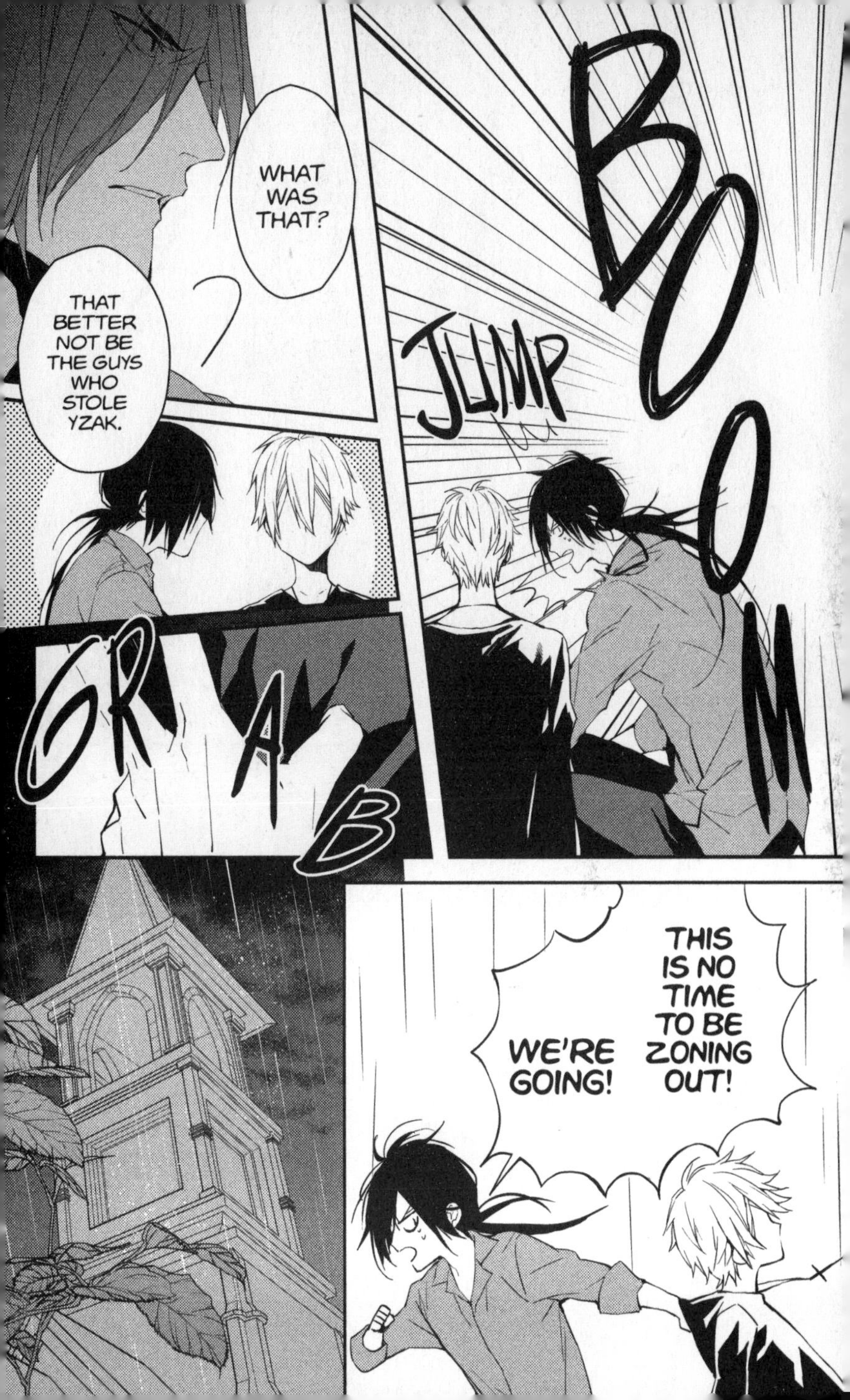
BOOM
JUMP
WHAT WAS THAT?
THAT BETTER NOT BE THE GUYS WHO STOLE YZAK.
GRAB
THIS IS NO TIME TO BE ZONING OUT!
WE'RE GOING!

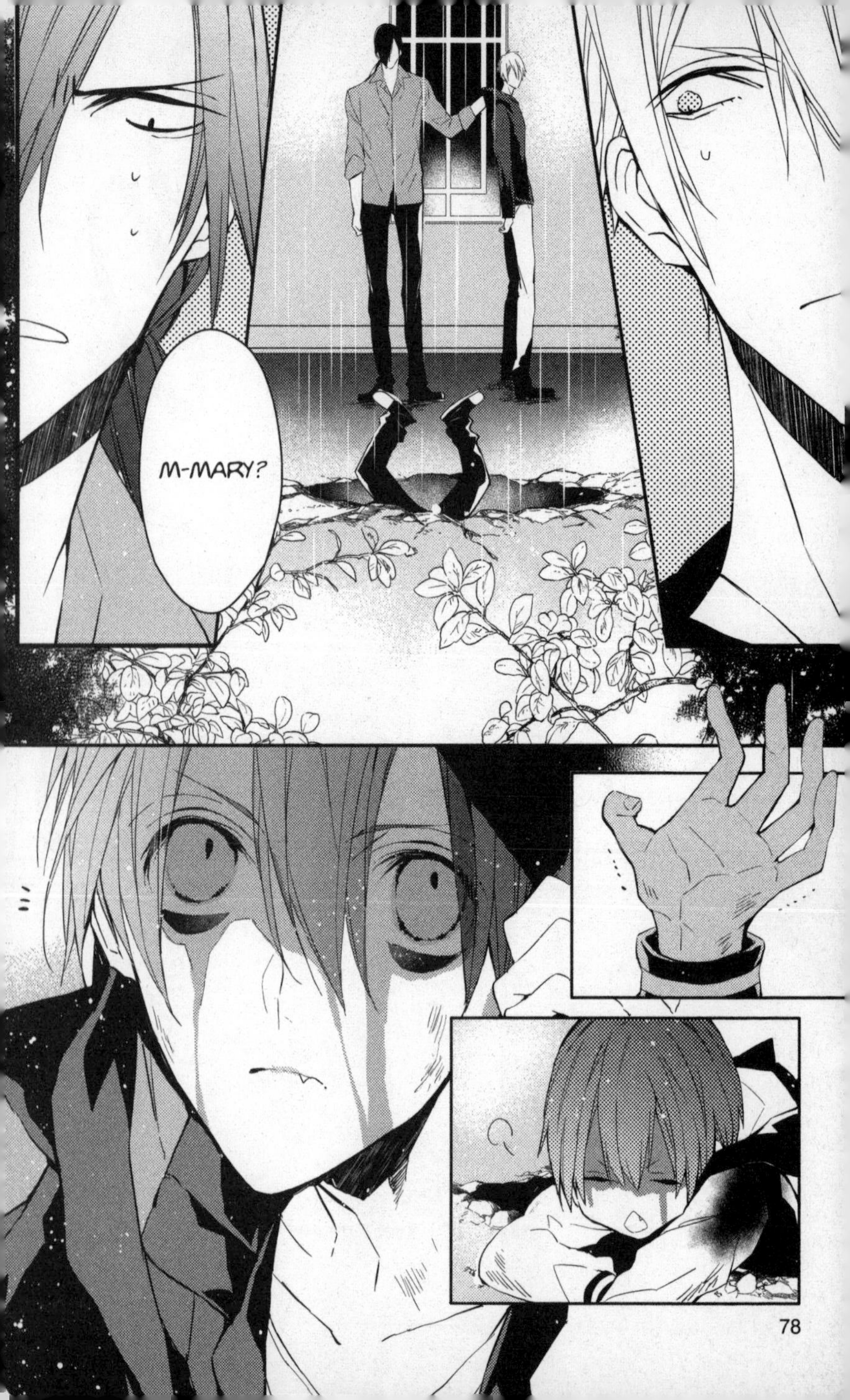
M-MARY?

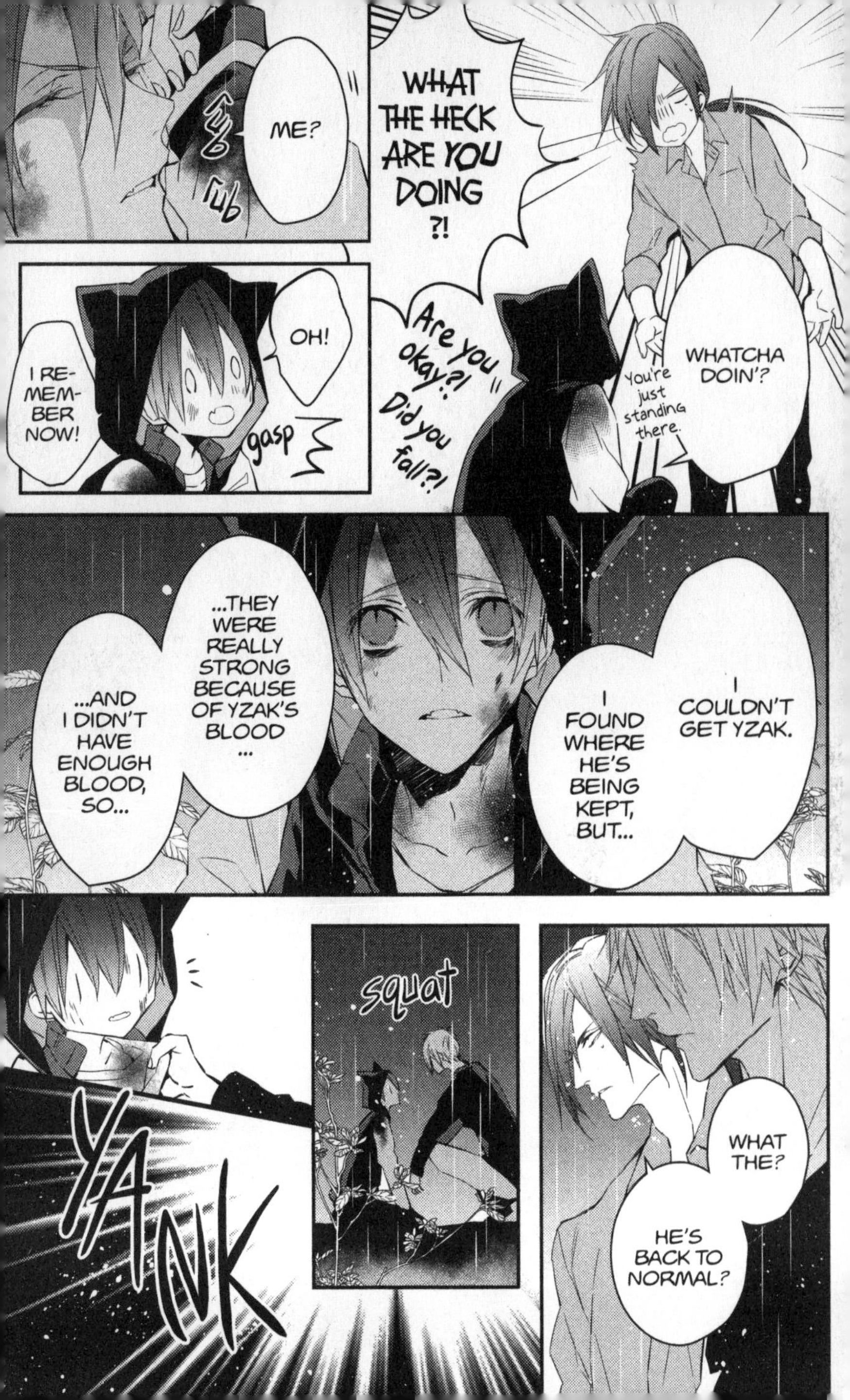
WHAT THE HECK ARE YOU DOING ?!
WHATCHA DOIN'?
You're just standing there.
Are you okay?! Did you fall?!
ME?
rub rub
OH!
I RE-MEM-BER NOW!
gasp
I COULDN'T GET YZAK.
I FOUND WHERE HE'S BEING KEPT, BUT...
...THEY WERE REALLY STRONG BECAUSE OF YZAK'S BLOOD ...
...AND I DIDN'T HAVE ENOUGH BLOOD, SO...
WHAT THE?
HE'S BACK TO NORMAL?
squat
YANK

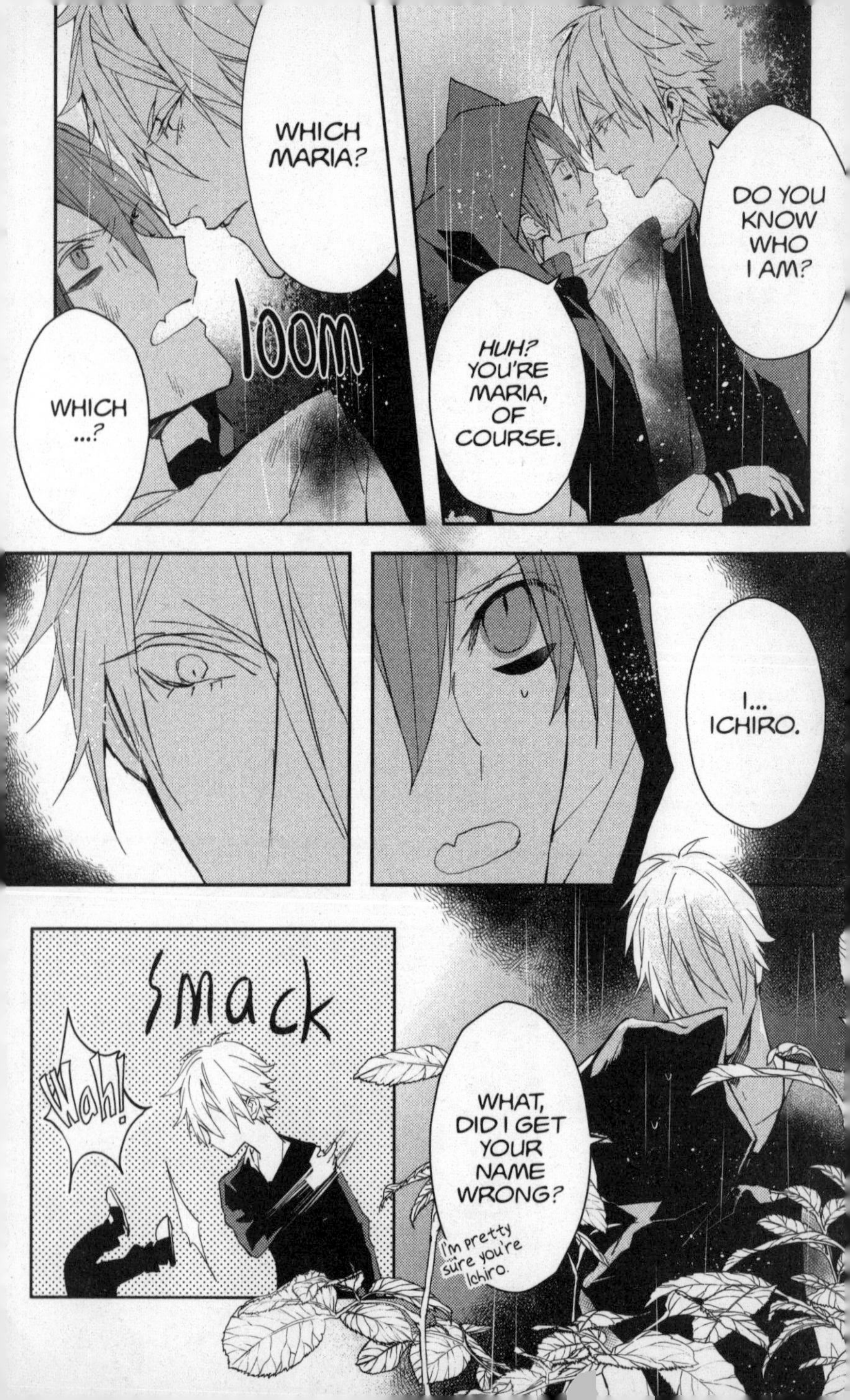
DO YOU KNOW WHO I AM?
HUH? YOU'RE MARIA, OF COURSE.
WHICH MARIA?
loom
WHICH ...?
I... ICHIRO.
WHAT, DID I GET YOUR NAME WRONG?
I'm pretty sure you're Ichiro.
Smack
Wah!

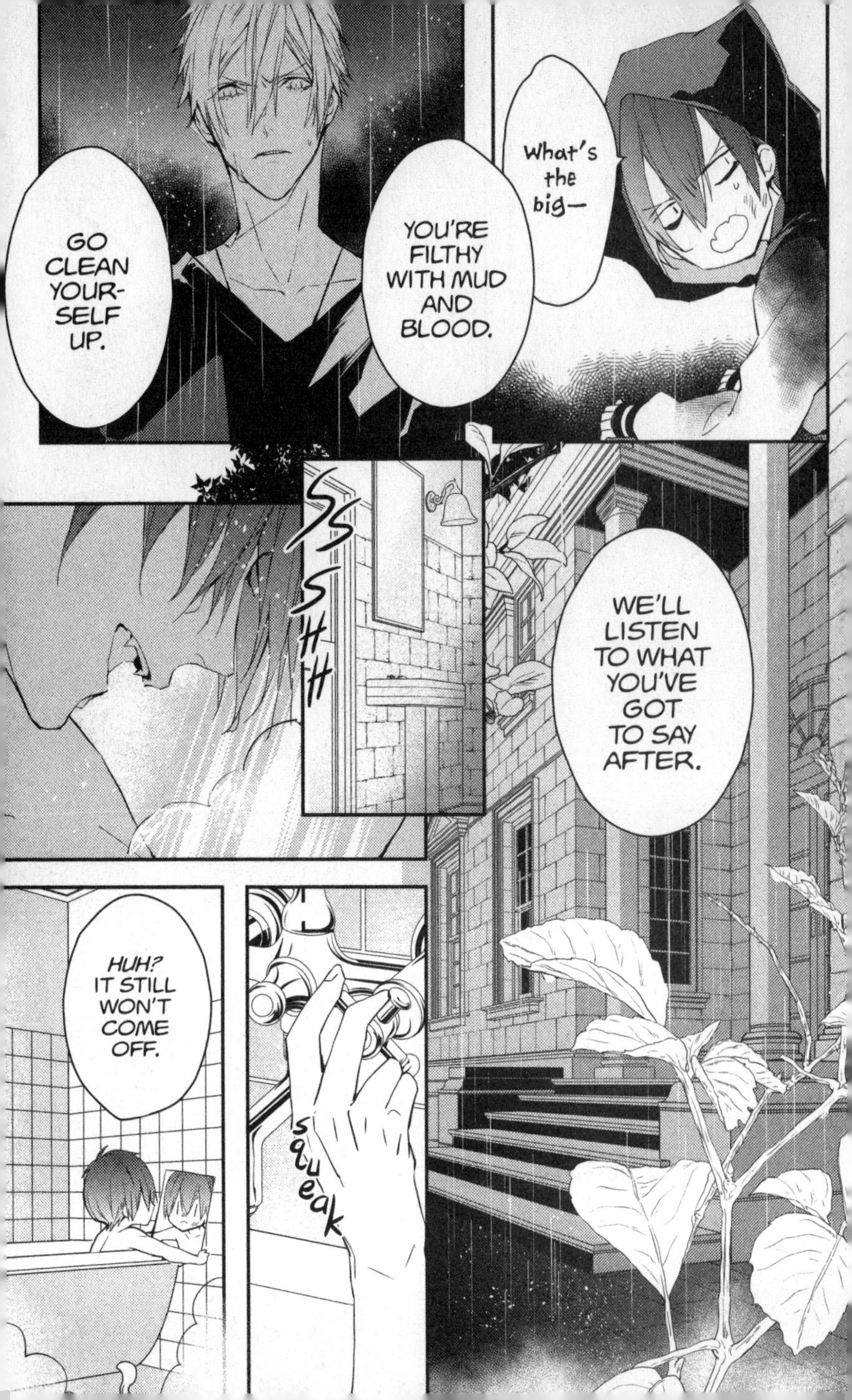
What's the big—
YOU'RE FILTHY WITH MUD AND BLOOD.
GO CLEAN YOURSELF UP.
WE'LL LISTEN TO WHAT YOU'VE GOT TO SAY AFTER.
SSSHH
squeak
HUH? IT STILL WON'T COME OFF.

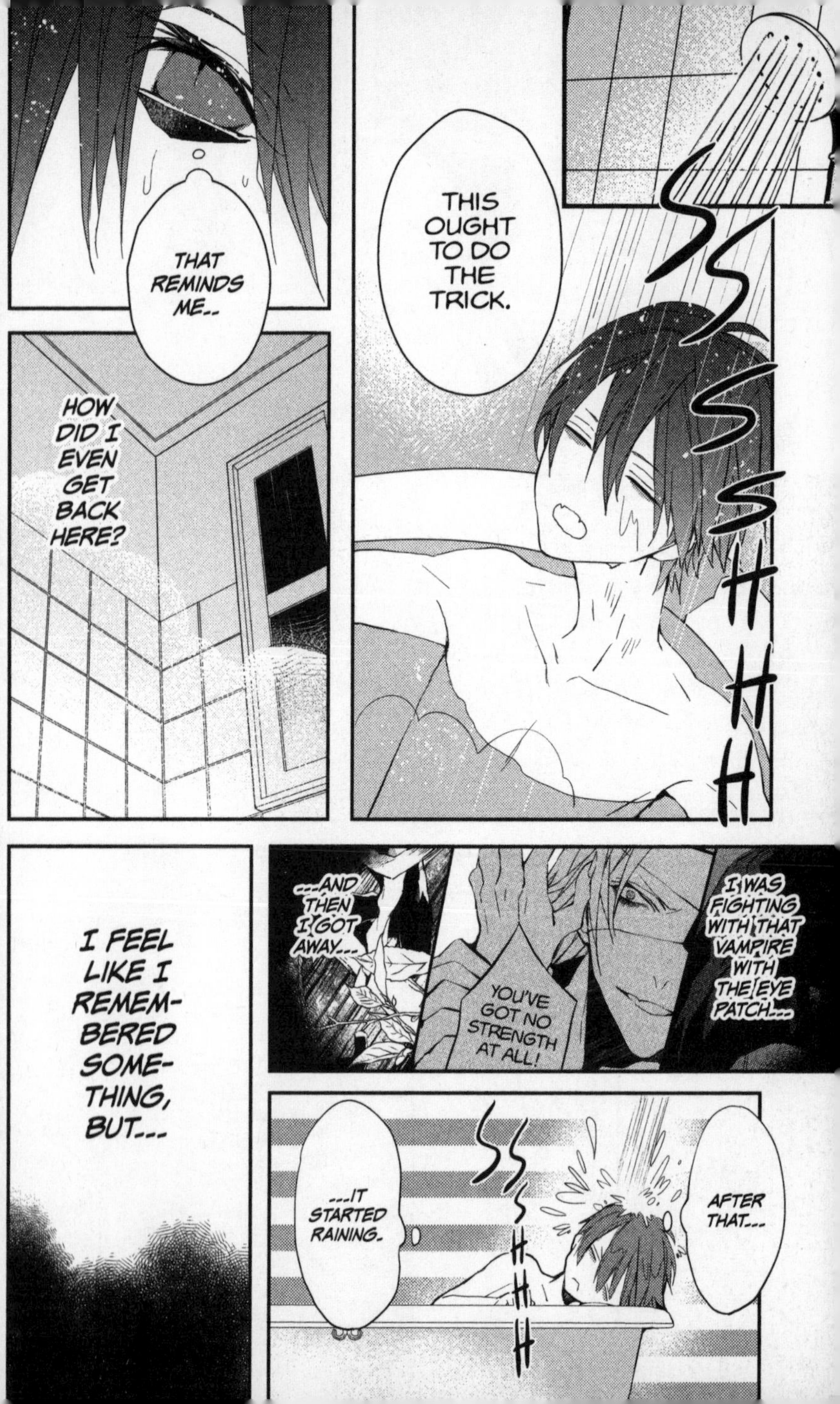
SSSSHHHH
THIS OUGHT TO DO THE TRICK.
THAT REMINDS ME...
HOW DID I EVEN GET BACK HERE?
I WAS FIGHTING WITH THAT VAMPIRE WITH THE EYE PATCH...
YOU'VE GOT NO STRENGTH AT ALL!
...AND THEN I GOT AWAY...
AFTER THAT...
SSHHHH
...IT STARTED RAINING.
I FEEL LIKE I REMEMBERED SOMETHING, BUT...

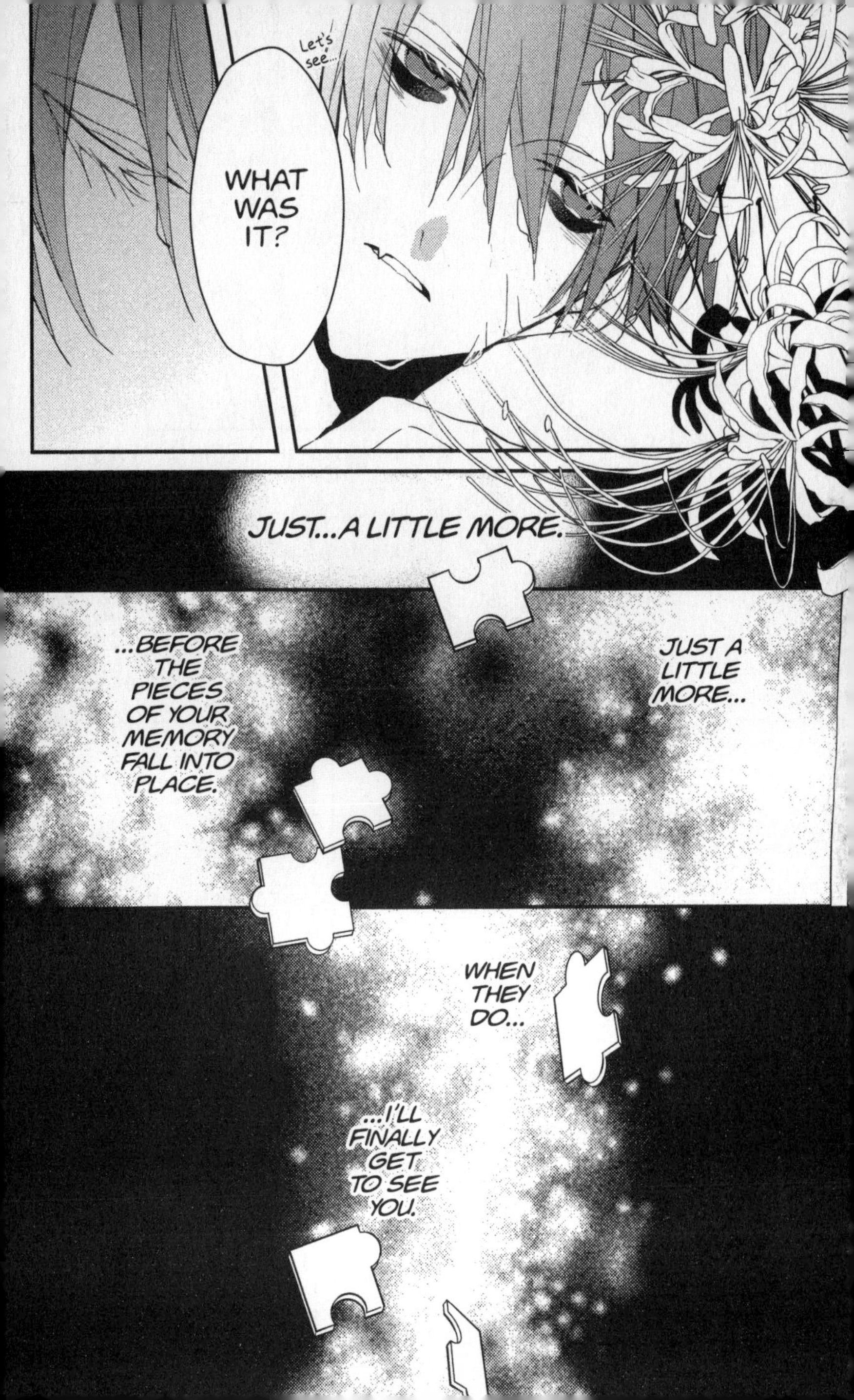

Let's see...
WHAT WAS IT?
JUST...A LITTLE MORE.
JUST A LITTLE MORE...
...BEFORE THE PIECES OF YOUR MEMORY FALL INTO PLACE.
WHEN THEY DO...
...I'LL FINALLY GET TO SEE YOU.

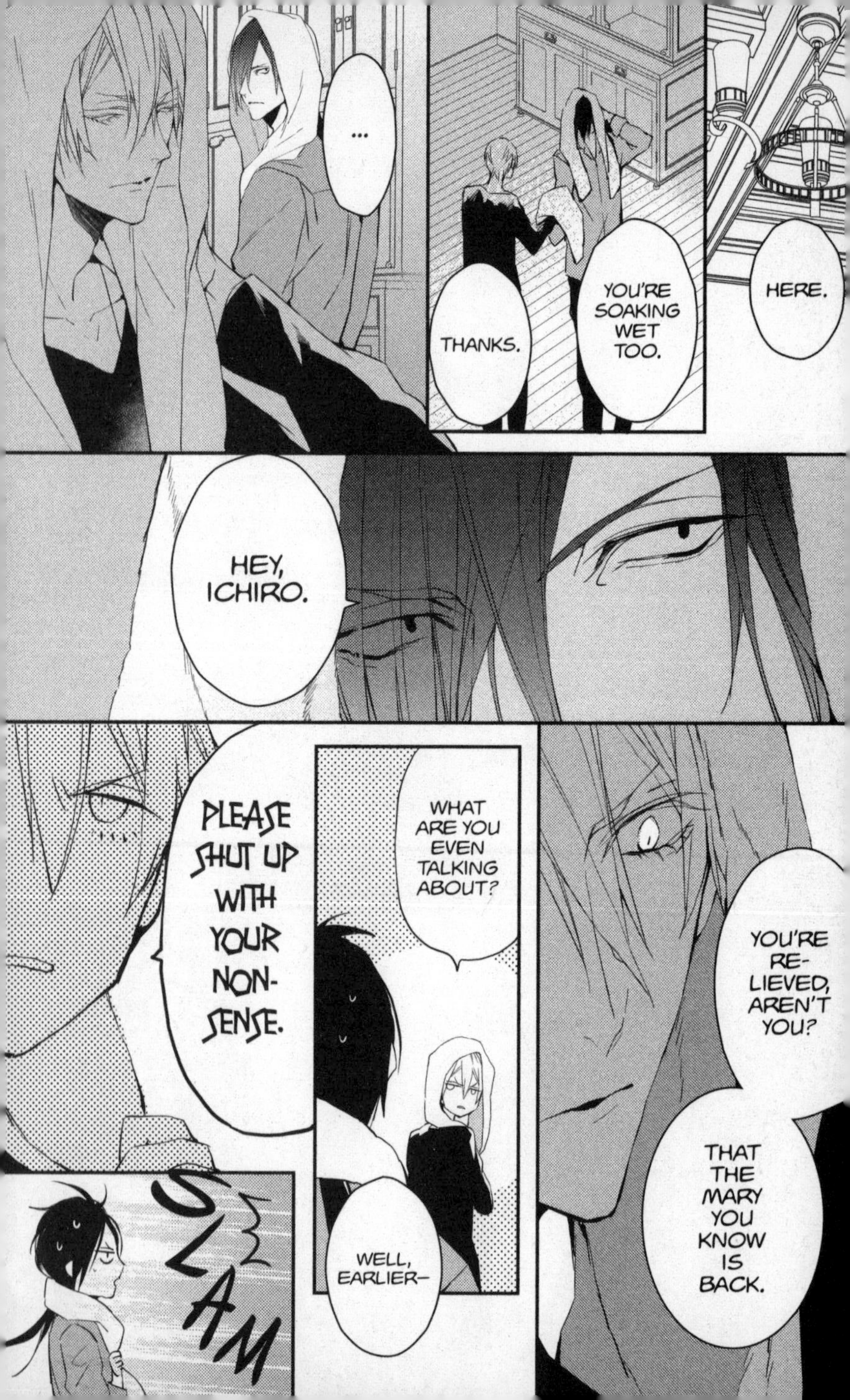
HERE.
YOU'RE SOAKING WET TOO.
THANKS.
...
HEY, ICHIRO.
YOU'RE RE-LIEVED, AREN'T YOU?
THAT THE MARY YOU KNOW IS BACK.
WHAT ARE YOU EVEN TALKING ABOUT?
WELL, EARLIER—
PLEASE SHUT UP WITH YOUR NON-SENSE.
SLAM

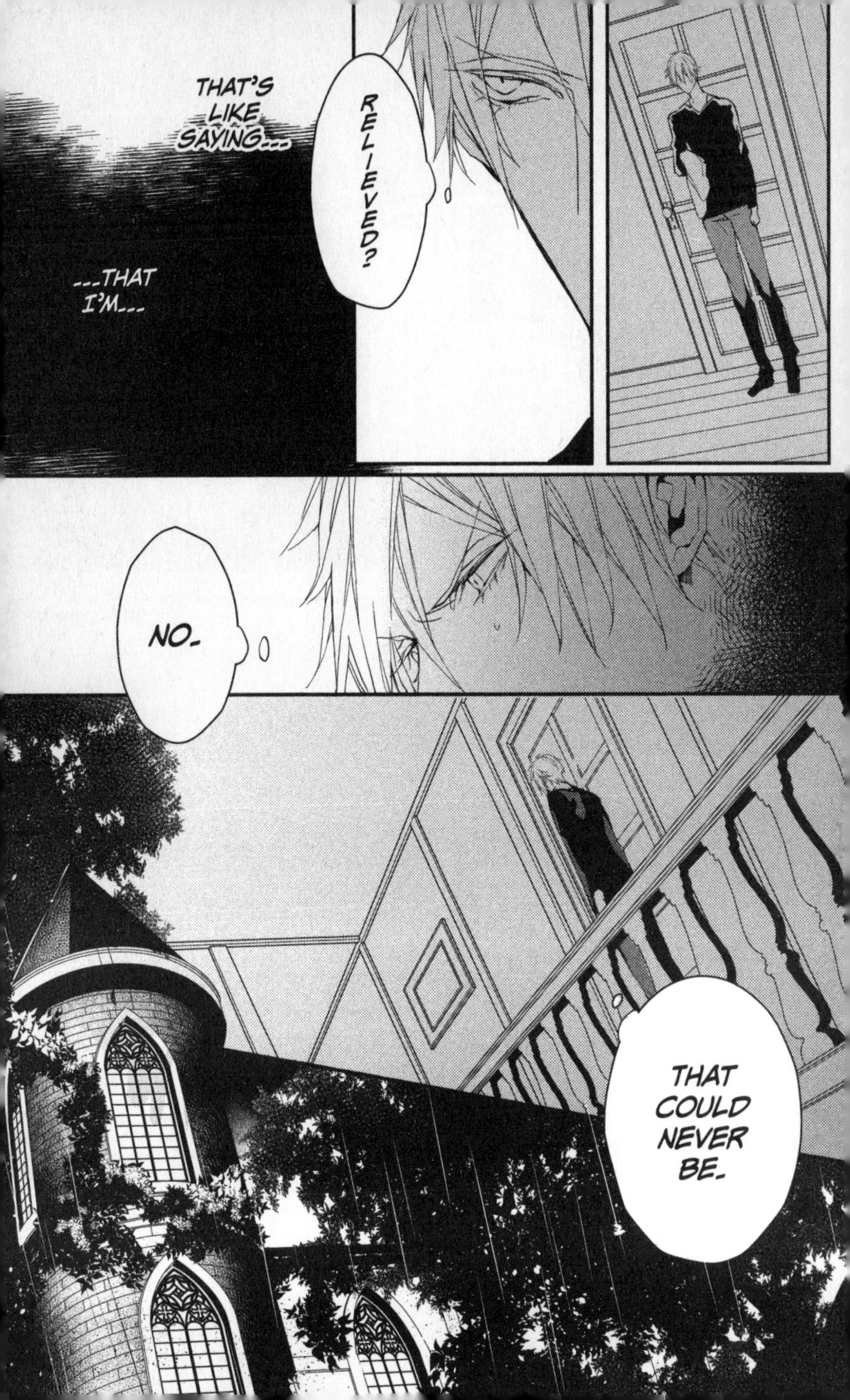
RELIEVED?
THAT'S LIKE SAYING...
...THAT I'M...
NO.
THAT COULD NEVER BE.

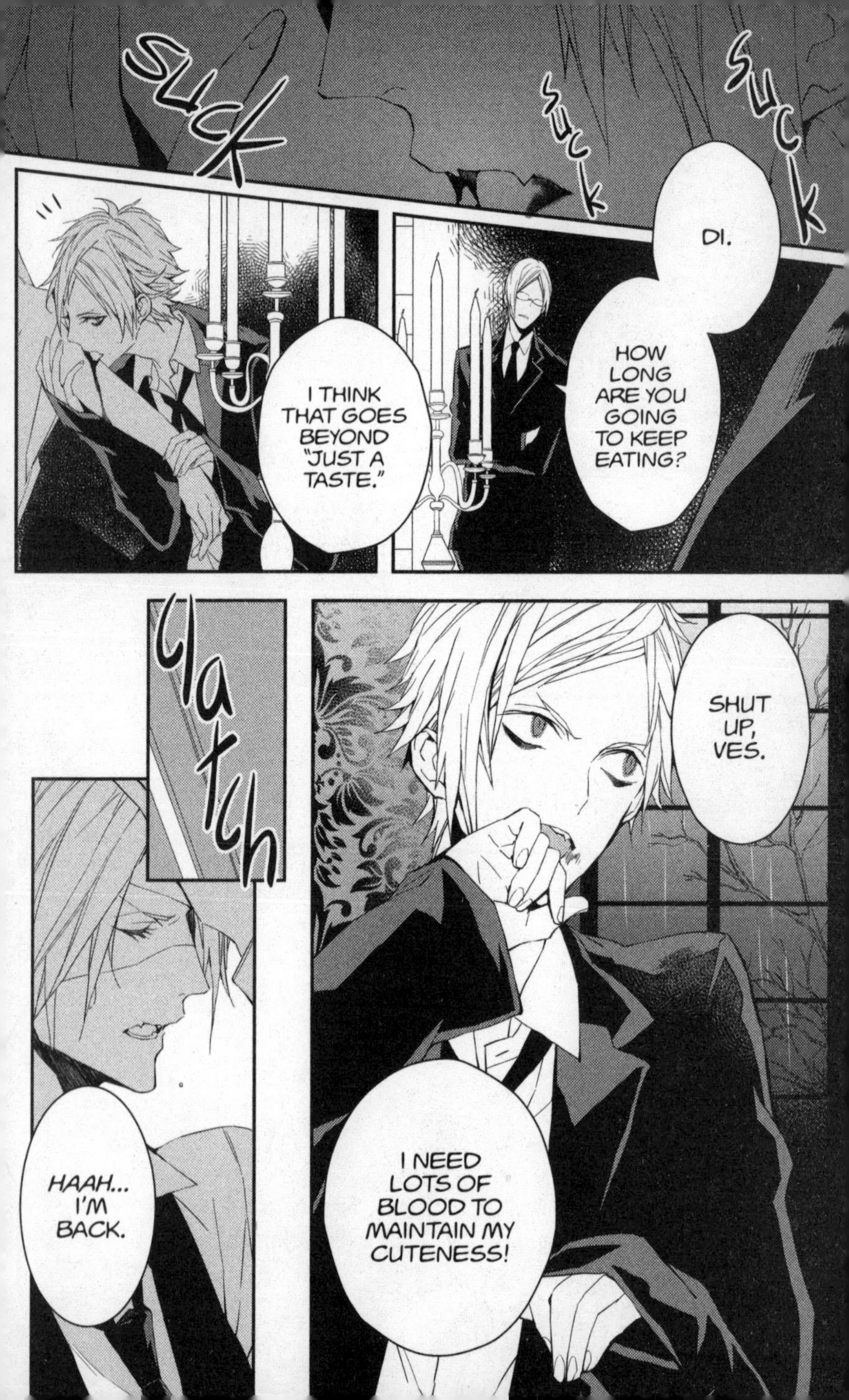
SUCK
suck
SUCK
DI.
HOW LONG ARE YOU GOING TO KEEP EATING?
I THINK THAT GOES BEYOND "JUST A TASTE."
SHUT UP, VES.
I NEED LOTS OF BLOOD TO MAINTAIN MY CUTENESS!
Glatch
HAAH... I'M BACK.

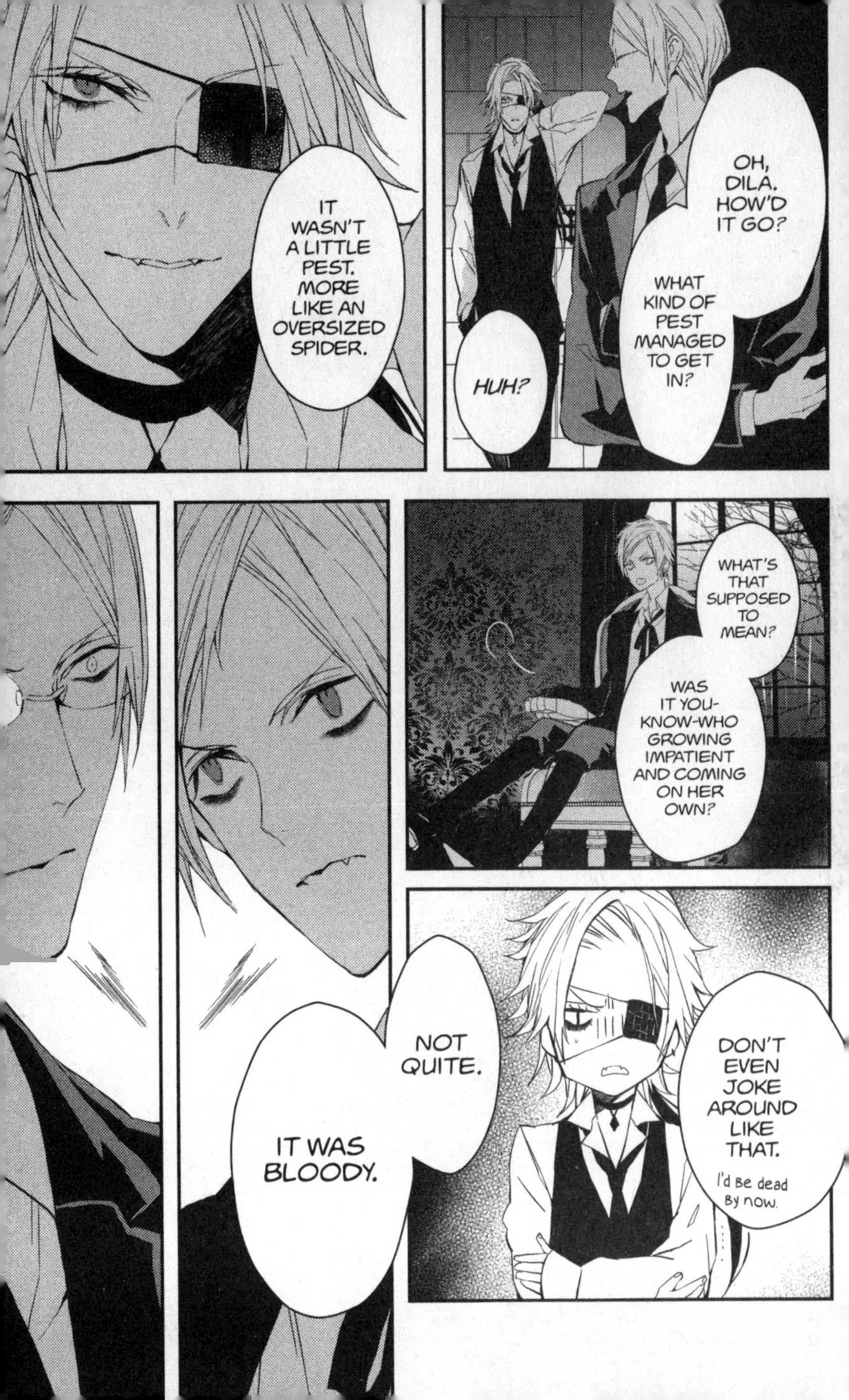
OH, DILA. HOW'D IT GO?
WHAT KIND OF PEST MANAGED TO GET IN?
HUH?
IT WASN'T A LITTLE PEST. MORE LIKE AN OVERSIZED SPIDER.
WHAT'S THAT SUPPOSED TO MEAN?
WAS IT YOU-KNOW-WHO GROWING IMPATIENT AND COMING ON HER OWN?
DON'T EVEN JOKE AROUND LIKE THAT.
I'd Be dead By now.
NOT QUITE.
IT WAS BLOODY.

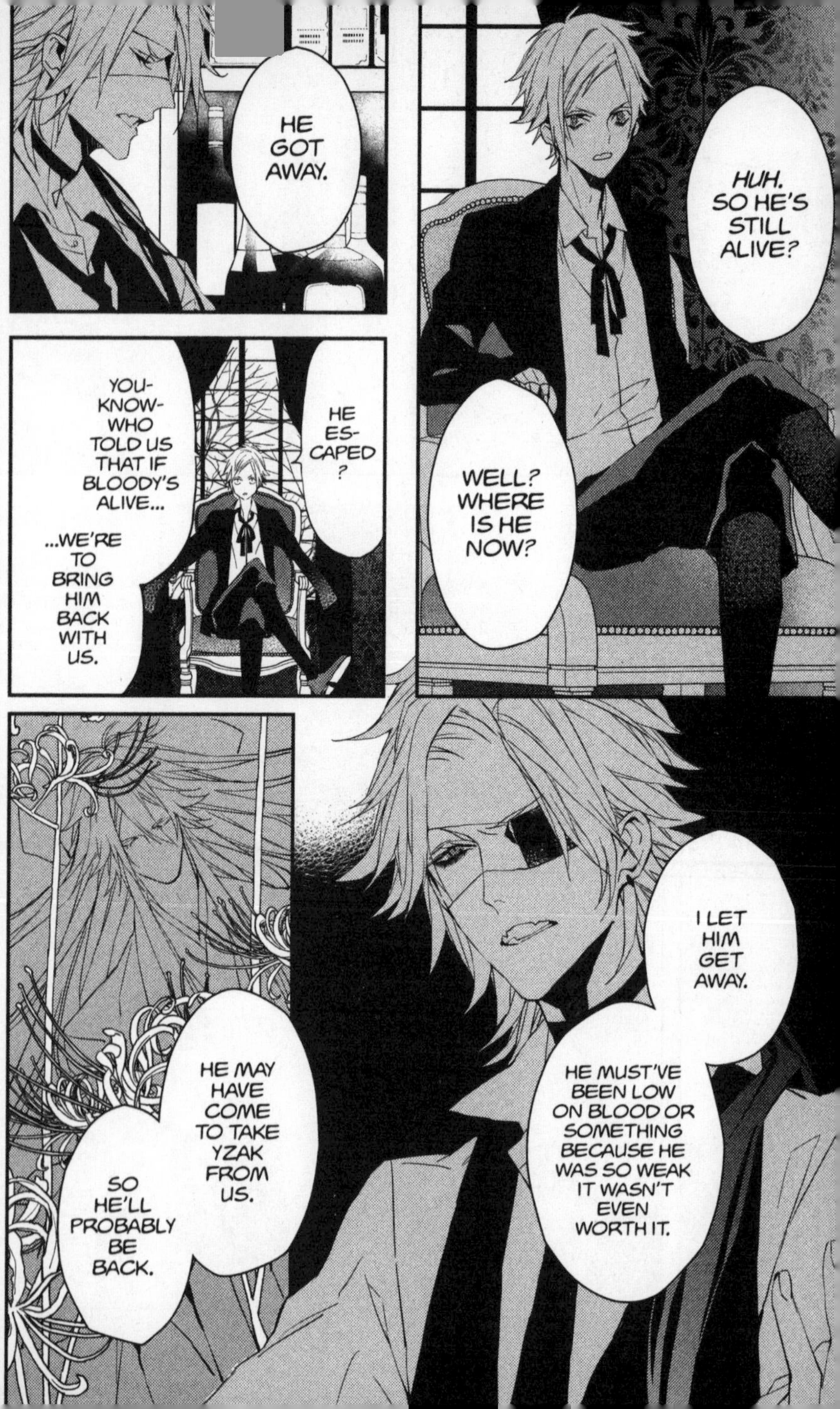
HUH. SO HE'S STILL ALIVE?
WELL? WHERE IS HE NOW?
HE GOT AWAY.
HE ESCAPED?
YOU-KNOW-WHO TOLD US THAT IF BLOODY'S ALIVE...
...WE'RE TO BRING HIM BACK WITH US.
I LET HIM GET AWAY.
HE MUST'VE BEEN LOW ON BLOOD OR SOMETHING BECAUSE HE WAS SO WEAK IT WASN'T EVEN WORTH IT.
HE MAY HAVE COME TO TAKE YZAK FROM US.
SO HE'LL PROBABLY BE BACK.

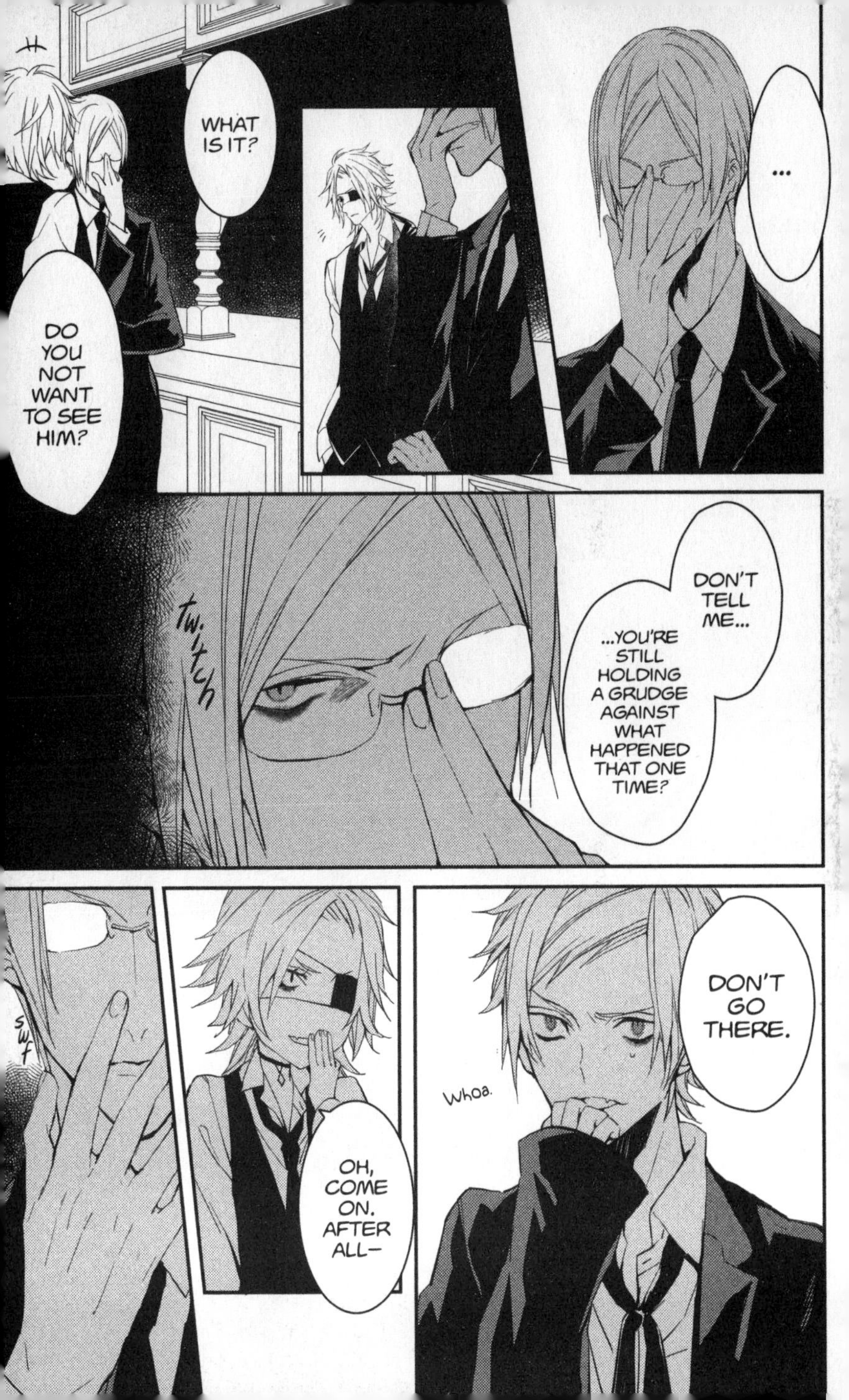
...
WHAT IS IT?
DO YOU NOT WANT TO SEE HIM?
DON'T TELL ME...
...YOU'RE STILL HOLDING A GRUDGE AGAINST WHAT HAPPENED THAT ONE TIME?
twitch
DON'T GO THERE.
Whoa.
OH, COME ON. AFTER ALL—
swf

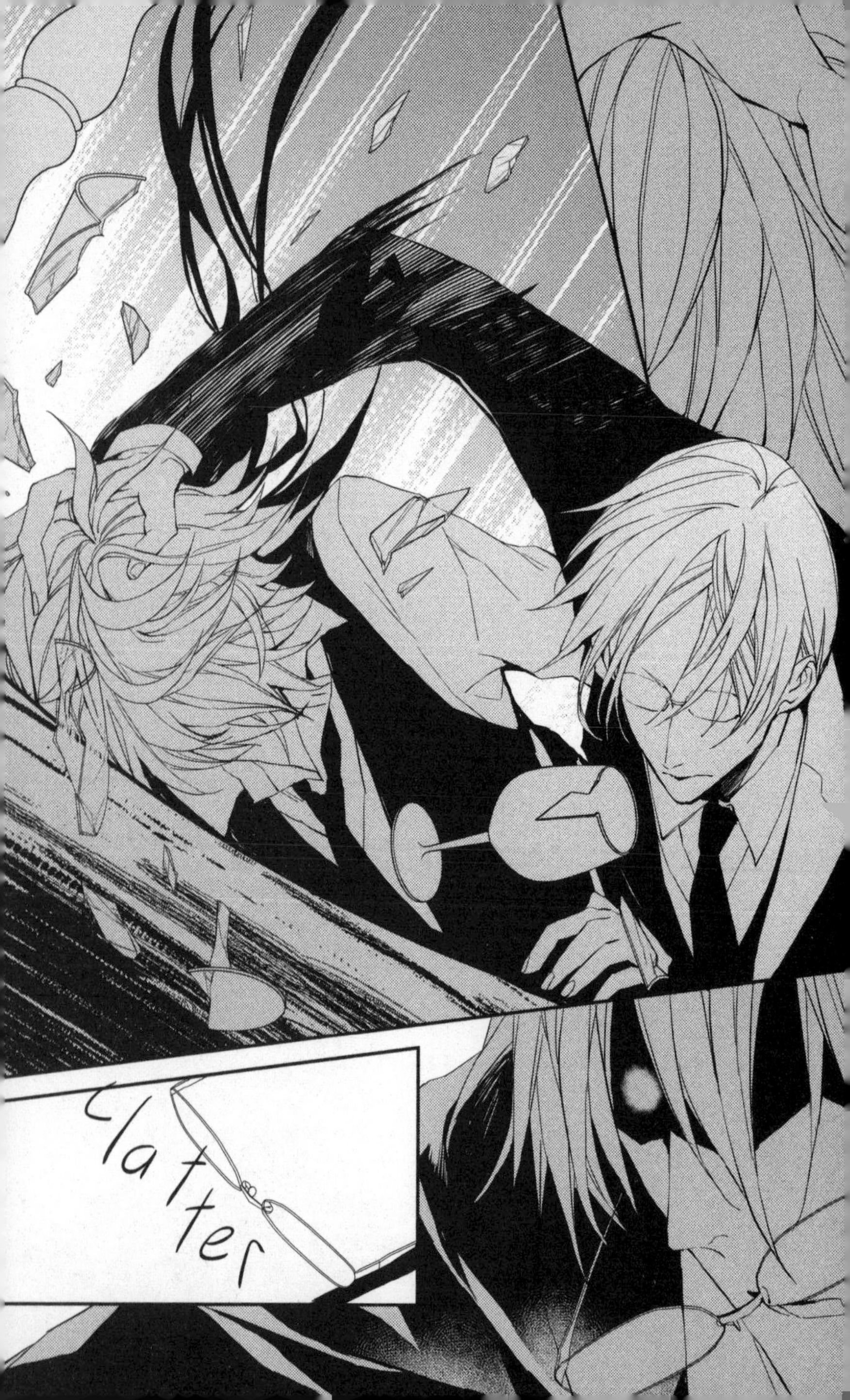
clatter

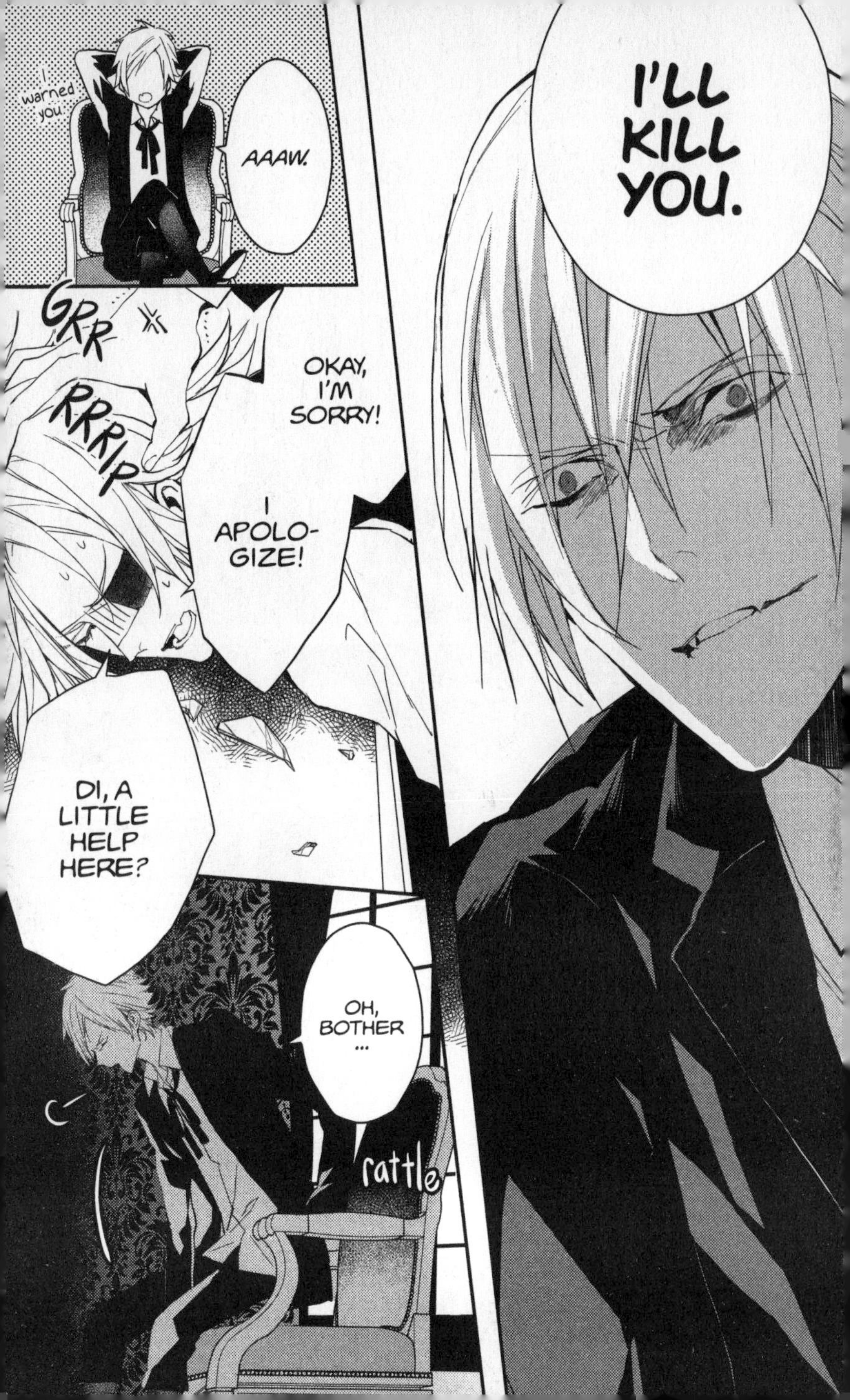
I'LL KILL YOU.
AAAW.
I warned you.
OKAY, I'M SORRY!
I APOLOGIZE!
GRRR
RRRIP
DI, A LITTLE HELP HERE?
OH, BOTHER ...
rattle

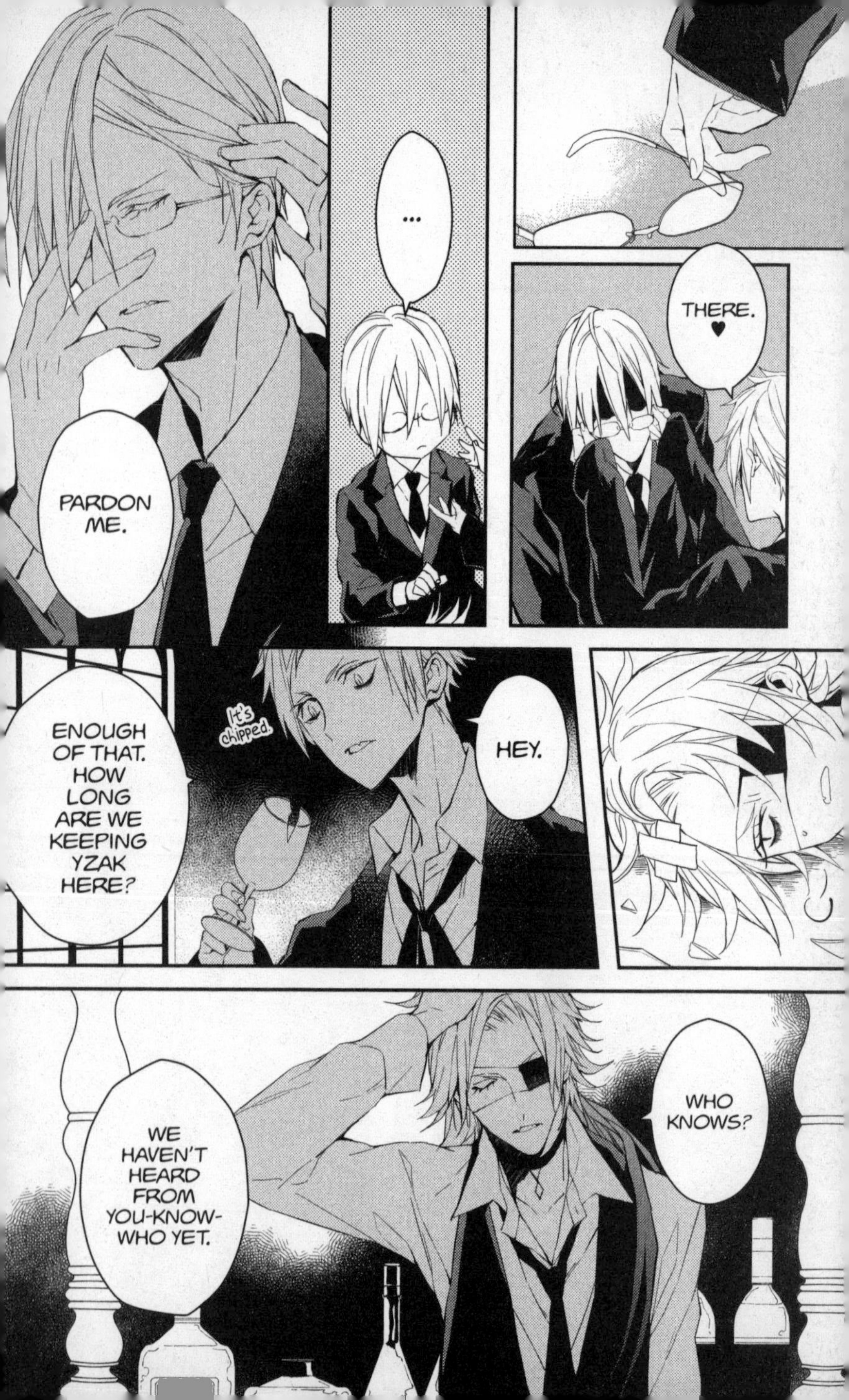
THERE. ♥
...
PARDON ME.
HEY.
It's chipped.
ENOUGH OF THAT. HOW LONG ARE WE KEEPING YZAK HERE?
WHO KNOWS?
WE HAVEN'T HEARD FROM YOU-KNOW-WHO YET.

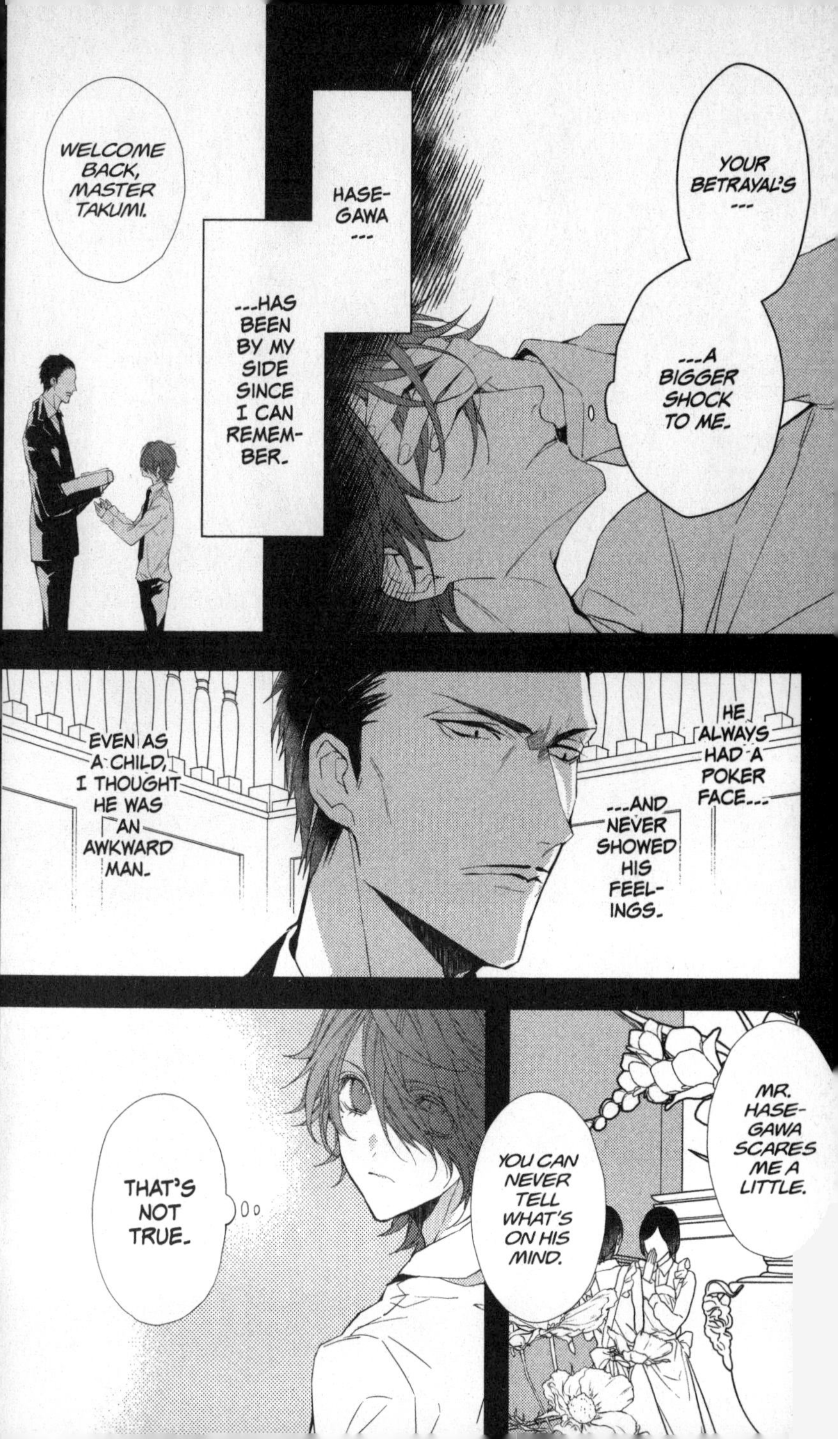
YOUR BETRAYAL'S...
...A BIGGER SHOCK TO ME.
HASE-GAWA...
...HAS BEEN BY MY SIDE SINCE I CAN REMEM-BER.
WELCOME BACK, MASTER TAKUMI.
HE ALWAYS HAD A POKER FACE...
...AND NEVER SHOWED HIS FEEL-INGS.
EVEN AS A CHILD, I THOUGHT HE WAS AN AWKWARD MAN.
MR. HASE-GAWA SCARES ME A LITTLE.
YOU CAN NEVER TELL WHAT'S ON HIS MIND.
THAT'S NOT TRUE.

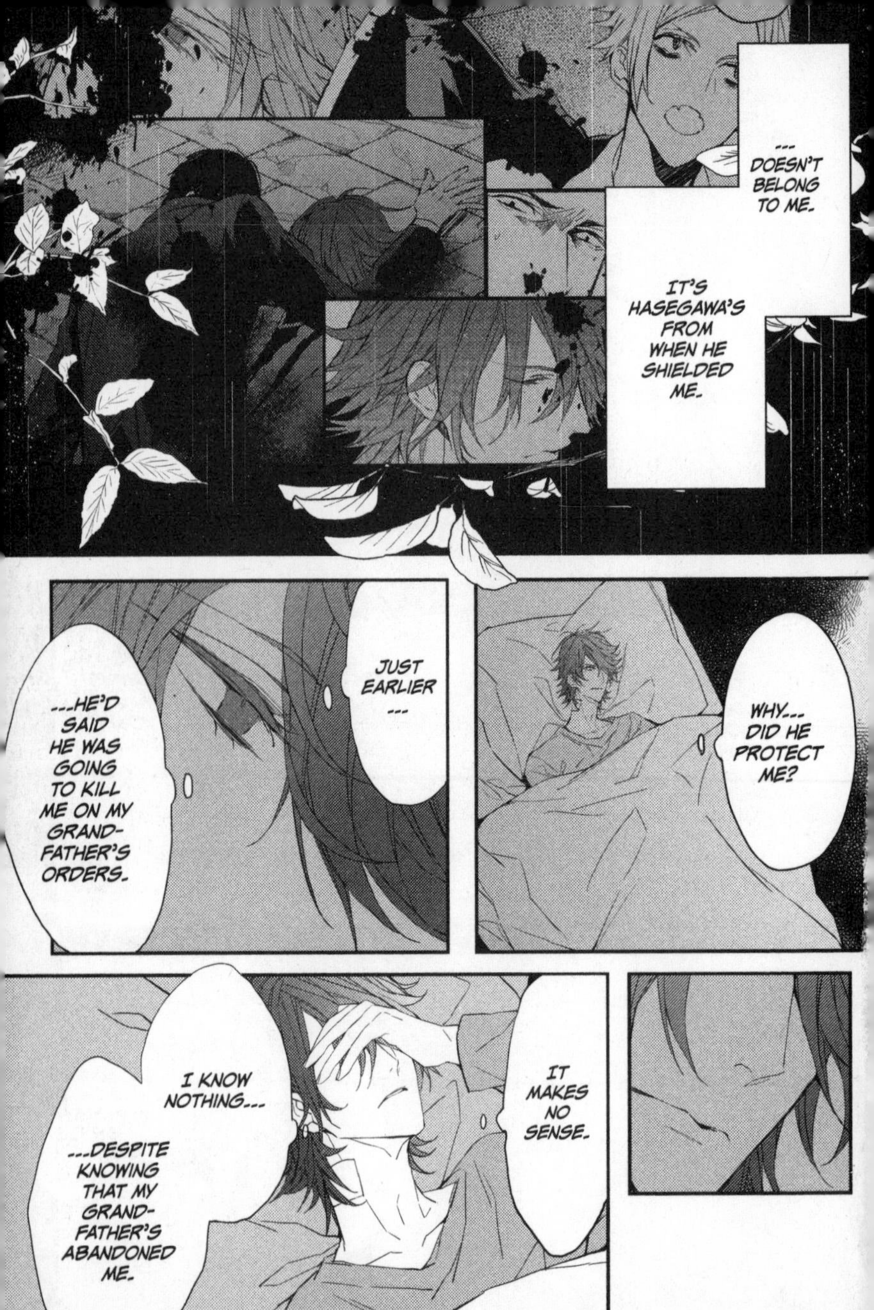
...DOESN'T BELONG TO ME.
IT'S HASEGAWA'S FROM WHEN HE SHIELDED ME.
WHY... DID HE PROTECT ME?
JUST EARLIER...
...HE'D SAID HE WAS GOING TO KILL ME ON MY GRANDFATHER'S ORDERS.
IT MAKES NO SENSE.
I KNOW NOTHING...
...DESPITE KNOWING THAT MY GRANDFATHER'S ABANDONED ME.

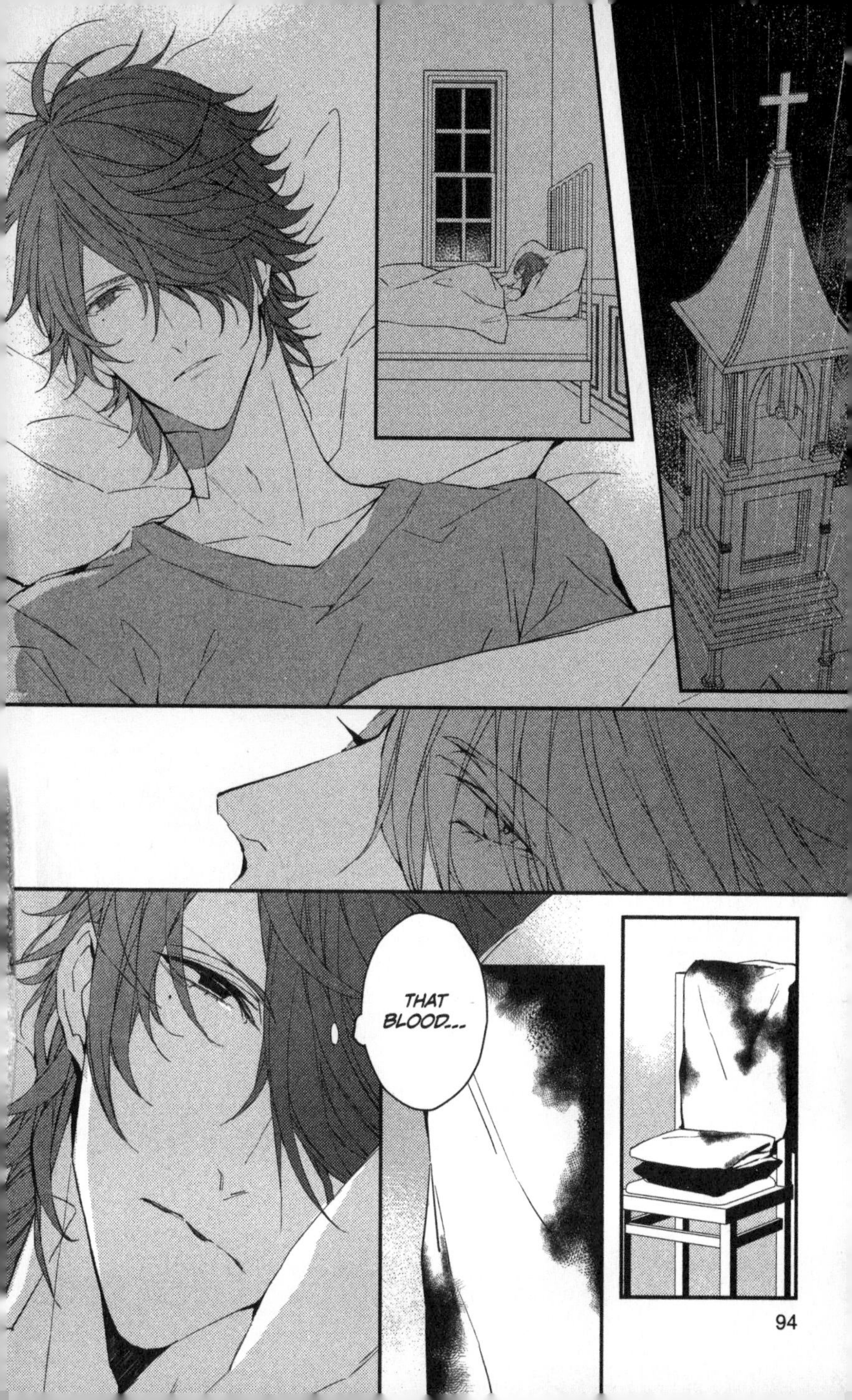
THAT BLOOD...

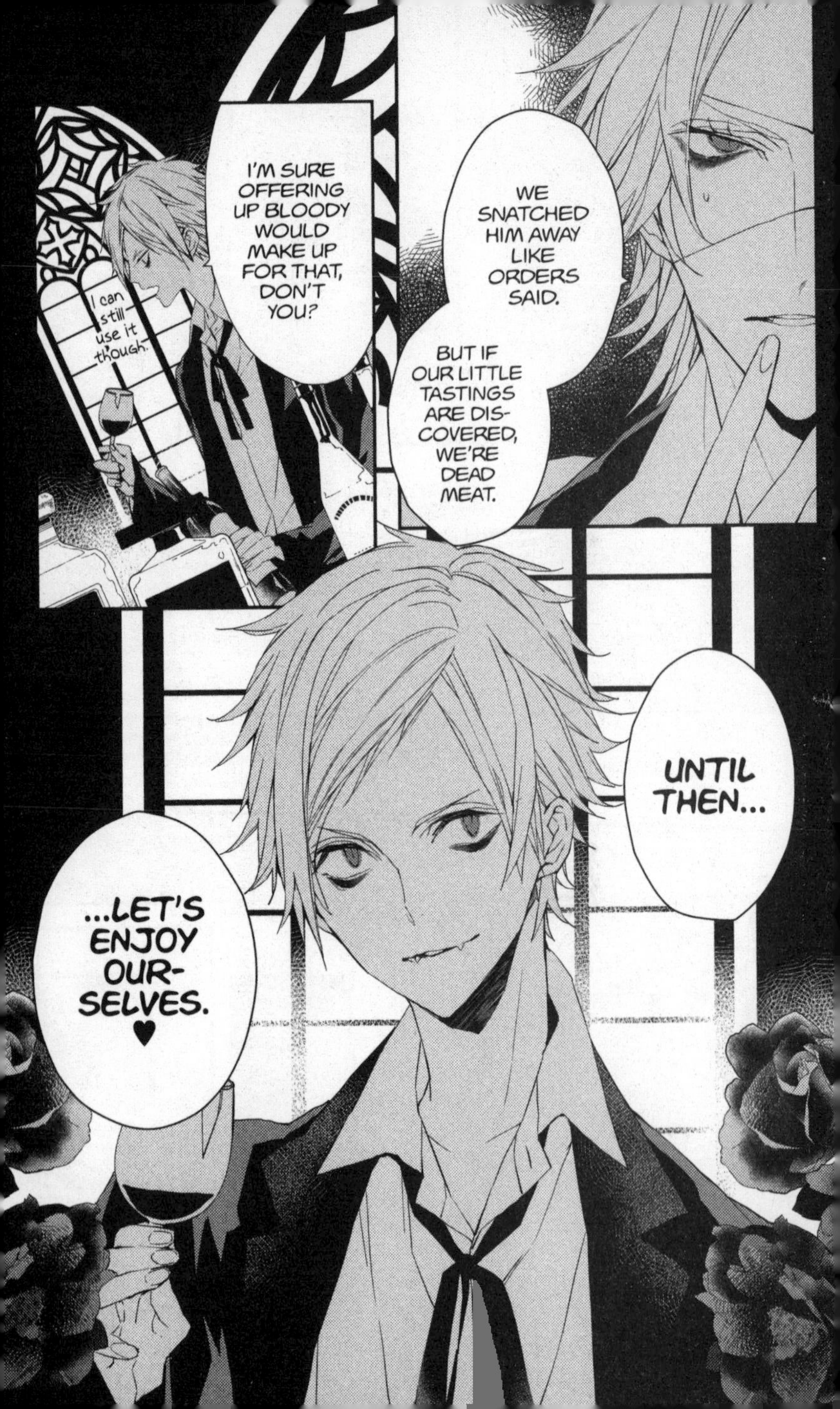
WE SNATCHED HIM AWAY LIKE ORDERS SAID.
BUT IF OUR LITTLE TASTINGS ARE DIS-COVERED, WE'RE DEAD MEAT.
I'M SURE OFFERING UP BLOODY WOULD MAKE UP FOR THAT, DON'T YOU?
I can still use it though.
UNTIL THEN...
...LET'S ENJOY OUR-SELVES. ♥

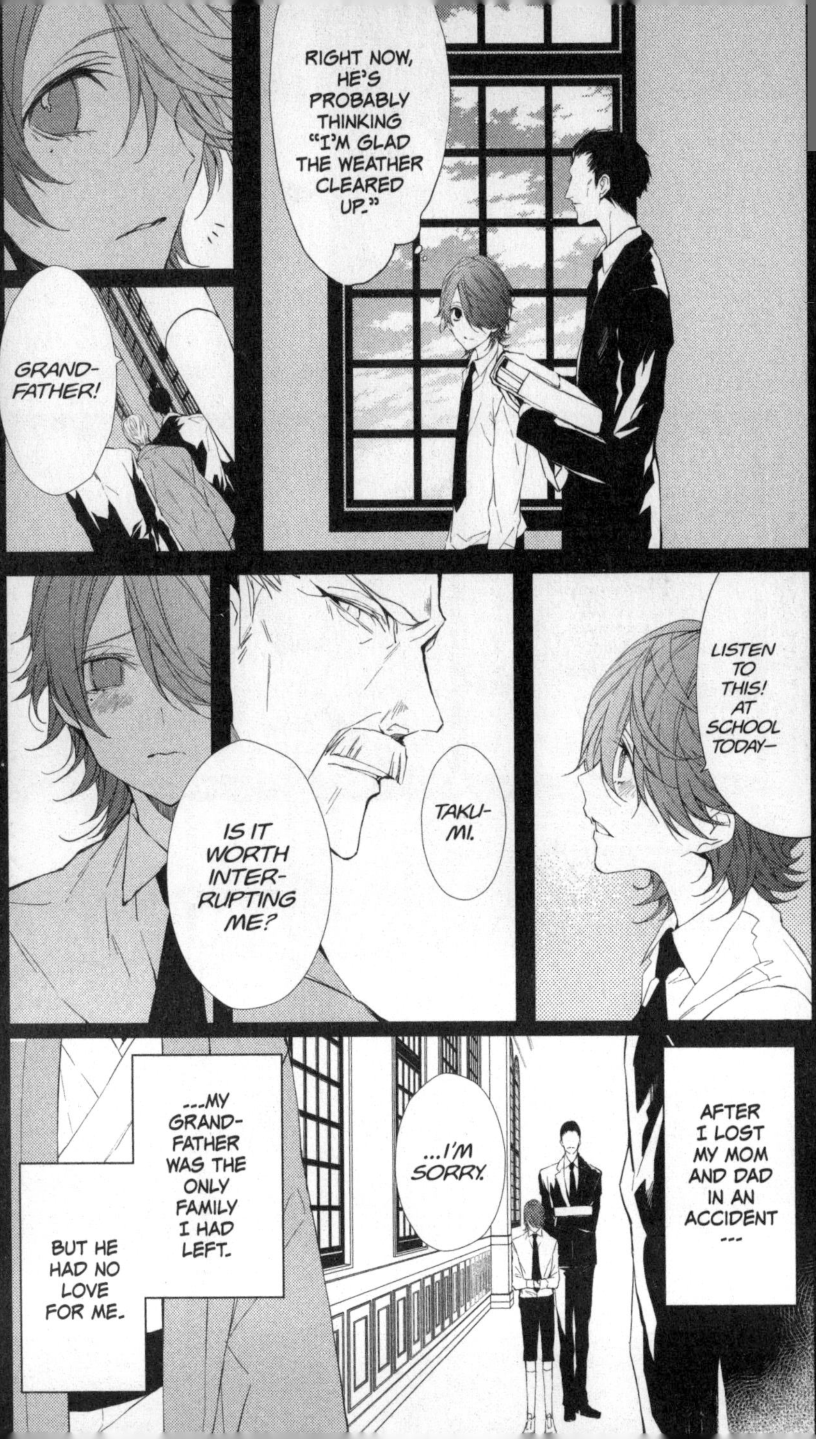
RIGHT NOW, HE'S PROBABLY THINKING "I'M GLAD THE WEATHER CLEARED UP."
GRAND-FATHER!
LISTEN TO THIS! AT SCHOOL TODAY—
TAKU-MI.
IS IT WORTH INTER-RUPTING ME?
AFTER I LOST MY MOM AND DAD IN AN ACCIDENT...
...I'M SORRY.
...MY GRAND-FATHER WAS THE ONLY FAMILY I HAD LEFT.
BUT HE HAD NO LOVE FOR ME.

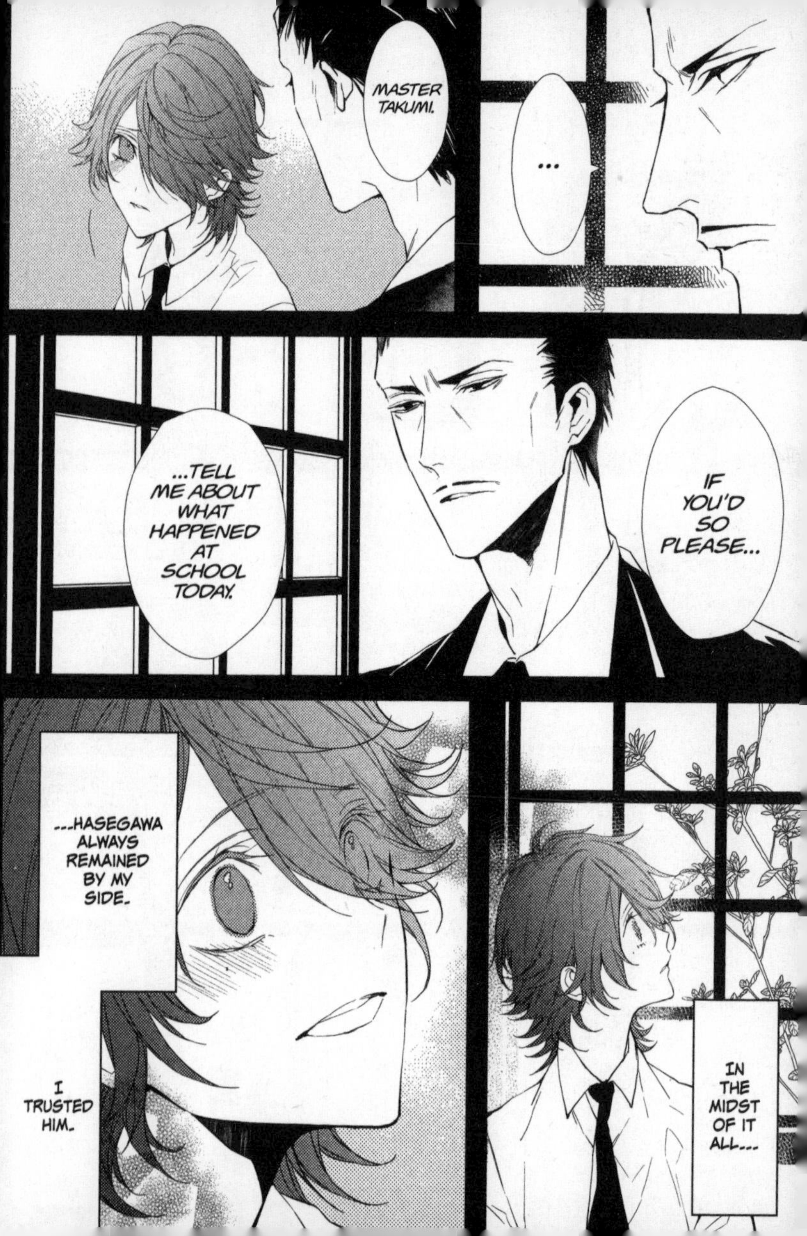
...
MASTER TAKUMI.
IF YOU'D SO PLEASE...
...TELL ME ABOUT WHAT HAPPENED AT SCHOOL TODAY.
IN THE MIDST OF IT ALL...
...HASEGAWA ALWAYS REMAINED BY MY SIDE.
I TRUSTED HIM.

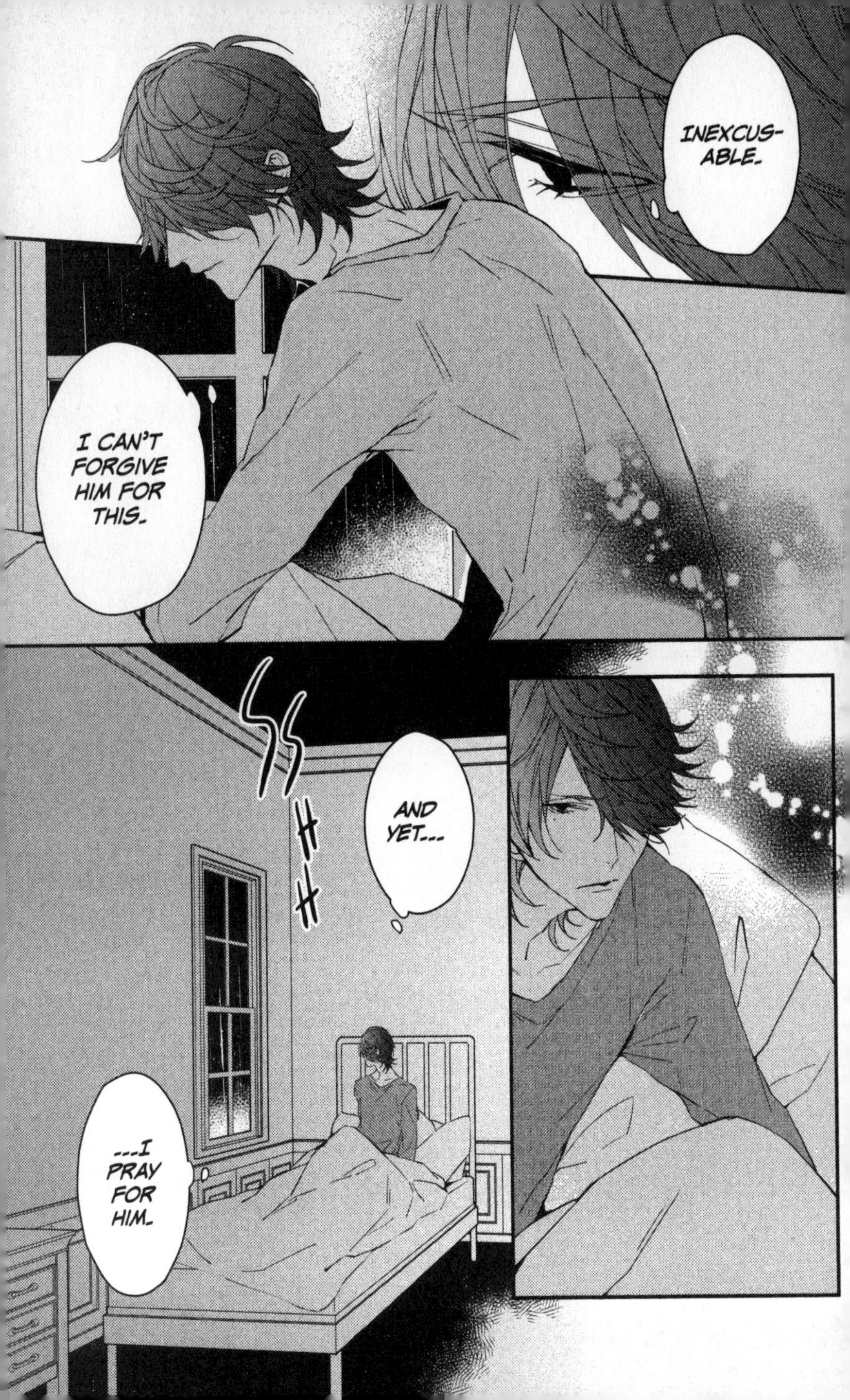
INEXCUS-
ABLE.
I CAN'T FORGIVE HIM FOR THIS.
SSHHH
AND YET...
...I PRAY FOR HIM.

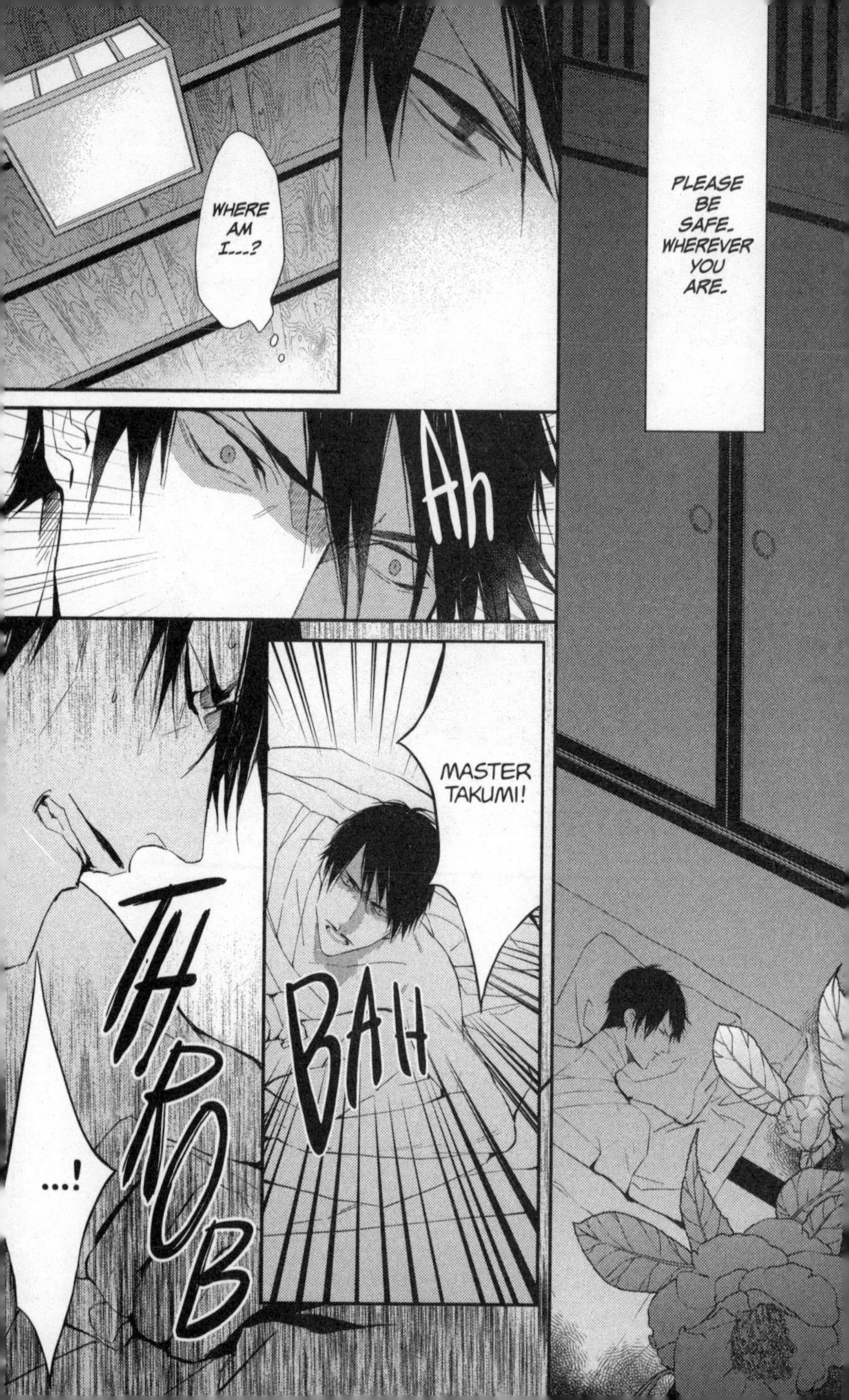
PLEASE BE SAFE. WHEREVER YOU ARE.
WHERE AM I...?
Ah
MASTER TAKUMI!
BAH
THROB
...!

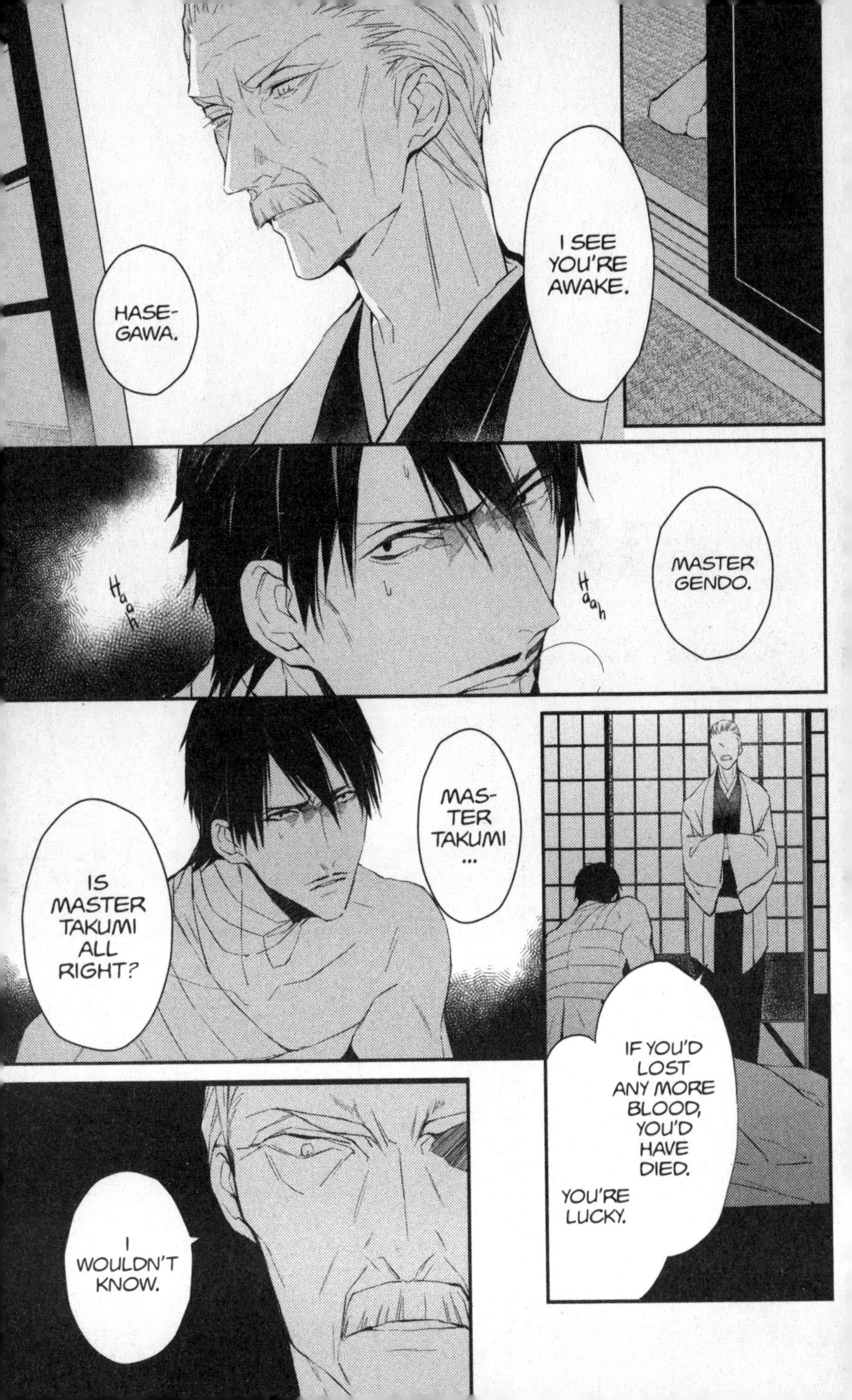
I SEE YOU'RE AWAKE.
HASE-GAWA.
Haah
MASTER GENDO.
Haah
IF YOU'D LOST ANY MORE BLOOD, YOU'D HAVE DIED.
YOU'RE LUCKY.
MAS-TER TAKUMI ...
IS MASTER TAKUMI ALL RIGHT?
I WOULDN'T KNOW.

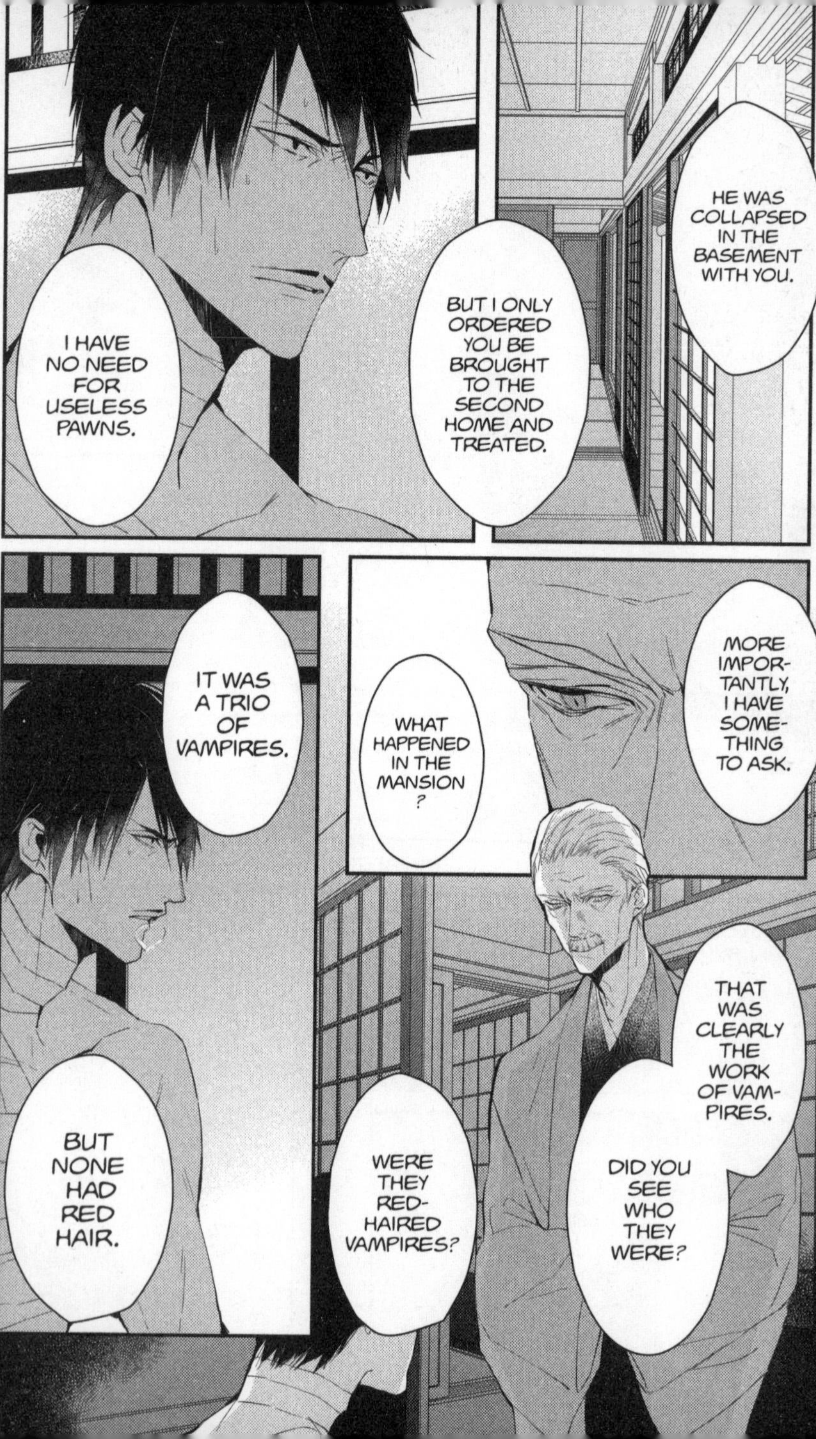
HE WAS COLLAPSED IN THE BASEMENT WITH YOU.
BUT I ONLY ORDERED YOU BE BROUGHT TO THE SECOND HOME AND TREATED.
I HAVE NO NEED FOR USELESS PAWNS.
MORE IMPORTANTLY, I HAVE SOMETHING TO ASK.
WHAT HAPPENED IN THE MANSION?
THAT WAS CLEARLY THE WORK OF VAMPIRES.
DID YOU SEE WHO THEY WERE?
WERE THEY RED-HAIRED VAMPIRES?
IT WAS A TRIO OF VAMPIRES.
BUT NONE HAD RED HAIR.

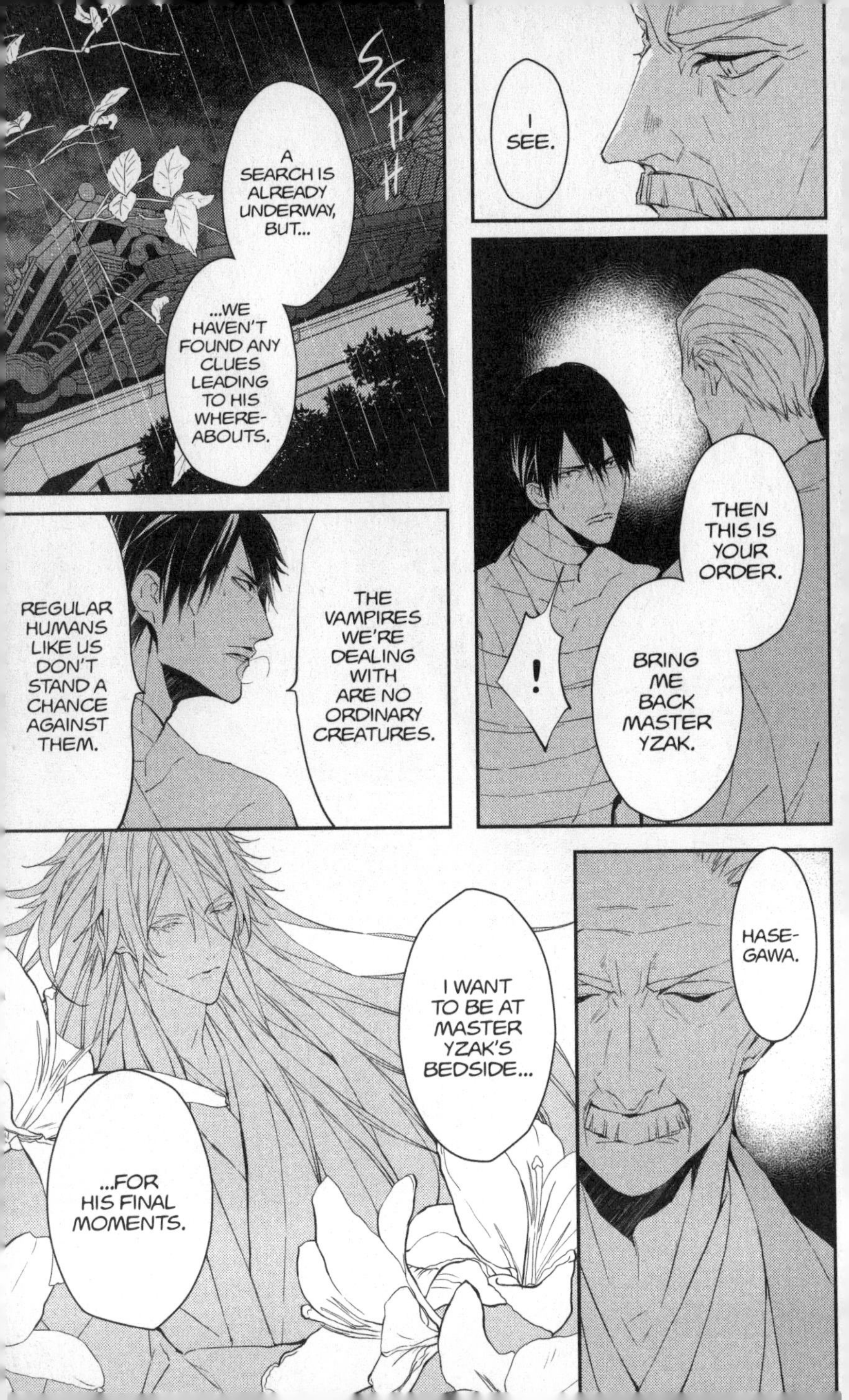
I SEE.
SSHH
A SEARCH IS ALREADY UNDERWAY, BUT...
...WE HAVEN'T FOUND ANY CLUES LEADING TO HIS WHERE-ABOUTS.
THEN THIS IS YOUR ORDER.
BRING ME BACK MASTER YZAK.
!
THE VAMPIRES WE'RE DEALING WITH ARE NO ORDINARY CREATURES.
REGULAR HUMANS LIKE US DON'T STAND A CHANCE AGAINST THEM.
HASE-GAWA.
I WANT TO BE AT MASTER YZAK'S BEDSIDE...
...FOR HIS FINAL MOMENTS.

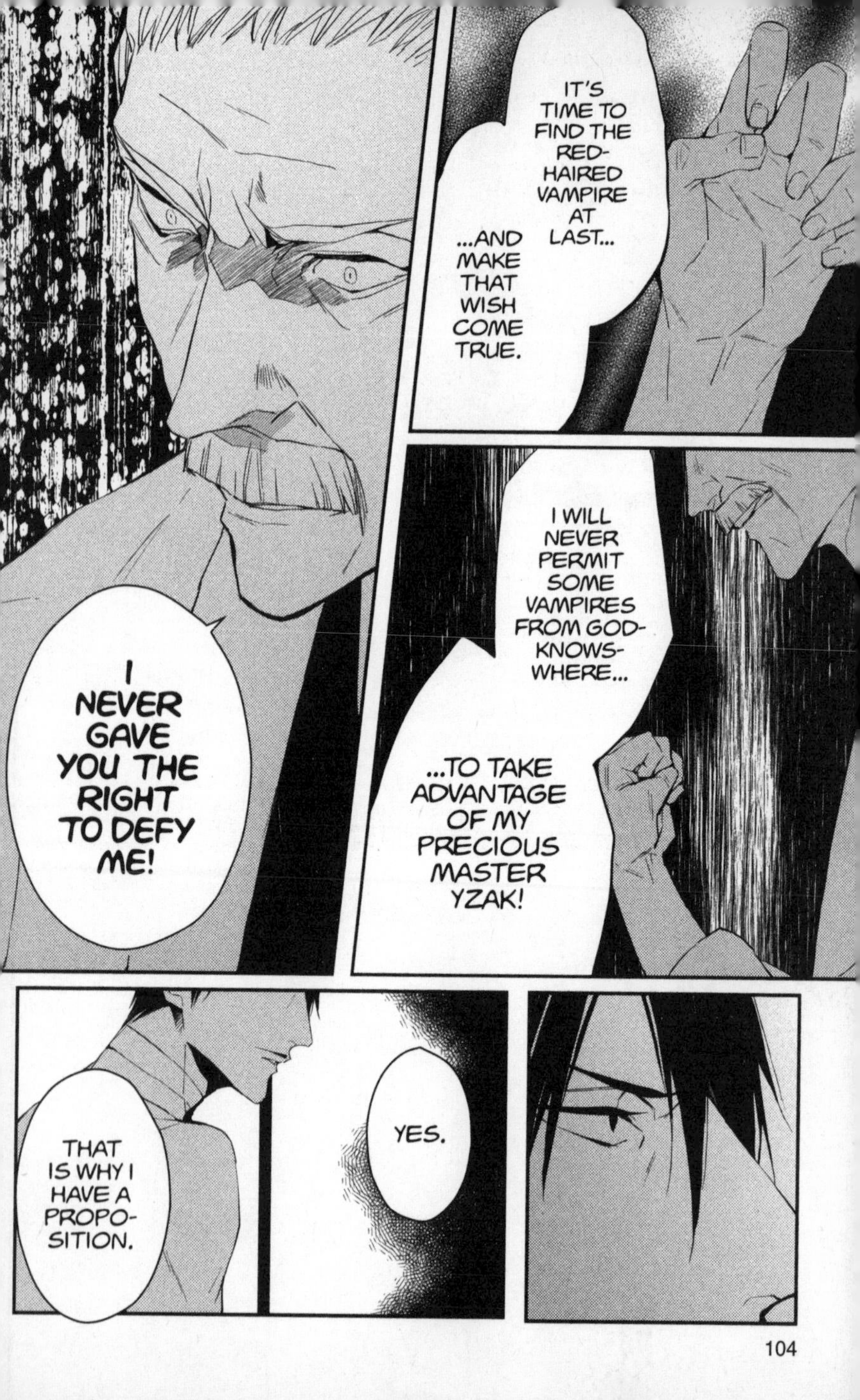
IT'S TIME TO FIND THE RED-HAIRED VAMPIRE AT LAST...
...AND MAKE THAT WISH COME TRUE.
I WILL NEVER PERMIT SOME VAMPIRES FROM GOD-KNOWS-WHERE...
...TO TAKE ADVANTAGE OF MY PRECIOUS MASTER YZAK!
I NEVER GAVE YOU THE RIGHT TO DEFY ME!
YES.
THAT IS WHY I HAVE A PROPOSITION.

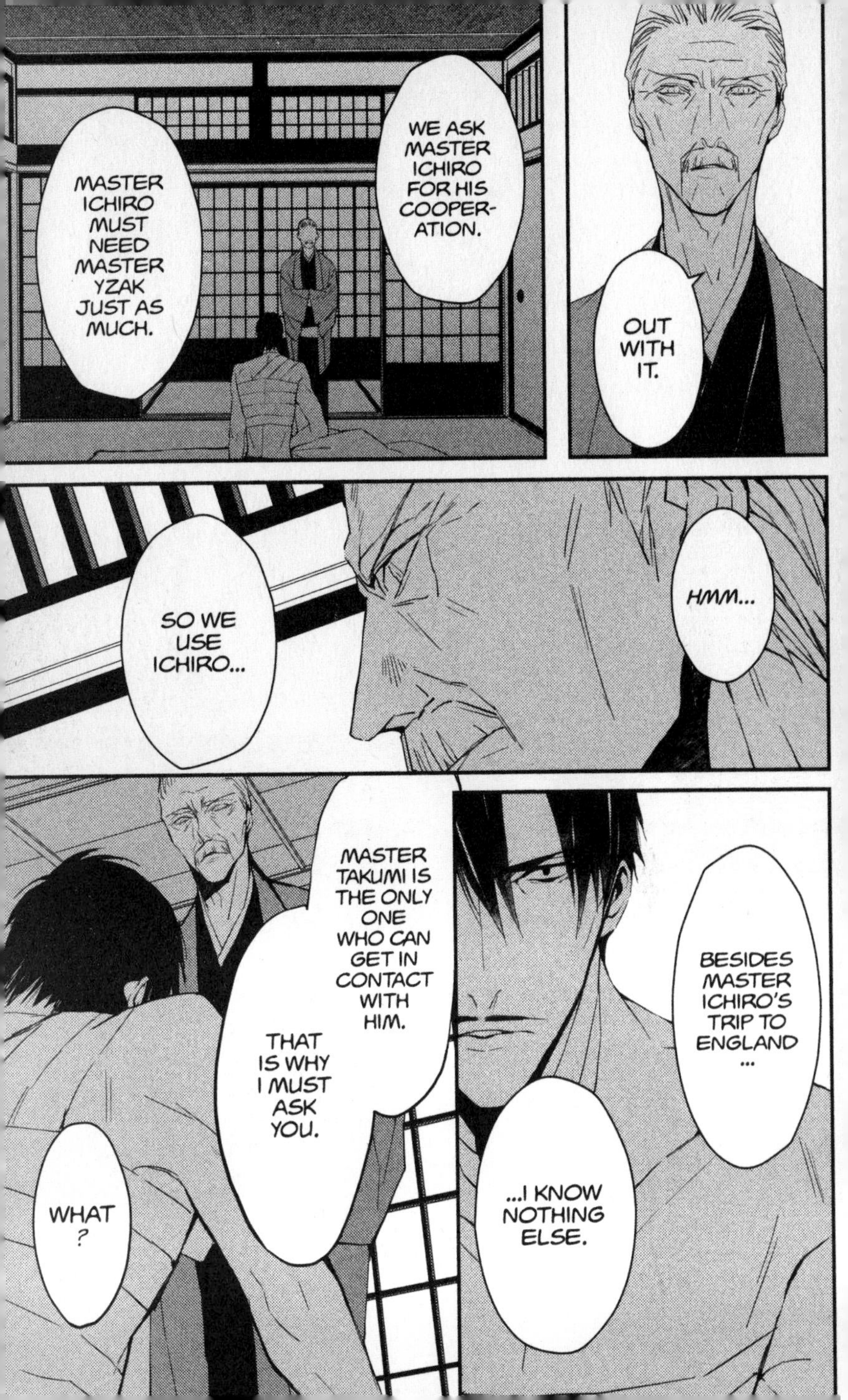
OUT WITH IT.
WE ASK MASTER ICHIRO FOR HIS COOPER-ATION.
MASTER ICHIRO MUST NEED MASTER YZAK JUST AS MUCH.
HMM...
SO WE USE ICHIRO...
BESIDES MASTER ICHIRO'S TRIP TO ENGLAND ...
...I KNOW NOTHING ELSE.
MASTER TAKUMI IS THE ONLY ONE WHO CAN GET IN CONTACT WITH HIM.
THAT IS WHY I MUST ASK YOU.
WHAT?

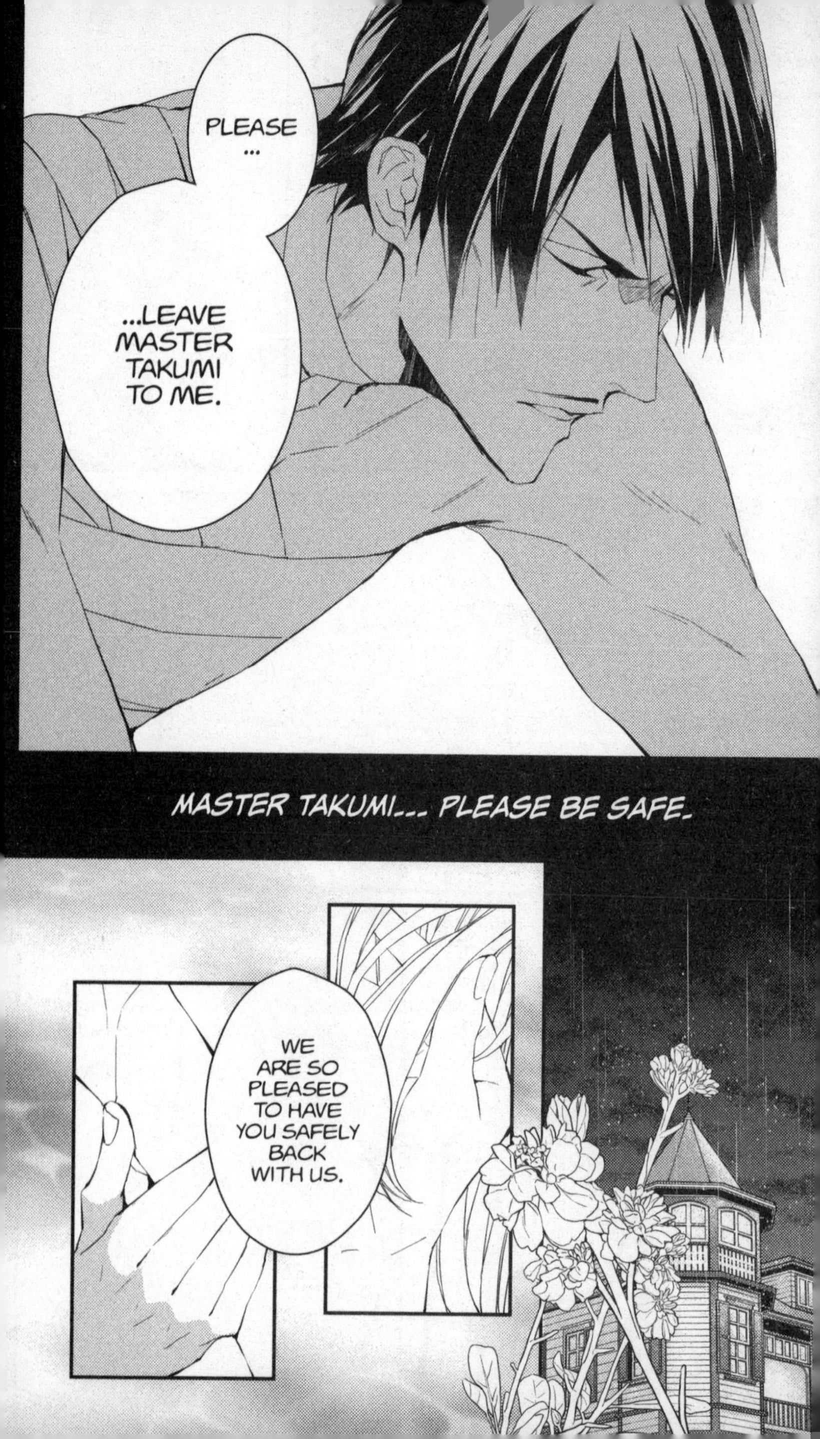
PLEASE ...
...LEAVE MASTER TAKUMI TO ME.
MASTER TAKUMI... PLEASE BE SAFE.
WE ARE SO PLEASED TO HAVE YOU SAFELY BACK WITH US.

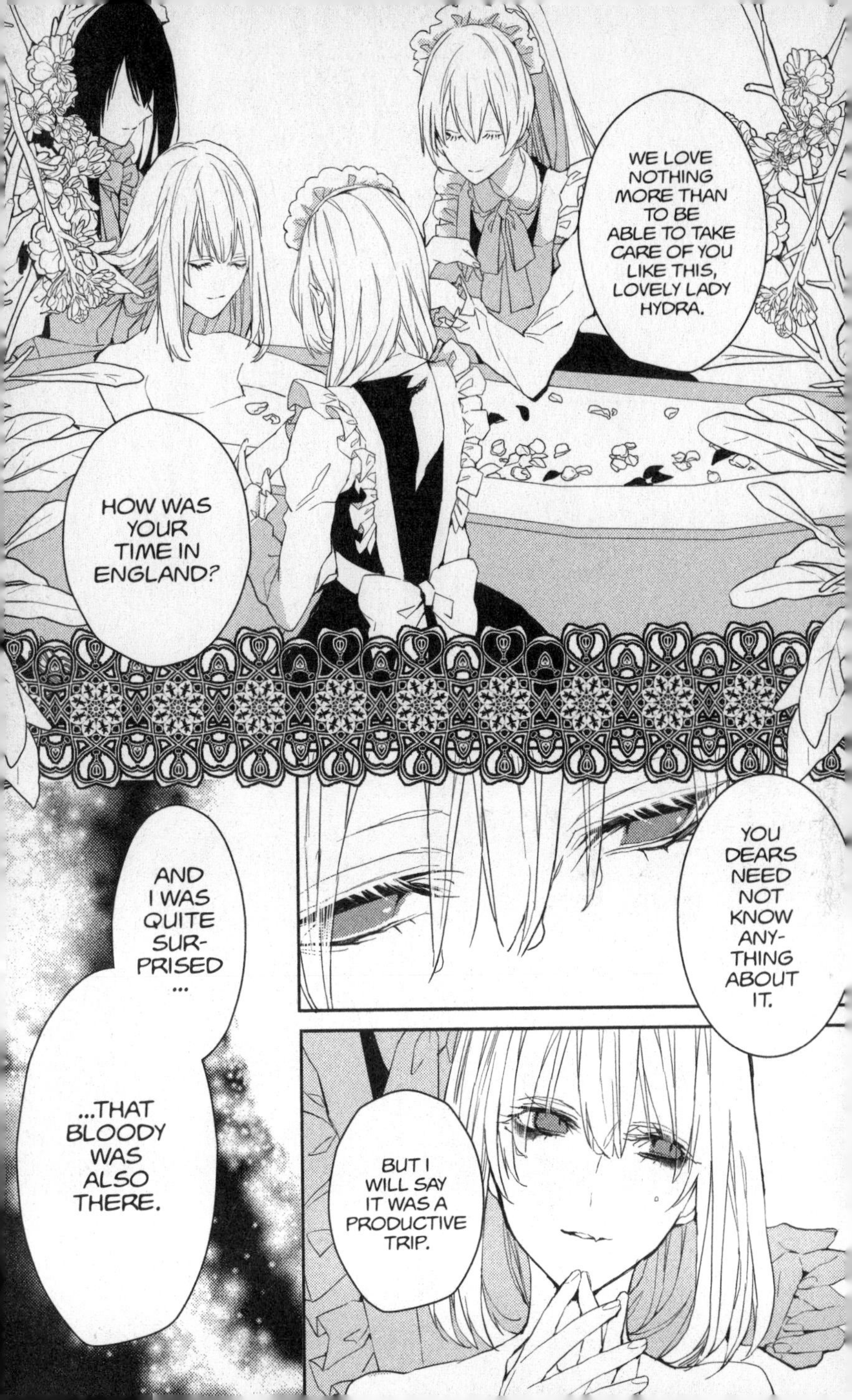
WE LOVE NOTHING MORE THAN TO BE ABLE TO TAKE CARE OF YOU LIKE THIS, LOVELY LADY HYDRA.
HOW WAS YOUR TIME IN ENGLAND?
YOU DEARS NEED NOT KNOW ANY-THING ABOUT IT.
BUT I WILL SAY IT WAS A PRODUCTIVE TRIP.
AND I WAS QUITE SUR-PRISED ...
...THAT BLOODY WAS ALSO THERE.

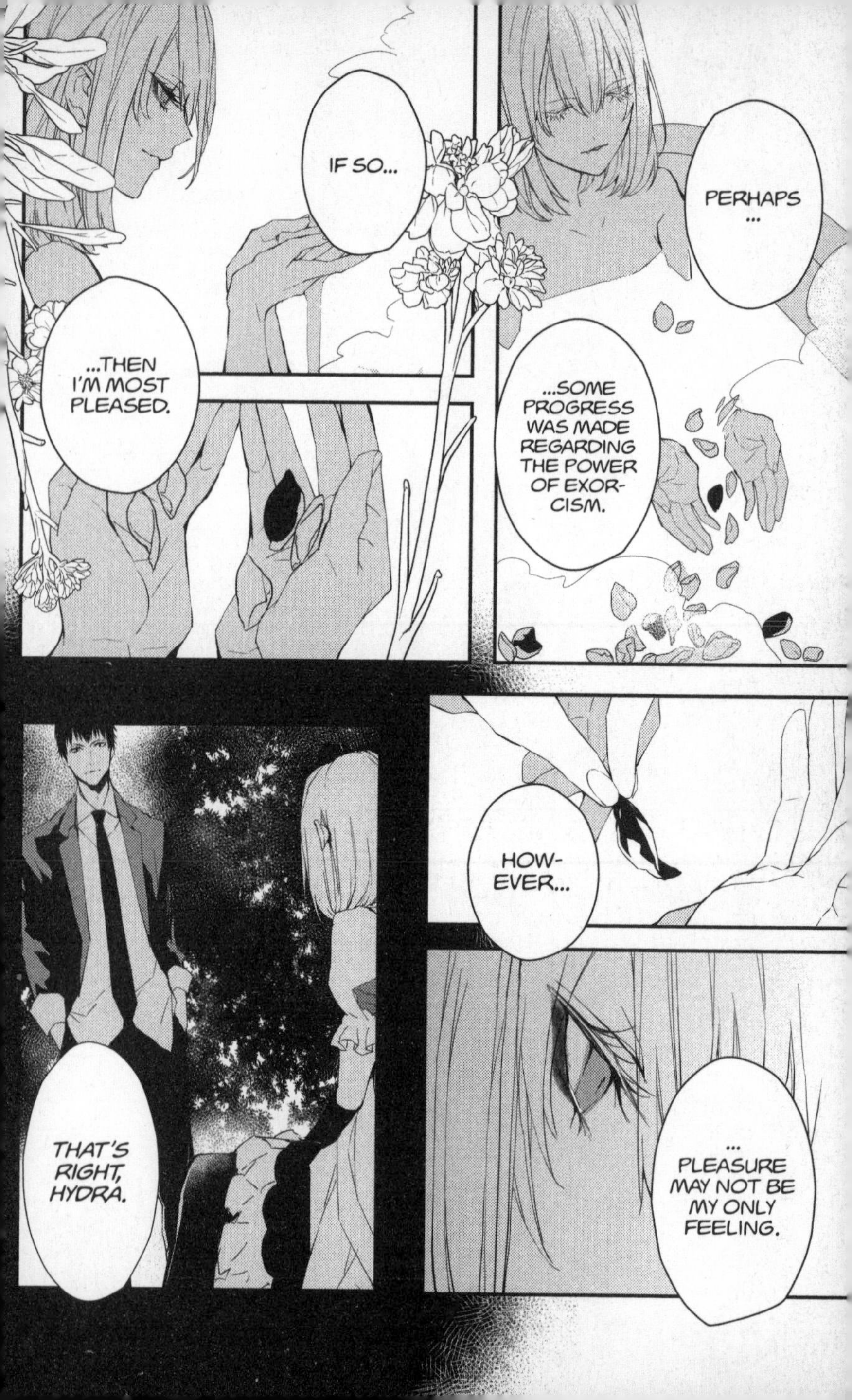
PERHAPS...
...SOME PROGRESS WAS MADE REGARDING THE POWER OF EXOR-CISM.
IF SO...
...THEN I'M MOST PLEASED.
HOW-EVER...
...PLEASURE MAY NOT BE MY ONLY FEELING.
THAT'S RIGHT, HYDRA.

IF I RAN INTO YOU, I THOUGHT I'D GIVE YOU A WARNING.
AND WHAT'S THAT?
IF IT'S SOME SILLY LITTLE THING, I'LL KILL YOU.
IT'S NOT SILLY.
IN FACT, IT MIGHT BE THE WORST NEWS YOU EVER HEAR.
THAT WOMAN ...
...IS ON THE MOVE AGAIN.

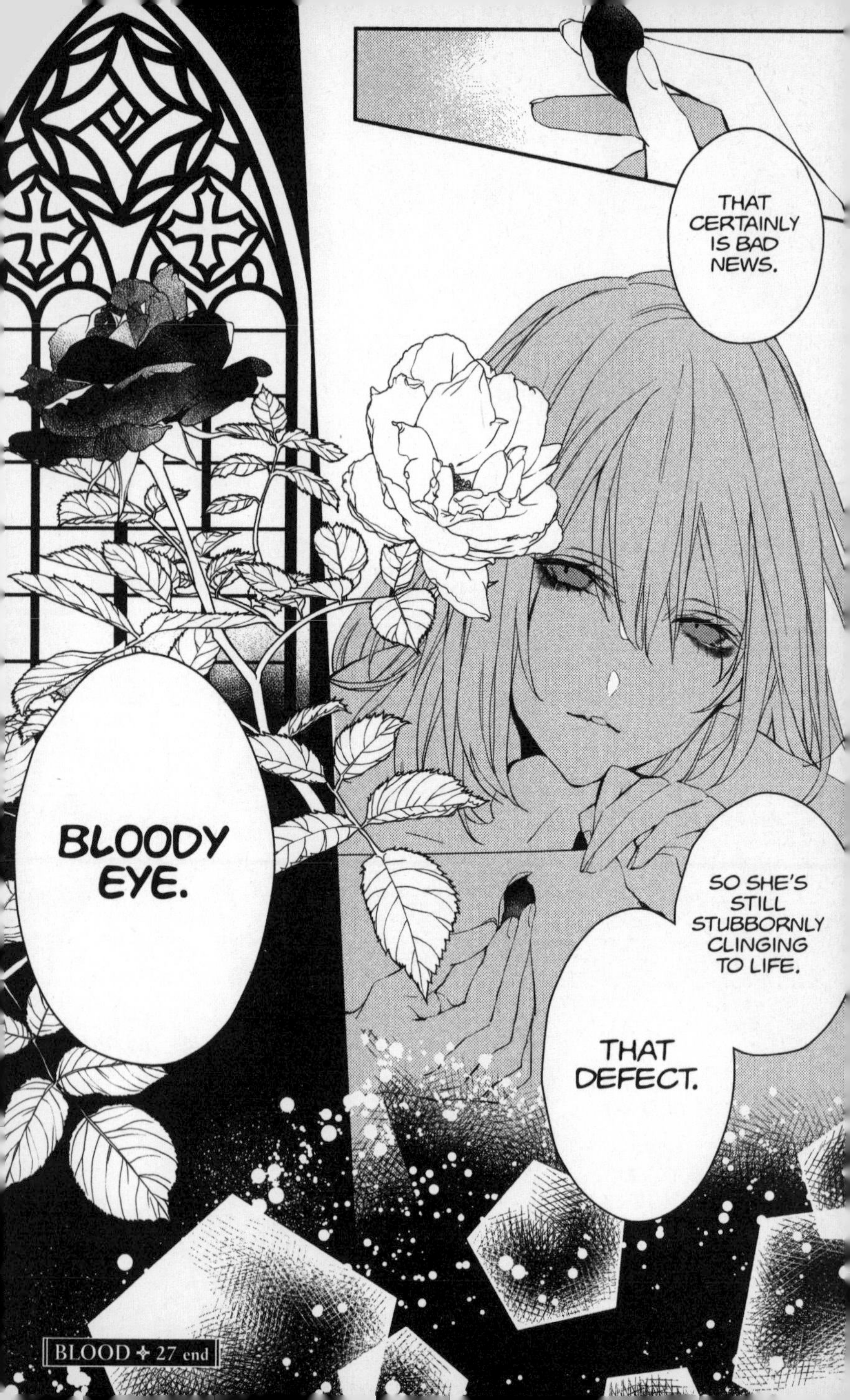
THAT CERTAINLY IS BAD NEWS.
SO SHE'S STILL STUBBORNLY CLINGING TO LIFE.
THAT DEFECT.
BLOODY EYE.
BLOOD ✦ 27 end

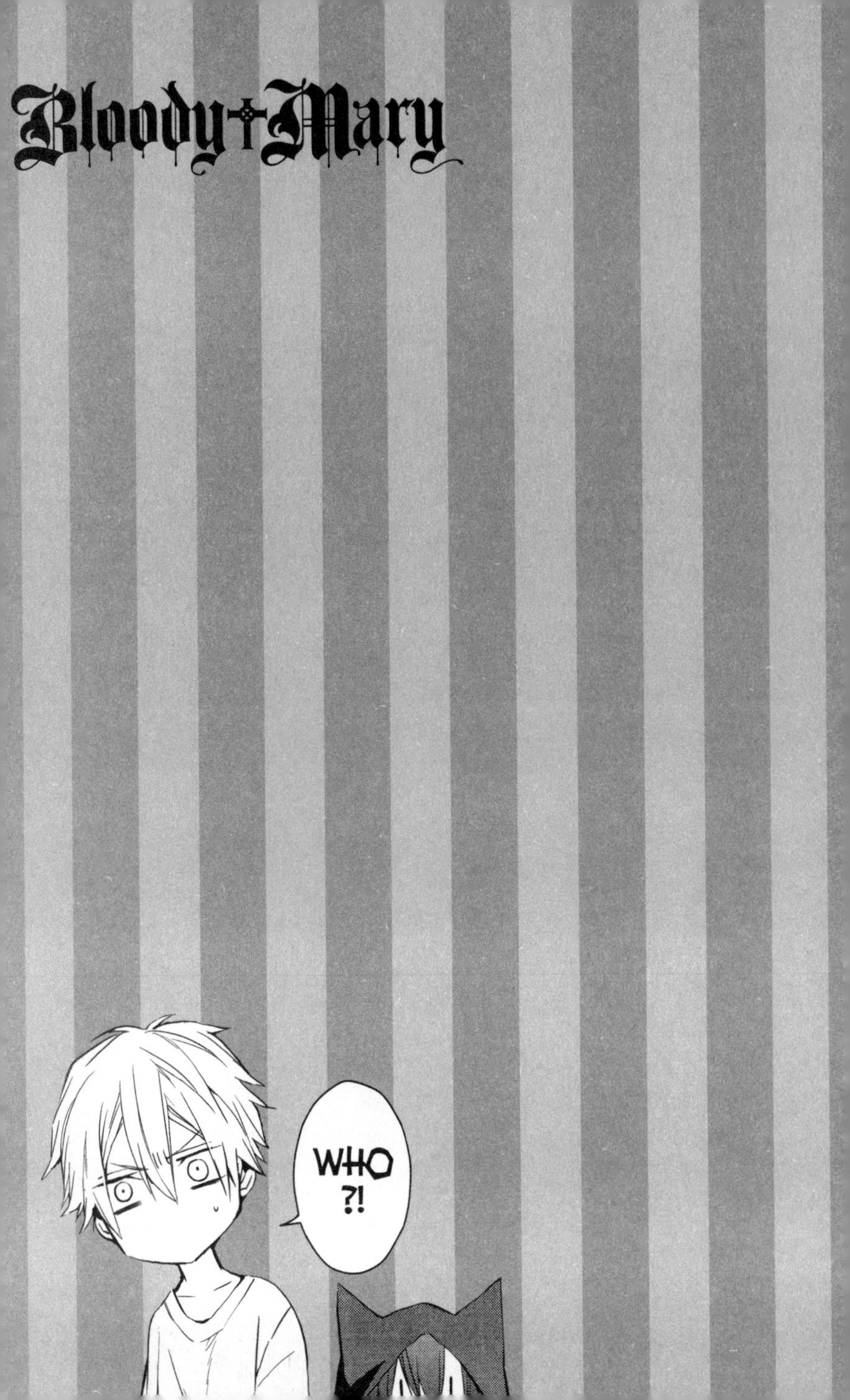
Bloody Mary
WHO ?!

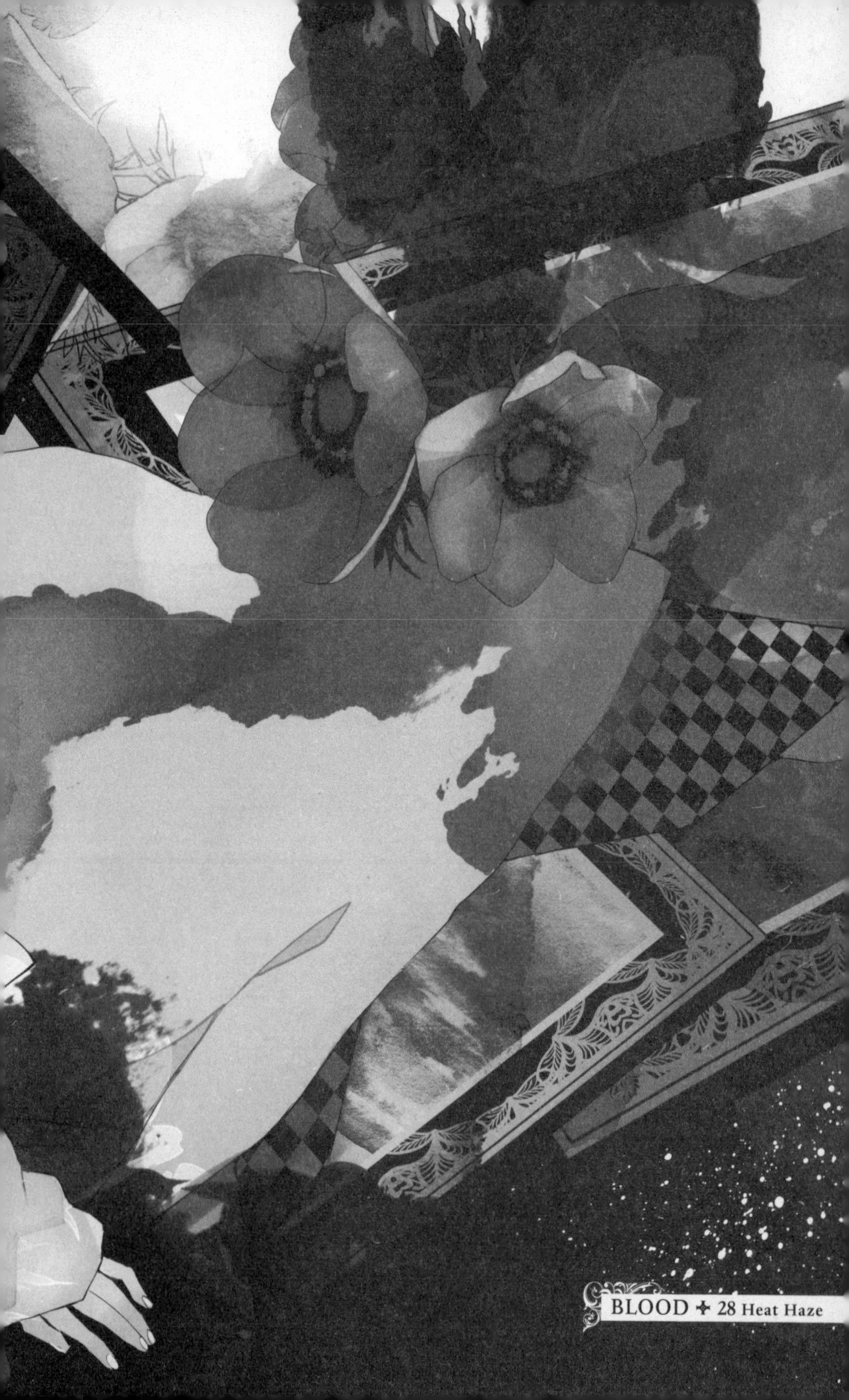
BLOOD ✦ 28 Heat Haze

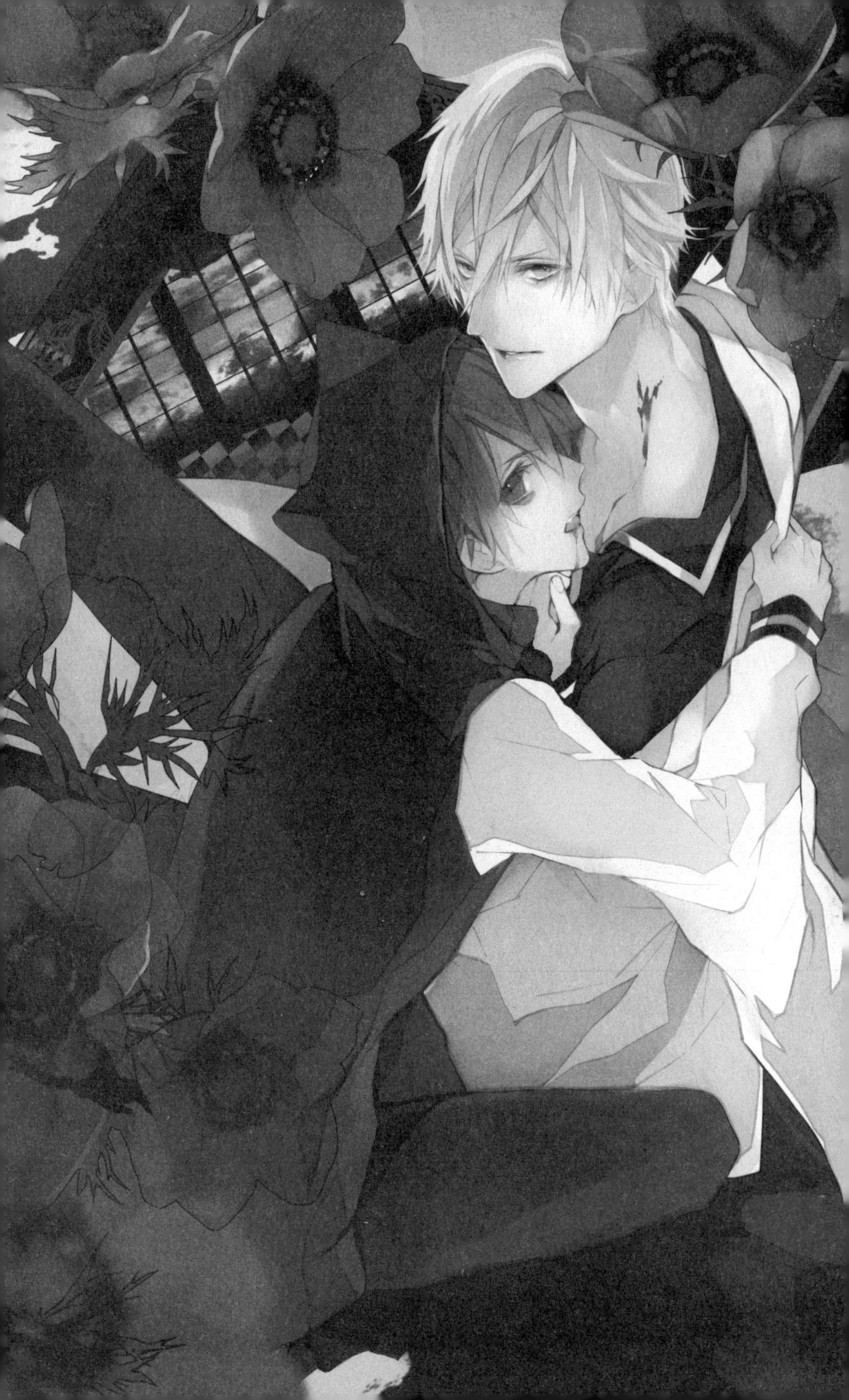

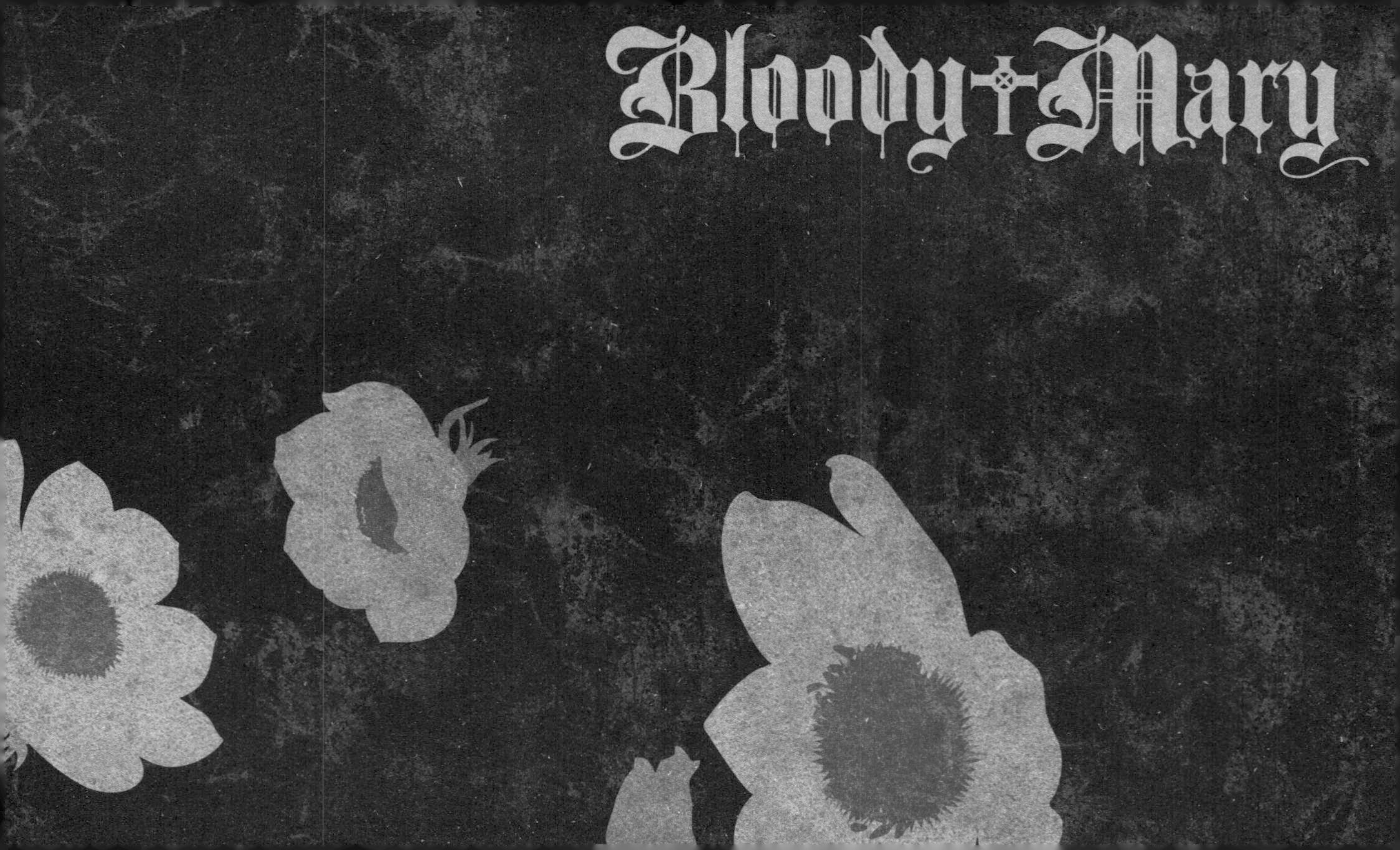
Bloody+Mary

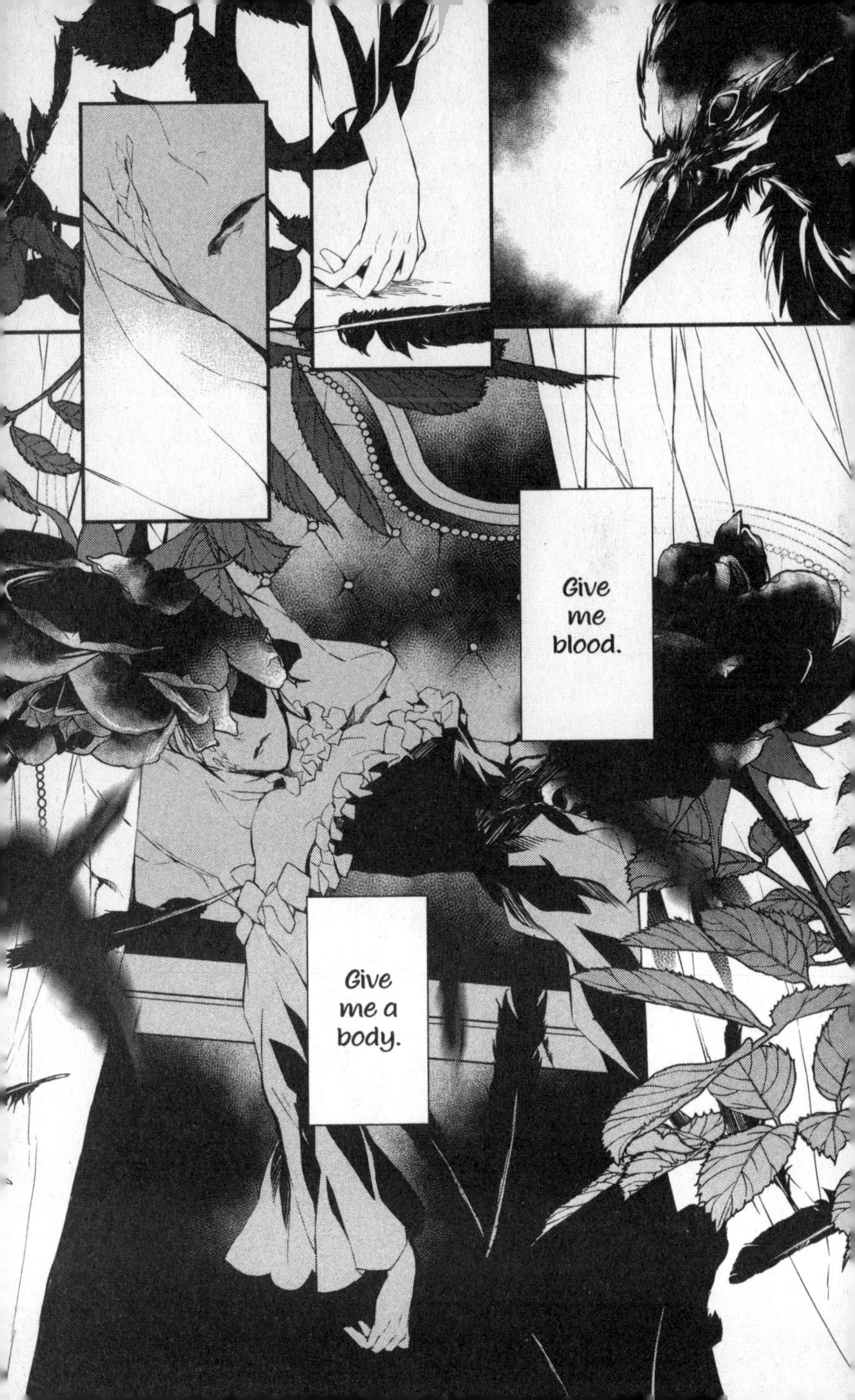
Give me blood.
Give me a body.

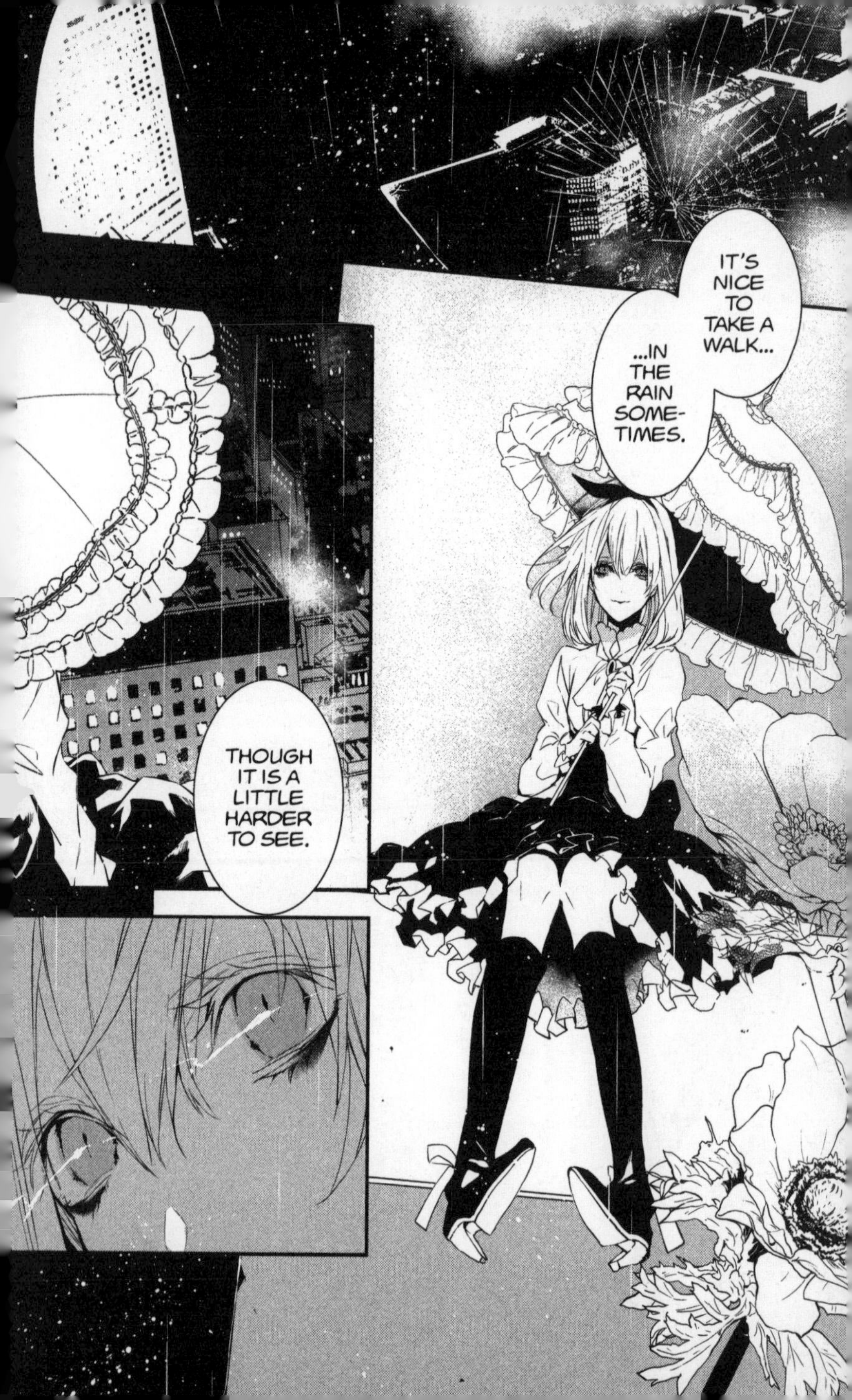
IT'S NICE TO TAKE A WALK...
...IN THE RAIN SOMETIMES.
THOUGH IT IS A LITTLE HARDER TO SEE.

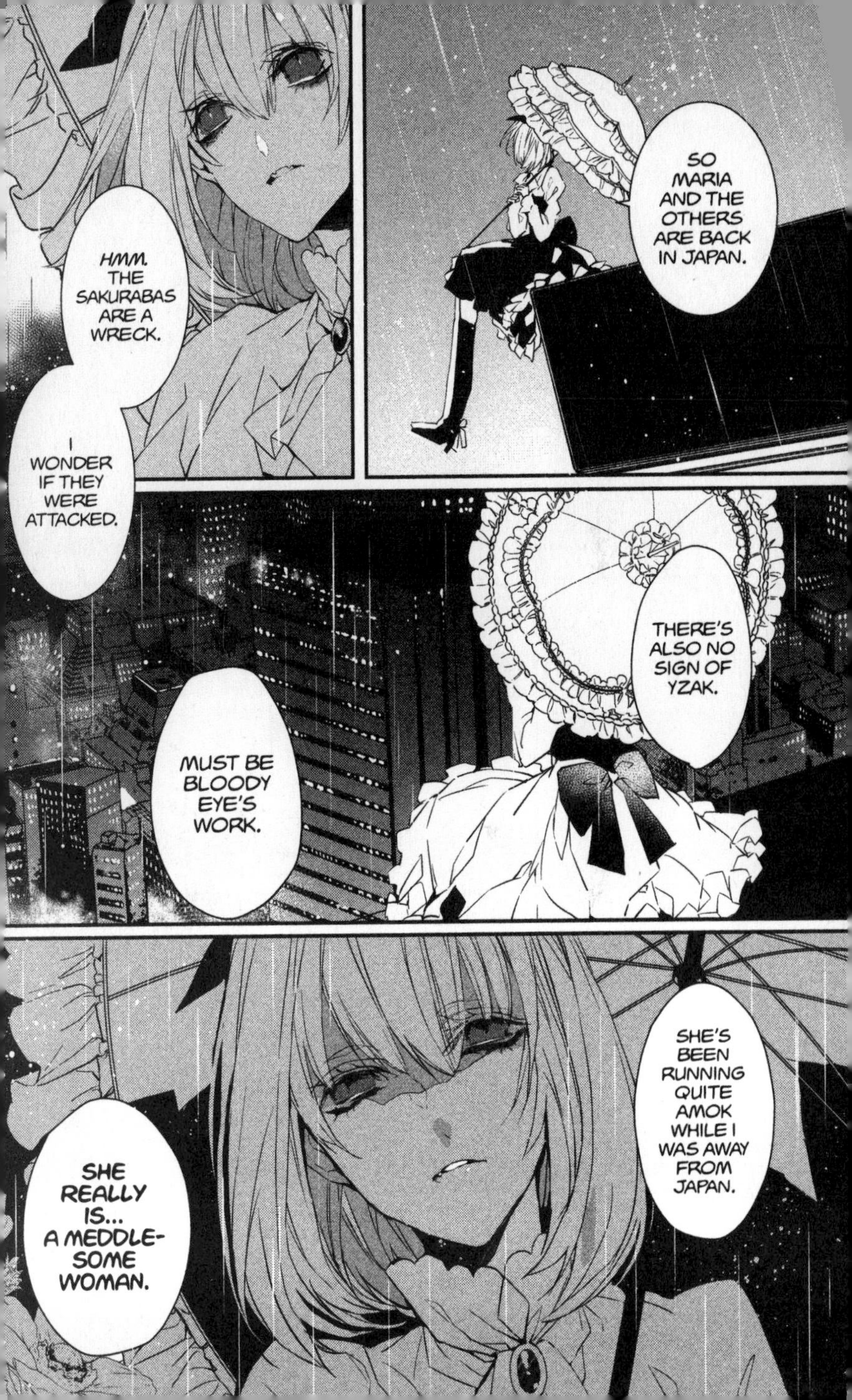
SO MARIA AND THE OTHERS ARE BACK IN JAPAN.
HMM. THE SAKURABAS ARE A WRECK.
I WONDER IF THEY WERE ATTACKED.
THERE'S ALSO NO SIGN OF YZAK.
MUST BE BLOODY EYE'S WORK.
SHE'S BEEN RUNNING QUITE AMOK WHILE I WAS AWAY FROM JAPAN.
SHE REALLY IS... A MEDDLE-SOME WOMAN.

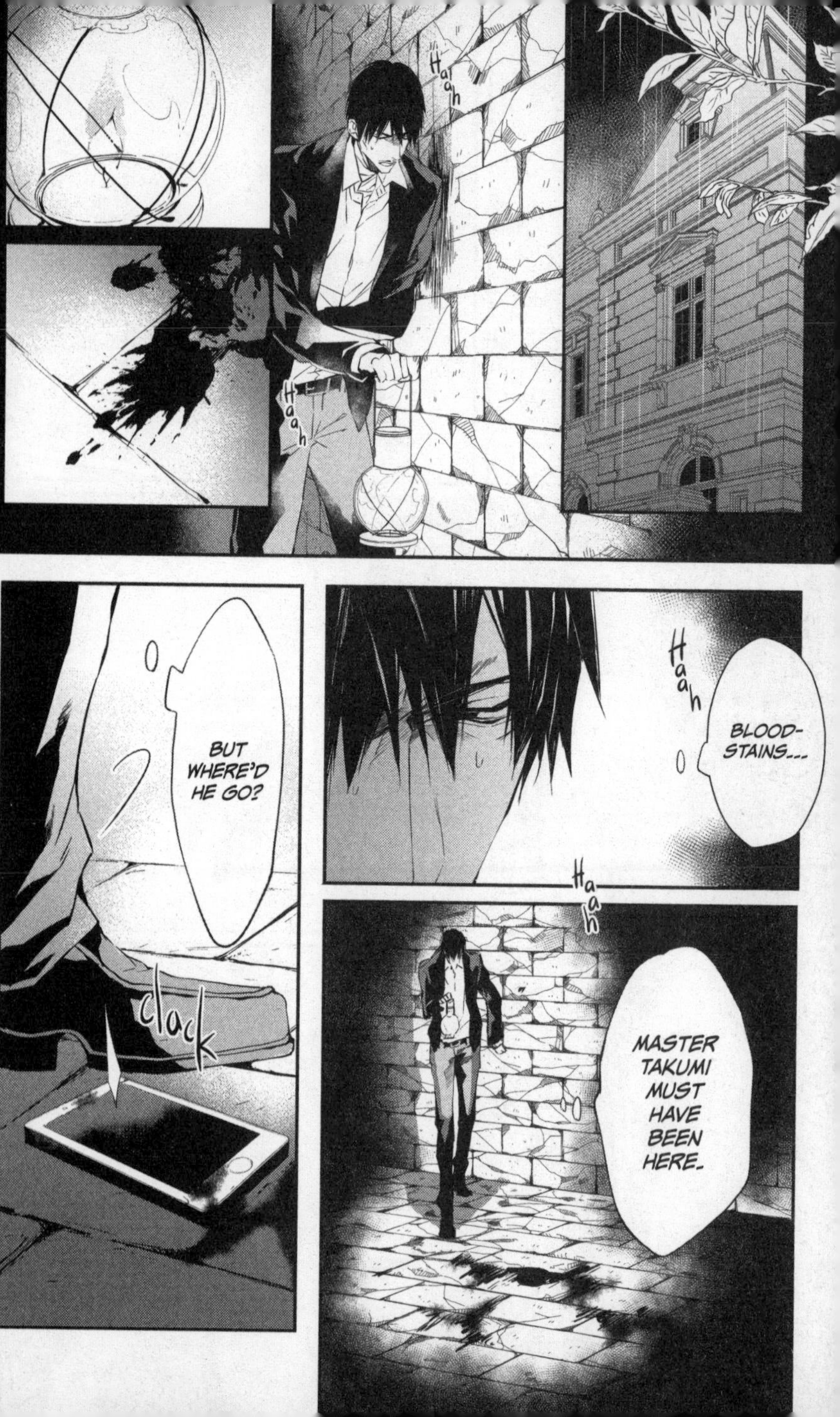
Haah
Haah
Haah
BLOOD-STAINS...
Haah
MASTER TAKUMI MUST HAVE BEEN HERE.
BUT WHERE'D HE GO?
clack

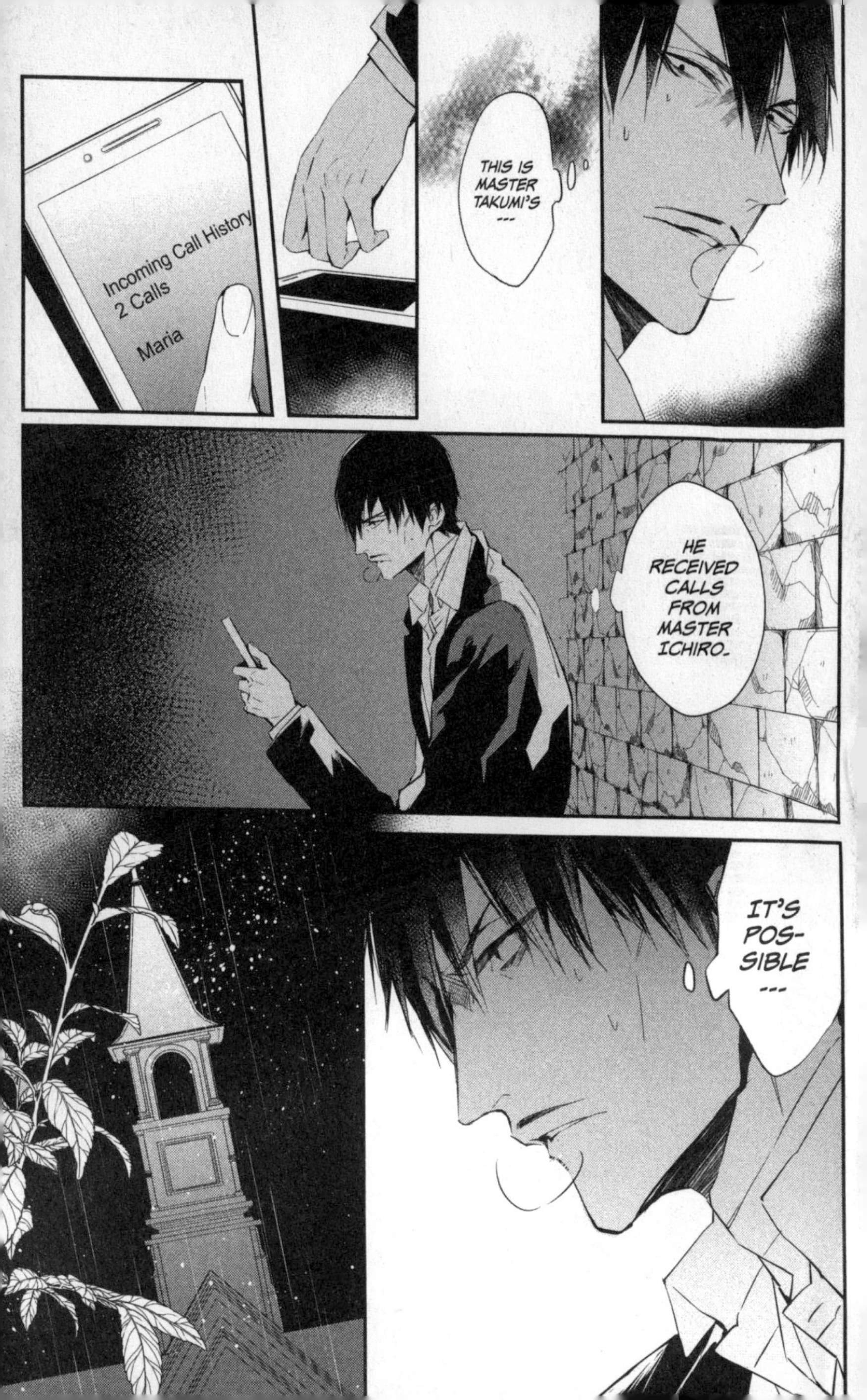
THIS IS MASTER TAKUMI'S ---
Incoming Call History
2 Calls
Maria
HE RECEIVED CALLS FROM MASTER ICHIRO_
IT'S POS-SIBLE ---

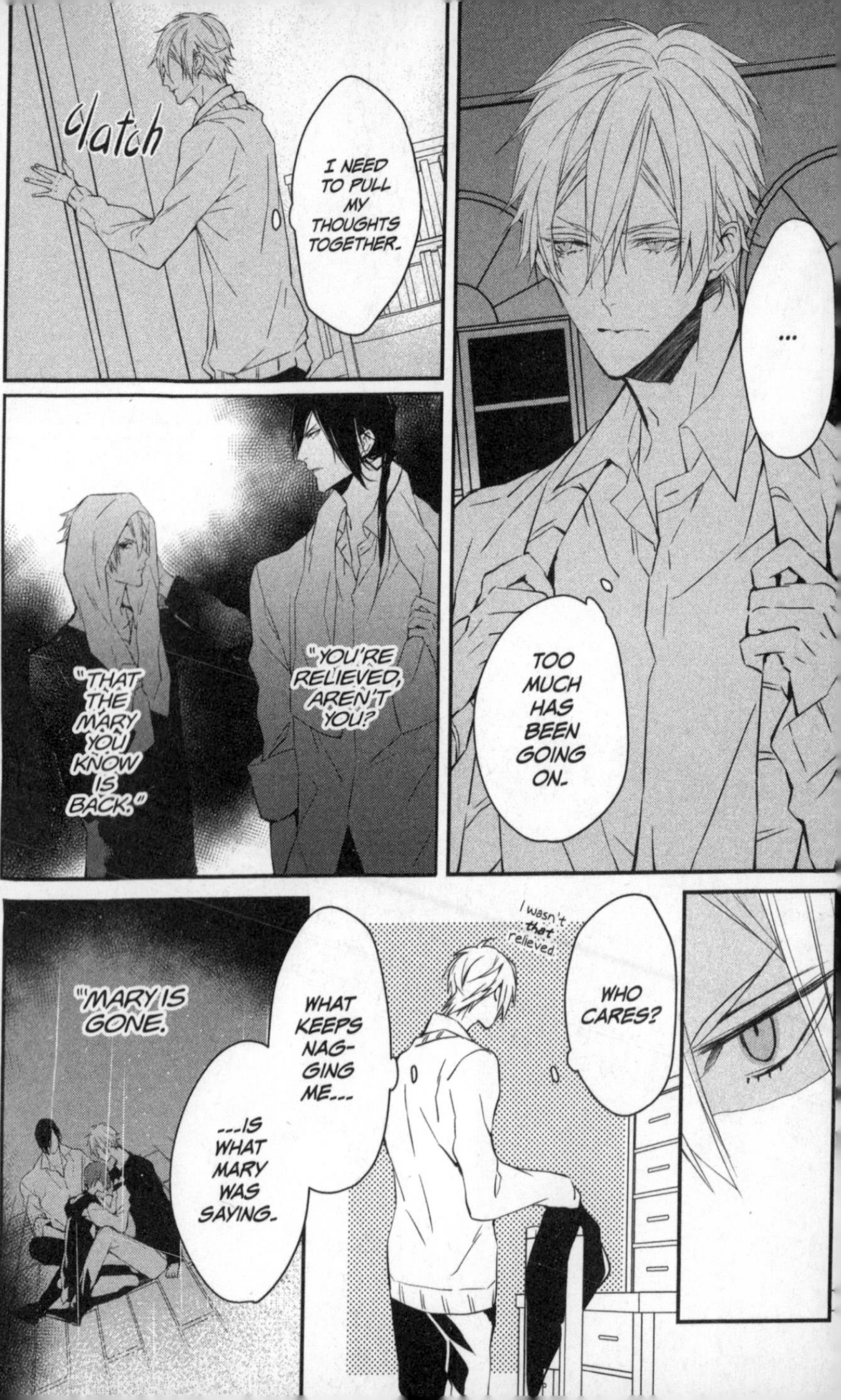
...
TOO MUCH HAS BEEN GOING ON.
Clatch
I NEED TO PULL MY THOUGHTS TOGETHER.
"YOU'RE RELIEVED, AREN'T YOU?
"THAT THE MARY YOU KNOW IS BACK."
WHO CARES?
I wasn't that relieved.
WHAT KEEPS NAG-GING ME...
...IS WHAT MARY WAS SAYING.
"MARY IS GONE.

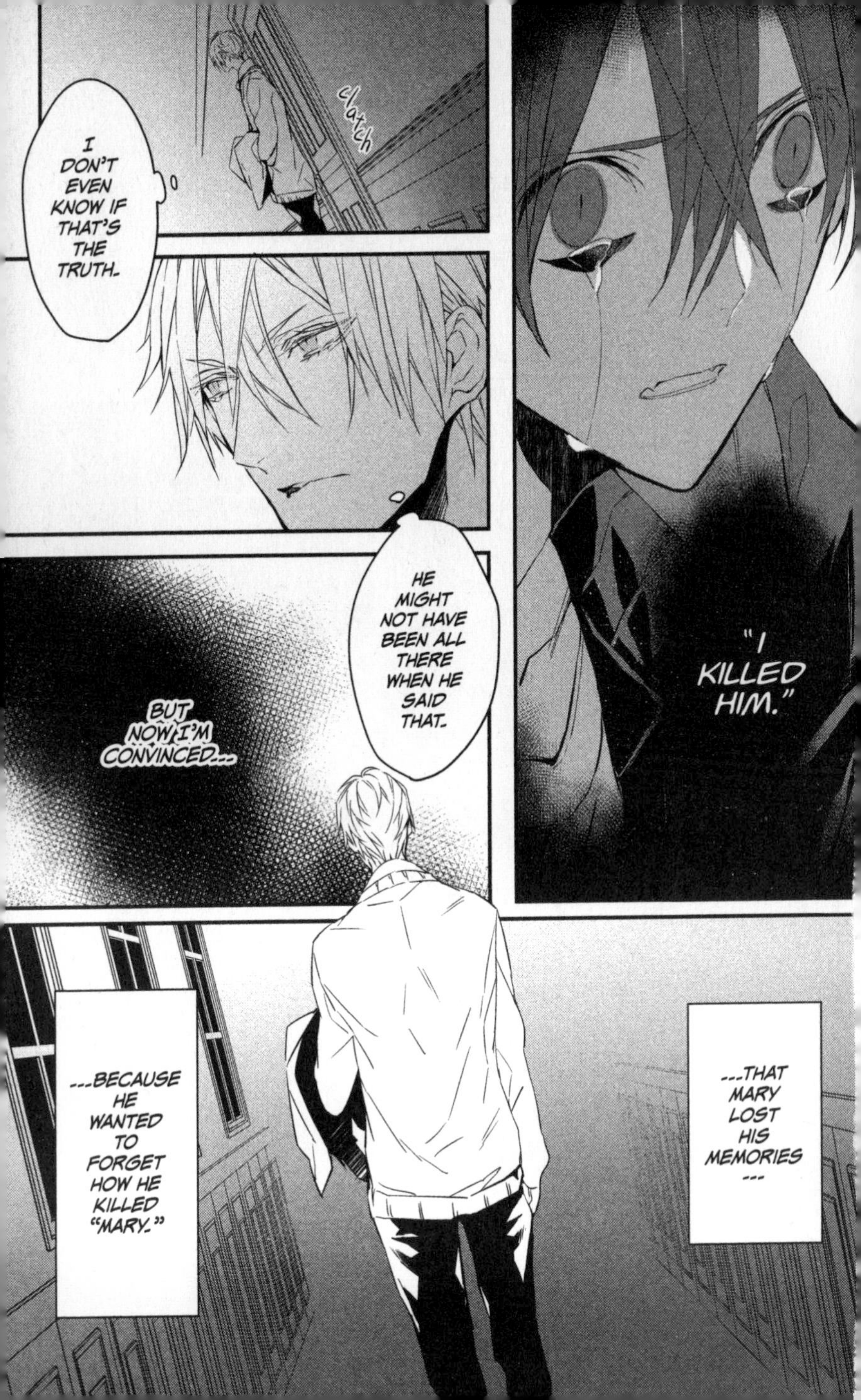

"I KILLED HIM."
clatch
I DON'T EVEN KNOW IF THAT'S THE TRUTH.
HE MIGHT NOT HAVE BEEN ALL THERE WHEN HE SAID THAT.
BUT NOW I'M CONVINCED...
...THAT MARY LOST HIS MEMORIES...
...BECAUSE HE WANTED TO FORGET HOW HE KILLED "MARY."

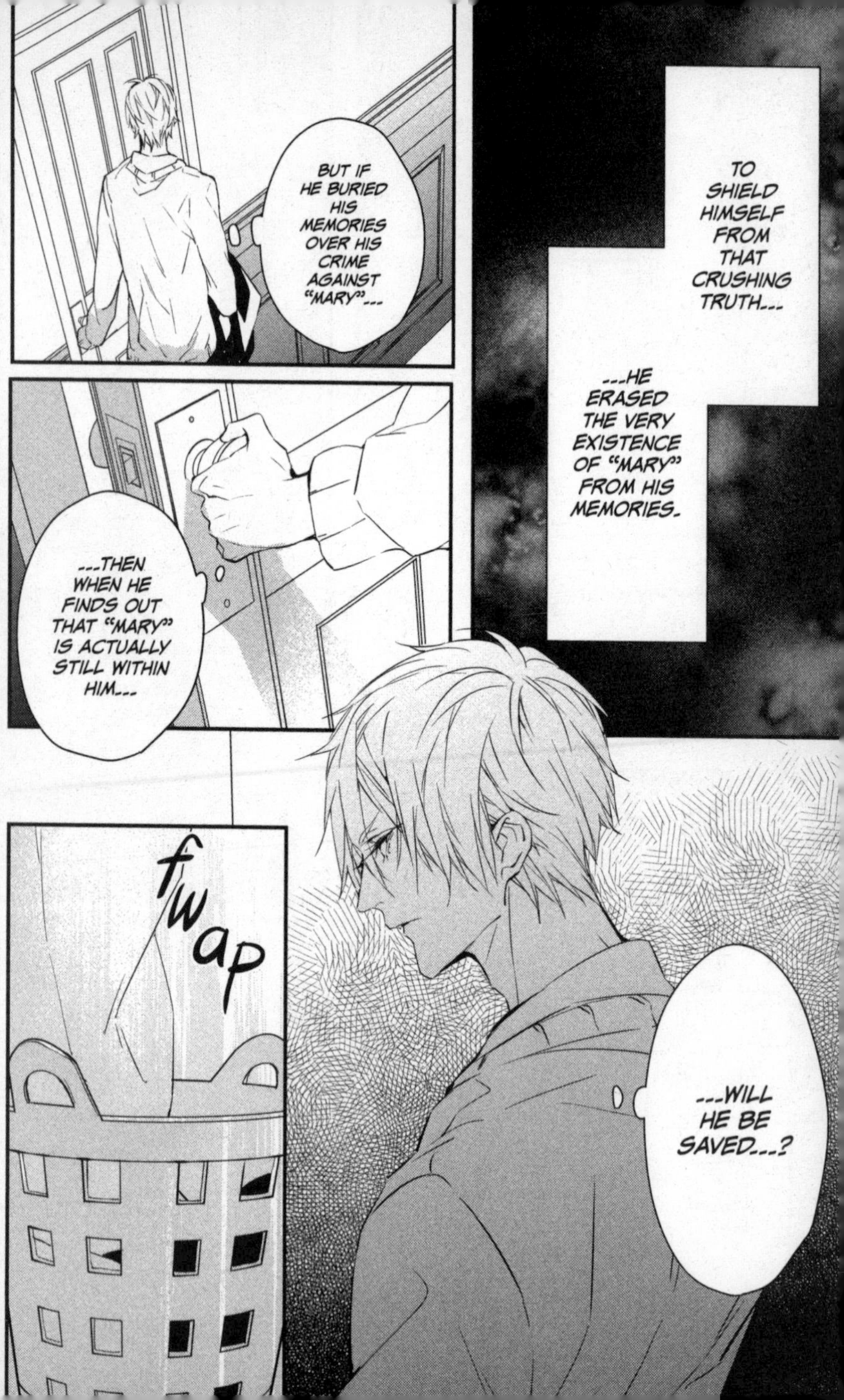
TO SHIELD HIMSELF FROM THAT CRUSHING TRUTH...
...HE ERASED THE VERY EXISTENCE OF "MARY" FROM HIS MEMORIES.
BUT IF HE BURIED HIS MEMORIES OVER HIS CRIME AGAINST "MARY"...
...THEN WHEN HE FINDS OUT THAT "MARY" IS ACTUALLY STILL WITHIN HIM...
...WILL HE BE SAVED...?
fwap

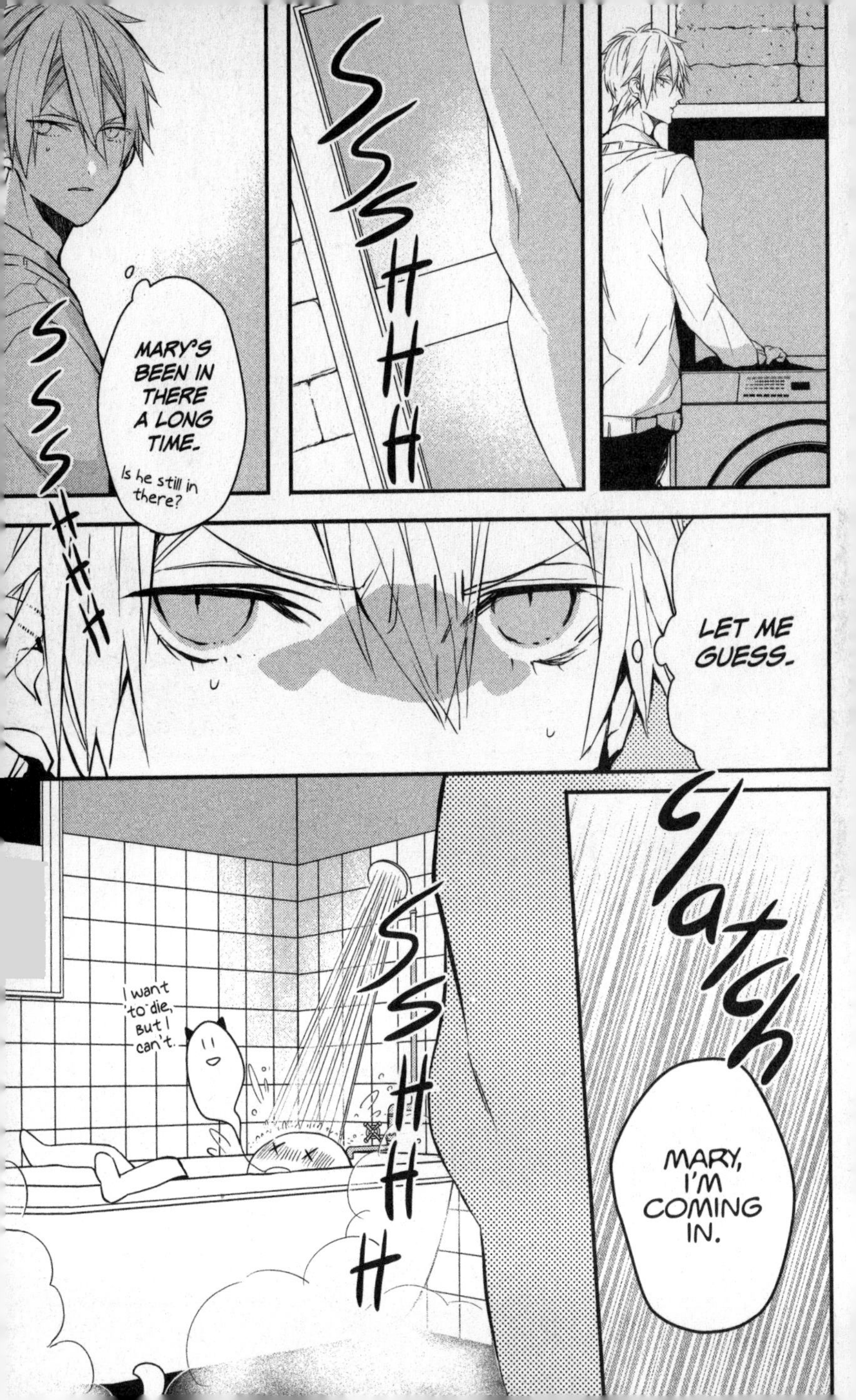
SSSHHH
MARY'S BEEN IN THERE A LONG TIME.
Is he still in there?
SSSHHHH
LET ME GUESS.
Clatch
MARY, I'M COMING IN.
SSHHHH
I want to die, but I can't.

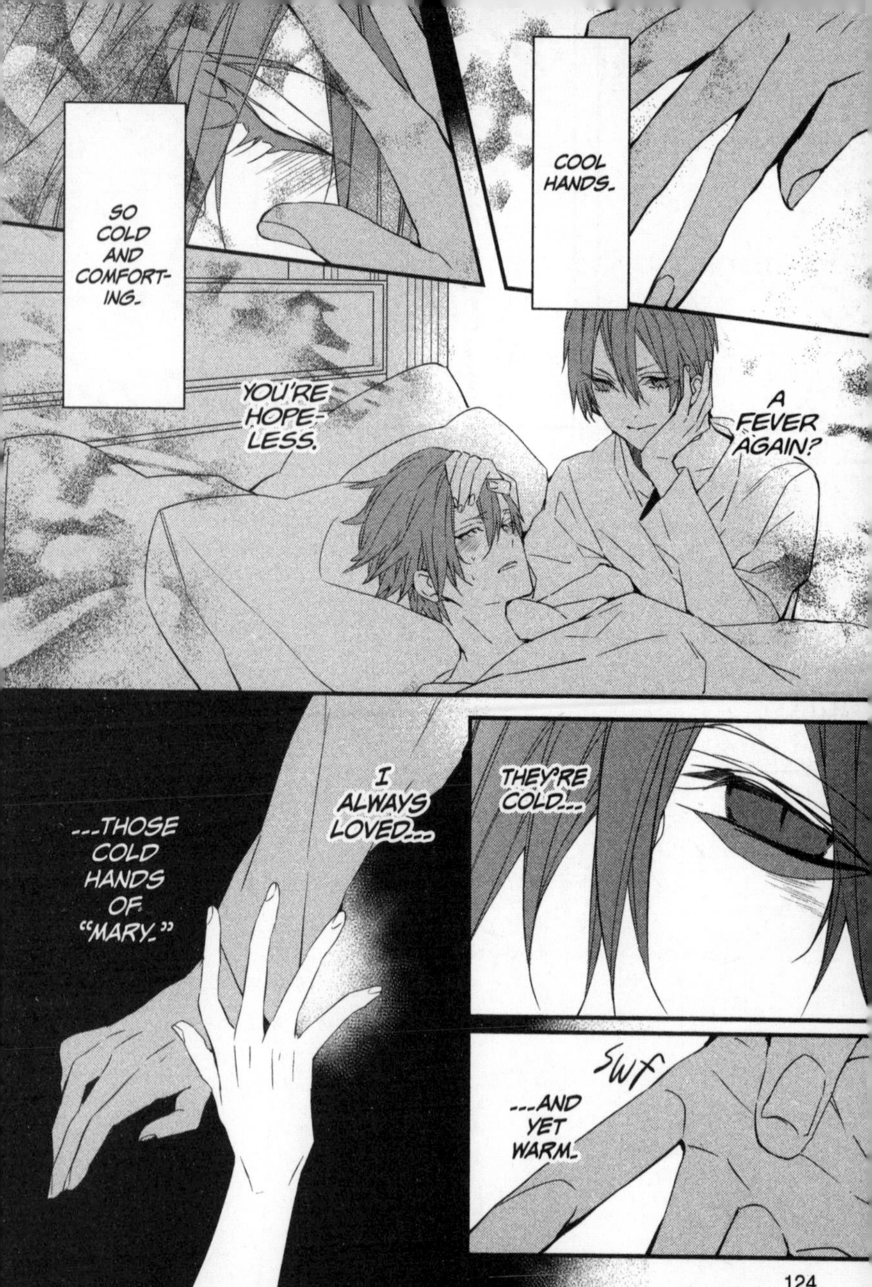
COOL HANDS...
SO COLD AND COMFORTING...
A FEVER AGAIN?
YOU'RE HOPELESS.
THEY'RE COLD...
SWF
...AND YET WARM...
I ALWAYS LOVED...
...THOSE COLD HANDS OF "MARY."

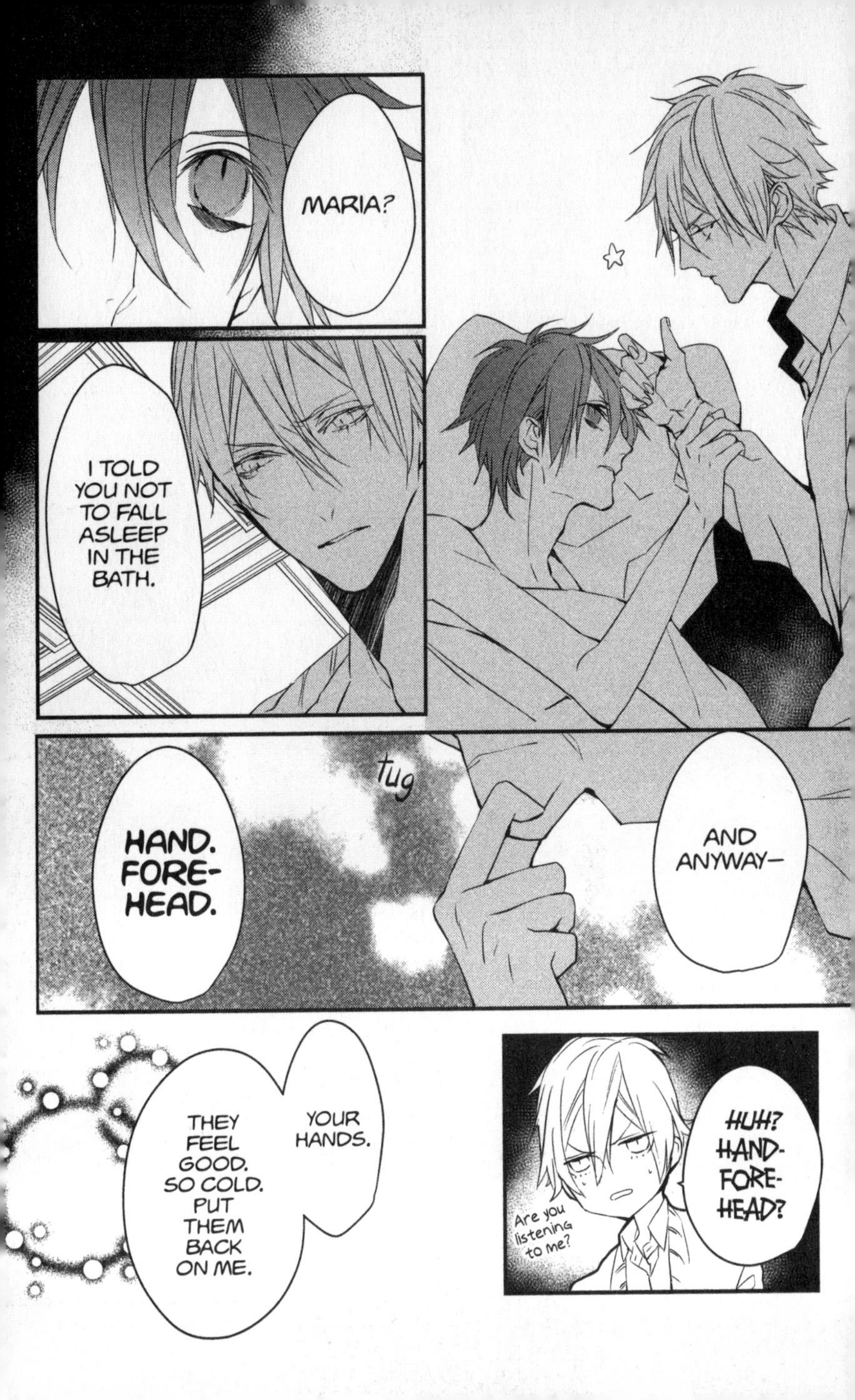
MARIA?
I TOLD YOU NOT TO FALL ASLEEP IN THE BATH.
AND ANYWAY—
tug
HAND. FORE-HEAD.
HUH? HAND-FORE-HEAD?
Are you listening to me?
YOUR HANDS.
THEY FEEL GOOD. SO COLD. PUT THEM BACK ON ME.

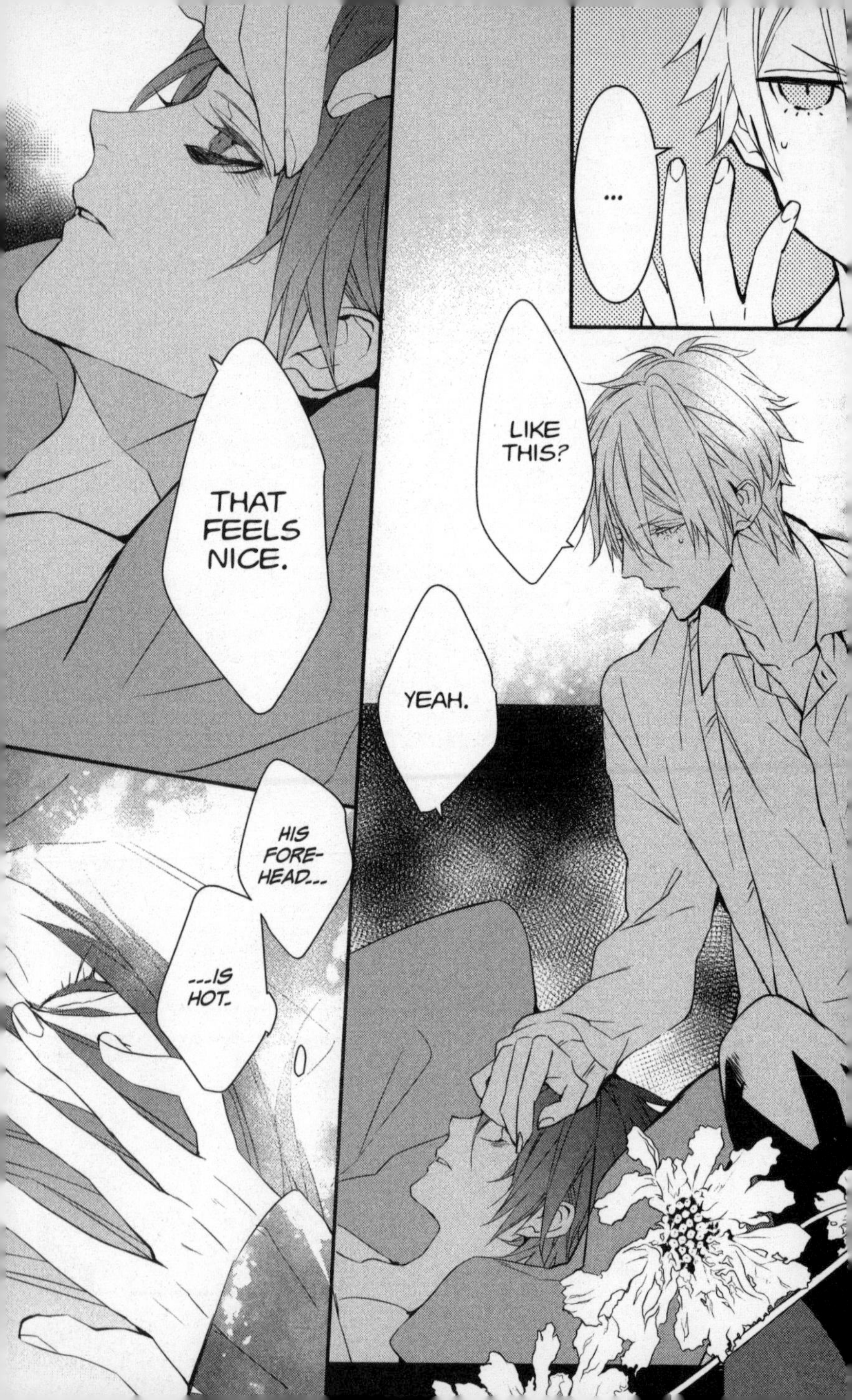
...
LIKE THIS?
YEAH.
THAT FEELS NICE.
HIS FORE-HEAD...
...IS HOT.

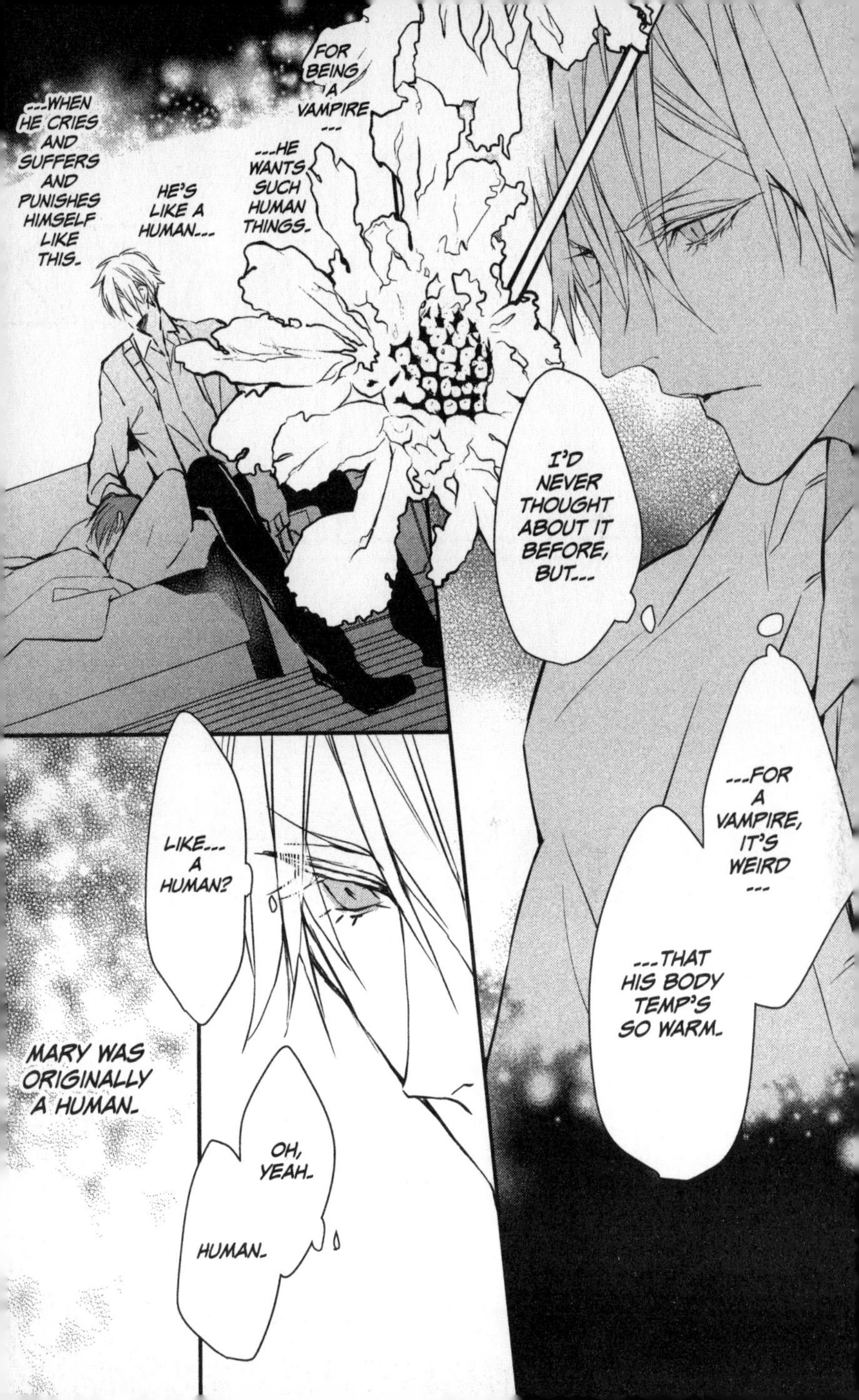
I'D NEVER THOUGHT ABOUT IT BEFORE, BUT...
...FOR A VAMPIRE, IT'S WEIRD...
...THAT HIS BODY TEMP'S SO WARM.
FOR BEING A VAMPIRE...
...HE WANTS SUCH HUMAN THINGS.
HE'S LIKE A HUMAN...
...WHEN HE CRIES AND SUFFERS AND PUNISHES HIMSELF LIKE THIS.
LIKE... A HUMAN?
OH, YEAH.
HUMAN.
MARY WAS ORIGINALLY A HUMAN.

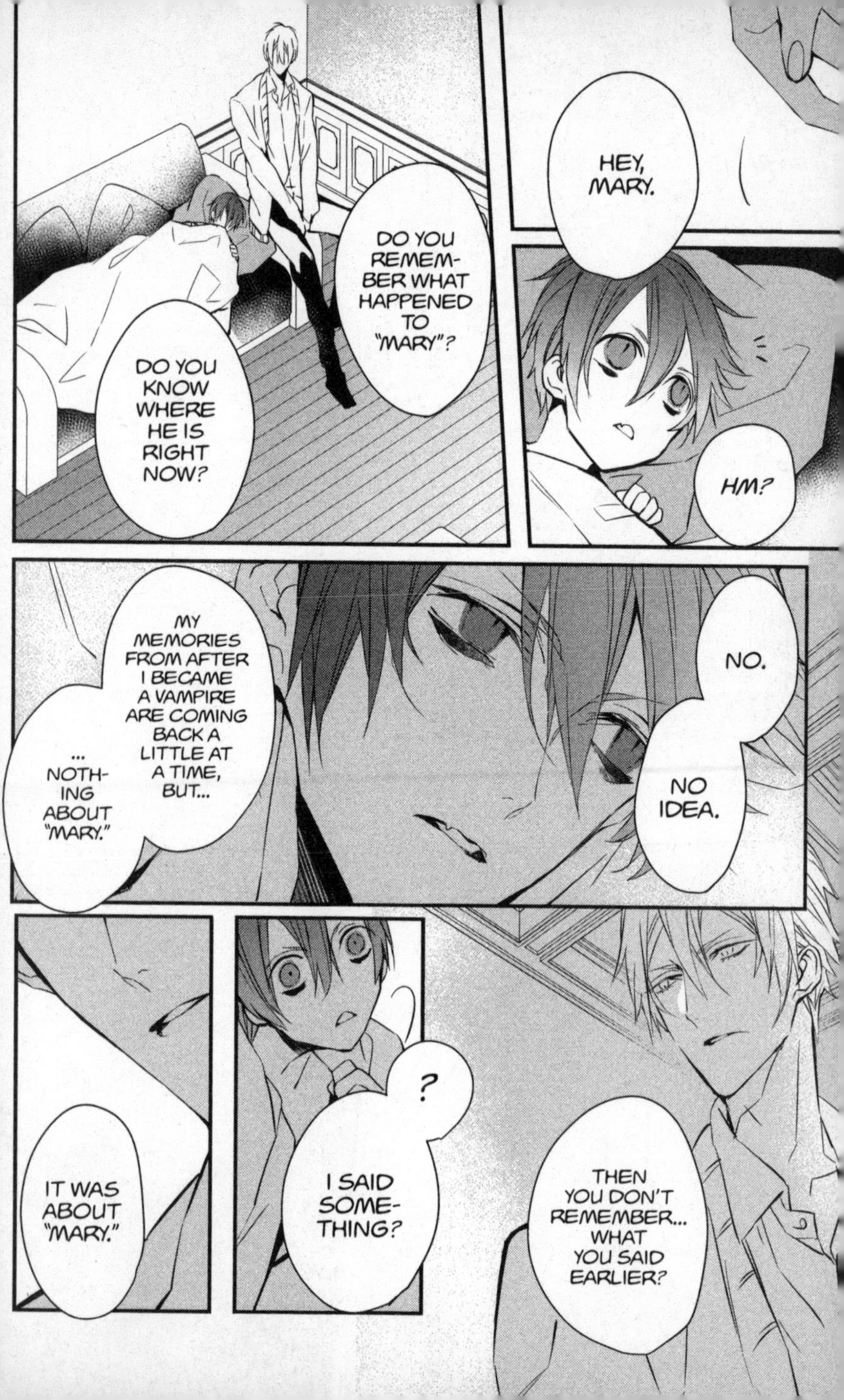
HEY, MARY.
HM?
DO YOU REMEM-BER WHAT HAPPENED TO "MARY"?
DO YOU KNOW WHERE HE IS RIGHT NOW?
NO.
NO IDEA.
MY MEMORIES FROM AFTER I BECAME A VAMPIRE ARE COMING BACK A LITTLE AT A TIME, BUT...
... NOTH-ING ABOUT "MARY."
THEN YOU DON'T REMEMBER... WHAT YOU SAID EARLIER?
?
I SAID SOME-THING?
IT WAS ABOUT "MARY."

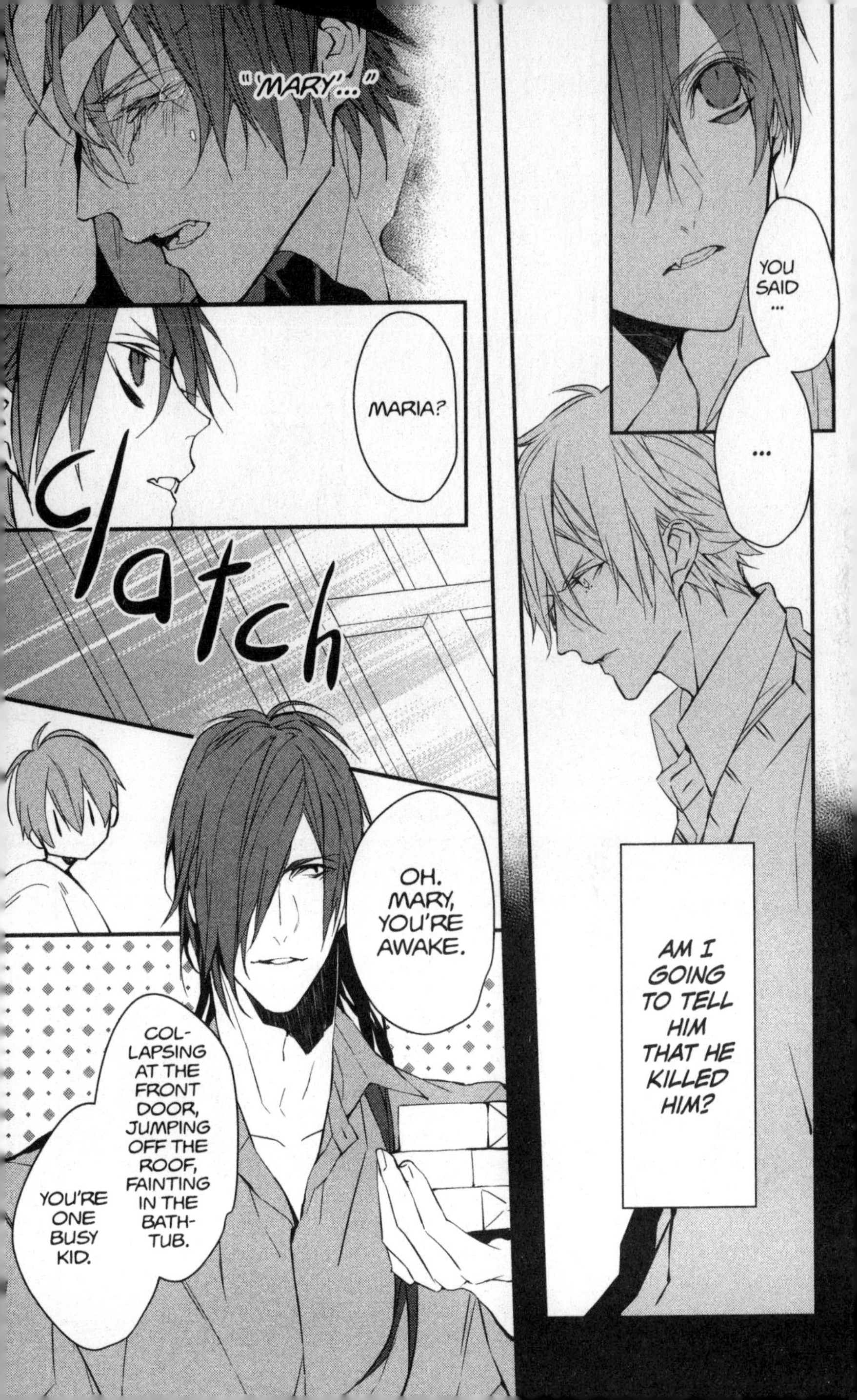
YOU SAID ...
...
AM I GOING TO TELL HIM THAT HE KILLED HIM?
"'MARY'..."
MARIA?
Clatch
OH. MARY, YOU'RE AWAKE.
COL-LAPSING AT THE FRONT DOOR, JUMPING OFF THE ROOF, FAINTING IN THE BATH-TUB.
YOU'RE ONE BUSY KID.

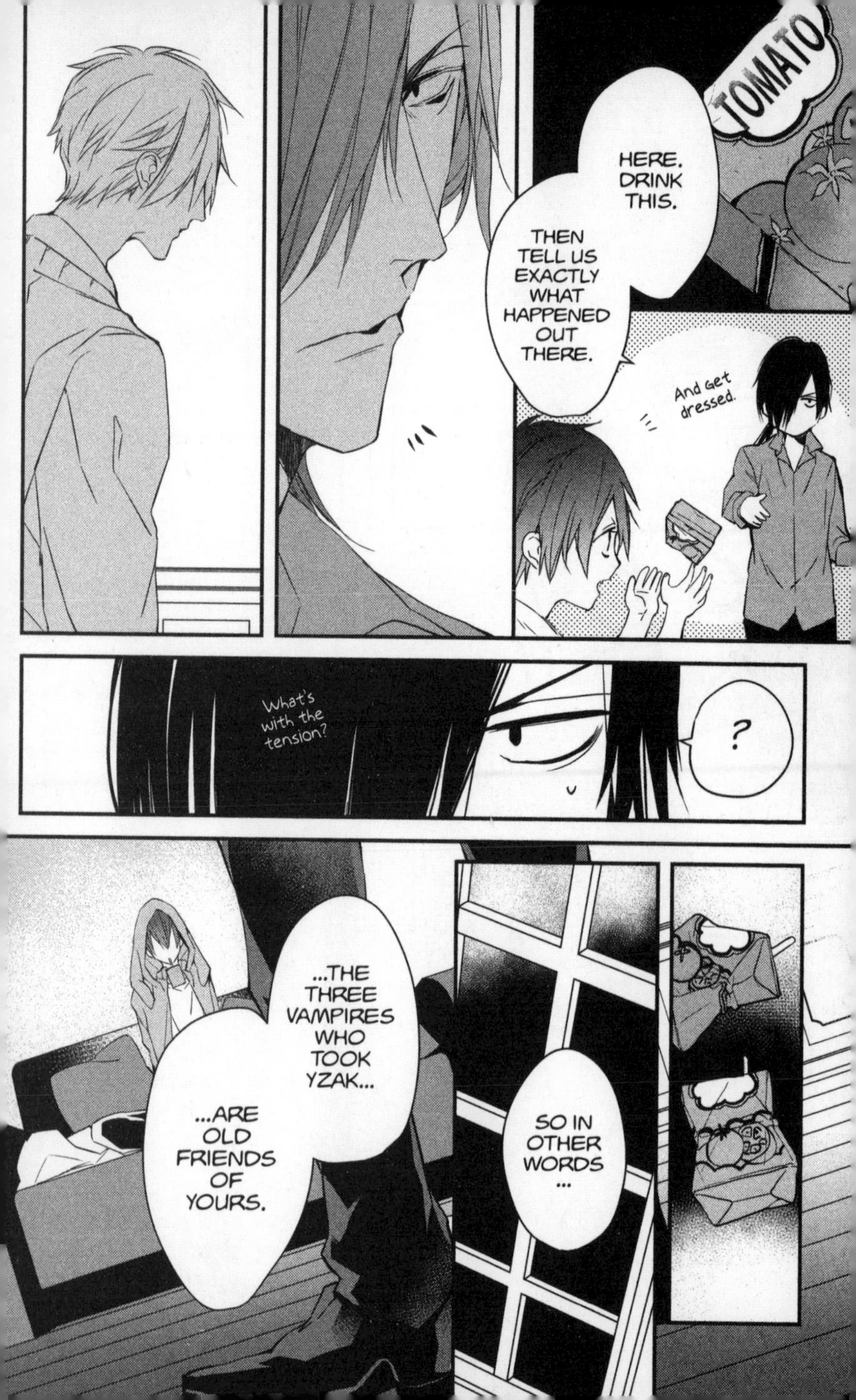
TOMATO
HERE. DRINK THIS.
THEN TELL US EXACTLY WHAT HAPPENED OUT THERE.
And get dressed.
?
What's with the tension?
SO IN OTHER WORDS...
...THE THREE VAMPIRES WHO TOOK YZAK...
...ARE OLD FRIENDS OF YOURS.

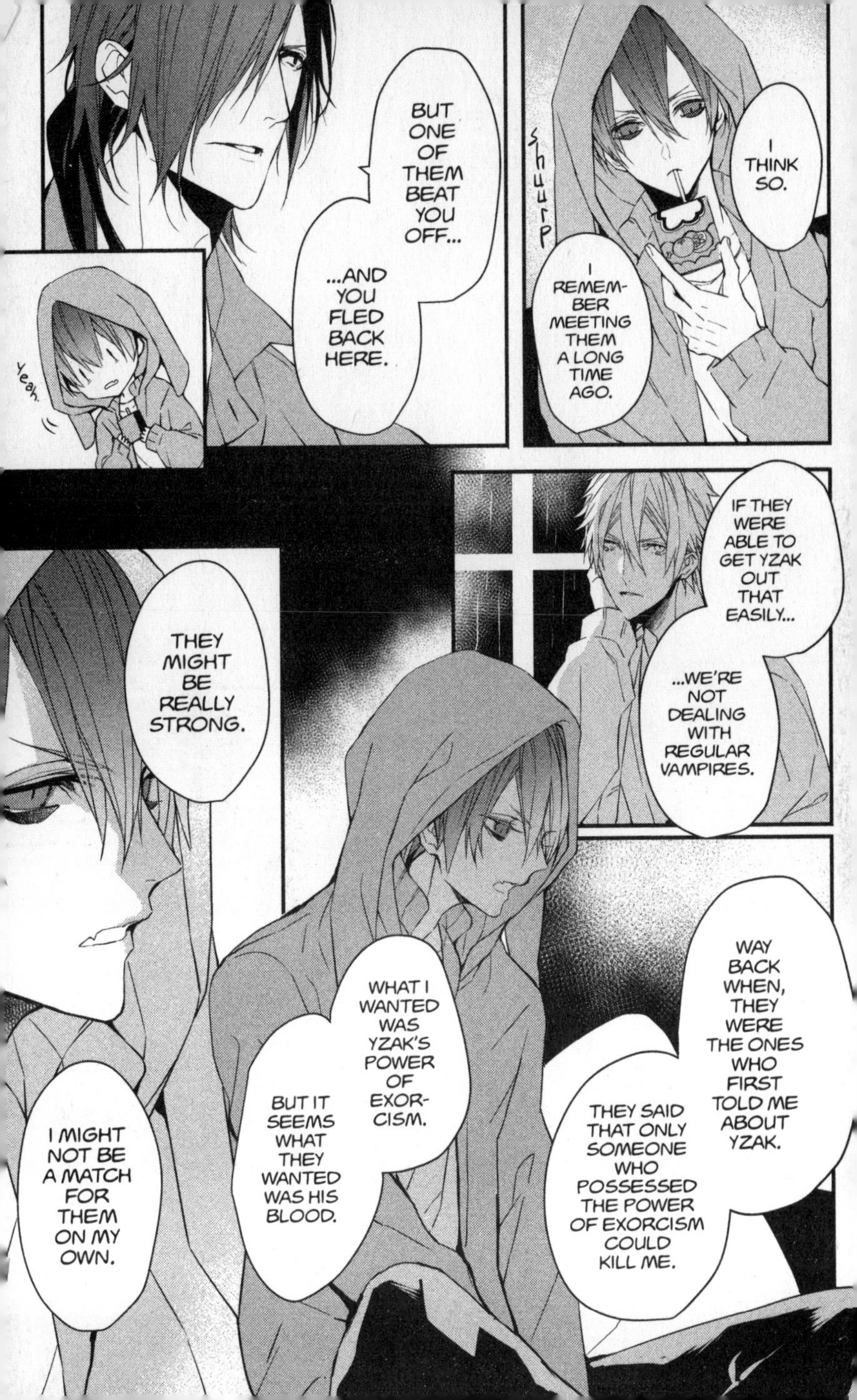
I THINK SO.
SHUURP
I REMEMBER MEETING THEM A LONG TIME AGO.
BUT ONE OF THEM BEAT YOU OFF...
...AND YOU FLED BACK HERE.
Yeah.
IF THEY WERE ABLE TO GET YZAK OUT THAT EASILY...
...WE'RE NOT DEALING WITH REGULAR VAMPIRES.
THEY MIGHT BE REALLY STRONG.
WAY BACK WHEN, THEY WERE THE ONES WHO FIRST TOLD ME ABOUT YZAK.
THEY SAID THAT ONLY SOMEONE WHO POSSESSED THE POWER OF EXORCISM COULD KILL ME.
WHAT I WANTED WAS YZAK'S POWER OF EXORCISM.
BUT IT SEEMS WHAT THEY WANTED WAS HIS BLOOD.
I MIGHT NOT BE A MATCH FOR THEM ON MY OWN.

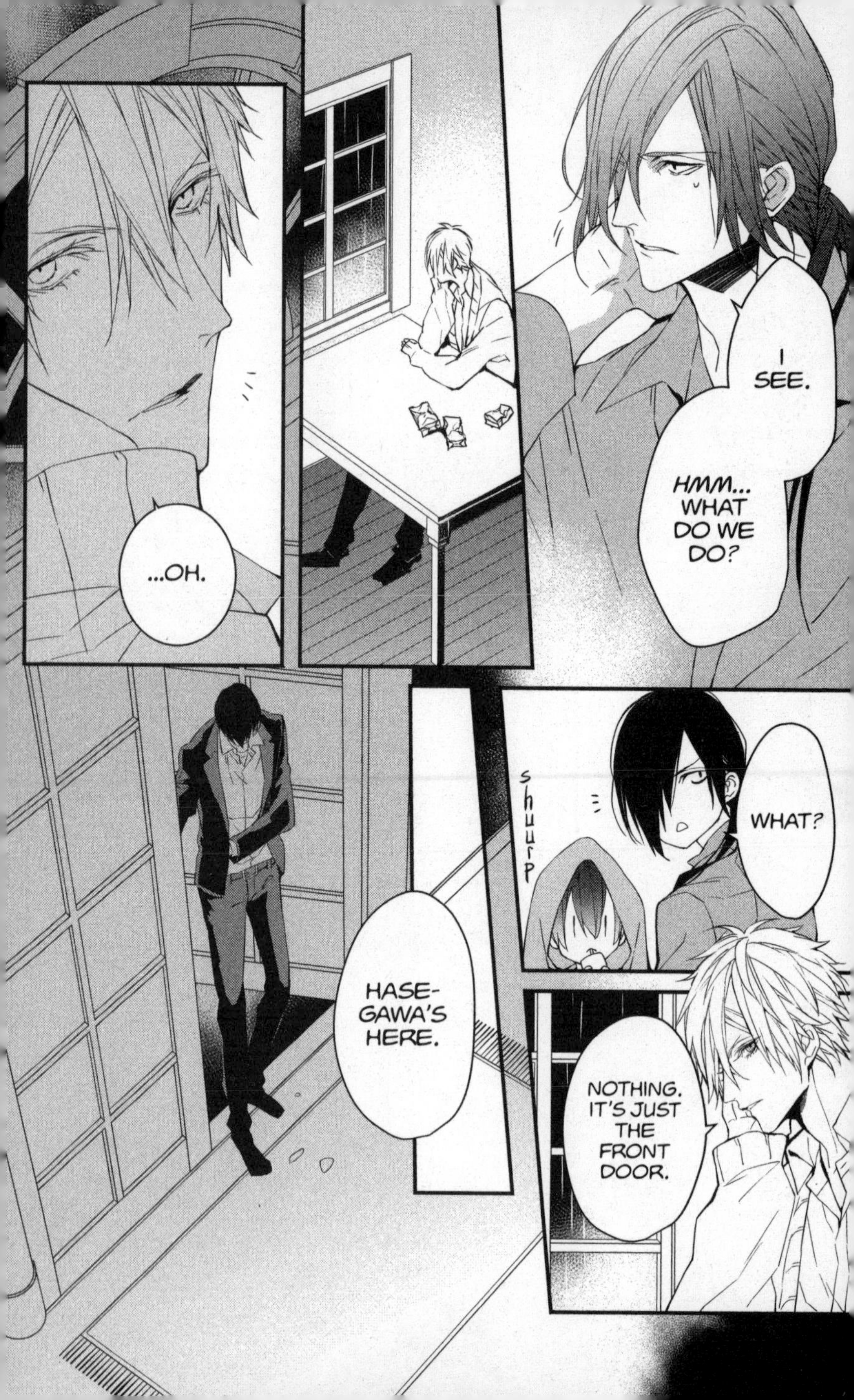
I SEE.
HMM... WHAT DO WE DO?
...OH.
WHAT?
SHUURP
NOTHING. IT'S JUST THE FRONT DOOR.
HASE-GAWA'S HERE.

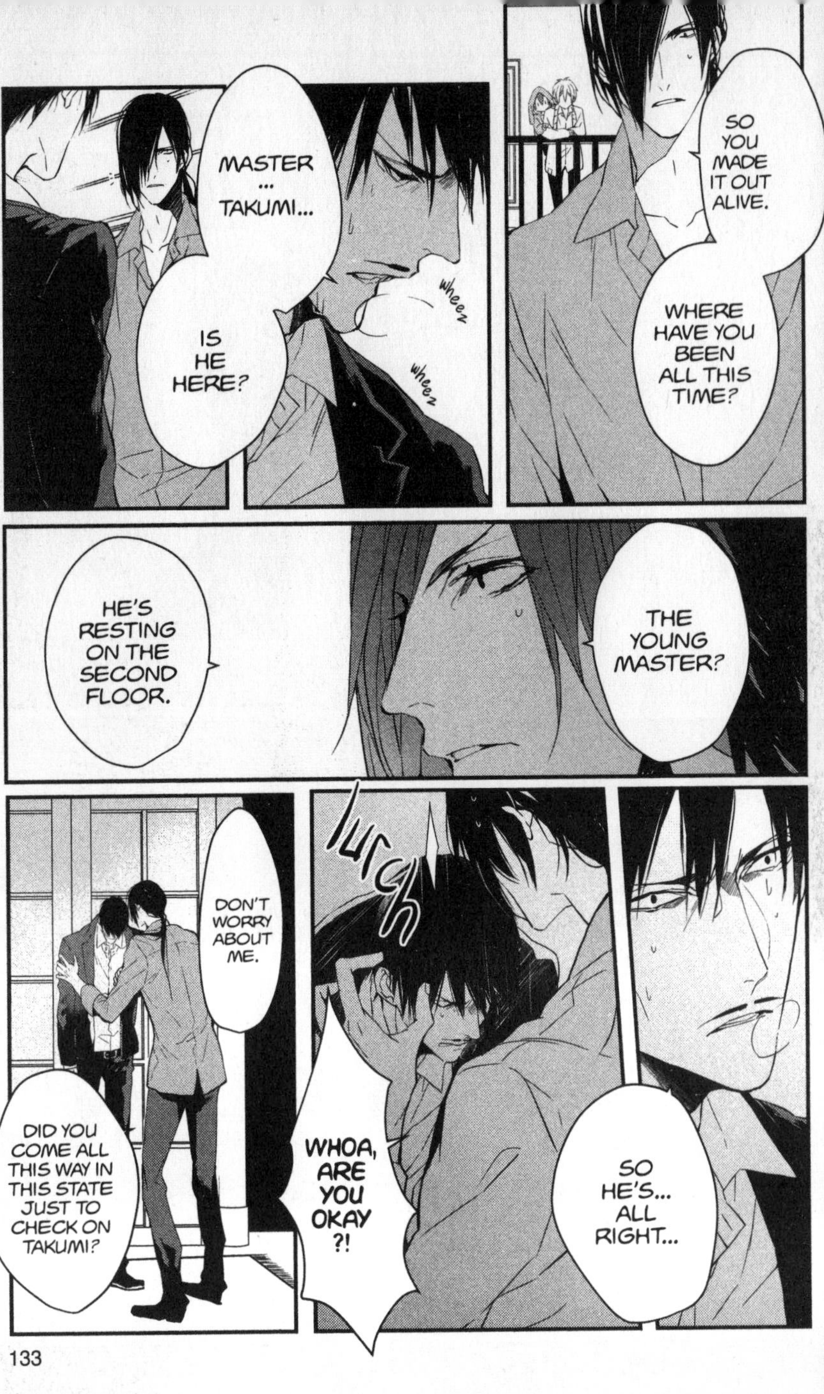
SO YOU MADE IT OUT ALIVE.
WHERE HAVE YOU BEEN ALL THIS TIME?
MASTER ... TAKUMI...
wheez
wheez
IS HE HERE?
THE YOUNG MASTER?
HE'S RESTING ON THE SECOND FLOOR.
SO HE'S... ALL RIGHT...
lurch
WHOA, ARE YOU OKAY ?!
DON'T WORRY ABOUT ME.
DID YOU COME ALL THIS WAY IN THIS STATE JUST TO CHECK ON TAKUMI?

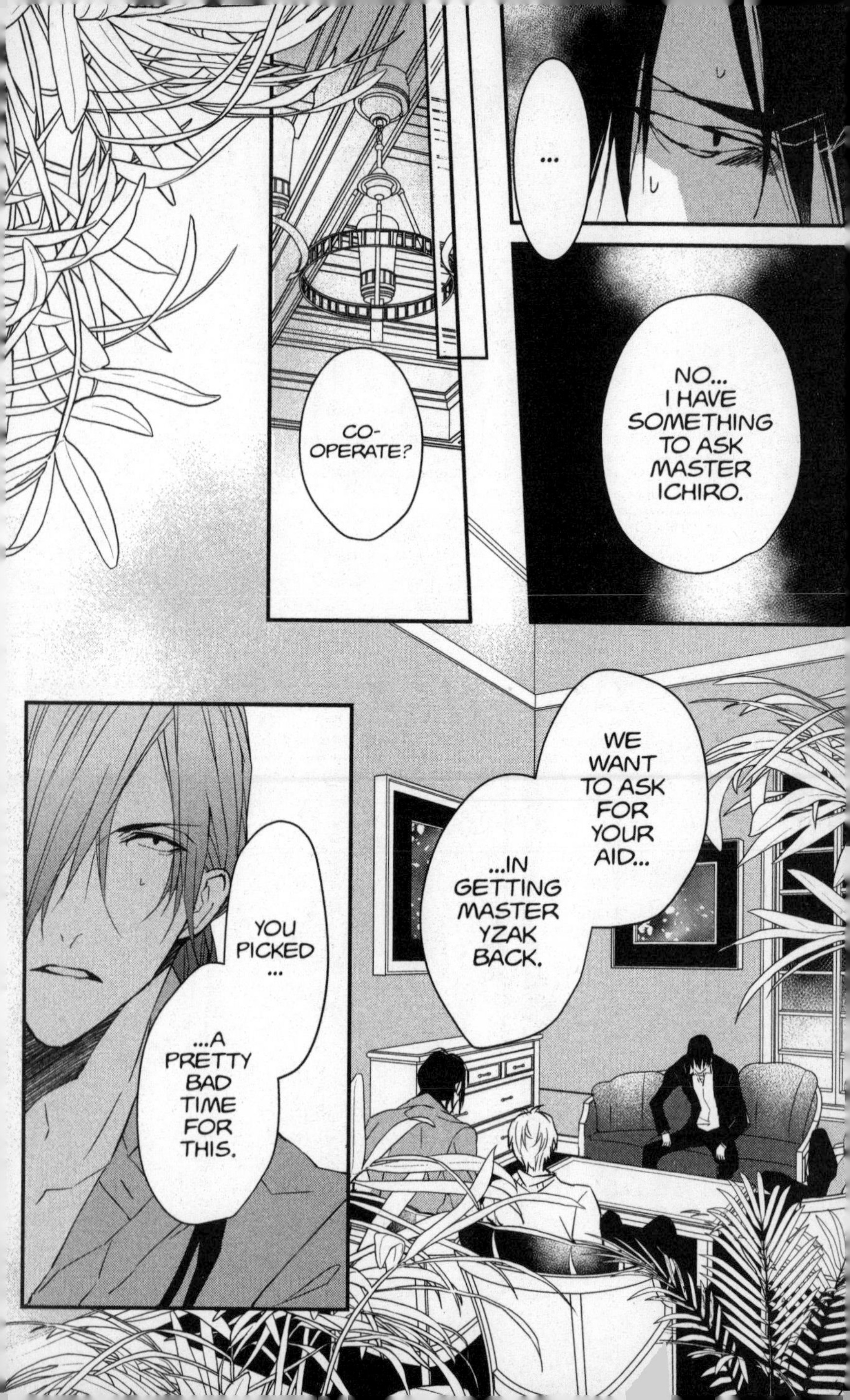
...
NO... I HAVE SOMETHING TO ASK MASTER ICHIRO.
CO-OPERATE?
WE WANT TO ASK FOR YOUR AID...
...IN GETTING MASTER YZAK BACK.
YOU PICKED ...
...A PRETTY BAD TIME FOR THIS.

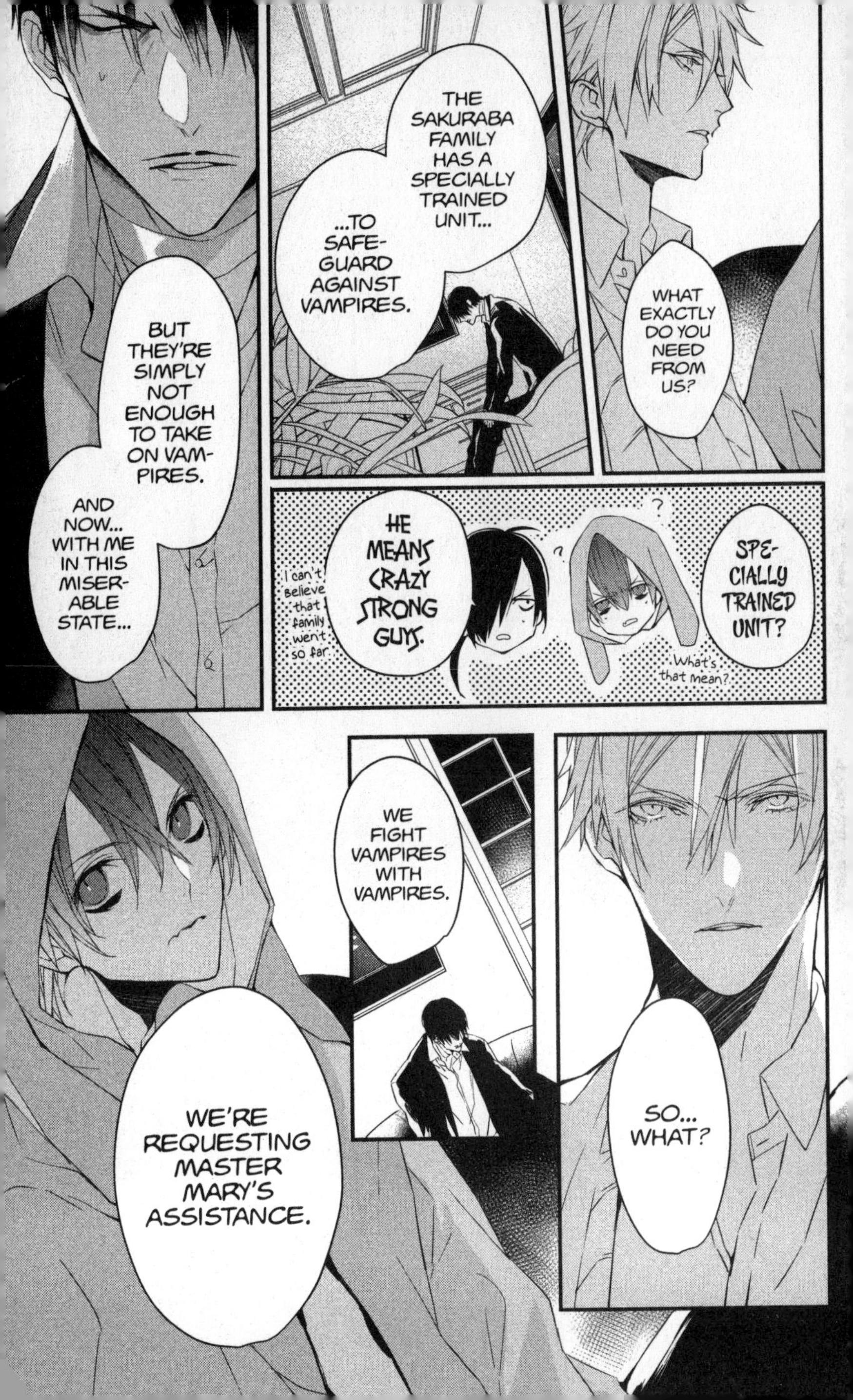
WHAT EXACTLY DO YOU NEED FROM US?
THE SAKURABA FAMILY HAS A SPECIALLY TRAINED UNIT...
...TO SAFE-GUARD AGAINST VAMPIRES.
SPE-CIALLY TRAINED UNIT?
What's that mean?
HE MEANS CRAZY STRONG GUYS.
I can't believe that family went so far.
BUT THEY'RE SIMPLY NOT ENOUGH TO TAKE ON VAM-PIRES.
AND NOW... WITH ME IN THIS MISER-ABLE STATE...
SO... WHAT?
WE FIGHT VAMPIRES WITH VAMPIRES.
WE'RE REQUESTING MASTER MARY'S ASSISTANCE.

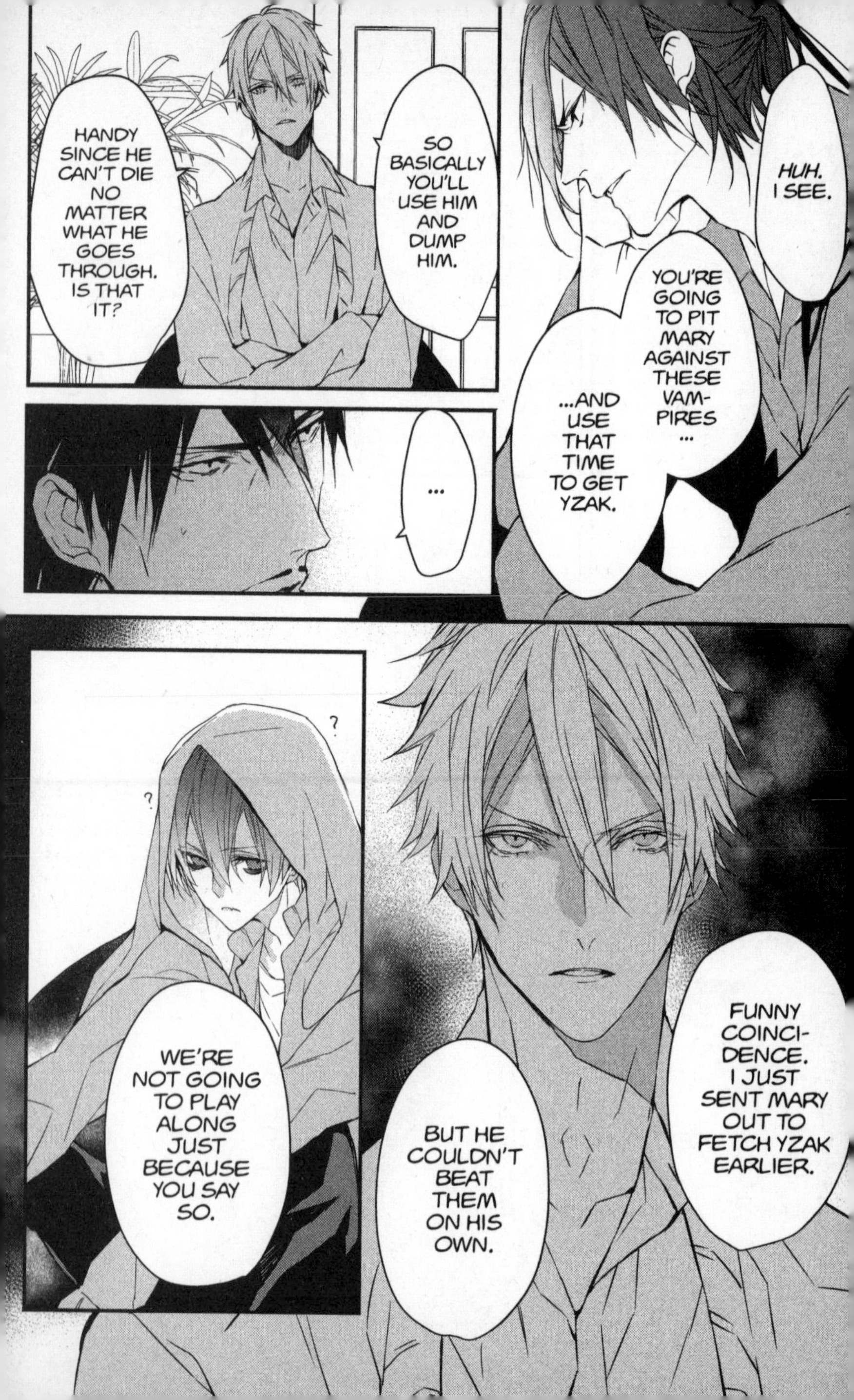
HUH. I SEE.
YOU'RE GOING TO PIT MARY AGAINST THESE VAMPIRES...
...AND USE THAT TIME TO GET YZAK.
SO BASICALLY YOU'LL USE HIM AND DUMP HIM.
HANDY SINCE HE CAN'T DIE NO MATTER WHAT HE GOES THROUGH. IS THAT IT?
...
FUNNY COINCIDENCE. I JUST SENT MARY OUT TO FETCH YZAK EARLIER.
BUT HE COULDN'T BEAT THEM ON HIS OWN.
?
?
WE'RE NOT GOING TO PLAY ALONG JUST BECAUSE YOU SAY SO.

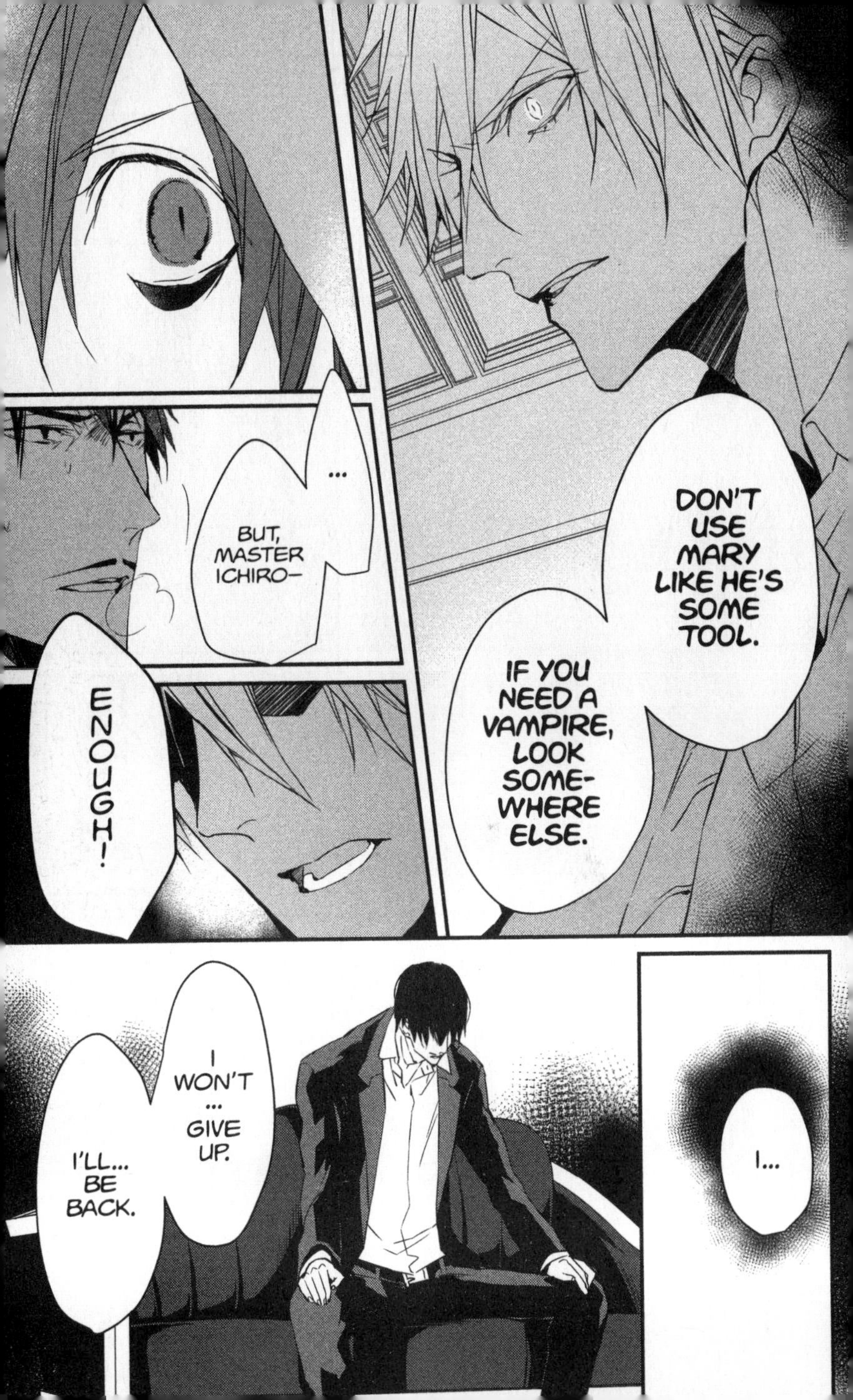
DON'T USE MARY LIKE HE'S SOME TOOL.
IF YOU NEED A VAMPIRE, LOOK SOME-WHERE ELSE.
...
BUT, MASTER ICHIRO—
ENOUGH!
I...
I WON'T ... GIVE UP.
I'LL... BE BACK.

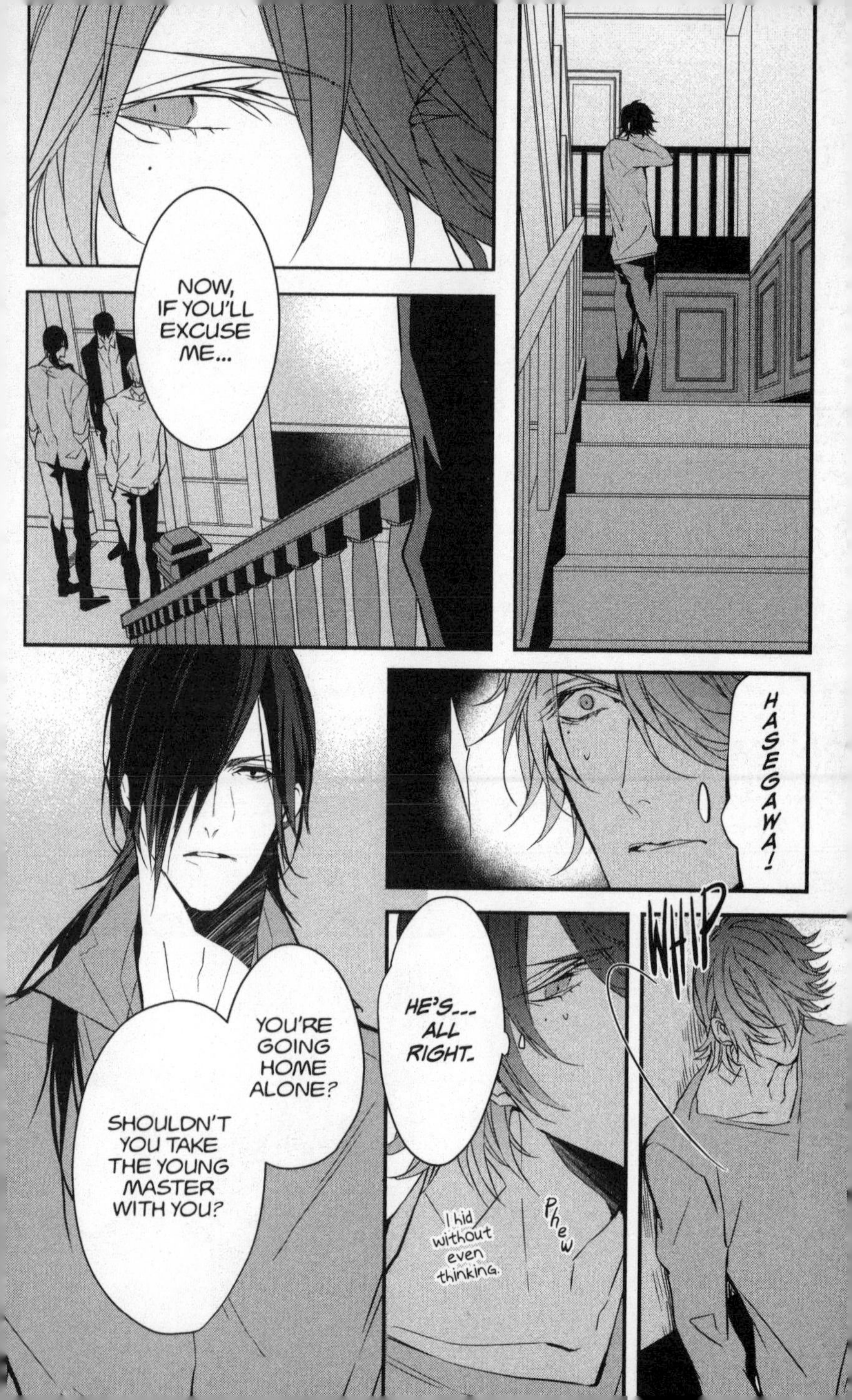
NOW, IF YOU'LL EXCUSE ME...
HASEGAWA!
WHIP
HE'S... ALL RIGHT.
Phew
I hid without even thinking.
YOU'RE GOING HOME ALONE?
SHOULDN'T YOU TAKE THE YOUNG MASTER WITH YOU?

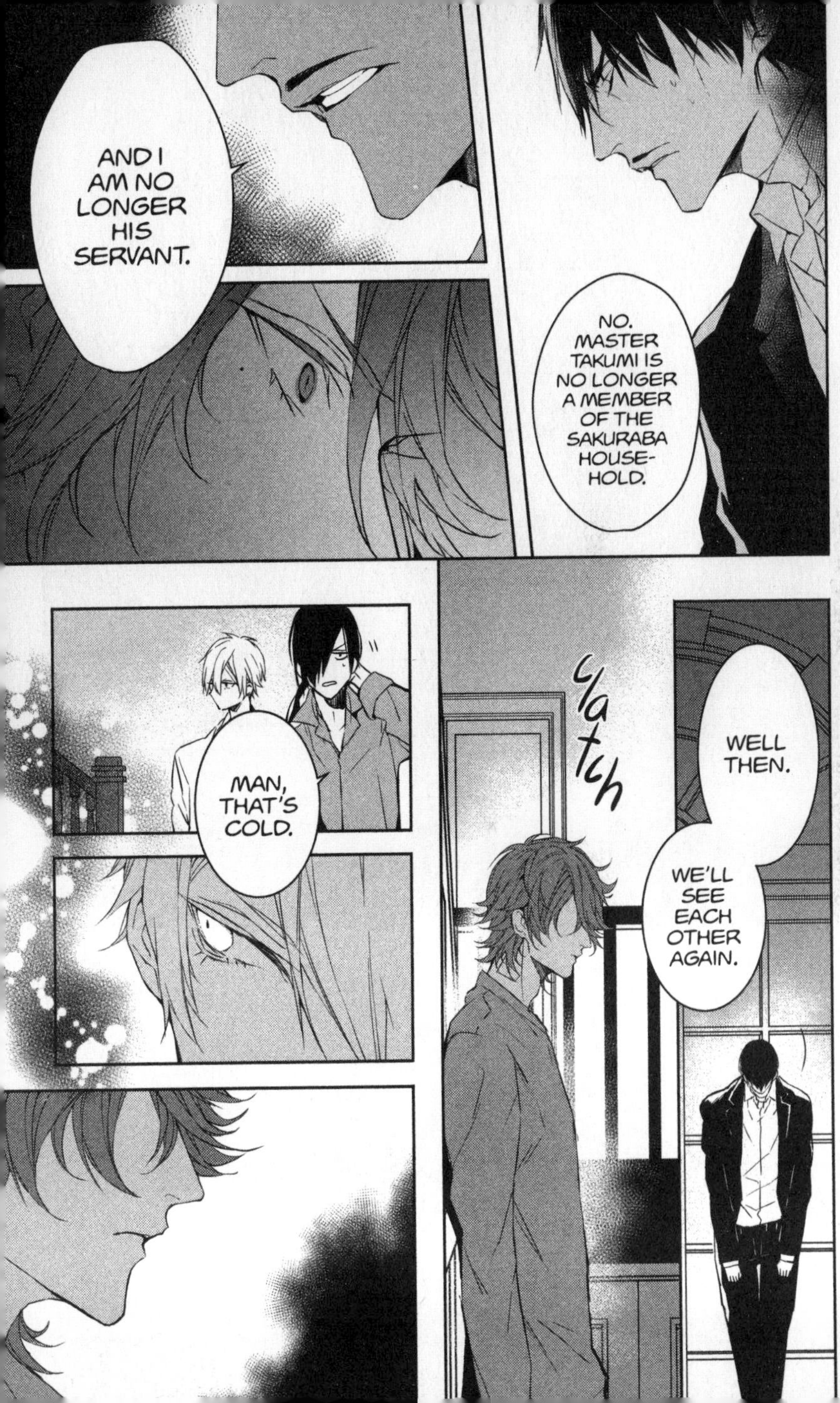
NO. MASTER TAKUMI IS NO LONGER A MEMBER OF THE SAKURABA HOUSE-HOLD.
AND I AM NO LONGER HIS SERVANT.
WELL THEN.
WE'LL SEE EACH OTHER AGAIN.
clatch
MAN, THAT'S COLD.

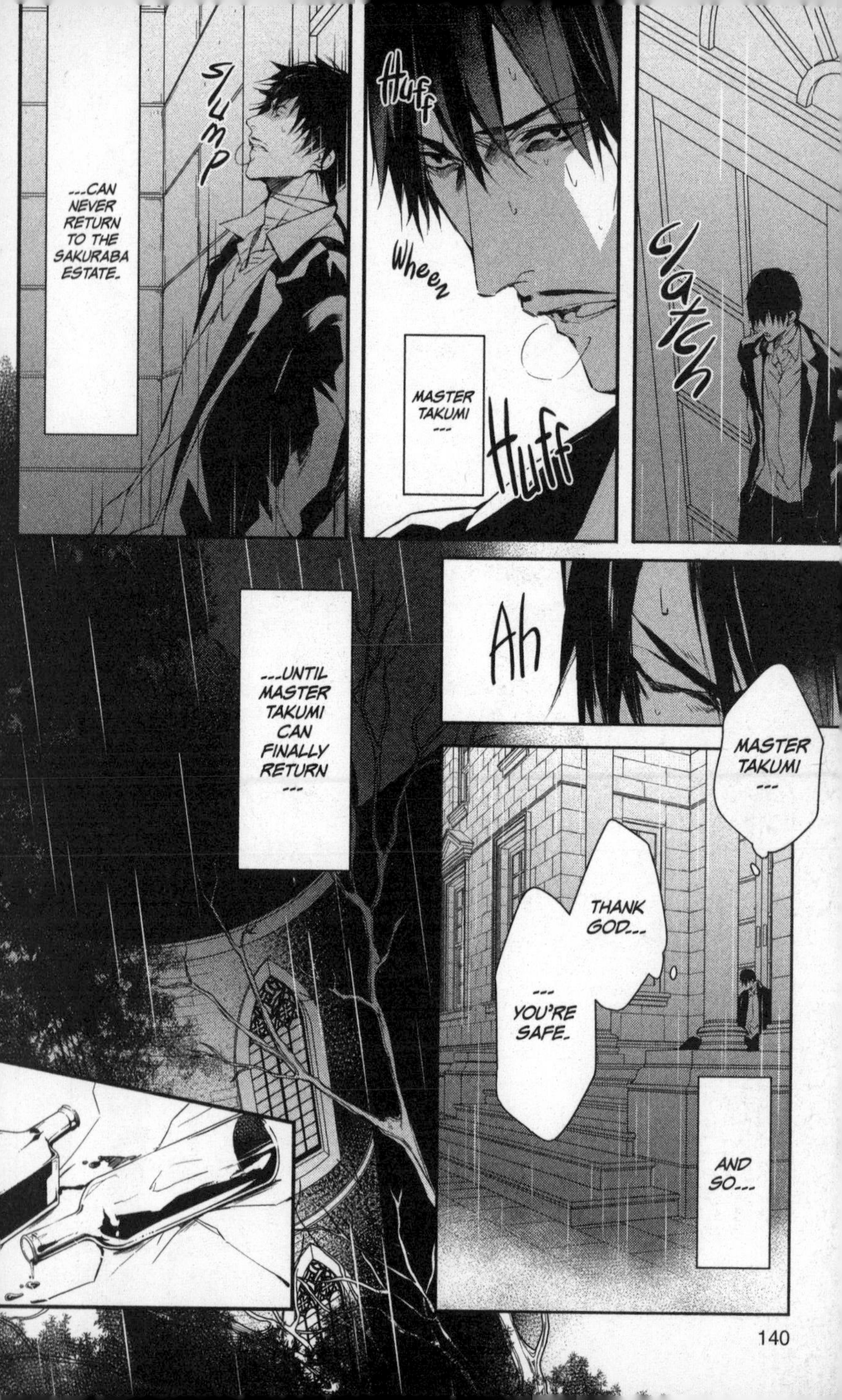
Clatch
Huff
Wheen
MASTER TAKUMI ---
Huff
SLUMP
---CAN NEVER RETURN TO THE SAKURABA ESTATE.
Ah
MASTER TAKUMI ---
THANK GOD...
--- YOU'RE SAFE.
AND SO...
---UNTIL MASTER TAKUMI CAN FINALLY RETURN ---

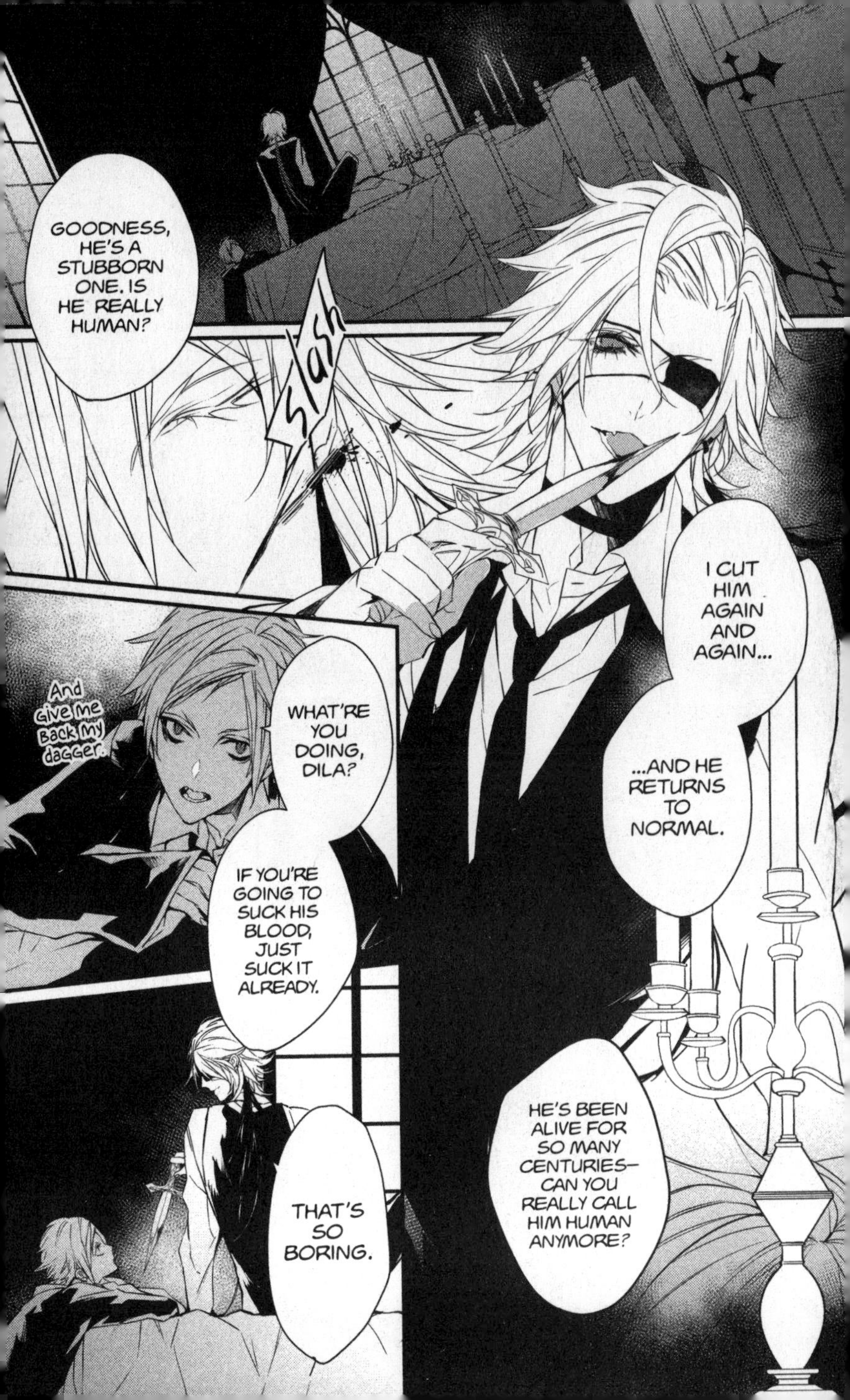
GOODNESS, HE'S A STUBBORN ONE. IS HE REALLY HUMAN?
slash
I CUT HIM AGAIN AND AGAIN...
...AND HE RETURNS TO NORMAL.
HE'S BEEN ALIVE FOR SO MANY CENTURIES— CAN YOU REALLY CALL HIM HUMAN ANYMORE?
WHAT'RE YOU DOING, DILA?
IF YOU'RE GOING TO SUCK HIS BLOOD, JUST SUCK IT ALREADY.
And Give me Back my dagger.
THAT'S SO BORING.

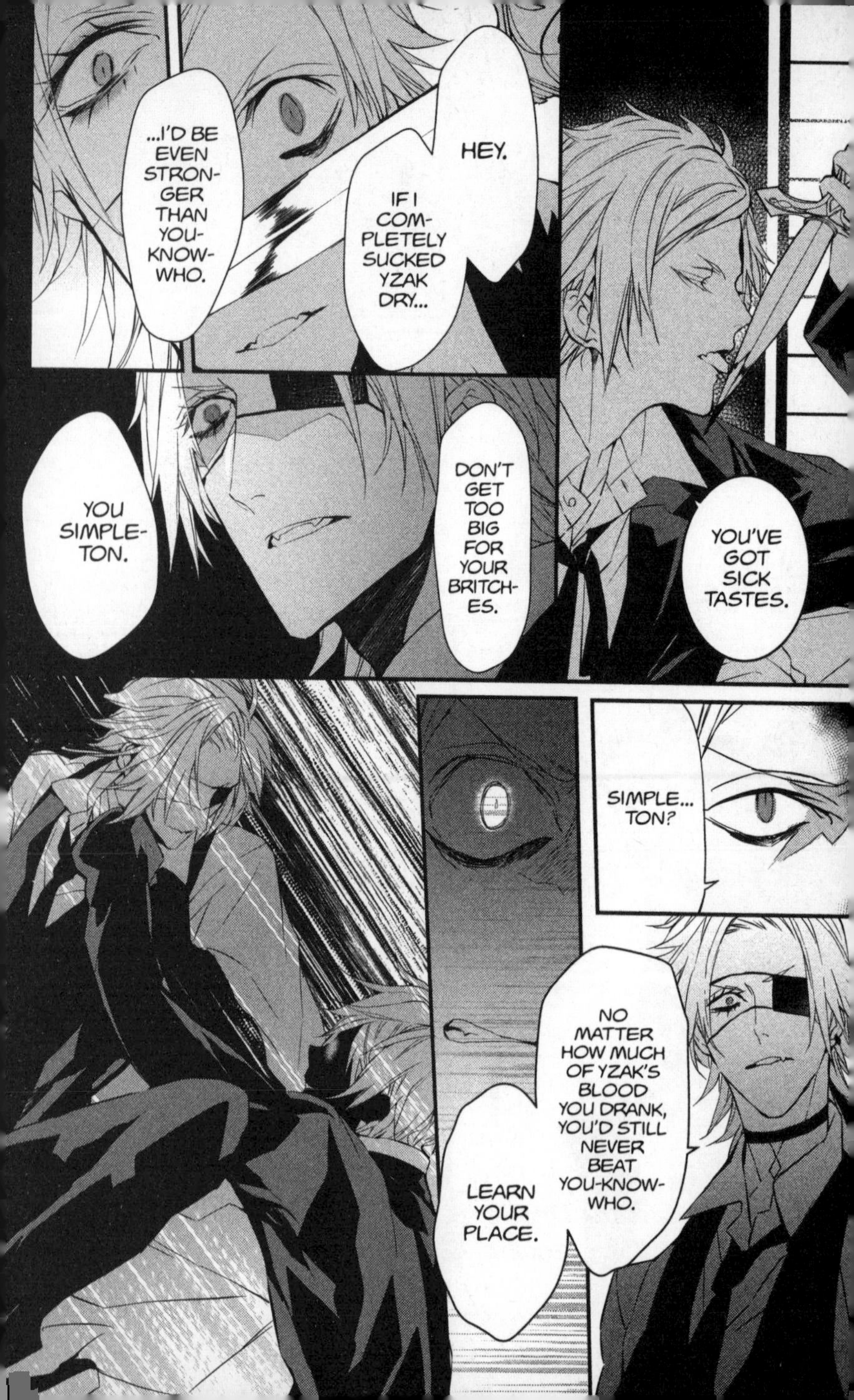
YOU'VE GOT SICK TASTES.
HEY.
IF I COMPLETELY SUCKED YZAK DRY...
...I'D BE EVEN STRONGER THAN YOU-KNOW-WHO.
DON'T GET TOO BIG FOR YOUR BRITCHES.
YOU SIMPLETON.
SIMPLE... TON?
NO MATTER HOW MUCH OF YZAK'S BLOOD YOU DRANK, YOU'D STILL NEVER BEAT YOU-KNOW-WHO.
LEARN YOUR PLACE.

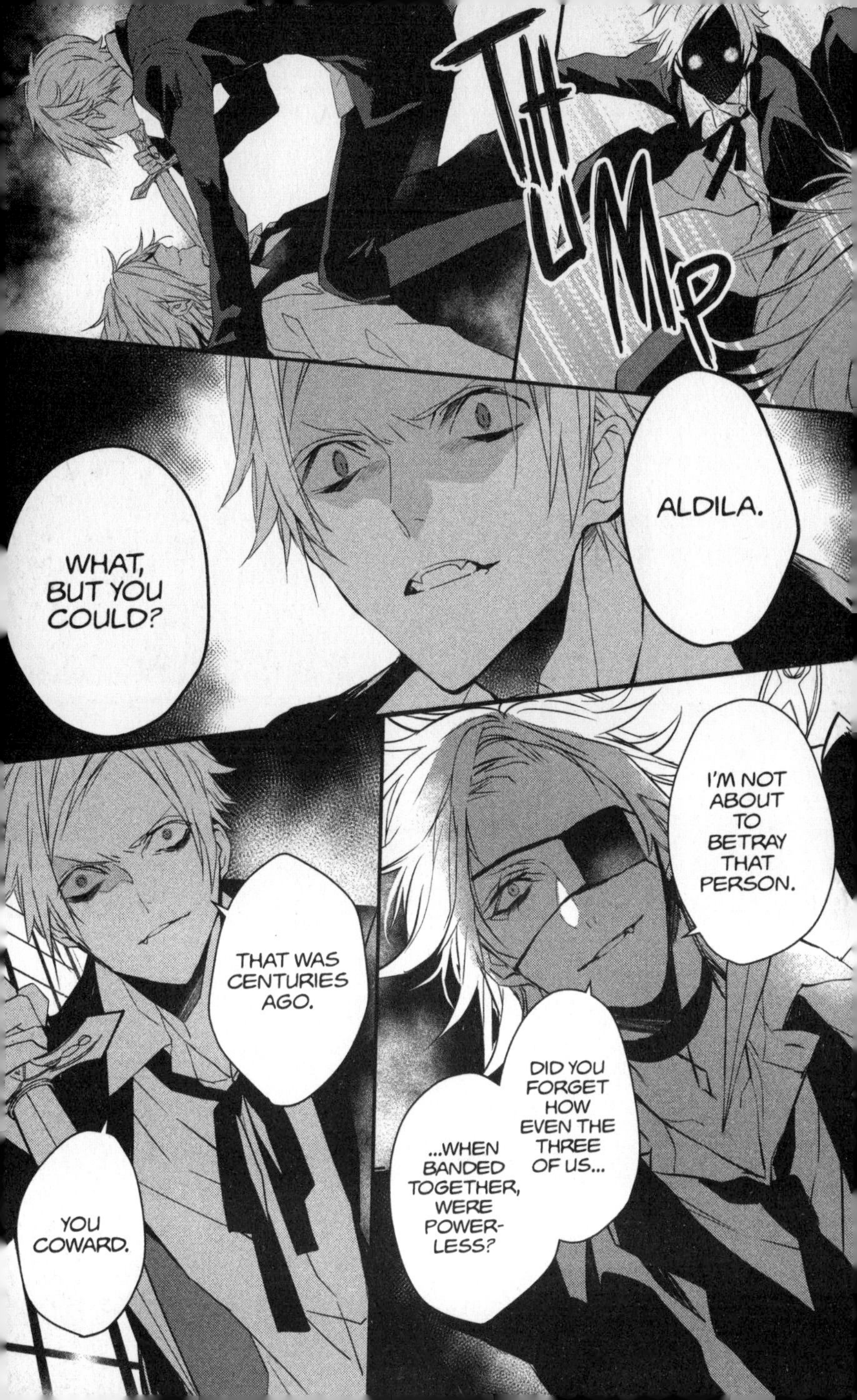
THUMP
ALDILA.
WHAT, BUT YOU COULD?
I'M NOT ABOUT TO BETRAY THAT PERSON.
DID YOU FORGET HOW EVEN THE THREE OF US...
...WHEN BANDED TOGETHER, WERE POWERLESS?
THAT WAS CENTURIES AGO.
YOU COWARD.

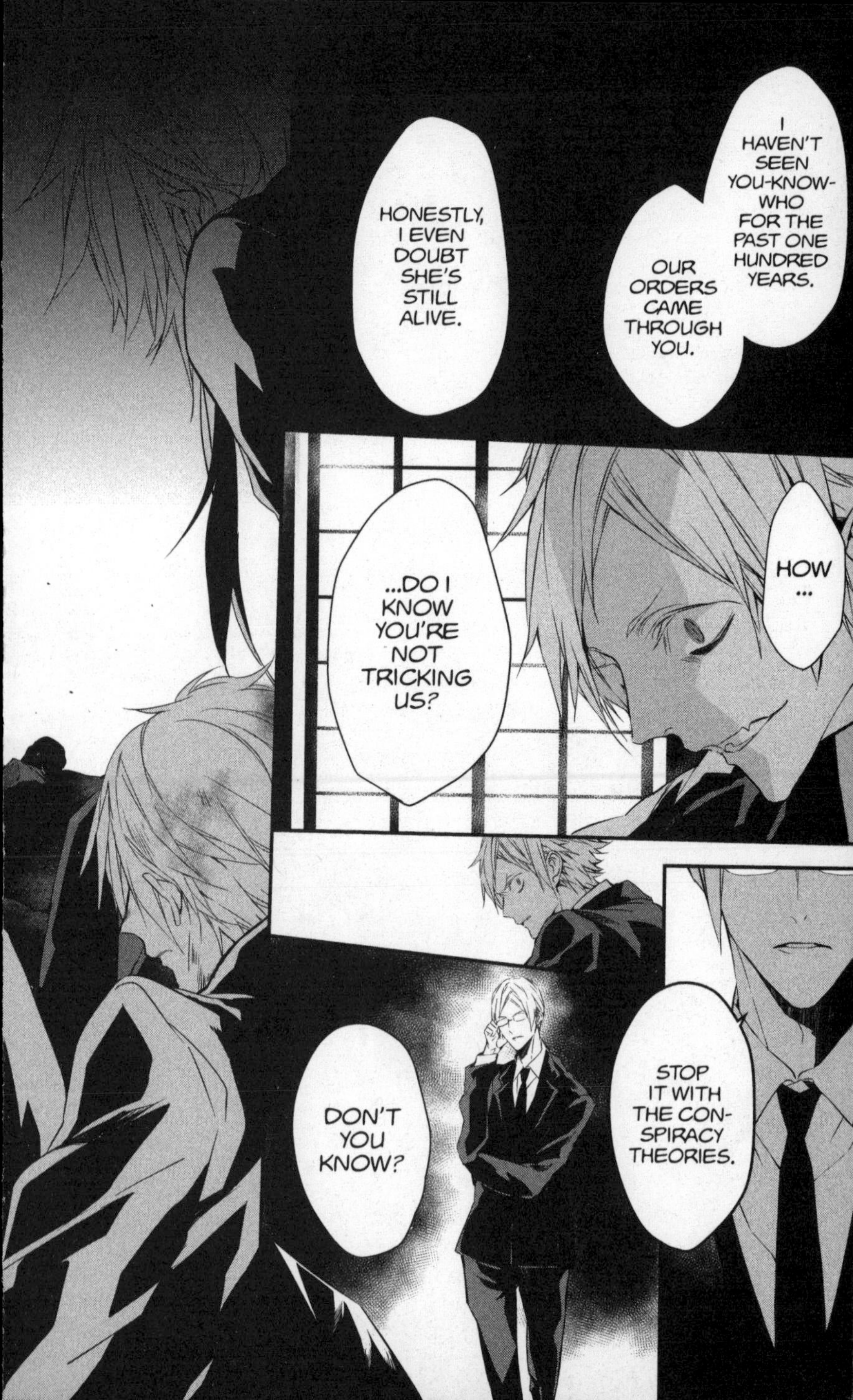
I HAVEN'T SEEN YOU-KNOW-WHO FOR THE PAST ONE HUNDRED YEARS.
OUR ORDERS CAME THROUGH YOU.
HONESTLY, I EVEN DOUBT SHE'S STILL ALIVE.
HOW...
...DO I KNOW YOU'RE NOT TRICKING US?
STOP IT WITH THE CON-SPIRACY THEORIES.
DON'T YOU KNOW?

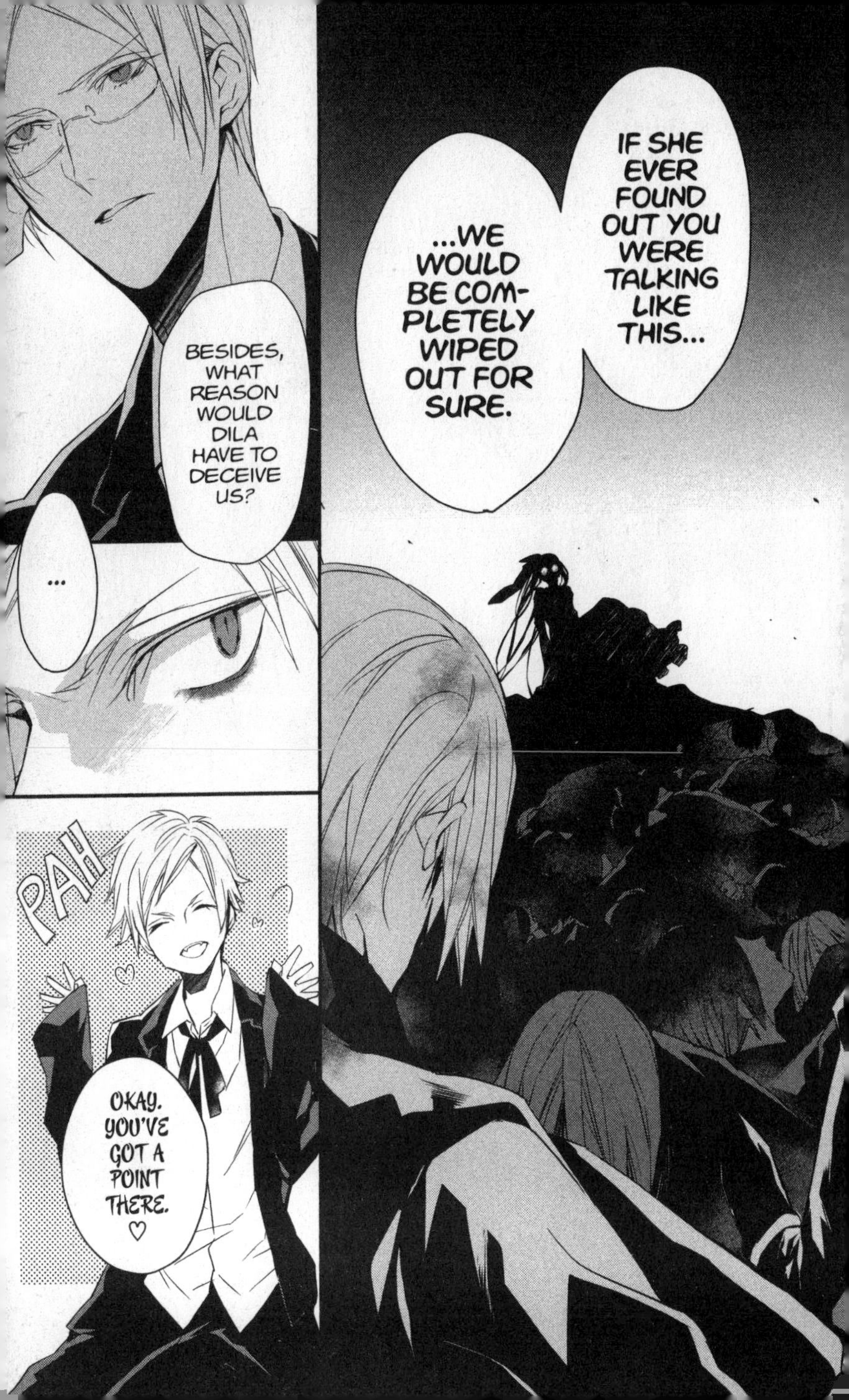
IF SHE EVER FOUND OUT YOU WERE TALKING LIKE THIS...
...WE WOULD BE COM-PLETELY WIPED OUT FOR SURE.
BESIDES, WHAT REASON WOULD DILA HAVE TO DECEIVE US?
...
PAH
OKAY. YOU'VE GOT A POINT THERE. ♡

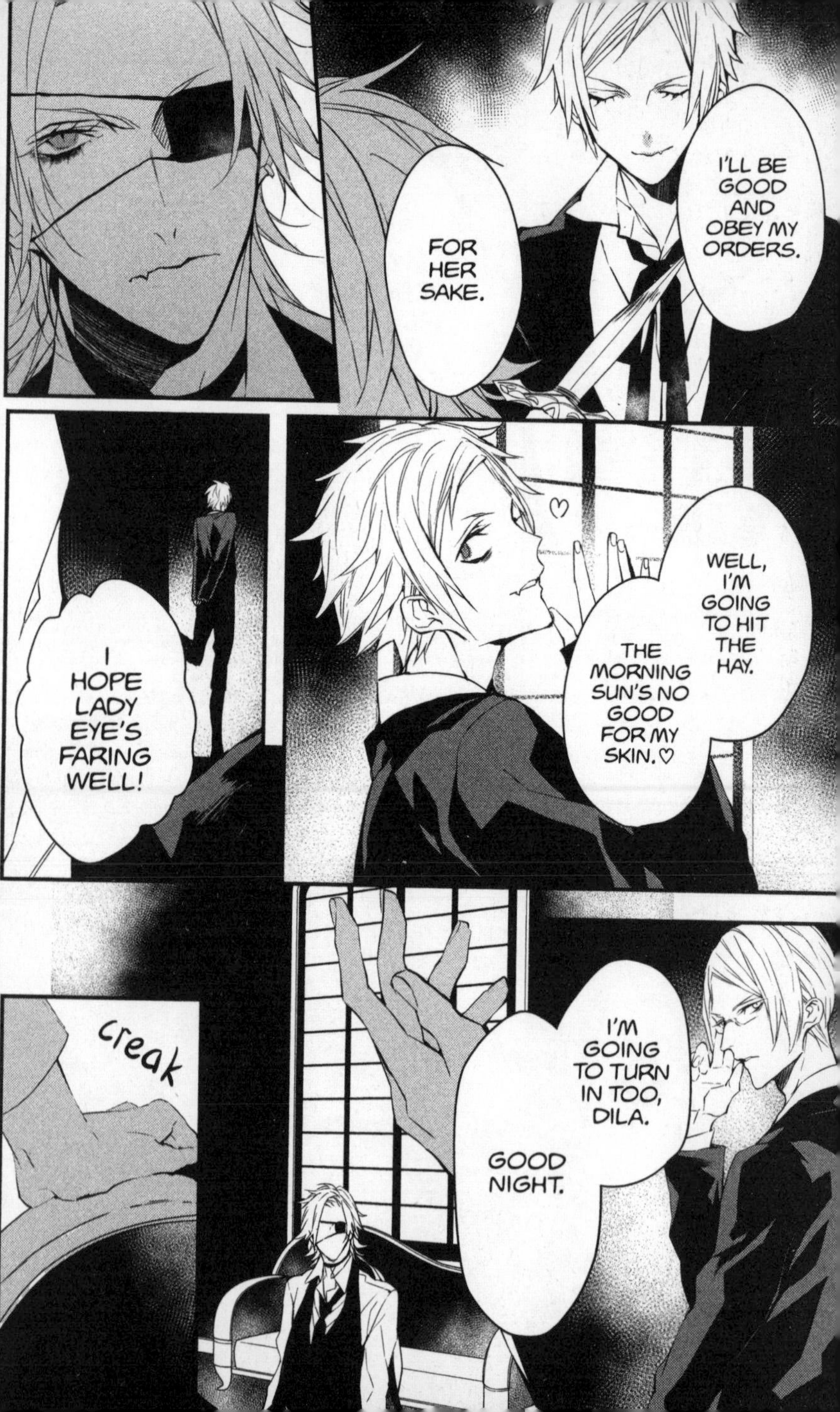
I'LL BE GOOD AND OBEY MY ORDERS.
FOR HER SAKE.
WELL, I'M GOING TO HIT THE HAY.
THE MORNING SUN'S NO GOOD FOR MY SKIN.♡
I HOPE LADY EYE'S FARING WELL!
I'M GOING TO TURN IN TOO, DILA.
GOOD NIGHT.
creak

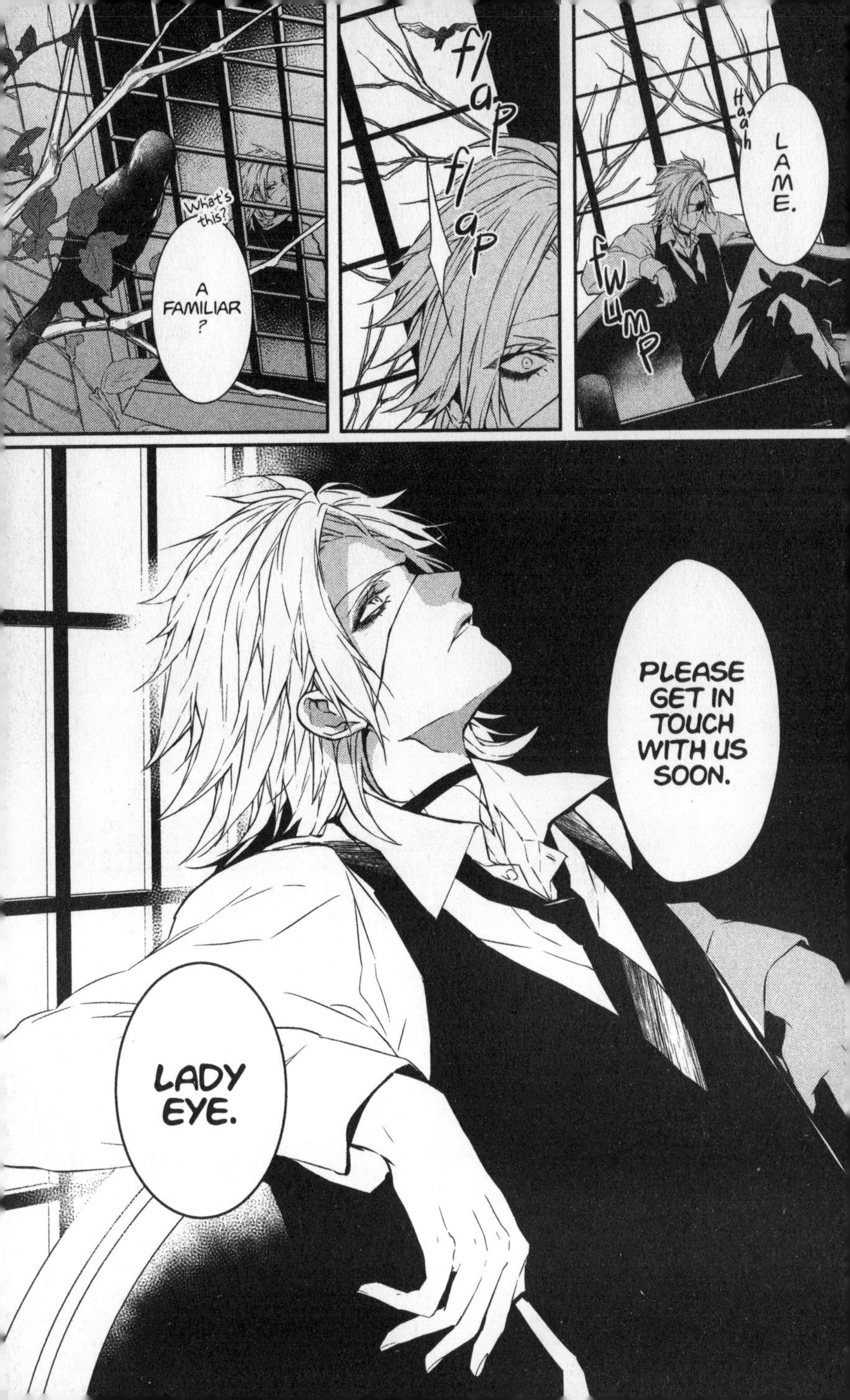
Haaah
LAME.
fwump
flap flap
What's this?
A FAMILIAR?
PLEASE GET IN TOUCH WITH US SOON.
LADY EYE.

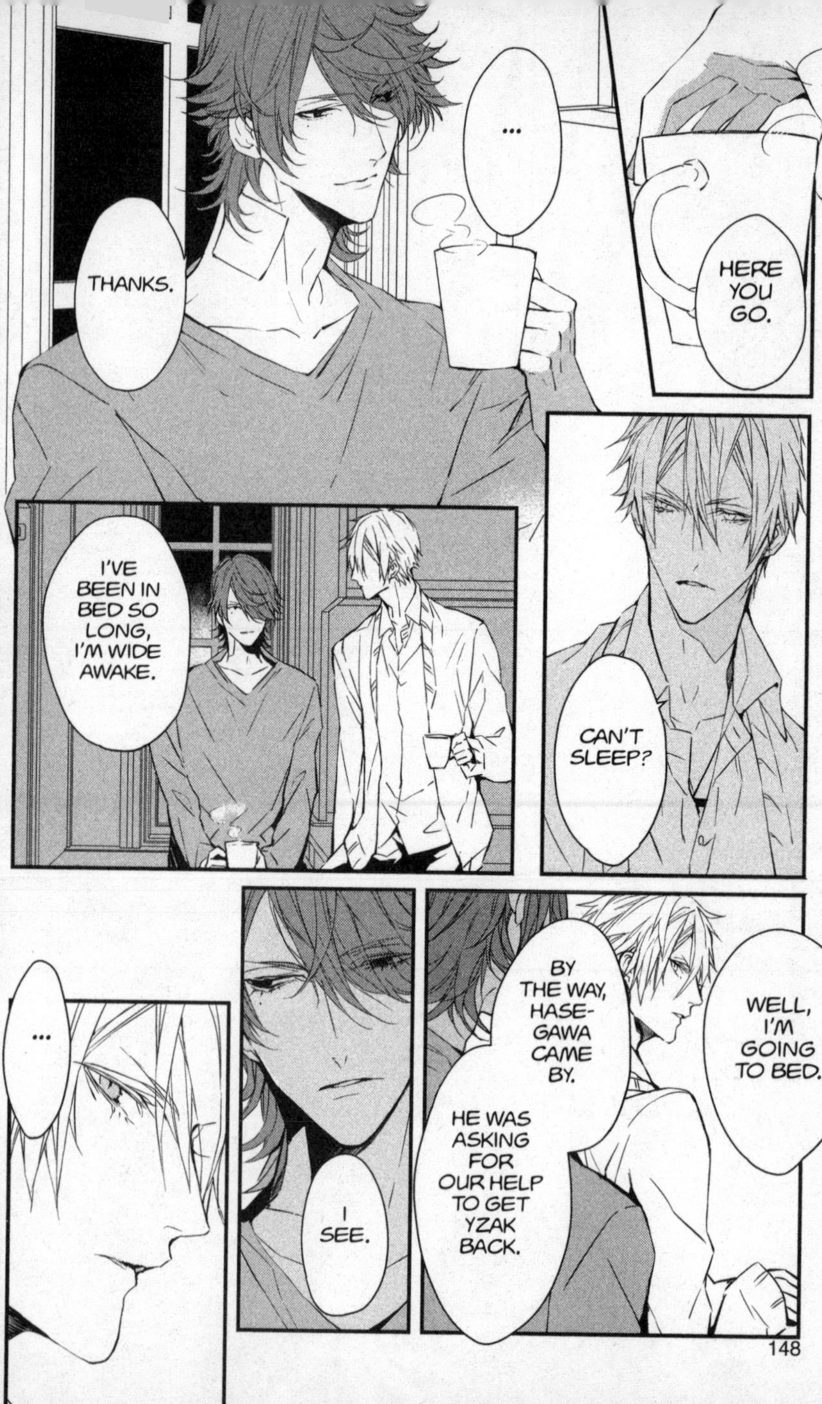
HERE YOU GO.
...
THANKS.
CAN'T SLEEP?
I'VE BEEN IN BED SO LONG, I'M WIDE AWAKE.
WELL, I'M GOING TO BED.
BY THE WAY, HASE-GAWA CAME BY.
HE WAS ASKING FOR OUR HELP TO GET YZAK BACK.
I SEE.
...

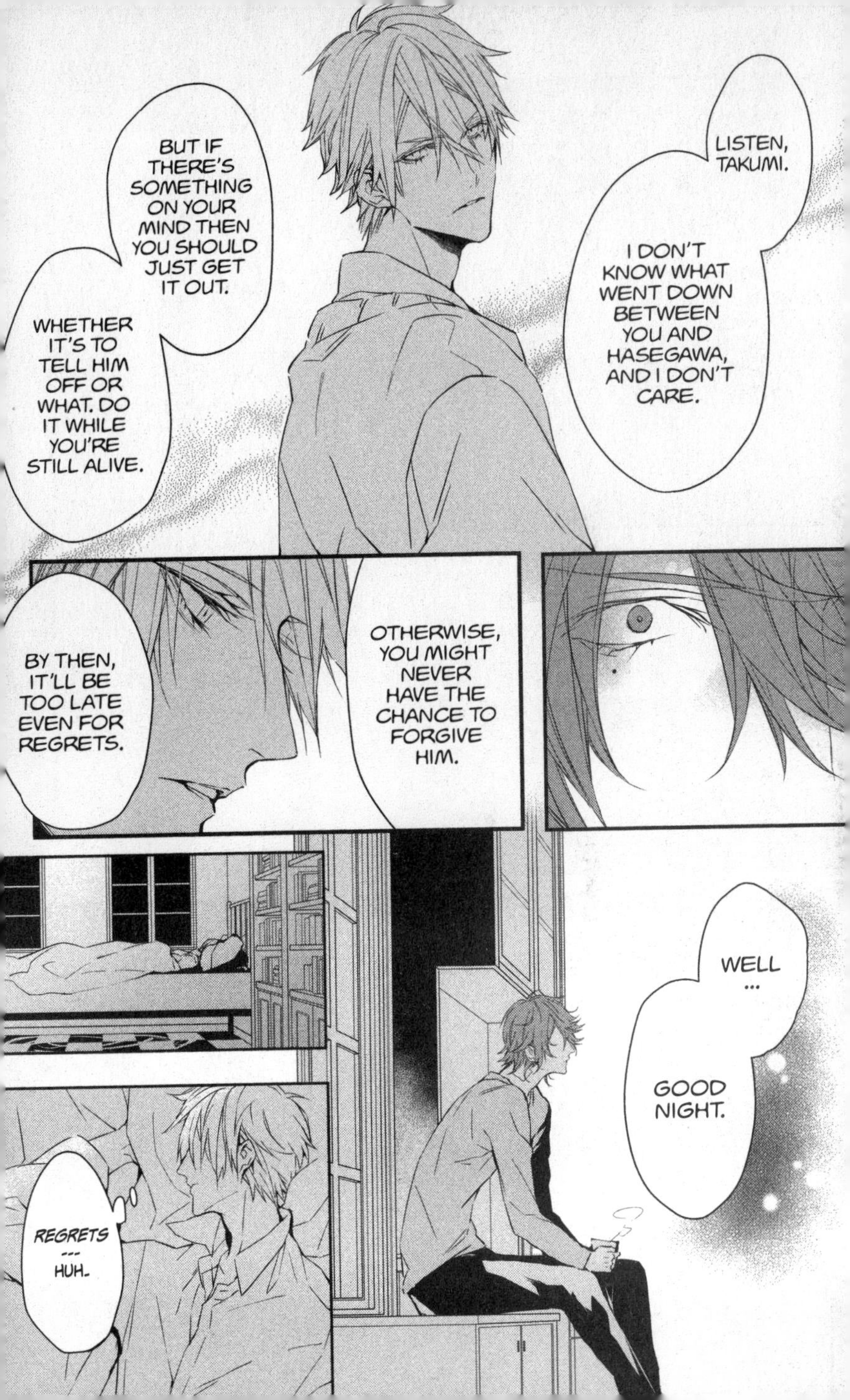
LISTEN, TAKUMI.
I DON'T KNOW WHAT WENT DOWN BETWEEN YOU AND HASEGAWA, AND I DON'T CARE.
BUT IF THERE'S SOMETHING ON YOUR MIND THEN YOU SHOULD JUST GET IT OUT.
WHETHER IT'S TO TELL HIM OFF OR WHAT. DO IT WHILE YOU'RE STILL ALIVE.
OTHERWISE, YOU MIGHT NEVER HAVE THE CHANCE TO FORGIVE HIM.
BY THEN, IT'LL BE TOO LATE EVEN FOR REGRETS.
WELL ...
GOOD NIGHT.
REGRETS --- HUH.

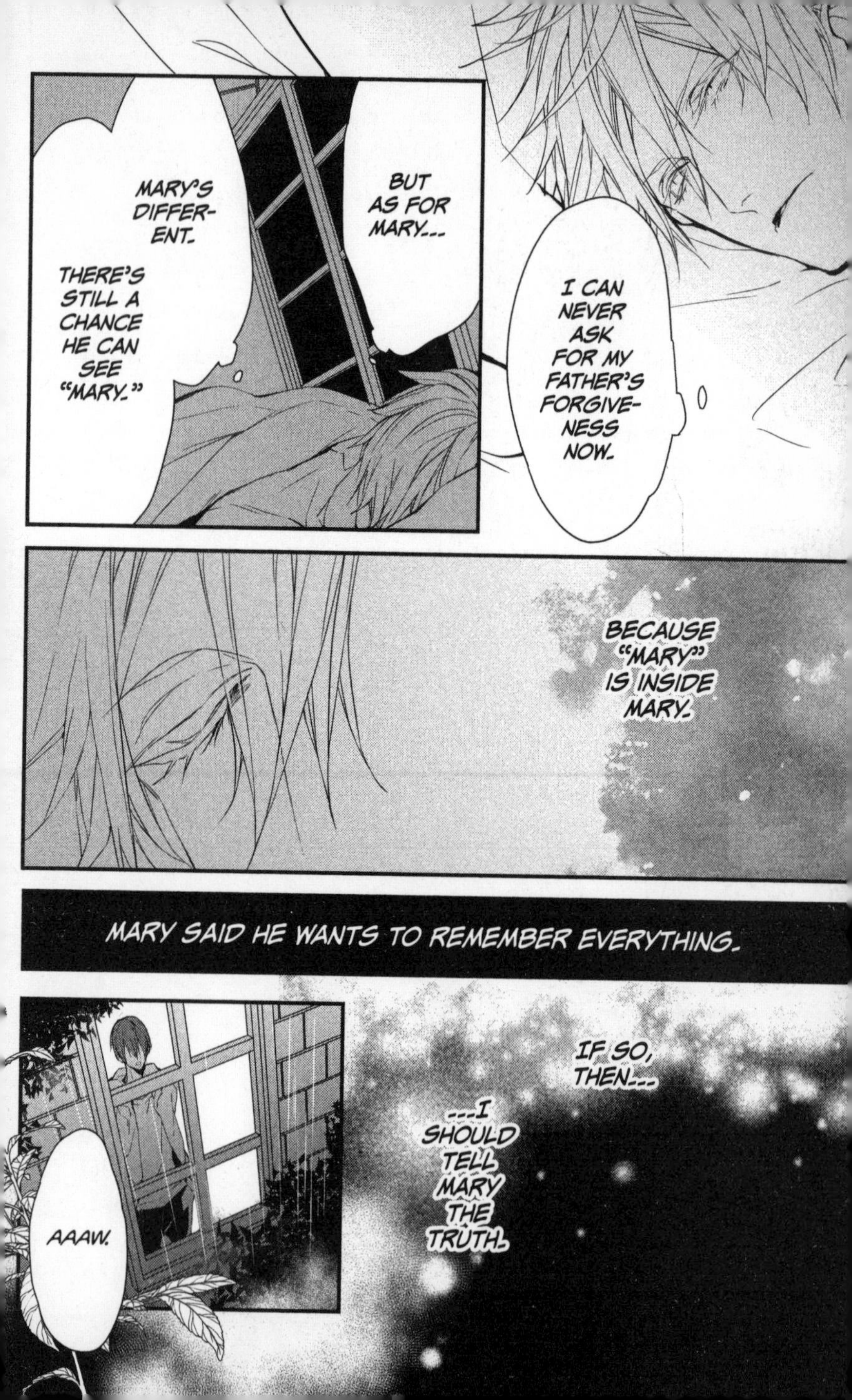
I CAN NEVER ASK FOR MY FATHER'S FORGIVENESS NOW.
BUT AS FOR MARY...
MARY'S DIFFERENT.
THERE'S STILL A CHANCE HE CAN SEE "MARY."
BECAUSE "MARY" IS INSIDE MARY.
MARY SAID HE WANTS TO REMEMBER EVERYTHING.
IF SO, THEN...
...I SHOULD TELL MARY THE TRUTH.
AAAW.

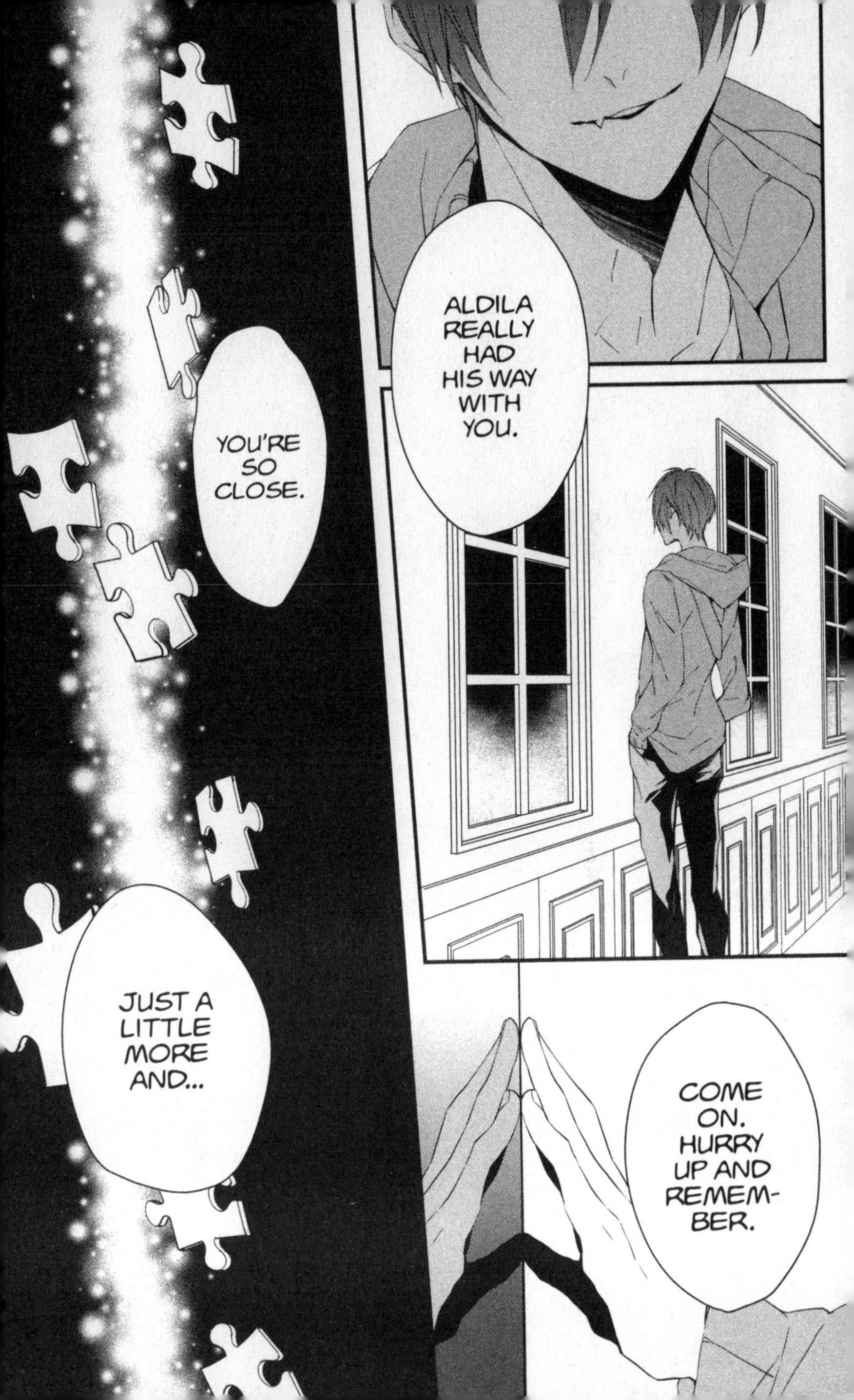
ALDILA REALLY HAD HIS WAY WITH YOU.
COME ON. HURRY UP AND REMEM-BER.
YOU'RE SO CLOSE.
JUST A LITTLE MORE AND...

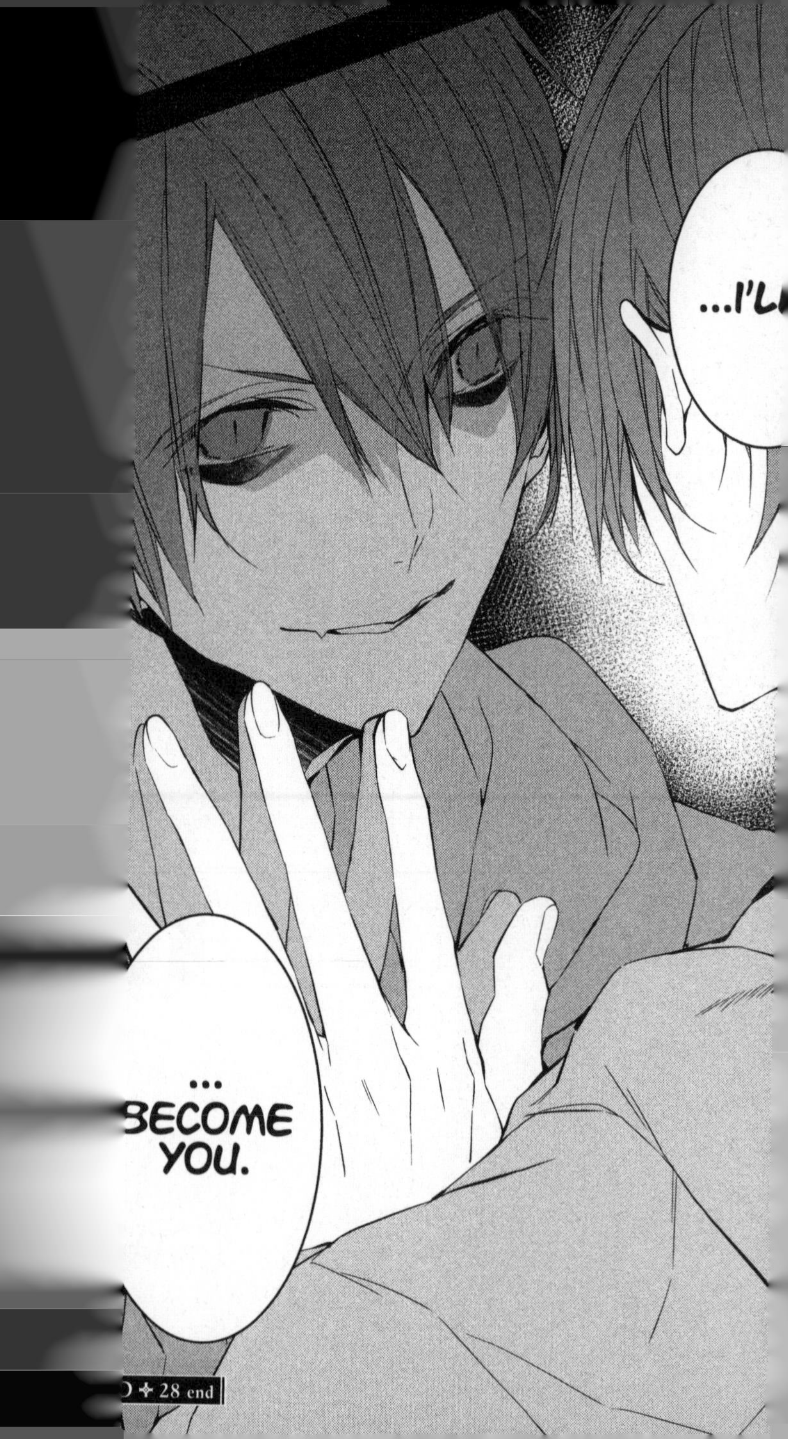
...I'L
...
BECOME
YOU.

✧ 28 end

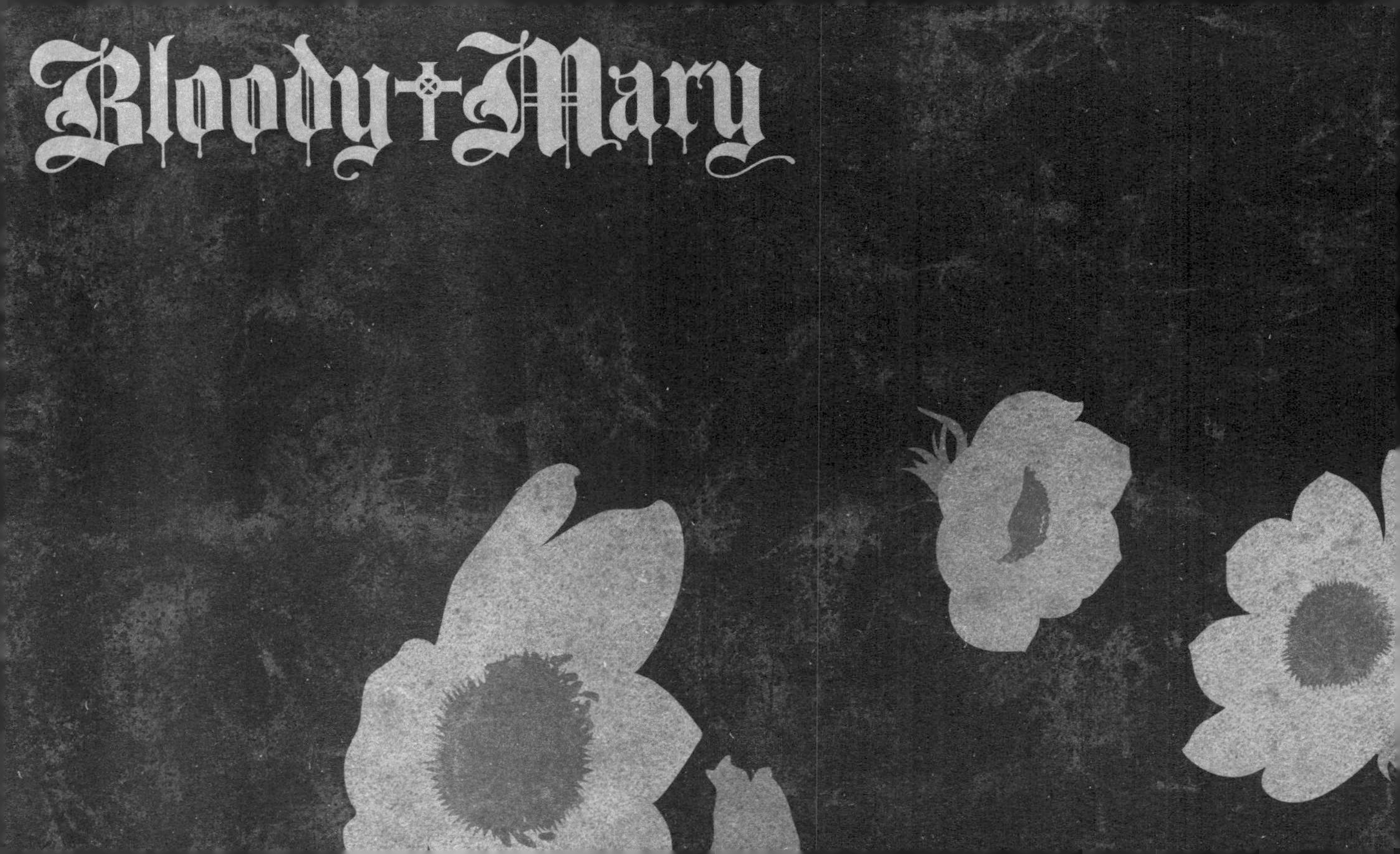
Bloody+Mary

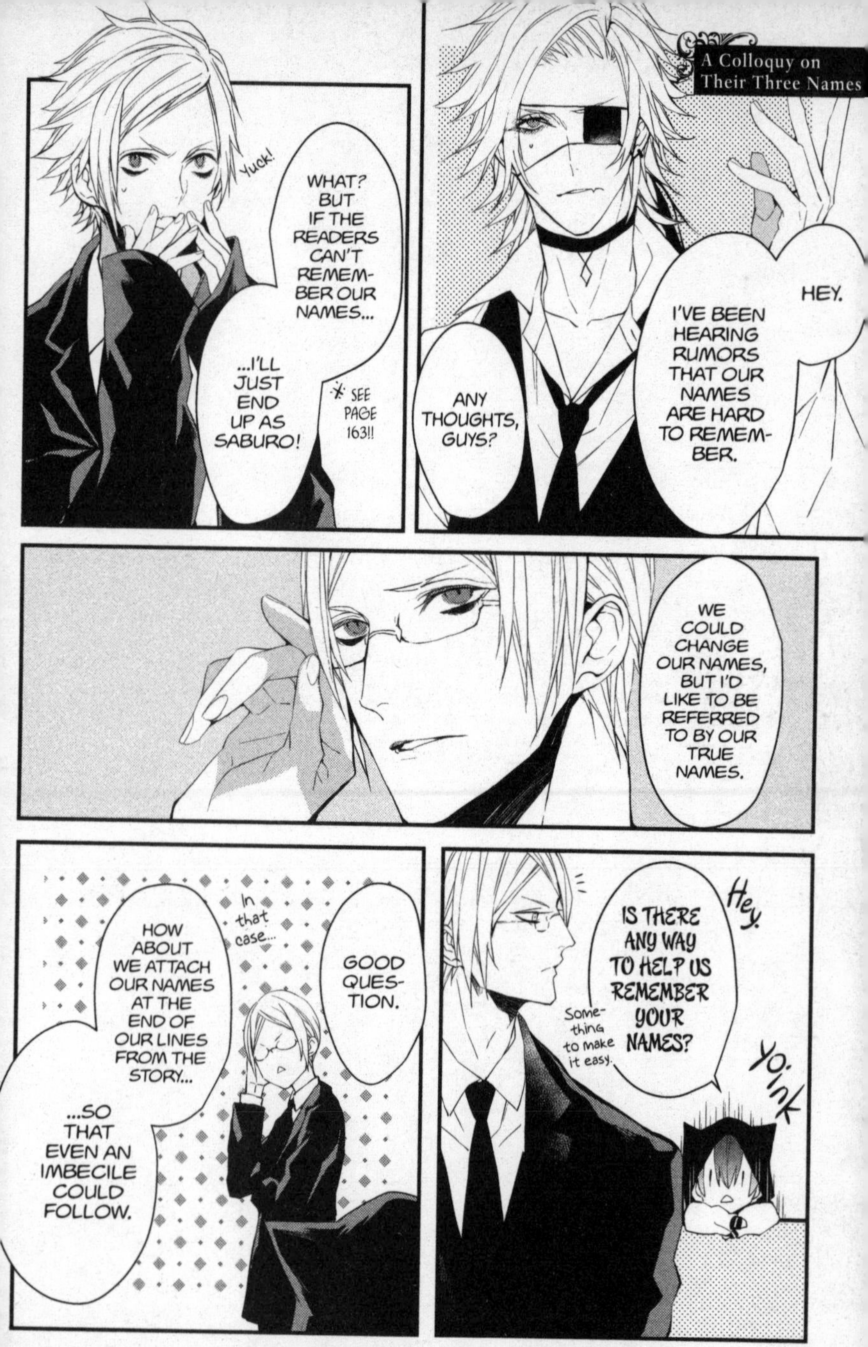
HEY.
I'VE BEEN HEARING RUMORS THAT OUR NAMES ARE HARD TO REMEMBER.
ANY THOUGHTS, GUYS?
Yuck!
WHAT? BUT IF THE READERS CAN'T REMEMBER OUR NAMES...
...I'LL JUST END UP AS SABURO!
※ SEE PAGE 163!!
WE COULD CHANGE OUR NAMES, BUT I'D LIKE TO BE REFERRED TO BY OUR TRUE NAMES.
Hey.
IS THERE ANY WAY TO HELP US REMEMBER YOUR NAMES?
Something to make it easy.
Yoink
GOOD QUESTION.
In that case...
HOW ABOUT WE ATTACH OUR NAMES AT THE END OF OUR LINES FROM THE STORY...
...SO THAT EVEN AN IMBECILE COULD FOLLOW.

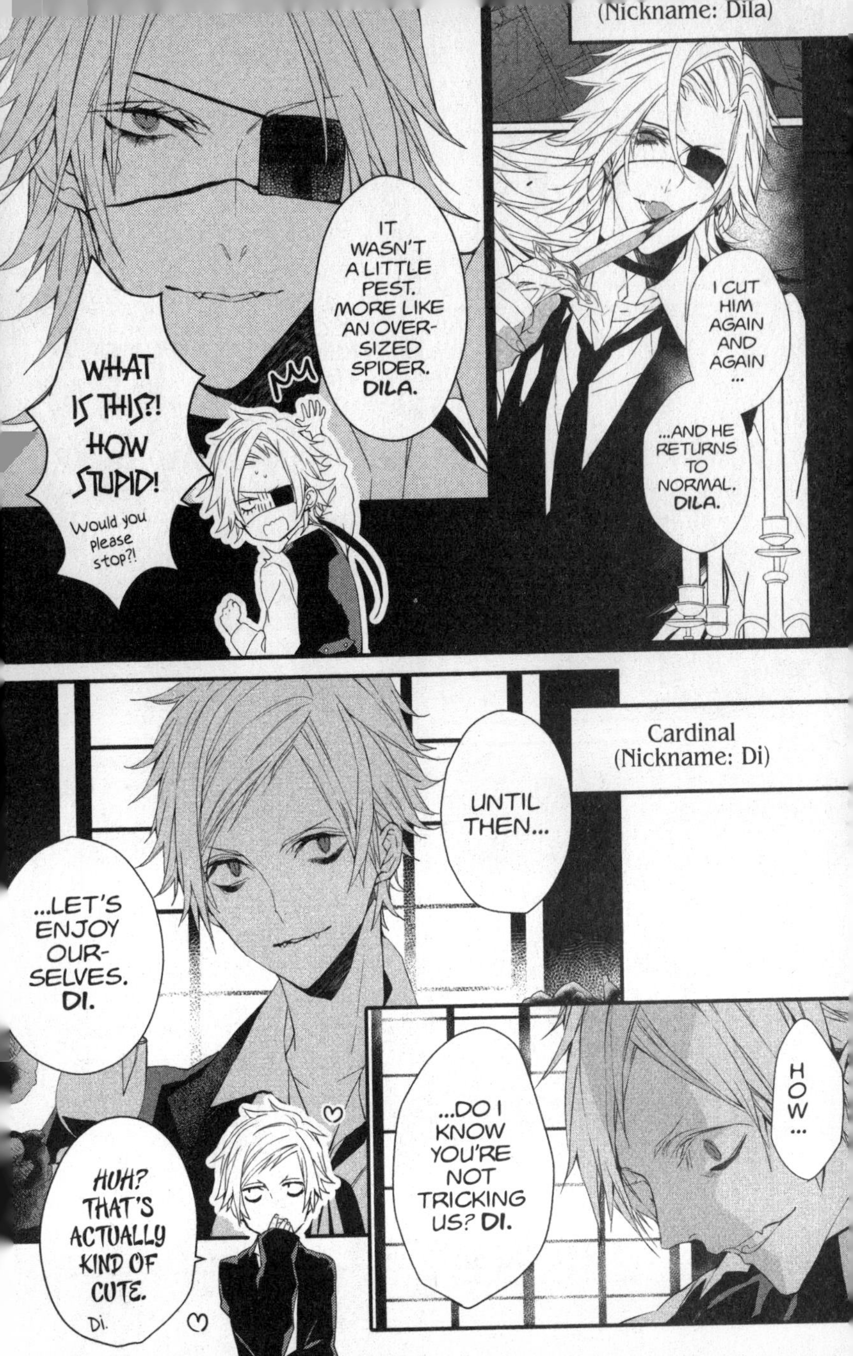
(Nickname: Dila)
I CUT HIM AGAIN AND AGAIN...
...AND HE RETURNS TO NORMAL. DILA.
IT WASN'T A LITTLE PEST. MORE LIKE AN OVER-SIZED SPIDER. DILA.
WHAT IS THIS?! HOW STUPID!
Would you please stop?!
Cardinal (Nickname: Di)
UNTIL THEN...
...LET'S ENJOY OUR-SELVES. DI.
HOW...
...DO I KNOW YOU'RE NOT TRICKING US? DI.
HUH? THAT'S ACTUALLY KIND OF CUTE.
Di.

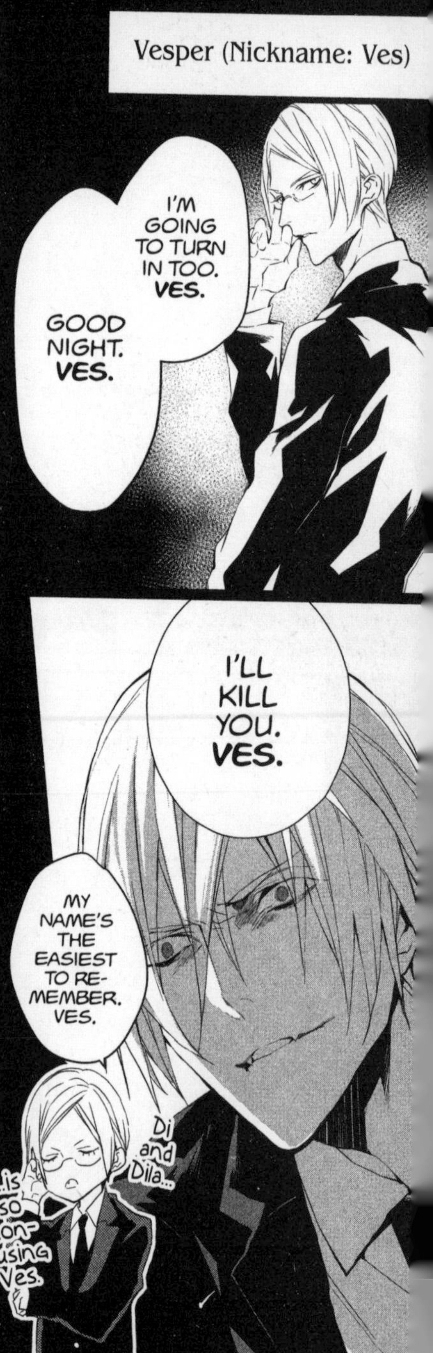
Vesper (Nickname: Ves)
I'M GOING TO TURN IN TOO. VES.
GOOD NIGHT. VES.
I'LL KILL YOU. VES.
MY NAME'S THE EASIEST TO RE-MEMBER. VES.
Di and Dila...
...is so con-fusing Ves.

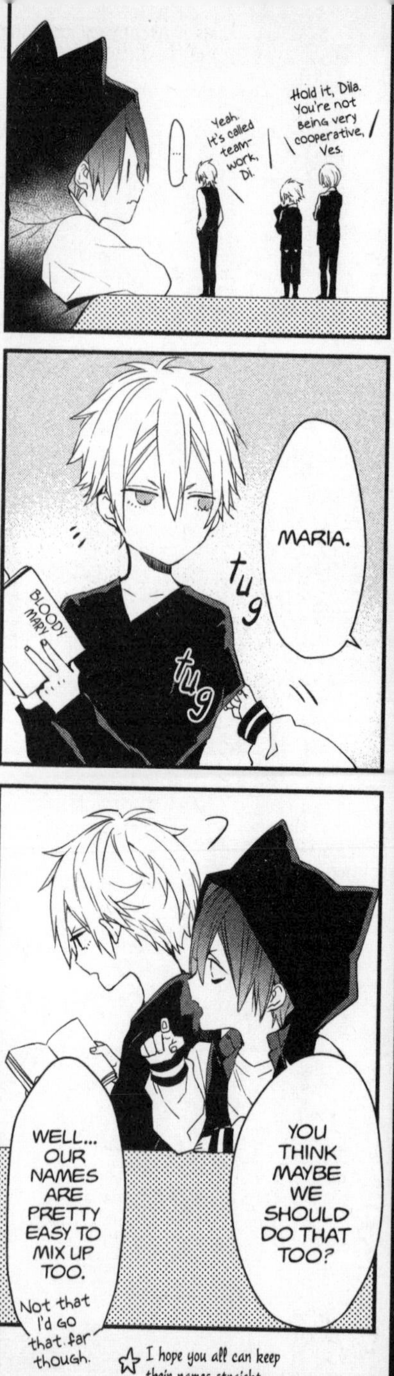
Hold it, Dila. You're not being very cooperative, Ves.
Yeah. It's called team-work, Di.
...
MARIA.
tug
BLOODY MARY
tug
YOU THINK MAYBE WE SHOULD DO THAT TOO?
WELL... OUR NAMES ARE PRETTY EASY TO MIX UP TOO.
Not that I'd go that far though.

☆ I hope you all can keep their names straight.

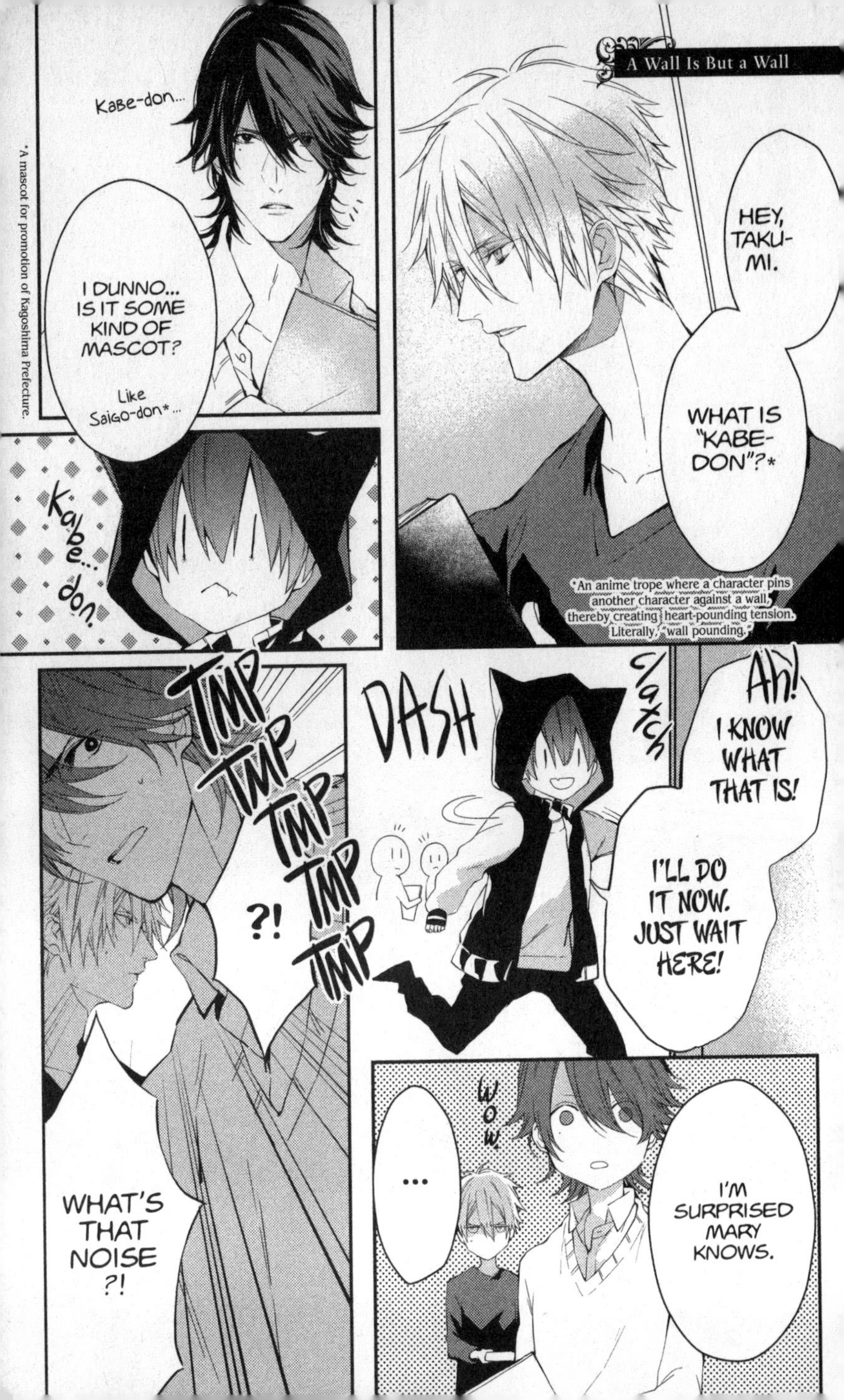
HEY, TAKUMI.
WHAT IS "KABE-DON"?*
*An anime trope where a character pins another character against a wall, thereby creating heart-pounding tension. Literally, "wall pounding."
Kabe-don...
I DUNNO... IS IT SOME KIND OF MASCOT?
Like Saigo-don*...
Kabe... don.
Ah! I KNOW WHAT THAT IS!
I'LL DO IT NOW. JUST WAIT HERE!
clatch
DASH
?!
TMP TMP TMP TMP TMP
WOW.
I'M SURPRISED MARY KNOWS.
...
WHAT'S THAT NOISE ?!

*A mascot for promotion of Kagoshima Prefecture.

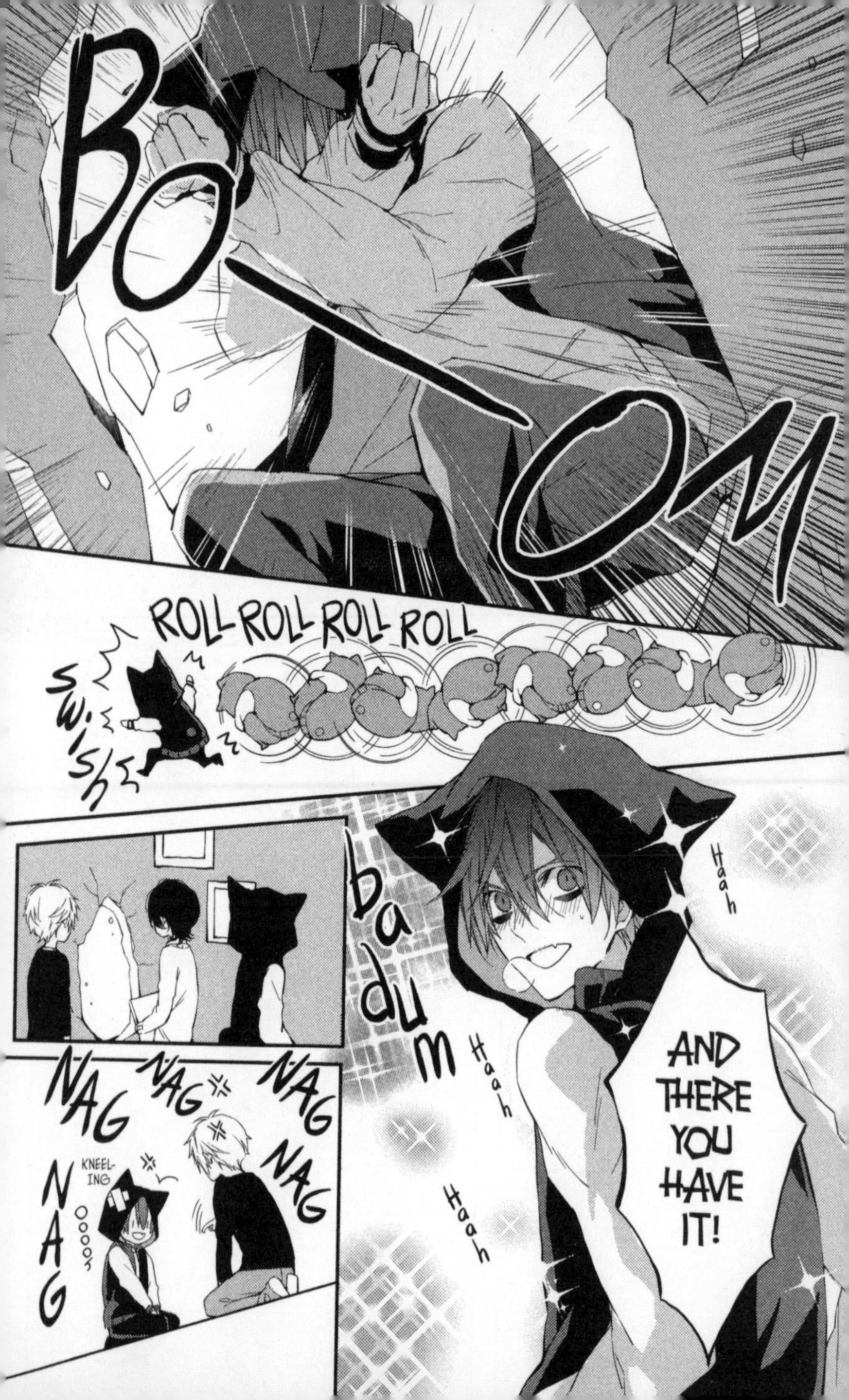
BOOM
ROLL ROLL ROLL ROLL
SWISH
Haah
AND THERE YOU HAVE IT!
ba dum
Haah
Haah
NAG NAG NAG NAG NAG NAG
KNEEL-ING
Oooo

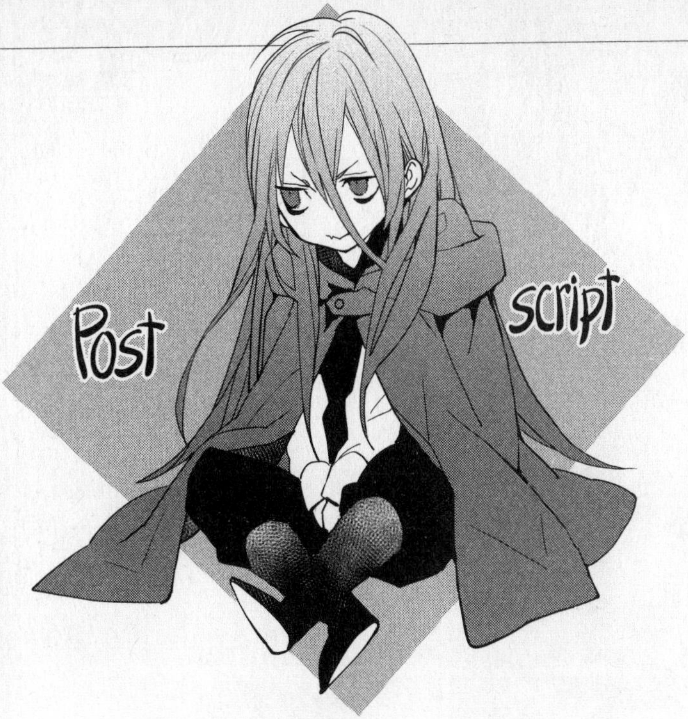
Post
script

Thank you for picking up *Blood Mary* volume 7!

- There's been a sudden influx of new characters. I hope you'll warmly welcome the vampire trio!
- The comic about kabe-don was something I got to draw as a bonus for *Asuka*-san! I remember having a lot of fun drawing Mary tumbling like a ball and then striking that pose at the end.
- As always, thank you so much for sticking with me on this. I'm working my hardest to bring you a story you can enjoy, so it'd make me super happy if we got to see each other in the next volume too.

Akaza Samamiya http://sama.ciao.jp/

SPECIALTHANKS

Mihoru / M-fuchi / H-gawa / T-mizu-sama / T-ko-sama /
Production Team/Support
Haruo / Sumida / M-ika / M-naga /
Editor S / Comics Editor H. N. / Designer / Everyone at Kosaido /
Everyone involved /
And everyone who reads this

## Ichiro Rosario di Maria

NAME

Ichiro
Rosario di Maria
(pictured at
nine years)

FAMILY

Father

HEIGHT

141 cm

Following in his father Yusei's footsteps,
he went to seminary to become a priest.
He began learning Latin.

## Takumi Sakuraba

**NAME**
Takumi Sakuraba
(pictured at ten years)

**FAMILY**
Grandfather

**HEIGHT**
148 cm

Some years ago, his father, heir to the Sakuraba family, passed away.

As a result, Takumi became the head of the Sakuraba family and began his study of aristocratic history.

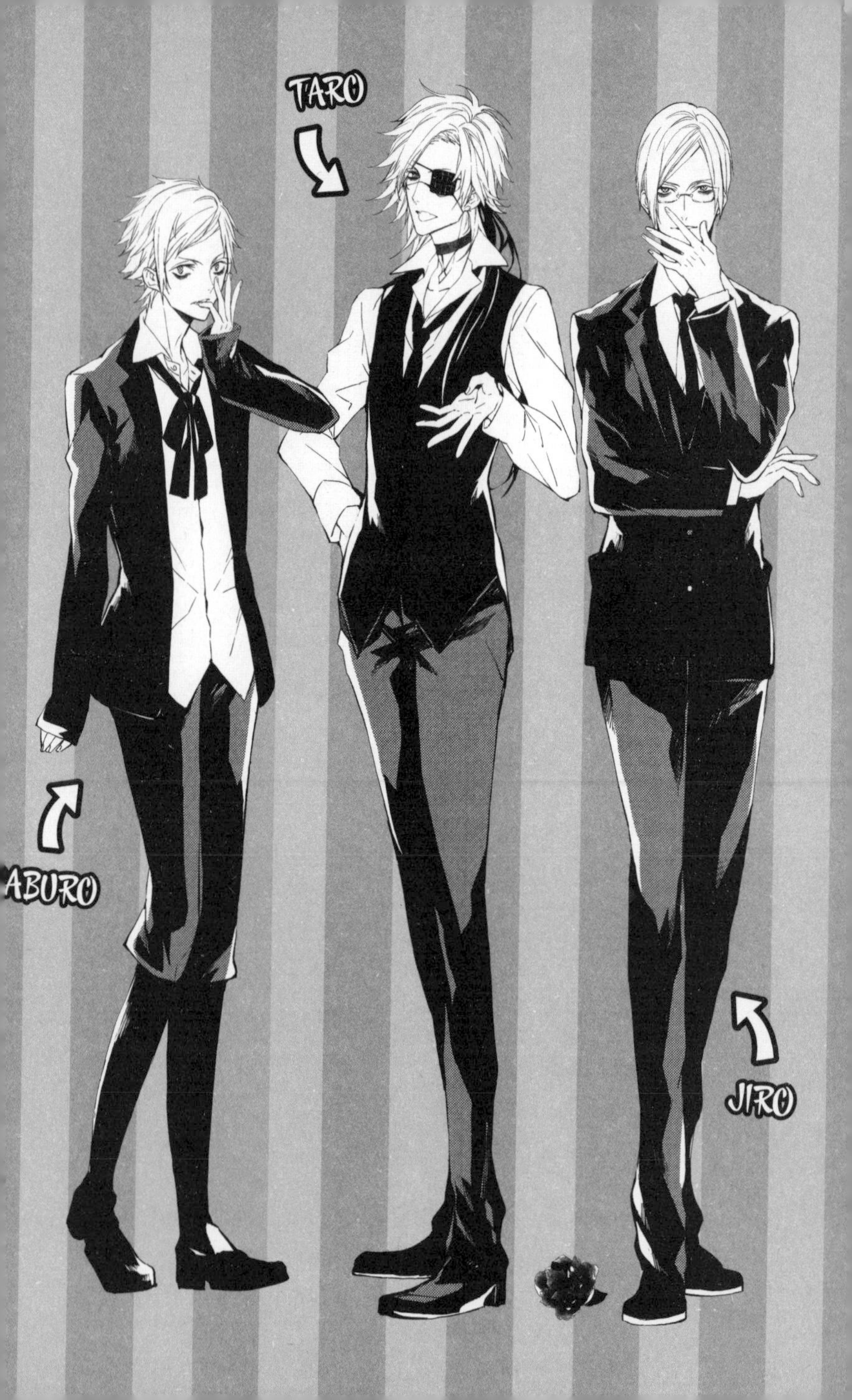
TARO
ABURO
JIRO

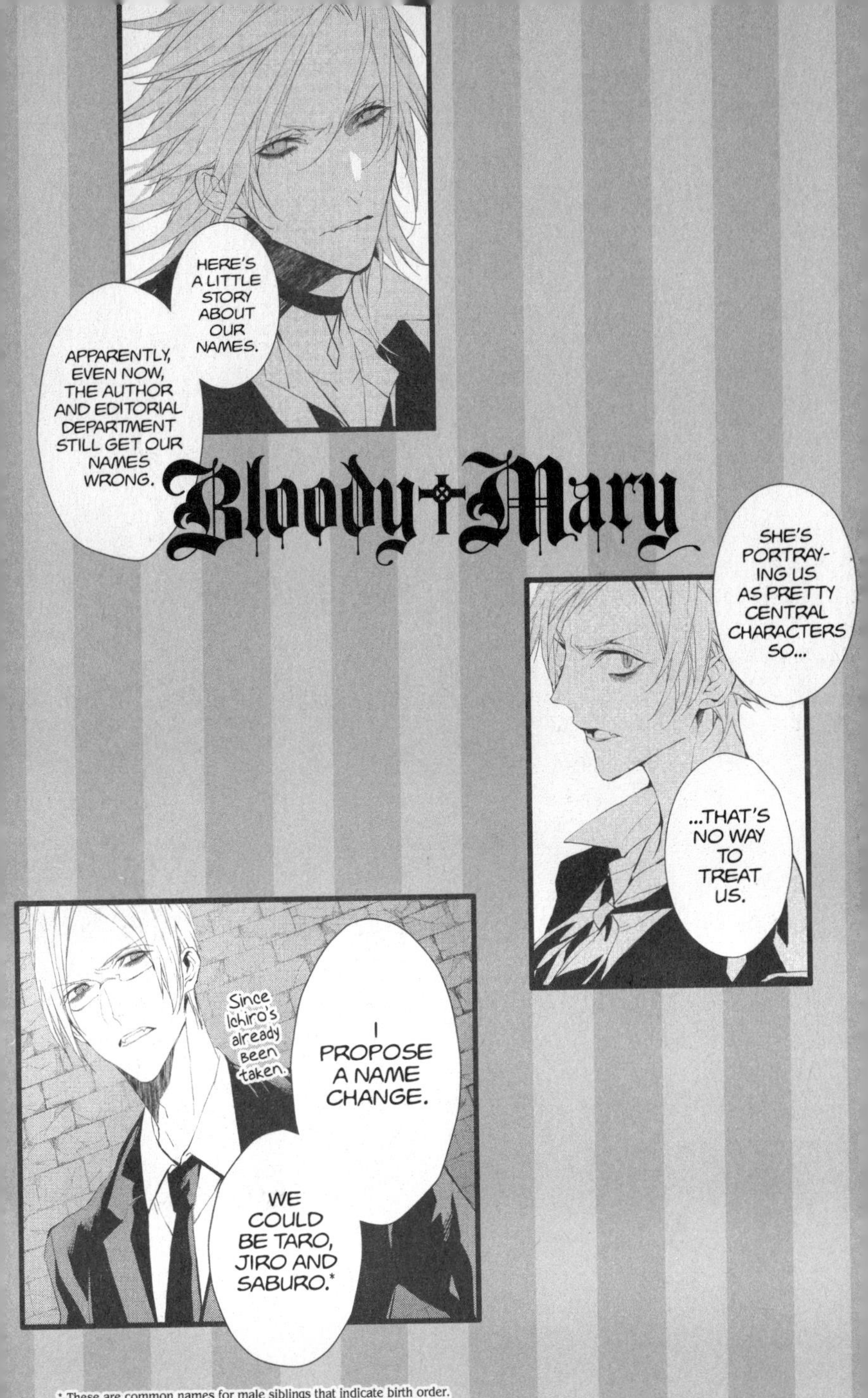
HERE'S A LITTLE STORY ABOUT OUR NAMES.
APPARENTLY, EVEN NOW, THE AUTHOR AND EDITORIAL DEPARTMENT STILL GET OUR NAMES WRONG.
Bloody+Mary
SHE'S PORTRAY-ING US AS PRETTY CENTRAL CHARACTERS SO...
...THAT'S NO WAY TO TREAT US.
I PROPOSE A NAME CHANGE.
Since Ichiro's already Been taken.
WE COULD BE TARO, JIRO AND SABURO.*

* These are common names for male siblings that indicate birth order.

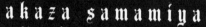

## akaza samamiya

Born November 7, Cancer, blood type B.
In volume 6, I wrote about how my cat
likes to wake me up. Well, I wanted to
let you know that she's changed her tactic
from biting me to making a lot of noise.
I wish she'd wake me up more gently.

# Bloody Mary
Volume 7
Shojo Beat Edition

**story and art by** Akaza Samamiya

**translation** Katherine Schilling
**touch-up art & lettering** Sabrina Heep
**design** Shawn Carrico
**editor** Erica Yee

BLOODY MARY Volume 7
© Akaza SAMAMIYA 2016
First published in Japan in 2016 by KADOKAWA
CORPORATION, Tokyo.
English translation rights arranged with KADOKAWA
CORPORATION, Tokyo.

The stories, characters and incidents mentioned
in this publication are entirely fictional.

No portion of this book may be reproduced or transmitted
in any form or by any means without written permission
from the copyright holders.

Printed in the U.S.A.

Published by VIZ Media, LLC
P.O. Box 77010
San Francisco, CA 94107

10 9 8 7 6 5 4 3 2 1
First printing, June 2017

www.viz.com    www.shojobeat.com

**PARENTAL ADVISORY**
BLOODY MARY is rated T for Teen and
is recommended for ages 13 and up.
This volume includes fantasy violence.
ratings.viz.com

A supernatural romance by the
creator of *Kiss of the Rose Princess*!

# The
# DEMON
# PRINCE
# of MOMOCHI
# HOUSE

*Story & Art by*
## Aya Shouoto

On her sixteenth birthday, orphan Himari Momochi inherits
her ancestral estate that she's never seen. Momochi House
exists on the barrier between the human and spiritual
realms, and Himari is meant to act as guardian between
the two worlds. But on the day she moves in, she finds
three handsome squatters already living in the house, and
one seems to have already taken over her role!

www.viz.com

ratings.viz.com

MOMOCHISANCHI NO AYAKASHI OUJI Volume 1 © Aya SHOUOTO 2013
MOMOCHISANCHI NO AYAKASHI OUJI Volume 3 © Aya SHOUOTO 2014

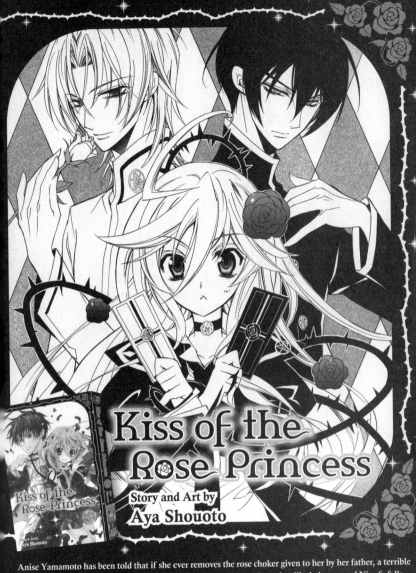

# Kiss of the Rose Princess

**Story and Art by Aya Shouoto**

Anise Yamamoto has been told that if she ever removes the rose choker given to her by her father, a terrible punishment will befall her. Unfortunately she loses that choker when a bat-like being named Ninufa falls from the sky and hits her. Ninufa gives Anise four cards representing four knights whom she can summon with a kiss. But now that she has these gorgeous men at her beck and call, what exactly is her quest?!

**$9⁹⁹ US / $12⁹⁹ CAN**

Shojo Beat

RATED TEEN
ratings.viz.com

www.viz.com

KISS OF ROSE PRINCESS Volume 1 ©Aya SHOUOTO 2009

# stop

YOU MAY BE READING THE

# wrong way

IT'S TRUE: In keeping with the original Japanese comic format, this book reads from right to left—so action, sound effects and word balloons are completely reversed. This preserves the orientation of the original artwork—plus, it's fun! Check out the diagram shown here to get the hang of things, and then turn to the other side of the book to get started!

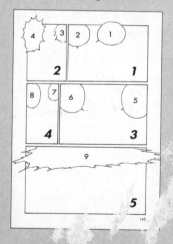